University Priorities and Constraints

Published by Economica, Ltd,
49, rue Héricart
75015 Paris
France

© *Economica Ltd, 2016*

All rights reserved

First published 2016

Printed in France

Luc E. Weber and James J. Duderstadt (eds)
University Priorities and Constraints
ISBN 978-2-7178-6857-9

University Priorities and Constraints

Edited by

Luc E. Weber

James J. Duderstadt

ECONOMICA

Glion Colloquium Series N°9
London • Paris • Genève

Titles in the Series

Governance in Higher Education, The University in a State of Flux,
Werner Z. Hirsch and Luc E. Weber, eds, (2001)

As the Walls of Academia are Tumbling Down,
Werner Z. Hirsch and Luc E. Weber, eds, (2002)

Reinventing the Research University,
Luc E. Weber and James J. Duderstadt, eds, (2004)

Universities and Business: Partnering for the Knowledge Economy,
Luc E. Weber and James J. Duderstadt, eds, (2006)

The Globalization of Higher Education,
Luc E. Weber and James J. Duderstadt, eds, (2008)

University Research for Innovation,
Luc E. Weber and James J. Duderstadt, eds, (2010)

Global Sustainability and the Responsibilities of Universities,
Luc E. Weber and James J. Duderstadt, eds, (2012)

Preparing Universities for an Era of Change
Luc E. Weber and James J. Duderstadt, eds, (2014)

University Priorities and Constraints
Luc E. Weber and James J. Duderstadt, eds, (2016)

Other publications of the Glion colloquium

The First Glion Declaration: The University at the Millennium,
The Glion Colloquium (1998)

The Second Glion Declaration: Universities and the Innovation Spirit,
The Glion Colloquium (2009)

Challenges Facing Higher Education at the Millennium,
Werner Z. Hirsch and Luc E. Weber, eds, American Council on Education/Oryx Press, Phoenix and IAU Press/Pergamon, Paris and Oxford, (1999)

CONTENTS

PREFACE		ix
CONTRIBUTORS		xv
CHAPTER 1	Glion Colloquium: A Retrospective *Peter Scott*	1
Part I	**The Role and Responsibility of Research Universities**	29
CHAPTER 2	Global Diversity in Higher Education Systems: The Divergent Fortunes of USA, Europe and Asia *Howard Newby*	31
CHAPTER 3	The Future of Universities — Academic Freedom, the Autonomy of Universities and Competition in Academia revisited *Bernd Huber*	45
CHAPTER 4	The Role of the University in Economic Development *Rebecca M. Blank*	61
CHAPTER 5	The social and political Responsibilities of research-intensive Universities: University Policies or Politics for Universities? *Alain Beretz*	71
CHAPTER 6	Learning to Think Critically *Lino Guzzella and Gerd Folkers*	85

Part II	**Intellectual Constraints**	101
CHAPTER 7	Creating Shared Value through Open Innovation Stefan Catsicas, Anne Roulin and Valerio Nannini	103
CHAPTER 8	The Evolution of globalized Higher Education Nicholas Dirks and Nils Gilman	117
CHAPTER 9	University Research comes in many Shapes Carlos H. de Brito Cruz	131
CHAPTER 10	Global Research Questions and Institutional Research Strategies Patrick J. Prendergast and Martina Hennessy	143
Part III	**Financial Constraints**	155
CHAPTER 11	A Business Model for the 21st Century European University Patrick Aebischer and Gérard Escher	157
CHAPTER 12	The Importance of Philanthropy Leszek Borysiewicz	171
CHAPTER 13	Converging Paths: Public and Private Research Universities in the 21st Century Ronald J. Daniels and Phillip Spector	183
CHAPTER 14	The University in the 21st Century Luc E. Weber	203
Part IV	**Structural Constraints**	215
CHAPTER 15	The Impact of China's Economic Rise on Global Higher Education Tony F. Chan	217
CHAPTER 16	Cities, Research Universities and the Economic Geography of Innovation Meric S. Gertler	235
CHAPTER 17	University Leadership and Governance Chorh Chuan Tan	249

CHAPTER 18	The Role of Universities and Social Needs in Times of Great Change	259
	Atsushi Seike	
Part V	**Human Constraints**	271
CHAPTER 19	From MOOCs to MOORs: a Movement towards Humboldt 2.0	273
	Yves Flückiger and Pablo Achard	
CHAPTER 20	Impact of Technology on Learning and Scholarship and the New Learning Paradigm	283
	Arnoud De Meyer	
CHAPTER 21	Adapting the University to the Constraints, Responsibilities and Opportunities of a New Age	297
	James J. Duderstadt	
CHAPTER 22	Reinventing Greatness: Responding to urgent global-level Responsibilities and critical university-level Priorities	307
	Ihron Rensburg	
CHAPTER 23	Intellectual Change: Creating the University of the 21st Century	319
	Linda P.B. Katehi	
Part VI	**Concluding Discussions**	331
CHAPTER 24	Glion Colloquium X Summary Chapter	333
	James J. Duderstadt and Luc E. Weber	

PREFACE

Since its launch in 1998, the Glion Colloquium has established itself as both a key international forum and a highly influential resource in addressing the challenges and responsibilities of the world's research universities. Held every two years, the forum brings together leaders of research universities, often joined by key figures from business and government, to consider together how the world's leading universities can meet the great challenges of the 21st century. Along the way, the forum also considers key issues related to research universities, including their management and financing, and issues of academic freedom and university relationships with private enterprise, governments and the wider public. The forum's intense discussions take place over three days in the tranquil setting of Glion-above-Montreux, Switzerland, and are based on papers prepared in advance by the participants. After the forum the papers are published both online and in books with worldwide circulation to give universities, governments and businesses practical access to cutting-edge analysis of the current and future state of the world's prominent research universities and of the major benefits these institutions can bring to society.

Over the past two decades, over 200 leaders of higher education, business and government agencies have participated in the Glion Colloquium to consider topics such as the rapidly changing nature of research universities, university governance, the interaction between universities and society, collaboration between universities and business, the globalization of higher education and how universities prepare to address the changes characterizing our times. The conferences have also considered the many global challenges requiring both the human and intellectual contributions of universities, e.g., global sustainability as the activities of humankind threaten the fragile balance of our planet; the widening gaps in prosperity, health and quality of life characterizing developed, developing and under-developed regions; the accelerating pace and impact of new technologies and the stability of the global economy in the face of questionable business practices, government policies and public priorities.

The papers presented and the associated discussions at each colloquium have subsequently been published in a series of books available through publishers and downloadable two years after publication in full-text format on the Glion Colloquium website at http://www.glion.org.

Yet, all of our universities also face highly diverse, complex, compelling responsibilities at the local and regional level that frequently take priority over broader global concerns because of our governance, financing and public responsibilities. For example, many institutions are challenged to address growing needs for advanced education of regional populations, e.g., the "massification" of higher education opportunities. Some institutions face intense political pressure, both external and internal, to move up the rankings of their academic reputation in various global or national surveys. Others are expected to place more emphasis on transferring the intellectual property developed through campus research into the marketplace to stimulate local economic activity. Some are expected to address urgent social issues, such as income inequality or the plight of underserved populations. And almost all universities are pressured to reduce the costs of their educational programs, particularly in an era when there are other pressing demands on both public tax revenues and household incomes.

Of course, they face a formidable challenge in appropriately balancing the priorities between local issues such as technology transfer, regional challenges such as creating an educational infrastructure to provide an adequate flow of students into universities with interests and aptitudes in science and engineering, and global challenges such as renewable energy technologies and global climate change. They also face many constraints, such as the resistance of the siloed medieval structure of academic disciplines to the rapid convergence of disciplines required in fields such as biomedical science, the impact of disruptive technologies (e.g., ICT) on teaching and research, or attracting the resources necessary to conduct graduate education and research at world-class levels. In fact, all too frequently, the ability to address internal constraints becomes a key factor in shaping the priorities of efforts to respond to external needs and opportunities.

In June 2015, two dozen leaders of many of the world's most distinguished research universities attended the Xth Glion Colloquium to consider how institutions determine the priorities of the diverse challenges that call upon their resources, the plans they had developed to address these challenges, and the internal constraints and complexities that must be overcome to succeed in these efforts.

Because of the great diversity of institutions and of the challenges they faced, it was felt important to engage the participants more deeply in determining the organization and design of the Xth Glion Colloquium. Several months before the meeting, invited participants were asked to propose a topic pertinent to one of the following five subtopics:

- The Role and Responsibility of Research Universities
- Intellectual Constraints
- Financial Constraints
- Structural Constraints
- Human Constraints

The final agenda for the meeting consisted of an opening session aimed at summarizing the history of the Glion Colloquium, followed by five sessions spanning the interests of the participants. A sixth and final session was then used to enable the participants to identify key issues and conclusions, as well as provide input on the organization of future Glion Colloquia.

This book is intended to provide a record of the Xth Glion Colloquium. **It begins with** a comprehensive analysis of the history of the Glion meetings by Peter Scott, one of its early participants and former Vice-Chancellor of Kingston University. Scott stresses that the Glion initiative has provided an unusually valuable contribution to higher education because it has created a sustained and documented conversation involving the leadership of many of the world's most distinguished universities over almost two decades, during which the environment for higher education has changed significantly. The geopolitical and economic order has shifted from economic growth in the 1990s as the Cold War ended, to the global financial crisis and recession in the new century, with aging populations in the West, the growth of Asian populations and influence in the East, and rapidly evolving technologies such as the Internet, social networking and the analytical tools of data analysis challenging the traditional paradigms of teaching and research. While universities have long emphasized the need for continuity and stability, today they are increasingly identified as key players in knowledge-driven economies that are increasingly dependent on their graduates and their research. The Glion Colloquium has provided a forum to consider not only the tensions and synergies between continuity and change, but also the impact of major forces reshaping the academy such as globalization, market competition and the shift from public to private financing.

This opening session set the stage for the next five sessions of the Glion Colloquium concerning the changing role and responsibilities of the world's universities as they face the changing constraints of intellectual change, shifting financial support, structural challenges and changing human needs. During **the first of these sessions** (Newby, Huber, Blank, Beretz and Guzzella), it was noted that today's universities are still caught in a triangular force field of demands for massification (enrolment growth), increased quality (as measured by league tables) and reducing the burdens on public financing. But the balance of such forces differs greatly among nations with aging populations demanding increased expenditures on health care and security, those with rapidly growing economics and populations demanding more education opportunity, and those seeking world-class quality capable of delivering the best graduates and research. It was noted that these frequently conflicting responsibilities were also challenging long-standing university traditions, such as academic freedom and autonomy in the conduct of teaching and research. To the core missions of education and scholarly research, society now demands that universities contribute more directly to economic growth and service through both applied research and educational programs more directly related to the needs of industry and the workplace. The unique characteristics and roles of research universities are increasingly challenged (if not ignored) by the broader and diverse needs of society.

The second session focused on the changing nature of the intellectual constraints on the university (Catsicas, Dirks, de Brito-Cruz and Prendergast). The growing scientific and technology needs for industry demand a more intimate relationship with universities, working together through open innovation paradigms that better address the rapid evolution of developing markets. Powerful forces of globalization similarly demand new paradigms for interaction among universities around the world rather than simply exchanging students and faculty. New paradigms are appearing, such as campuses involving co-location of activities from universities scattered about the globe to facilitate more intimate collaboration rather than the traditional approach of individual institutions sprinkling several branch campuses in far-flung locations. The urgency and complexity of global issues have stimulated efforts for universities to join together in international research collaboration in addressing global research questions that span not only science and technology, but also social, economic and political issues that require global collaboration.

The third session concerned the rapidly changing financial environment for higher education (Aebischer, Borysiewicz, Daniels and Weber), as the traditionally strong public support for higher education, because of its value as a public good, was increasingly being challenged by the perception of a college education as an individual benefit that should be paid by student fees. To be sure, much of the world still provides government financing as the major support for public universities, but the increasingly significant role played by private universities (including for-profit organizations) raises the possibility of a convergence of not only public and private financing, but also the missions and character of these institutions. Key here is the growing importance of philanthropy in support of higher education, a long tradition in the United States because of its favourable tax treatment of both charitable giving and endowment earnings, but increasingly important in both Europe and Asia.

These financial challenges are occurring in an environment characterized by increasing globalization, competition, technology and economic needs, all changing at an increasing pace that threatens the traditional approaches to not only teaching and research, but also to the way that universities are led and governed.

The fourth session addressed other structural constraints (Chan, Gertler, Tan and Seike) such as the implications of the rapid growth both of educational capacity and needs of nations in Asia and Africa, the role that cities played in providing the intellectual, economic and social environment particularly conducive to the excellence of research universities, and the challenges to traditional autonomy so important for high-quality teaching and research as the university became an ever more important institution in the achievement of national prosperity and security.

The fifth session addressed the changing needs of society, driven by forces such as disruptive technologies, growing populations and economic inequities (Flückiger, De Meyer, Duderstadt, Rensburg and Katehi). The impact of rapidly evolving technologies, such as social networking and analytics on teaching and research was considered, with important new applications such as MOOCs (massive open online courses) and MOORs (massive open online research) to provide extremely large populations with learning and research opportunities and the analytical capacity to perform empirical research on massive data sets. Such approaches are not only capable of serving large populations, particularly seeking continuing education, but also demanding new skills on the part of college graduates. But growing needs for learning at the college level, both because of rapidly growing populations in regions such as Asia and Africa, and lifelong learning opportunities because of rapidly changing workforce requirements, will require new technologies and perhaps even new types of learning institutions to serve global needs.

The final session brought all of the participants together to discuss many of the key themes and conclusions arising during the Glion X Colloquium. Among these themes were how to address the growing needs for affordable and sustainable educational opportunities for growing populations, the inequities in educational opportunity driven both by current public policy (e.g., intergenerational competition for public resources) and economic capacity, the balance between the autonomy and accountability for research universities as they become more central players in knowledge-driven economies, the impact of disruptive technologies on learning and scholarship, and the need for universities to join together in collaborative efforts to address major global needs, such as climate change, disease and poverty.

There was a uniform belief that the Glion Colloquium was extremely important for providing an opportunity not only for university leaders to join together to consider such issues, but, moreover, for building and sustaining relationships and collaboration among the leading research universities of the world.

The Xth Glion Colloquium was arranged under the auspices of the University of Geneva and enabled through the generous support of the Swiss State Secretariat for Education, Research and Innovation, the Swiss Federal Institutes of Technology of Zurich and Lausanne (ETH Zurich and EPFL), and the University of Geneva. We are also particularly grateful for the efforts of those who contributed to the colloquium and to the production of this book, in particular Natacha Durand, head of admissions at the University of Geneva, and Gerlinde Kristahn, Ph.D. candidate, as well as Edmund Doogue in Geneva, who provided rigorous editorial assistance.

Finally, participants from both this and earlier Glion Colloquia would particularly like to acknowledge the important role that Marianne Weber has played in organizing and hosting events for the Colloquium participants and their guests. Indeed, these activities have provided a remarkable opportunity to build lasting relationships among university leaders that have been important to the future of higher education.

Luc E. Weber
University of Geneva

James J. Duderstadt
University of Michigan

CONTRIBUTORS

ACHARD, Pablo
After a Ph.D. in particle physics, Pablo Achard carried out research in computational neurosciences. Since 2009, he has been working at the University of Geneva's Rectorate where he is in charge of, among other duties, strategic planning and foresight. In this position, he has developed the university's MOOC program. He is currently deputy to Rector Flückiger.

AEBISCHER, Patrick
Patrick Aebischer has been the president of the Ecole Polytechnique Fédérale de Lausanne, EPFL, since 1999. He was trained as an MD (1980) and a neuroscientist (1983) at the Universities of Geneva and Fribourg. From 1984 to 1992, he was Professor of Medical Sciences at Brown University. In 1992, he became Professor and Director of the Surgical Research Division and Gene Therapy Center at CHUV, the Lausanne University Medical School Hospital in Lausanne. He is the founder of three biotechnology companies. He is a member of the boards of Lonza and Nestlé, and chairs the Novartis Venture Fund.

BERETZ, Alain
Alain Beretz is a member of the Pharmacology faculty of the University of Strasbourg. He was Vice-President in charge of technology transfer (2001-2006), and then President of the Louis Pasteur University in Strasbourg (2007-2008). He was elected in 2009 as the first president of the University of Strasbourg, resulting from the innovative merger of the three previous universities. He was reelected in 2012 for a second four-year term, and in May 2014 became the Chair of the League of European Research Universities (LERU).

BLANK, Rebecca M.
Rebecca M. Blank is chancellor at the University of Wisconsin-Madison. An economist by training with a Ph.D. from MIT, she served as Dean of the

Gerald R. Ford School of Public Policy at the University of Michigan. She was a member of President Clinton's Council of Economic Advisors, and served as Undersecretary, Deputy Secretary and Acting Secretary of the U.S. Department of Commerce under President Obama.

BORYSIEWICZ, Leszek

Professor Sir Leszek Borysiewicz is the 345th Vice-Chancellor of the University of Cambridge. He was Chief Executive of the U.K.'s Medical Research Council from 2007, and from 2001 to 2007 was at Imperial College London, where he served as Principal of the Faculty of Medicine and later as Deputy Rector. Professor Borysiewicz was knighted in the 2001 New Year's Honours List for his contribution to medical education and research into developing vaccines, including work towards a vaccine to combat cervical cancer.

CATSICAS, Stefan

Stefan Catsicas was appointed Executive Vice President for Innovation, Technology and R&D, and Chief Technology Officer of Nestlé S.A., effective 1 September 2013. He started his career as the Head of Neurobiology at the Glaxo Institute for Molecular Biology in Geneva. Returning to academia, he joined the University of Lausanne as Professor and Chairman of the Cell Biology and Morphology Institute, and later as Vice-President Research and Professor of Cellular Engineering at the Swiss Federal Institute of Technology in Lausanne. In 2005 he co-founded a private group of biotechnology companies and his passion for education brought him back to academia in 2011 as Provost and Executive Vice President of the King Abdullah University of Science and Technology.

CHAN, Tony F.

Professor Tony F. Chan assumed the presidency of HKUST on 1 September 2009. His scientific background is in Mathematics, Computer Science and Engineering. He was formerly Dean of Physical Sciences at UCLA and Assistant Director of the Mathematical and Physical Sciences Directorate at US NSF. Professor Chan is an elected member of US NAE, a senior member of IEEE and an elected fellow of both SIAM and AAAS. He is a member of the Board of Trustees of KAUST in Saudi Arabia, President's Advisory Council of KAIST in South Korea, and Scientific Advisory Board of UVienna in Austria. He was one of the world's most cited mathematicians.

DANIELS, Ronald J.

Ronald J. Daniels is the 14th president of Johns Hopkins University, America's first research university. Since taking office in 2009, he has focused his leadership on three overarching themes — interdisciplinary collaboration, individual excellence and community engagement — which are now cornerstones to the university's strategic vision through 2020, and to Hopkins' $4.5 billion fundraising campaign. A law and economics scholar, Daniels is author or editor of seven books and dozens of scholarly articles.

De BRITO CRUZ, Carlos H.
Brito Cruz has a doctorate in Physics. He was a visiting researcher in Rome, Paris, and at the AT&T's Bell Laboratories. He was the Rector of the State University of Campinas (Unicamp) and the President of the São Paulo Research Foundation (FAPESP). Brito Cruz is a member of the Brazilian Academy of Sciences and of the Order of the British Empire (OBE). He has been the Science Director at FAPESP since 2005.

De MEYER, Arnoud
Professor De Meyer is President of Singapore Management University and previously Director of Judge Business School at the University of Cambridge, and Founding Dean of INSEAD's Asia Campus in Singapore. Professor De Meyer has an MSc in Electrical Engineering, an MBA and a Ph.D. in Management from the University of Ghent in Belgium. He is an external director of Dassault Systèmes SA (France). In Singapore, he serves on several Boards including the National Research Foundation, Singapore International Chamber of Commerce and Temasek Management Services.

DIRKS, Nicholas B.
Nicholas B. Dirks is the Chancellor of the University of California, Berkeley, and the former executive vice president for the arts and sciences and dean of the faculty at Columbia University. A historian and anthropologist of South Asia, Dirks is the author of numerous books, including *The Hollow Crown: Ethnohistory of an Indian Kingdom* (1987), *Castes of Mind: Colonialism and the Making of Modern India* (2001) and, most recently, *Autobiography of an Archive: A Scholar's Passage to India* (2015).

DUDERSTADT, James J.
Dr James J. Duderstadt is President Emeritus and University Professor of Science and Engineering at the University of Michigan. A graduate of Yale and Caltech, Dr Duderstadt's interests include nuclear science, applied physics, computer simulation, science policy and higher education. He currently teaches science and technology policy at Michigan, while chairing the National Academies Division on Policy and Global Affairs and directing the Millennium Project, a research centre concerned with the impact of over-the-horizon technologies on society.

ESCHER, Gérard
Gérard Escher obtained his diploma in Biology at the University of Geneva, and his Ph.D. (Neuroscience, 1987) at the University of Lausanne, where he

led a research group working on synapse formation, after a postdoctoral fellowship at Stanford University. For 10 years he worked as Scientific Advisor and Assistant Director at the Swiss State Secretariat for Education and Research. Since 2008 he has served as the senior advisor to Patrick Aebischer.

FLÜCKIGER, Yves

Yves Flückiger has been full professor at the Department of Economics of the University of Geneva since 1992. Vice-rector of this institution for eight years, in July 2015 he became Rector. His scientific interests include international, education and labour economics, and more specifically unemployment analysis, migration policies, income inequality and discrimination and working conditions in diverse labour markets. He has authored many books and more than 120 publications in international scientific journals.

FOLKERS, Gerd

Gerd Folkers studied Pharmaceutical Sciences and attained a doctorate in 1982 in pharmaceutical chemistry. In 1991 he was appointed Professor for Pharmaceutical Chemistry at the ETH in Zurich. The emphasis of his research was the molecular design of bioactive compounds and their application for a personalized therapy of tumours and diseases of the immune system. He served at the Research Council of the Swiss National Science Foundation from 2003 to 2011. Since 2004 he has been head of the Collegium Helveticum, a joint project of ETH Zurich and University of Zurich for the study of new scientific perspectives in transdisciplinary processes. Since 2012, Gerd Folkers has been a member of the Swiss Science and Innovation Council, serving as its Vice-President since 2014.

GERTLER, Meric

Professor Meric Gertler is one of the world's foremost urban theorists and policy practitioners. He is widely known as an expert on innovation, creativity and culture as drivers of prosperity and the economic dynamism of city-regions. He began his term as the 16th President of the University of Toronto in November 2013. Prior to that, he served as the Dean of the Faculty of Arts and Science, where he championed many innovations in undergraduate teaching and learning. He is a Professor of Geography and Planning, the Goldring Chair in Canadian Studies, and co-founder of a large research program at the Munk School of Global Affairs at the University of Toronto. He has authored or edited seven books and he is a Fellow of the Royal Society of Canada, a Fellow of the Academy of Social Sciences (U.K.), and a Corresponding Fellow of the British Academy.

GILMAN, Nils

Nils Gilman is the Associate Chancellor of the University of California, Berkeley, and an intellectual historian. He is the author of *Mandarins of the*

Future: Modernization Theory in Cold War America (2004) and the co-editor of *Humanity: An International Journal of Human Rights, Humanitarianism, and Development*. Dr Gilman holds a B.A. (1993), M.A. (1995) and Ph.D. (2000) in History from UC Berkeley.

GUZZELLA, Lino

Lino Guzzella has been President of ETH Zurich since January 2015 and full professor of Thermotronics since 1999. From 2001 to 2003, he headed the Department of Mechanical and Process Engineering, and, from mid-2012 until the end of 2014, he was Rector of ETH Zurich. After receiving his mechanical engineering diploma in 1981 and his doctoral degree in 1986 from ETH, he held several positions in industry. His research focuses on novel approaches in system dynamics and control of energy conversion systems. Control-oriented systems modeling, dynamic optimization and feedback control design methods are the main area of research. He is a member of the Swiss Academy of Engineering Sciences and is involved in various international and national research bodies.

HENGARTNER, Michael

Michael Hengartner, a Swiss-Canadian citizen, was born in St Gallen, Switzerland in 1966 and grew up in Québec City, Canada. He studied biochemistry at the Université Laval in Québec City. After earning his PhD at the Massachusetts Institute of Technology with Nobel laureate H. Robert Horvitz, he was head of a research group at the Cold Spring Harbor Laboratory in the USA from 1994 to 2001. In 2001, he was appointed professor for molecular biology at the newly created Ernst Hadorn Chair at the Institute of Molecular Life Sciences, University of Zurich. From 2009 to 2014, he acted as dean of the Faculty of Science. He is now Rector of the University of Zurich.

HENNESSY, Martina

Martina Hennessy is a Consultant Physician in St James Hospital Dublin, and Professor of Medical Education in Trinity College Dublin. She is the Director of the Trinity International Development Initiative, and in 2014 she was appointed Associate Dean of Research in the university with responsibility for progressing the Global Research Question in collaboration with other university officers.

HUBER, Bernd

Professor Dr Bernd Huber is Professor for Public Finance and, since 2002, President of Ludwig-Maximilians-Universität (LMU) München. Among his numerous posts, he is also a member of several advisory and strategic councils, of the Scientific Council to the German Ministry of Finance and of the Board of Directors of Venice International University. He was chairman of the League of European Research Universities from 2008 until 2014 and served as referee for the Excellence Initiatives in Spain and France.

KATEHI, Linda P. B.

Before being named the first woman chancellor at the University of California, Davis in August 2009, Linda P. B. Katehi held high leadership and faculty positions at the University of Illinois at Urbana-Champaign, Purdue University and the University of Michigan. She earned her bachelor's degree in electrical engineering from the National Technical University of Athens, Greece, in 1977, and her master's and doctoral degrees in electrical engineering from UCLA in 1981 and 1984.

NANNINI, Valerio

Valerio Nannini joined Nestlé as the Senior Vice President, Head of Strategies and Performance, effective 1 April 2014. In this role, he fosters and drives a cross-functional culture of innovation that is fast, effective and efficient across all Nestlé markets globally. He started his career in Nestlé Italy and has helped build, establish and reorganize various markets within Nestlé in different geographies across various Technical, Supply Chain and R&D functions in India, Thailand, Indonesia, South Africa, Switzerland and Singapore.

NEWBY, Howard

Sir Howard Newby was Vice-Chancellor of the University of Liverpool from 2008 to January 2015. Prior to this, he was Vice-Chancellor of the University of the West of England (UWE) in Bristol, the Chief Executive of the Higher Education Funding Council for England (HEFCE), Vice-Chancellor of the University of Southampton and Chairman and Chief Executive of the Economic and Social Research Council (ESRC).

PRENDERGAST, Patrick J.

Patrick Prendergast was elected by the academic staff and student representatives as the 44th Provost of Trinity College Dublin in 2011. Prior to that he was the Vice-Provost/Chief Academic Officer, and the Dean of Graduate Studies. He is an engineer by profession, and was Professor of Bioengineering before becoming Provost. He is a member of the Royal Irish Academy, and an International Fellow of the Royal Academy of Engineering. He has published extensively on medical device design.

RENSBURG, Ihron

Prof Ihron Rensburg has been, since 2006, the Vice Chancellor of the University of Johannesburg. He served as South Africa's National Planning

Commissioner, Chairperson of the Southern African Vice Chancellors Association, Chairperson of Higher Education South Africa, Chairperson of the Ministerial Committee on Student Accommodation in South African Universities, Member of the Ministerial Committee on the Funding of South African Universities, Councillor of the Association of Commonwealth Universities and Board Member of the Commonwealth of Learning.

ROULIN, Anne

Anne Roulin is responsible for Nutrition, Health & Wellness (NHW) and Sustainability within R&D based at Nestlé HQ in Switzerland. In this role, she works across Nestlé R&D in over 30 centres globally to embed NHW and sustainability at the earliest phase of the product development cycle. Previously she was Global Head of Packaging for Nestlé and prior to Nestlé she founded and built up a company specialized in package development, after spending 10 years with Tetra Pak in Switzerland, the United States and Italy.

SCOTT, Peter

Peter Scott is Professor of Higher Education Studies at the UCL Institute of Education. He is also Treasurer of the Academia Europaea. He was Vice-Chancellor of Kingston University in London from 1998 until 2010, and a member of the board of the Higher Education Funding Council for England. Previously he was Professor of Education at the University of Leeds, and a journalist as an editorial writer at *The Times* and Editor of *The Times Higher Education Supplement*.

SEIKE, Atsushi

President of Keio University since 2009, Atsushi Seike was previously a consultant at RAND Corp and Visiting Principal Research Officer at the Economic Research Institute of the Economic Planning Agency. He also chairs the Council for the Promotion of Social Security System Reform and Policy Studies Group for an Aged Society for Japan, is the President of the Japan Association of Private Universities and Colleges, and serves as a member of WEF's Global University Leaders Forum and Global Agenda Council on Ageing.

SPECTOR, Phillip

Until September 2015, Phil Spector was the Vice President for Strategic Initiatives at Johns Hopkins University, working on a range of policy questions relating to the future of higher education. Before that, he was Senior Advisor to the Legal Adviser at the U.S. Department of State and Senior Counsel to Senator Hillary Rodham Clinton. He is a graduate of Yale Law School and Swarthmore College. He is now a consultant specializing in strategic policy development.

TAN, Chorh Chuan

Professor Tan Chorh Chuan is the President of the National University of Singapore; Chairman of National University Health System; Deputy Chairman of Singapore's Agency for Science, Technology and Research; and a Director of the Monetary Authority of Singapore. A physician-scientist by training, he is active on several international fora including the World Economic Forum's Global University Leaders Forum, which he chaired for a two-year term.

WEBER, Luc E.

Luc Weber was professor of Public Economics at the University of Geneva and an adviser to Swiss governments. Since 1982, he has been deeply involved in university management and higher education policy in the capacity of vice-rector, then of rector, of the University of Geneva, as well as Chairman of the Swiss Rectors' Conference. More recently, he served on the Steering Committee for Higher Education and Research of the Council of Europe, the International Association of Universities and the European University Association.

CHAPTER 1

Glion Colloquium: A Retrospective

Peter Scott

INTRODUCTION

Two Declarations, nine books, 180 chapters, 2,400 pages published over a 15-year span from 1999 to 2014 — by any standards the outputs of the regular meetings of the Glion Colloquium, held in Glion itself with the exception of one held in California, have provided a major stimulus to new thinking about the future of higher education during a crucial period in its development. Now a tenth book, including this chapter, has been published based on the proceedings of the most recent Colloquium held in Glion in June 2015. Participants in successive colloquia and authors of the contributions to these nine books comprise many of the leading figures in American and European universities and, since 2007, from other world regions, notably East Asia — and also many of the leading higher education researchers and commentators in both continents, as well as business leaders. It is difficult to recall a similar initiative that has been sustained over such a long period and has mobilized so many higher education leaders and thinkers on both sides of the Atlantic. And it is an initiative that is still very much live, current and continuing. As has already been indicated, the tenth colloquium was held in June 2015 and another is planned for 2017.

The scope and scale of the Glion process make it difficult to categorize easily its impact on policy-making and wider influence. Its outputs have been too varied and wide-ranging to be pigeon-holed neatly. What might have appeared a lack of focus has actually provided to be a source of strength, although its centre of gravity has perhaps been on the preoccupations and concerns of the

American research university, and its European analogues, rather than on the mass-participation higher education systems that have developed since 1960. Glion's outputs have also reflected radical shifts in the wider higher education environment, so a tighter focus might have led to premature redundancy. When the first colloquium was held in 1998, the Bologna Declaration had not yet been signed and the modernization of European higher education had barely begun (Bologna Declaration, 1999). On the other side of the Atlantic it was still possible — just about — to believe that the reductions in direct State funding, and resultant rapid rise in tuition, were reversible. The idea of the "public university" was still strong, and the inevitability of a shift towards the idea of a higher education "market" not yet assured. In the middle of the second decade of the 21st century new policy contexts have emerged, and maybe new orthodoxies have become established, that would have been difficult to anticipate at the end of the last century — even if, in many instances, the Glion outputs have been remarkably prescient.

More broadly the successive colloquia have spanned a period of fundamental change in the world's geopolitical and economic orders. The first meetings were held still in the afterglow of optimism generated by the collapse of Communist rule in central and Eastern Europe (and the transition to majority rule in South Africa) and by the move towards an "ever closer union" within the European Union culminating in the 2007 Lisbon Treaty (European Council, 2007). Even the violence of disintegrating Yugoslavia could be diminished if not entirely dismissed as the unfinished business of long-ago Balkan disputes. Francis Fukuyama's claim that we had reached the "end of history" was still almost plausible (Fukuyama, 1992). But a new age of pessimism, and threat, quickly succeeded, dramatically heralded by 9/11. The dormant Cold War was succeeded by a more frightening "war on terror", which has continued to this day. Its impacts in terms of security and surveillance, and curbs on immigration and creeping xenophobia, have not yet been fully digested.

The global, and most national, economies followed a similar trajectory. The liberalization of the 1980s and 1990s seemed to have produced a new economic order characterized by permanent growth, which had made redundant old cyclical patterns of boom and bust. The way in which the bursting of the dot.com bubble was contained appears as proof of its core stability. The stagnation of the Japanese economy in the 1990s was dismissed as an event in a "faraway country", with no worrying implications for the more fortunate and favoured nations of the "old" West and its satellite economies. But the global banking crisis of 2008 and subsequent recession shattered these illusions and destroyed that stability. Many countries have lost up to a decade of economic growth. Welfare states have been shrunk by austerity policies (and the public universities and mass higher education systems they nurtured have suffered correspondingly), while banking and other corporate reforms have stalled. New conceptualizations have been developed in this new age of (public) austerity, such as the shift from the "tax state" up until the 1980s, through the "debt state" of the 1990s and 2000s to the "consolidation state" of the 2010s. The welfare state has gone into (terminal?) decline to be succeeded by a new enthusiasm for "shrinking" the state. More fundament social changes have resulted, with the young facing diminished prospects compared with their parents (and grandparents). This shift, unprecedented since the days of the early industrial revolution, has impacted especially forcefully on students faced with higher tuition fees.

It is this period of turbulence and transition that is spanned by the Glion colloquia. It was not only a time of transition in higher education; the (decisive?) shift towards more "market" systems has already been mentioned, but perhaps of even greater significance has been the heightened perception of the importance of globalization, and its multiple impacts on universities. It was also a time of fundamental geopolitical and economic (and also social) transformations that are still incomplete. And, of course, these processes, within higher education and wider society, were closely related, as political change impacted on higher education policy (especially in the context of funding) and as science and technology transformed economic structures and possibilities. Both processes are reflected in Glion's published outputs. However, Glion also demonstrated some enduring continuities, essential preoccupations that have not been changed even by such dramatic events as 9/11 or the banking crash. Higher education generates its own transformations, notably through the dynamism of scientific research, but also evident in wider intellectual developments, that are not simply the impression of external factors, political, economic and cultural, however epoch-making. The Glion colloquia illustrate this dialectic between change and continuity that has always characterized the development of higher education.

The remainder of this paper is divided into three sections. The first is a brief, and inevitably impressionistic, sketch of some of the key changes that have taken place in the higher education environment since the late 1990s. The second is a more detailed discussion of the outcomes of each of the Glion meetings — not forgetting, of course, the Glion Declaration and its later iterations. The third is an attempt to suggest some general themes that can be extracted from the nine books and 2,400 pages, and to relate these themes to other initiatives in higher education. It also offers a provisional judgment on the wider significance of the Glion process, both looking back to its beginnings and evolution and looking forward to how it may be able to contribute to the future evolution of higher education policy, and thought, in Europe and the United States.

THE HIGHER EDUCATION ENVIRONMENT

The detailed experiences of American and European universities have diverged over the past two decades, but common themes can also be identified (especially with regard to the dilemmas facing research universities). The major divergences have been that in the United States disinvestment by State Governments has gathered pace with the result that now most major State universities receive substantially less than 20% of their revenue directly from their States. As a result, tuition fees have been increased, although these increases have led to criticism that the middle classes are being priced out of (elite) higher education (National Centre for Education Statistics, 2012). Such criticism is especially strong in the case of private research universities, despite their provision of generous scholarships and commitment to needs-blind admissions. At the same time, similar political circumstances have led to downward pressure on the Federal budget. As a result, the focus on alumni contributions and private and corporate donations has increased. Private for-profit institutions (such as the Apollo Group-owned University of Phoenix), although not in serious competition with mainstream public and private research universities, have also acquired an enhanced role. Despite poor completion rates, they have come to consume an increased share of the budget for student support.

The experience in Europe has been different. Although Government expenditure has declined in proportional if not actual terms, the pressure on university budgets has been less intense. In a few European countries, notably the United Kingdom, tuition fees have been substantially increased. But in most only limited progress has been made towards shifting the funding burden from taxpayers to students (and graduates). Indeed, in Germany tuition fees charged in some *lander* have been abolished. Even in the U.K., state-funded loans have been provided to enable students to pay their fees, so no up-front payment is required and generous repayment terms are available. In some Central and Eastern European countries, notably Poland and Hungary, private institutions have flourished and now enrol large numbers of students. But across Europe more generally private institutions have struggled to establish themselves, posing little challenge to public research universities but rather concentrating on low-cost vocational courses. Instead the major Europe-wide phenomenon has been the Bologna process which began in 1998 as a limited exercise in the harmonization of course structures, student credentials and quality assurance arrangements, but has acquired an impressive momentum of its own (with, again, the — partial — exception of the U.K.) It has stood proxy for the wider modernization of European higher education, and also acquired new links with European strategies for research and innovation. Substantial reordering of the formal relationship between universities and the

State has been undertaken, while new, more selective funding policies have been introduced (of which the *Excellenz* initiative in Germany is the most high-profile, but by no means the only example).

These divergent experiences raise the question of whether European higher education continues to defer to American models of development — in short, whether it is still subject to a process of Americanization — or whether it has developed its own models. Clearly American models were influential in the reform of Swedish universities, despite their (initial) social democratic flavour, in the 1970s and also of higher education in the Netherlands. They were also influential in the reshaping of higher education systems in post-Communist Central and Eastern Europe. Nor can there be any doubt about the continuing attractiveness of American models, pre-eminently that of the research university, in a global context — although whether this attractiveness is greater in Asia than in Europe remains an interesting question. However, the resistance of major European systems to American influences — for example, in France, Germany and Italy — has probably been increased by the development of the Bologna process (despite the fact that it introduced the apparently "Anglo-American" two-cycle bachelors-masters pattern and also the fact that this process has sometimes been interpreted, by student organizations among others, as an exercise in neoliberal marketization).

However, it would be misleading to allow these differences to overshadow the very substantial commonalities of experience between North America and Europe, which were highlighted in the Glion colloquia. These commonalities include: first, funding (but also efficiency); secondly, system design (and, in particular, the role best played by markets) and also the role of the State (if no longer necessarily as predominant funder then as regulator); thirdly, purposes including new research strategies and practices (and, in particular, the strengthening of links to innovation) and new patterns of teaching (in terms both of a tilt towards vocationalism and employability and also of new methods and patterns of delivery); fourthly, burgeoning performance cultures reflected in both officially generated metrics and, perhaps more powerfully, league tables; and, finally, globalization (in both positive terms — for example, the strengthening of global science and global recruitment of academic talent — and more negative terms — for example, growing concerns about immigration and the impact of so-called "fundamentalism").

Funding & efficiency

As has already been indicated, the debates about the future funding of higher education have taken different forms, or had different emphases, on opposite shores of the Atlantic. But the key issue is a common one, how to create sustainability funding systems when public funding can no longer be relied upon and escalating fees encounter growing resistance, whether from students, their parents and graduates or from political parties.

One interesting question is whether Europe will eventually move towards greater reliance on tuition fees — and, therefore, is simply a laggard rather than following a different path. In England higher education was "free" between 1962 and 1998 (for full-time undergraduates and some postgraduates) and few would have anticipated the relatively easy acceptance of student fees (it is important to recognize that fees are still not charged in Scotland and at a lower level in Wales, so it is misleading to talk of a common U.K. approach to student fees and higher education funding). It is possible, therefore, to imagine that other European countries may also lose their present inhibitions about abandoning (virtually) "free" higher education — in parallel perhaps with their acceptance of more flexible labour markets. A second interesting question, more relevant in the U.S., is whether there are limits to increasing fee levels against a background of stagnant middle-class incomes — and, crucially, whether these limits are being approached. It is possible that, over the long haul, any limits may make it difficult to rely on fee income as the main substitute for constrained State support. Student debt already exceeds consumer debt in the U.S., and there is growing political criticism of inflation-busting fee increases. There are even allegations that much of the revenue raised by fees is not used for the (direct) benefit of students (Campos, 2015). On both sides of the Atlantic, universities may have to learn to live with less reliable, and predictable, income streams. "Sustainable" funding may be difficult to achieve.

It is also worth noting that the debate about the funding of universities has been dominated by income, both aggregates and sources, or by volume, the difficulty of funding greatly extended higher education systems that enrol mass student populations. Far less attention has been paid to reducing costs, whether by improving operational efficiency or by increasing productivity. Yet it can be argued that the real funding crisis has arisen more because of the rapidly increasing costs of providing higher education, especially in high-cost research universities than because of curbs on public funding or resistance to higher tuition fees. Although not caught in the same anti-productivity trap as healthcare due to improved drug and other treatment (and, therefore, to longer lifespans), universities have also had to cope with serious cost pressures. Most forms of learning technology have been additional to more traditional forms of instruction, and have added rather than reduced cost. Some alternative, mainly for-profit, providers have been able to target low-cost subjects and develop new lower-cost delivery systems. But that option has not been available to established research universities with reputations for excellence to defend. Encouraging students to behave as consumers, even in the absence of high fees, may also have driven up costs, because of higher expectations about the standard of facilities. This process is still perhaps more advanced in the United States, but the same pressures can be observed in Europe, driven to some extent by league tables. Finally many universities are "over-trading" in research, despite their best efforts to secure funding that reflects the full economic cost of research. Under the conditions that prevail in modern higher education systems, and especially in research universities, market competition may have had a tendency to drive up costs rather than produce greater efficiency.

System Design & the Role of the State

It has become commonplace to argue that the mass, and largely public, systems of higher education within which institutional missions were clearly demarcated through "master plans" and similar policy and legal instruments, which dominated the second half of the 20th century, are in the process of being superseded in the early 21st century by market systems, often with substantial involvement by private for-profit institutions and in which even public institutions are increasingly taking on entrepreneurial roles.

At best this is too simple a characterization. First, higher education systems have proved to be remarkably resilient, and institutional landscapes as remarkably stable. These systems have been modified by new funding patterns, generally the result of shortfalls in public support, and also by policies that have made it easier for alternative providers to compete with public (or not-for-profit private) universities. But the higher education systems established in most U.S. States, and the institutional patterns in most (Western) European countries, that date from the second half of the 20th century, are still recognizably the same. It seems premature to conclude that "systems", whether highly structured as in parts of the U.S. or evolutionary as is more generally the case in Europe, have had their day and been replaced by free-wheeling markets.

Secondly, the impact of market-like policies has been strongly differentiated depending on the type and level of institution. In most cases research universities form the elite components of their national systems, both in the make-up of their student bodies and their scholarly and scientific prowess. As such they have been to some degree "above" any market competition that may have influenced the behaviour of mass-access and teaching-oriented institutions. Although, as has already been indicated, their income streams have been re-proportioned, total budgets have continued to increase. The market competition they have experienced, in particular for academic talent but also for reputation, has not been contained with national systems but has been played out on an international stage. Although most have become more involved in various forms of entrepreneurial activity — for example, top-end executive programmes, research commercialization and technology transfer — the major stimulus has as often come from the State as from the market sector.

Far from retreating, the State has often played a more activist role with regard to universities. Public funding may have been constrained, although the degree to which this has been generally true can be questioned. International statistics do not support the idea that the State has disinvested in higher education and research on a significant scale, at any rate as measured in GDP shares. And, as has been pointed out, substantial sums of publicly generated resources continue to flow to universities through a number of routes. However, it remains true that conventional forms of public funding have been unable to keep pace with the needs of higher education. But, if the State has a more limited role as a (direct) funder of universities, in many countries it has increased its influence in two other respects.

The first is as the orchestrator of national, or Europe-wide, innovation strategies in which research universities in particular are expected to play pivotal roles. Much of the funding may come from non-State sources, but the State has often been the prime mover of such strategies. The second is as a regulator. Already the development of mass systems with a diversity of institutional types and missions had placed greater emphasis on explicit quality measures — now supplemented, of course, by the drive to provide more transparent "customer" information to support market-like policies in some countries. The opening-up of higher education to new and alternative providers has also created a greater need for the more explicit regulation of the more mixed public-private higher education systems that are emerging. The devolution of administrative responsibilities once discharged by State bodies to universities may have had a similar effect. In the 21st century the State has typically taken over a number of roles, some of which could be said to create conflicts of interest — still as a substantial funder of public institutions, as the dominant designer of higher education systems, as the orchestrator of innovation strategies, as regulator, as an (over-mighty?) "customer" acting on behalf of students and other stake-holders. Yet the plurality of State roles has yet to be recognized in terms of a renegotiated relationship with higher education.

Purposes — Teaching & Research

In the domains of both teaching and research, there appears to have been a sharp shift towards viewing the core purposes of higher education in more instrumental terms. Students are now more likely to be regarded, and treated, as "customers", even when they are not expected to pay significant tuition fees. Universities have been redefined as "service" organizations. At the same time the quality of graduates is now more likely to be defined in terms of their "employability" in the labour market. Both trends have been contested, of course. Critics of the trend towards treating students as "customers" point out that, even if a university education can reasonably be regarded as a "purchase", it is nearly always a one-off "purchase"; that students cannot be held to "know best" (they have come to be educated not to consume); that students must themselves contribute to their own learning through complex processes of peer learning and the co-production of skills and knowledge. Critics of the heightened emphasis on "employability" as the major success criterion point out the naivety of believing that most mismatches in the labour market can be resolved by "supply-side" solutions; and also that the 21st-century graduate labour market has become increasingly fragmented with some graduates (typically those with already extensive social capital and who have attended elite universities) able to look forward to successful, and lucrative, careers, while other graduates face insecure and fractured futures (Brown, Lauder & Ashton, 2008). Yet, despite these powerful counter-critiques, both trends appear to have become well entrenched — not only in political discourse, but in institutional practices and priorities.

A similar process can be observed with regard to research. The centrality of higher education, and in particular of research universities, in the global knowledge economy has led not only to heightened emphasis on the contribution universities can make to meeting the demand for highly skilled professional workers, but also an equally strong emphasis on the contribution that research can make to innovation (and so to economic growth) and to social well-being. Re-conceptualizations of the processes of knowledge generation, such as powerful utility of the "triple helix" of State, industry and universities or the evolution of more distributed and reflexive forms of so-called "Mode 2" knowledge production, have emphasized the closer linkages between university-based research, technology and innovation (Etzkowitz, 2008 and 2014; Gibbons *et al.*, 1994; Nowotny, Scott & Gibbons, 2001 and 2003). Where once scientific research (and scholarship) were seen as producing economic and social benefits through a complex chain of mediating links, now the tendency is to see the relationship between research and benefits in terms of less complicated, and only lightly mediated, links. This is apparent in universities, with the growth of science and technology parks, spin-in and spin-out companies and rebalancing of pure and applied research (and also, perhaps, the emphasis on recovering the full economic cost of research). It is also apparent in Government, with the increasing popularity of integrated innovation strategies and assessments of research that embrace not only its scientific quality but also its "impact" (to use the language employed in the U.K.'s Research Excellence Framework, but also a feature of other selective funding regimes). Once again, the objections to over-instrumentalized research policies — such as the traditional assertion that universities are best at curiosity-driven research, or that linear accounts of research-technology-innovation chains are too simple and even naive — appear to carry little weight. The paradoxical result is that any enhanced autonomy that research universities may gain from more diverse funding systems for teaching may be more than cancelled out by their close conscription within State-directed innovation systems.

Performance, Metrics and League Tables

The fourth trend is towards much greater emphasis on the measurement of performance. This can be observed at many levels — from management of the performance of individual academic staff through setting quantifiable targets, through departmental budgets (and internal institutional allocation methodologies) determined increasingly by metrics, and the growth of contract funding in research (a trend powerfully reinforced by the development of more entrepreneurial models of higher education), to the growing popularity of whole-institution "contracts" between universities and state authorities. These trends are apparent within most higher education systems. Indeed, some of the best examples of explicitly contractual funding arrangements between universities and the state can be found in Western Europe (where public funding of higher education has remained at a high level — perhaps not a coincidence?)

However pervasive the use of performance measurement has become at individual, departmental, institutional and national levels, the limits of metrics such as citation scores and impact factors have been recognized by most public authorities. A recent report in England rejected the idea that such metrics could replace more traditional forms of peer review in subsequent REFs (Wilsdon et al., 2015). But no such restraint has been shown in the proliferation of league tables, most of which have been produced by media and other commercial organizations (although one of the most prominent has been produced by a Chinese university, Jia Tong University in Shanghai) (Rauhvargers, 2011; Marope, Wells & Hazelkorn 2013; Marginson, 2014). Of course, rankings are not new. Those produced by US News and World Report date back several decades. Nor, of course, is the unofficial ranking of individual professors, although this has been given a new intensity with the rise of the internet and social networking. However, league tables have acquired a new influence over institutional behaviour, particularly perhaps in the case of research universities because a ranking in the top 50, 100 or 200 is crucial to their status and success. And not only universities but also governments. In most respects, "official" metrics are now overshadowed by "unofficial" league tables.

There are several sources of this enthusiasm for performance measurement, metrics and (most of all) league tables. But perhaps the most significant are the rise of so-called "audit society", a phenomenon that can now be observed throughout both the market and public sectors and which some writers have attributed to the deconstruction of older notions of trust rooted in professional expertise (Power, 1997). Almost as significant, and closely linked, has been the simultaneous rise of a "market" culture within most higher education systems, as has happened more widely across the public sector (such as the privatization of energy and transport companies), which has required the development of much stricter accountability regimes.

Globalization

The final trend that has affected all higher education institutions, whatever their differences in funding or legal status, has been globalization. The impact on research universities, because of their international reach and reputations, has perhaps been greatest and most direct. However, "globalization" is as often employed as a media mantra as a precise analytical tool. Even when it is more fully described, it is generally used to denote the impact of the liberalization of markets — financial, labour, all kinds, the "abolition" of time and space, the spread of global "brands" — in short, a single path of (inevitable and benign) development. In reality globalization is a bundle of phenomena that impact in different ways on universities.

The most obvious is the flows of international students, and academic staff. The recruitment of international students may provide a key economic input for those institutions that charge high tuition fees and, across North America and Europe, also provides academic capacity that might be difficult to sustain if it relied solely on "domestic" demand. This is especially true in the case of Ph.D. students and post-doctoral and early-career researchers. The higher education and research systems in these countries depend critically on the import of academic talent — from Asia, the Middle East, Africa and Latin America. These imbalances not only raise important issues related to equity and balanced development (and the avoidance of geopolitical disorder), but also questions about how long America and Europe will be able to continue to import academic talent on the required scale. It is already clear that several Asian countries may soon cease to export students (and staff) and may instead need to become importers to feed the development of their dynamic university and research systems. At the very least, these flows are likely to become less unbalanced in future.

A second manifestation of globalization is the growth of offshore campuses. Nottingham in the U.K. and New York University in the U.S. are perhaps the most active and successful institutions in developing transnational education. But very many American and European universities are now engaging in less full-blown international activities — such as the validation of teaching programmes in other countries or membership of international networks of (usually like-minded and equal-rated) institutions. Transnational education raises a number of complex issues — legal and jurisdictional, financial and organisational, cultural and scientific and, of course, ethical. Yet its attractions are obvious — as an alternative form of globalization when (and if) more traditional flows of international students, scientists and scholars reduce.

Two final, perhaps less desirable, aspects of globalization have also become more prominent. One is the explosion of global league tables that has already been discussed. The second is the impact of uglier forms of globalization on universities and research — the rise of so-called "fundamentalism" which, while rejecting the liberal and secular values of the "West", nevertheless employ global technologies (and "brands") to promote their cause; but also the rising tide of opposition to immigration in many European countries and also, although less categorically perhaps, the United States. The rise of "fundamentalism" is a sharp reminder of the divorce between processes regarded in America and Europe as inextricably linked, the modernization of society and the economy through economic development and modernity (or the political and cultural values associated with the Enlightenment). This divorce had already become clear in parts of East Asia, notably China. It may also have been present in the so-called "culture wars" notably in the United States on issues such as climate change, evolution and stem cell research. The rising tide of opposition to immigration has also been a sharp reminder that the international flows of students, scientists and scholars, so critical to the success of many research universities, are only one part of much larger flows of low-skilled migrants and refugees.

THE GLION PROCESS

Beginnings and ends: 1998 and 2013 compared

The first Glion colloquium was held in May 1998, and its proceedings were published in *Challenges Facing Higher Education at the Millennium*, edited by Werner Hirsch and Luc Weber, in the following year (Hirsch & Weber, 1999). This represented the starting point of the Glion process. The ninth Glion colloquium was held in June 2013, and its proceedings were published last year in *Preparing Universities for an Era of Change*, and the editors were Luc Weber now joined by Jim Duderstadt (Weber & Duderstadt, 2014). It is interesting to compare not only the content but also the "tone" of the two colloquia and their published proceedings to determine what has changed — but also what has stayed the same. For that reason the 1998 and 2013 colloquia perhaps deserve more extended analysis than the intervening meetings.

The first thing that is striking is the similarity of titles — challenges and change. This sense that universities have been subject to a process of almost permanent revolution, which far from abating is becoming more intense (and also more volatile and less predictable), is now pervasive. It has been ground into the mentality of modern higher education system, to such an extent that evidence of continuity, and enduring values, is often ignored — although this too can be glimpsed throughout the Glion process.

Right at the start in the first colloquium the organizers, and orchestrators, nailed their colours to the mast of change. They contrasted two rival views of how higher education should approach the future — the first emphasizing the need for continuity and stability (if not, quite, for universities to be left alone); and the second, which they endorsed, adopting a more activist approach embracing "major affirmative steps" (in short, for universities to embrace future challenges). The second approach has become key to the ethos of Glion in the intervening years. But, at the first and subsequent meetings, the tension between evolution and revolution, which echoed this contrast between stability and active engagement, remained. Change may have been inevitable, but what form would it take? For example, James Duderstadt, in an important contribution to the first volume, argued that U.S. higher education faced two starkly different futures — a pessimistic scenario he labelled "massive restructuring" (market-driven mediocrity, unbundling of core university responsibilities and what would now be termed "commodification"); and an optimistic scenario he labelled a "culture of learning" in which existing institutions would rise successfully to meet new challenges, particularly with regard to the learning needs of their students.

Helpfully Luc Weber, one of the key Glion orchestrators, summarized the key challenges identified by the participants in the first colloquium. These he grouped under nine headings:

- Environment (the impacts of globalization and technology were especially emphasized);
- Mission (the need for responsive and responsible universities able to open up new publics and industry, while continuing to focus on producing critical citizens rather than just expert "technicians");
- Challenges to research universities (notably the growing tension between teaching and research, and the relentless drive towards specialization in research in the quest for excellence);
- Competition (not only "external" competition from rival, for-profit, providers, but also "internal" competition generated by the commercialization of teaching research);
- Students and teaching (focussing on the lack of progress towards equal, or fair, access despite mass expansion, and the challenges of lifelong learning);
- Academic profession (the changing role of teachers as what would now be termed "facilitators of learning", an over-faithfulness to disciplines and the tension between specialization and multi-disciplinarily);

- Finance (declining traditional, especially public, funding quickening the search for alternative income, and the need to curb escalating costs);
- Governance (an endorsement of "shared governance", but with stronger leadership, streamlining decision-making and, for State universities, greater autonomy).

In this manner the challenges to be met by "major affirmative steps" were set out right at the start of the Glion process. It is a list that has clearly stood the test of time. But there may also have an intriguing shift on "tone". In 1998 Frank Rhodes expressed optimism in his chapter on the "The New University". In it he offered an ideal portrait of the new American university able to reconcile shared governance with strong leadership, private funding with public responsibility, campus localism with global reach, autonomy with networks of partners, a strong knowledge and research focus with student centredness, new technology with traditional community, quality and excellence with efficiency and a professional and expert orientation with humanity. Today, perhaps, it would be more difficult to feel so confident about the possibility of such reconciliations. Instead there would be greater fears that these competing (contradictory?) forces would fragment the university itself.

The latest volume (apart from the present book), the proceedings of the 2013 colloquium, perhaps demonstrates this shift towards pessimism. Although not going so far as to characterize the research university as an endangered species, it highlights some of the key threats to its vitality. These include ageing populations in those world regions where research universities are concentrated, especially in Western Europe but also in North America (where overall population growth conceals reductions in shrinking proportions of the social elites with which research universities have been most closely associated); new technologies that simultaneously enable and disrupt (for example, obliterating temporal and spatial constraints and in the process challenging traditional paradigms of learning); funding challenges produced by the rising cost of teaching and research and shrinking tax bases resulting from slower economic growth and taxpayer resistance (and, at the same time, growing sensitivity about above-inflation increases in tuition fees); and the impact of global markets that subvert organizational norms and structures by promoting out-sourcing and, more radically, the unbundling of academic activities once regarded as inextricably entwined.

Taken together these threats may pose an existential challenge to research universities, despite their dominance of global league tables. In the first session of the 2013 colloquium, a panel of three university leaders — James Duderstadt (Michigan), Heather Munroe-Blum (McGill) and Howard Newby (Liverpool) — reflected on the recommendations made in a gloomy report from the National Academies of Science, Engineering and Medicine in the United States which identified a triple abandonment — by Government no longer committed to investment in university research; by corporations no longer willing to sustain world-leading research capacity themselves while relying on under-funded university capacity; and by the universities themselves unable to achieve the levels of efficiency and productivity required to remain globally competitive. In short, a gloomy prognosis to which the academies' remedies — more coherent innovation strategies, an end to the erosion of public funding, increased efficiency, streamlined regulation, reforms in graduate education and more emphasis on science, technology, engineering and mathematics — seemed as much exhortatory as practical.

Another contribution at the 2013 colloquium by Hunter Rawlings, revealingly entitled "How to Answer the Utilitarian Assault on Higher Education", struck an even more pessimistic note. In it he attempted to answer widespread criticism that large numbers of American college students appeared to be achieving only limited "learning gains" as measured by standardized tests — and therefore often lacked the skills required in the expanding graduate labour market. Paradoxically this — alleged — under-achievement had not been accompanied by any significant decline in the earnings premium that graduates enjoy. This may suggest that this pervasive discourse of "crisis", not confined to the United States, reflects not so much the economic realities of the labour market, but the rise of political hostility towards higher education, fuelled by alarmist media interventions. Recently *The Economist* devoted a special report to higher education with the provocative title "The whole world is going to university. Is it worth it?" (*The Economist*, 2015). There is only limited evidence that the employers of graduates support an even tighter focus on vocational skills and competences, at any rate as demonstrated through their hiring preferences.

However, the shift from a largely supportive political environment towards a more sharply critical one is a phenomenon that many higher education systems in North America and, to a more limited degree, Western Europe have experienced (but which is largely absent in South and East Asia). This may pose particular challenges to universities, especially established research universities, which have traditionally regarded themselves as closely aligned with political and social elites and state agencies and structures — "insiders", it might almost be said. Perhaps this loss of "respect" is as important a factor in explaining any feelings of disenchantment, and contributing to a sense of "crisis", as any state disinvestment in higher education (which, although real enough in parts of the United States, has not really been experienced in Europe where higher education budgets have generally suffered much less than other publicly funded services — and is certainly not evident in China, Korea and other Asian countries with rapidly developing higher education systems to match their dynamic economies).

Generalizations are certainly treacherous, although potentially they can be illuminating. However, a comparison of the content, and, crucially, "tone" of the first and the latest Glion colloquia suggests three tentative conclusions.

- The first is that, now as then, higher education systems in general, and research universities in particular, are caught up in a process of ceaseless change — to which they can respond either minimally or with enthusiasm (the latter being the strong preference of most Glion participants, although not necessarily of the academic/faculty colleagues across all disciplines, notably the humanities and some social sciences);
- The second is that American universities appear to be facing greater, and perhaps more hostile, political challenges than their European peers — more immediate threats to funding and also sharper public criticism. They are more on the defensive — and this cannot be fully accounted for by the popularity of polemical literature in the United States compared with the staider literary traditions of Europe; nor perhaps by the fact that in Europe the future of higher education has remained an essentially second-order political issue. At first sight this is a paradoxical conclusion to reach because American research universities continue to dominate global league tables, and their scientific and scholarly excellence and productivity are probably greater than at any time in their history. Perhaps, against the odds, the Bologna process has been able to breathe new life, and confidence, into European universities;
- The third, and incontestable, conclusion is the clear evidence of the rise of Asian higher education. This is reflected not only in the increasing number of Asian participants and contributors in more recent Glion colloquia (which has mirrored growing Asian participation in most other international higher education forums) but also the unmistakable sense of optimism prevailing in, and political and public support enjoyed by, most successful Asian universities.

Evolving agendas 2000-2011

The intervening six colloquia, and proceedings, covered a wide range of topics. Their titles, and the sequence, tell an interesting story. First, in 2001 came *Governance in Higher Education*, with the suggestive subtitle "the University in Flux", which concluded with the Glion Declaration 2000 (Hirsch & Weber, 2001). A year later the title chosen for the book based on the preceding colloquium was *As the Walls of Academia are Tumbling Down*, a series of essays on the opening-up of the research universities (Hirsch & Weber, 2002). In

2004 the theme was *Reinventing the Research University*, a title that clearly described the preoccupations of the preceding colloquium (Weber & Duderstadt, 2004). Two years later the focus had both narrowed and broadened out — *Universities and Business: Partnering for the Knowledge Society* (Weber & Duderstadt, 2006). In 2008 the focus was wider still, on *The Globalization of Higher Education* — although this topic had already been covered in contributions to earlier colloquia (Weber & Duderstadt, 2008). In 2010 it was back to the economy — *University Research for Innovation* (Weber & Duderstadt, 2010). Then in 2012 a new priority emerged, reflecting its urgency and topicality — *Global Sustainability and the Responsibility of Universities* (Weber & Duderstadt, 2012).

Each colloquium built on the discussions held in the preceding, creating both a strong sense of continuity of issues (and concerns) and also an impressive momentum. But the arc of the colloquia, which began and has ended (for the moment) with change and challenges, also seems to indicate an increasing preoccupation with the external environment rather than focusing on the internal dynamics, and dilemmas, of the research university. Although the first three colloquia certainly addressed broad topics, notably the lowering of the "walls" between research universities and their enveloping environment and consequently the need to "reinvent" them, the focus was an inward gaze, on how research universities needed to adapt. The following four colloquia had a wider, more outside-in perspective — on links with industry, globalization, innovation and sustainability. It may only be coincidence that this shift coincided, approximately, with the collapse of the neoliberal world order (rather as the late 1970s and 1980s witnessed the collapse of the post-war welfare-state Keynesian world order).

'Governance in Higher Education'

The second colloquium in 2000, the only one to be held outside Glion in Del Mar in California, focused on three major themes — recent trends in university governance, fundamental principles of governance and ways in which governance might be improved — all against the background of the evolving mission and responsibilities of the research university in the new century discussed in an opening presentation by Frank Rhodes, President of Cornell for 18 years and a Glion stalwart. Governance was considered both in a broader sense — the role of the President (Rector, Vice-Chancellor) and other executive managers, as well as the ebb and flow of "shared governance" with faculty members was included, along with the responsibilities of university boards — but also perhaps a narrower sense — although the governance of European universities was discussed, the focus was on the governance of U.S. research universities (conveniently so perhaps as the next decade would see major changes in many European countries as Ministries loosened their grip on universities, while patterns of governance in the U.S. have been more stable).

Among the dilemmas identified during this colloquium, two were especially notable. The first was whether governance in higher education, and in particular of research universities, was — or should be — distinctive and different from other types of public and social institution. The consensus reached is perhaps best summed up as "yes — but". Yes, because there was general agreement that universities flourished best with the minimum possible intervention from external stakeholders, especially the State (a view that was perhaps easier to sustain in 2000 than it is 15 years later). But, because it was accepted that university governance was highly complex — embracing both formal legal instruments and informal patterns of behaviour; multi-layered (institution and department); and with multiple actors (students — and alumni, faculty — junior as well as senior, administration — and not only the President/Rector and their senior colleagues, boards — external and internal members, State authorities — as funders and/or regulators, employers and communities). The second dilemma was whether it was possible to devise a general theory of university governance. Luc Weber, for example, discussed the application of lessons from the economic theory of federalism, such as the well-established European principle of subsidiarity. Henry Rosovsky preferred a more pragmatic approach — not too much democracy, a commitment to shared governance and recognition that governance structures were simply a means to the true end, the enhancement of teaching and research. But there was general agreement that getting governance right, and improving decision-making, provided a key enabling framework within which universities could respond to the challenge of change.

'As The Walls of Academia are Tumbling Down'

The third colloquium was held back in Glion in the summer of 2001. Its theme was the increasing permeability of the university, hence the somewhat worried title. This title may have reflected some ambivalence about the degree to which this should be resisted or welcomed, although the general will among the participants (and the contributors to the subsequent book) leaned towards the latter (more optimistic) view. This permeability was seen as both an external and internal phenomenon — external in the sense that universities, and especially research universities, were now increasingly regarded by both the State and industry as key instruments of innovation (which was reflected both in additional scrutiny, unwelcome perhaps, but also increasing largesse, in the form of sponsored research); and internal in the sense that the growth of interdisciplinary courses (and multi-disciplinary research) was tending to erode traditional departmental boundaries and also that the application of new technologies was beginning to challenge existing divisions of labour between teachers, their students and those responsible for providing learning support.

Research universities were now best regarded as part of complex networks, notably with regard to applied research and technology transfer but also lifelong learning. James Duderstadt presciently considered the future of the university in the digital age — a theme which, of course, has assumed every greater salience as the years have gone by. Luc Weber wrote about the universities' responsibilities in an age of an increasing competition — another theme that has gone from strength to strength (and now has become a dominant motif of both policy discourse and institutional practice in contemporary higher education). The potential, and dangers, of new alliances between universities and high-technology companies were discussed by Werner Hirsch — and concrete case-studies of such alliances were offered from ETH in Zurich and also San Diego. Whatever residual regrets there may have been in the overthrow of the "walls of academia", there seemed to be little nostalgia for the idea of the university as an ivory tower. The 21st century had firmly arrived. This third colloquium, like the second on governance, set an agenda — a list of topics and themes that would be developed later in the Glion process.

'Reinventing the Research University'

The fourth colloquium was again held in Glion two years later. The title chosen for the subsequent book proclaimed its radical agenda — not to restore or renew or even to reform but to reinvent the research university. As with governance there were clear differences between America and Europe. Just as U.S. universities, public or private, had powerful governing boards while formal organs of university governance were less well developed in most of Europe, so the research university was a familiar and established category in the U.S. (and, indeed, formally enshrined in the influential Carnegie classification of institutions — even divided into two divisions) while in Europe the emergence of an elite group of research intensive universities was — and perhaps still is — more tentative. So key contributions came from Robert Zemsky and James Duderstadt, offering an American perspective, and Luc Weber and Pavel Zgaga, illuminating the rather more complex European perspective.

It is somewhat of a simplification — but perhaps the challenge facing American research universities was one of reform, to enable them to meet new post-millennial challenges, while in Europe the prospect was of a more radical process — of invention as much as reinvention. The — comparative — underdevelopment of Europe's leading universities was also raised by Frans van Vught in a challenging contribution on "Closing the European

Knowledge Gap? Challenges for European universities in the 21st century". This, it should be remembered, was two years before European heads of government committed themselves, hubristically as it turned out, to making Europe the most advanced high-technology region in the world by 2010 in the Lisbon Declaration. This specifically European perspective was complemented by Wayne Johnson's expansive discussion of new "knowledge chains", in which of course research universities featured prominently, in his chapter on the globalization of research and development. It is also worth noting that another contribution from Zemsky raising for the first time in the Glion process a topic that is now of consuming, even obsessive, interest in worldwide higher education, the need to classify (and rank?) universities according to their functions and market positions. In both van Vught's and Zemsky's (second) contribution, key contours of future policy debates were first sketched.

'Universities and Business: Partnering for the Knowledge Society'

The fifth Glion colloquium in 2005, once again held overlooking Lake Geneva, had a broader range of participants, which is reflected in the subsequent book published a year later. University leaders from both sides of the Atlantic were again there in force (one of the strengths of the Glion process has been the remarkable continuity of university participants, offering a fascinating insight into how ideas have developed within this leadership cadre). But they were joined by key industrial leaders — notably Peter Brabeck-Lemathe, chief executive and president of the leading Swiss (and multinational) company Nestlé. This twin-track approach was highlighted by two rather than one summary chapters, from Brabeck-Lemathe (based on an after-dinner talk he gave at the symposium) as well as from the editors, James Duderstadt and Luc Weber. But it was perhaps the title of one chapter, by William Wulf, "A Mosaic of Problems" that best summed up the eclectic range of issues under discussion — a case-study of regional development in Austin, Texas, and Lausanne in Switzerland; the threat of declining demand for science and engineering courses, and best practice in business-industry collaboration (by Richard Lambert, a former Editor of the *Financial Times* and later the Director General of the Confederation of British Industry, who headed a national enquiry into this very topic). Bertie Andersson also offered a critical analysis of European research policy which in the wake of the Lisbon Declaration had acquired an urgent topicality. However, no one challenged the need for closer university-industry links, although many acknowledge the difficulty of exploiting them to the full. The banking crisis, and subsequent economic recession, still lay in the future.

In their concluding summary Duderstadt and Weber highlighted both the common issues that research universities faced on both sides of the Atlantic

— for example, declining demand for science and engineering courses (for which they, like many commentators held secondary schools responsible) — and also the, perhaps more significant, differences. The theme of European "underdevelopment", first raised by Frans van Vught in the previous colloquium, was reintroduced. In their view three specific challenges faced European universities. The first was the need to accept some degree of formal stratification; not all universities could aspire to research eminence without diluting the financial, scientific and human resources that could be made available. The second, which followed from the first, was the comparative lack of comprehensive research universities with a critical mass of excellence across most disciplines; to a greater extent than the U.S. with its tradition of big land-grant State universities and private "Ivy League" institutions, the European university landscape was populated by specialist institutions such as ETZ in Zurich or the London School of Economics. The third, which followed from the first two, was the need to create an environment that encouraged "world-class" institutions (incidentally the first time that this now ubiquitous label was employed in the Glion process); the clear implication was that uniform State funding regimes needed to be supplemented — by alternative income streams (including student fees).

'The Globalization of Higher Education'

Globalization, its opportunities, challenges and discontents, had featured in several earlier Glion colloquia. But it was the primary focus of the sixth colloquium held in 2007. As a result the range of participants, and later authors, was extended beyond the U.S. and (Western) European participants who had been the stalwarts of these earlier colloquia. Australia, Japan, Russia, China, Singapore, Korea and Brazil were all offered as case-studies. The colloquium itself was an (even more) comprehensive event. Eighteen nations, and all five continents, were represented. But this did not mean that perennial concerns were forgotten. Two contributions, by Georg Winkler and Patrick Aebischer and Jean-François Ricci, reprised worries about the under-development of (continental) European universities in the emerging, and intensifying, global competition. Were they "falling behind", and were their organizational patterns unsuited to meeting the challenges of globalisation? Concerns were also expressed about the difficulty facing American universities in balancing global, regional and national demands. Robert Zemsky even asked, provocatively, whether "our reach has exceeded our grasp" in taking a second look at higher education as a global enterprise. But the general flavour of the discussion, as represented in the subsequent book, was that universities were still behind the curve, comfortable with familiar processes of internationalization (such as flows of international students, scientists and scholars) but troubled by the potentially much more disruptive influence of globalization.

Nevertheless most contributors accepted that globalization was pre-eminently an economic and technological phenomenon, the development of world markets based on global divisions of labour (and powered above all by advances in information technologies). The cultural and geopolitical aspects of globalization were only hinted at. Only one contributor, John Waterbury, looked at the dark side of globalization and discussed how universities should respond to violent situations. This was perhaps the first occasion in which the shadow of 9/11, and subsequent conflicts in Iraq and Afghanistan, had fallen on the Glion discussions — but only fleetingly. On this wider canvass should universities simply confine themselves to being responsive, meeting the need of the high-tech global knowledge economy for skills and research, or should they seek instead to be responsible by reasserting core values, not only values of science and reason but also human and social values as well? This key question was filed under "future business".

'University Research for Innovation'

Ten years on from the original colloquium participants in the ninth colloquium, and contributors to the subsequent book, published in 2010, were in retrospective mood. Frank Rhodes compared and contrasted the challenges facing research universities at the beginning of the Glion process in 1999 with the challenges they faced a decade later. Nothing had happened in the intervening period, in his view, to doubt their centrality in the society, economy and culture of the 21st century, and he continued to reject Peter Drucker's prediction that they would become "relics". But he accepted that the research university now had to operate in a colder climate — in terms of external forces such as heightened geo-political (and military) conflict and post-crisis/post-crash economic environment, but also in terms of threats to funding and changing student constituencies. However, he remained an optimist — "adversity as opportunity" was a favourite phrase — and that optimism was reflected in the second Glion Declaration on "Universities and the Innovative Spirit" which he took the lead in drafting.

Although the focus was on university research for innovation, the actual scope was much broader than the university-industry links that such a title might have suggested — in two senses. First, alongside topics that might have been expected — the role of industry in fostering innovation, a review of national innovation strategies and (in greater detail) an account of the German Excellence initiative — broader topics were also covered. These included a, perhaps counter-intuitive, emphasis on scientific curiosity and the transformative impact of fundamental research, from Jean-Lou Chameau and Carol Carmichael (both from CalTech), a discussion of the dynamic between *bildung* and innovation, and an assertion that community engagement was a powerful catalyst for social innovation. Secondly, the focus was no longer so tightly on North America and Western Europe. Latin America, Singapore and Saudi Arabia were also included as case studies, the last in the form of a detailed account of the development of the King Abdul Azziz University of Science and Technology. Wider still, perhaps, Jamil Salmi discussed the challenges of establishing "world-class" (that label again) universities in the developing world. Finally the fundamental character of innovation was discussed in three contributions, indicating that in the fluid 21st-century world it could not be taken as an unproblematic "given".

'Global Sustainability and the Responsibilities of Universities'

The second-to-last Glion colloquium focused on sustainability — in its widest sense to embrace not only climate and environment, usually regarded as the key topics, but also the economy, poverty and health. In the first contribution Luc Weber emphasized the key role played by the humanities and social sciences to address these wider concerns. Sustainability was no longer an issue to be addressed through cutting-edge science and technology. It was also a state of mind, even a core value (especially perhaps among the latest generation of students). This highlighted one of the key contrasts, both of which concerned timescales. The first was the tension between older generations who had benefited from 20th-century economic growth (expressed through material culture) who were reluctant to attach the same priority to sustainability as their children (or grandchildren). The second was the difficulty of reconciling political timescales, often limited to little more than five years, with the longer, quasi-geological, timescales over which topics such as climate change operated, even as they accelerated to their irreversible conclusions. In his contribution Georg Winkler emphasized the breadth of sustainability challenges by pointing to those identified by the European Commission — climate change, health care, ageing populations and finite resources (for example, in energy and water).

Given the breadth of the colloquium's focus on sustainability it was inevitable that an equally wide range of topics was addressed. Some were familiar (and "safe"?), such as the contribution that university research can make to understanding and solving some of these problems. Others were equally familiar (but perhaps less "safe"?), such as the role that universities might play in educating global citizens who, of course, were likely also be passionate advocates for sustainability which might potentially bring them — and universities — into sharper conflict with powerful political and industrial forces with a vested interest in short-term perspectives (and profits?) A third set of topics was perhaps more self-interested — how to ensure that research universities were themselves sustainable in terms of political, and public, support and of funding. The sheer breadth of topics inevitably made it difficult to produce neat and coherent answers. Sustainability comprises too many strands — scientific, technical, political, economic, cultural and even moral. But the colloquium succeeded not only in highlighting this as one of the most important, if not the most important, challenges facing research universities, but also in illuminating these many strands.

COMMON THEMES AND CONCLUSIONS

The most important, and lasting, achievement of the series of Glion colloquia is that it has amounted to more than just a series of seminars; it perhaps deserves to be labelled a "process", not of course in the scale of significance of the Bologna process (with which, intriguingly, it has been contemporary), but nevertheless a sustained and coherent intervention in our shared understanding of the challenges facing higher education in the 21st century. This is true in at least three senses.

- First, at the core of Glion has been a group of influential individuals who have been active participants and contributors at several seminars (and in a few cases throughout). As a result it has been possible to observe the evolution of their views and perspectives over a period of more than 15 years. Such consistency of key personnel is unusual. One of the criticisms of the way in which higher education policies have been developed over the past two or three decades in many countries is that policy "memories" have become more and more foreshortened. The consequences of this foreshortening have been not simply the direct loss of experience — supposedly "new" initiatives often grind out old themes and are sometimes doomed to the same disappointments — but also perhaps an erosion of core values, that sense of the fundamental qualities and characteristics especially of research universities. This may have contributed to the divisions between faculty members, who retain this understanding and allegiances, and the policy and management "class" for whom everything is (always?) in flux (and may even make of a virtue of their ignorance of the past). The Glion process has bridged that divide;
- Secondly, Glion has offered a commentary on the tensions, but also synergies, between continuity and change. It is possible to regard the colloquia as a sustained conversation on this theme, the dialogue between what must endure and what must change. Right at the start the ambition was to confront challenges positively and creatively, but without abandoning the bedrock values of the research university. The titles of the individual colloquia signal an emphasis on challenges

to universities to change and adapt to new circumstances (although their novelty can perhaps be exaggerated — are the pressures to respond to globalization, and the urgent need for universities to "service" the emerging global knowledge-based economy, really more pressing and urgent than the massive social pressure experienced by higher education between the 1950s and 1970s?) However, many of the individual contributions make the case for continuity, not in a defensive or conservative sense but simply in a spirit of sustaining the university's (perhaps unique) capacity to transform the lives of their individual students and wider societies through critical enquiry (whether through teaching or research and scholarship);

- Thirdly, Glion has focused, not exclusively but predominantly, on the research university. Since the 1960s the policy focus has often been on the development of mass higher education systems. In some countries, traditional research universities have somewhat stood aside from the process, either because their position was protected within formally differentiated systems as has been the case in many American state-wide systems (although, of course, this did not preclude massive expansion of student numbers) or, in the case of Central and Eastern Europe, massification had to wait until the collapse of Communist regimes after 1989. In other countries, most especially perhaps in (continental?) Western Europe, even the most traditional universities have been swept up in the shift towards mass access (and, paradoxically, expansion has been more limited in non-university institutions). More recently, as the policy focus has shifted towards competitiveness in the global knowledge economy, research universities have received renewed emphasis — but often largely in terms of their research (and research moreover that seemed to relate to enhanced competitiveness). But generally their wider educational and cultural significance has not received the same emphasis (or has even become matter for a regret, and even apology, on grounds of social equity). In the eyes of many policy-makers, it seems, they are regarded essentially as "knowledge factories". The value of the Glion process has been to draw attention to research universities, in all their variety, in a more holistic manner.

The Glion process spanned a period of changes in the tectonic plates of global higher education. One has already been discussed — the, perhaps rather surprising, recovery of the European university led by, but by no means exclusively attributable to, the Bologna reforms (Scott, 2012; Crosier & Parveva, 2013). The trials of massification, compounded by the tightening of State budgets as post-war solidarities (and commitment to the welfare state and/or social market), had thrown many European universities on the defensive by the 1990s. The most established research universities had perhaps suffered more than more recently established institutions. Bologna may have helped them, along with the wider higher education systems in which they were embedded, recover their poise. Of course, other forces have been at work, notably the impact of global rankings of universities that (misleadingly) have understated the quality of many (continental) European universities and which have galvanized political action. Nor has it been an altogether comfortable process, as national policies such as the *Excellenz* initiative in Germany and more recently the French Government's policy of concentration and mergers of universities in major cities have upset long-standing conventions about the relationship between universities and the State. But the overall impact of the Bologna process and national reforms, has been to give European universities a new sense of direction — and a new policy language (even if it is a language disapproved of by some academic traditionalists) (European Commission, 2011; Olsen & Maassen, 2007). Of course, not everyone agrees that European universities are now able fully to meet the global challenges that face them (Ritzen, 2009). It may also have helped to create more of a level playing field between Europe and the United States. The funding challenges facing many American research universities, although they have done little to dent their global dominance, have perhaps had some impact on institutional morale — and produced a more reflective, and even self-critical, mood among their leaders (Smelser, 2013). The proceedings of the Glion colloquia, which began essentially as a transatlantic dialogue, suggest that policy insights, and even policy borrowing, have not always been one-way.

The second shift in the tectonic plates of world higher education, of course, has been the rise of East Asia — China, Korea, Singapore, Malaysia and (possibly) India to join Japan among the world's leading players. This is reflected clearly in the Glion process. New voices increasingly joined in what had begun as a transatlantic dialogue. With each successive colloquium it has been possible to observe a gradual shifting in the centre-of-gravity in world higher education, a shift that has taken place — or is taking place — also on the wider stages of geopolitics and the global economy. Of course, this shift should not be exaggerated. Much of the interest in East Asia expressed through the Glion process has been focused on the opportunities available to American and European universities rather than to a recognition that the baton has truly passed to that world region. University voices from other world regions also remain muted. One surprising silence is from Central and Eastern Europe where perhaps the earlier enthusiasm produced by the collapse of Communist rule has abated. Latin America, Africa, much of the Middle East (outside the oil-rich Arabian peninsula and Gulf States) continue to be zones of silence. The university world remains centred on the North Atlantic.

However, the abiding significance of the Glion process (so far) has been the commentary it has provided on the shift from the overwhelming post-war emphasis on building mass higher education systems, certainly in response to new workforce demands from increasingly post-industrial economies but predominantly to build more open, inclusive, opportunity-focused and perhaps more equal societies, to a 21st-century emphasis on the "knowledge economy" characterized by global competitiveness and accompanied perhaps by an increasing degree of social pessimism as environmental risks and geopolitical threats have accumulated and older forms of solidarity have been shredded. The research university has been in a commanding position to provide such commentary — prospectively as one of the most powerful agents of global competitiveness through its production of highly skilled graduates and outputs of research; but also retrospectively as a key institution in building national identities and shaping cultures (and also as an incubator, and preserver, of the values associated with modernity as they have emerged in the North Atlantic world over the past two centuries — and which are assumed, perhaps arrogantly, still to be transcendent).

REFERENCES

Bennetot Pruvot, E. & Estermann, T (2014). *DEFINE Thematic Report: Funding for Excellence*, European University Association, Brussels.

Bologna Declaration (1999). The European Higher Education Area: Joint Declaration of the European Ministers of Education, 19 June 1999, Bologna.

Brown, P., Lauder, H. & Ashton, D. (2008). "Education, Globalisation and the Future of the Knowledge Economy", *European Educational Research Journal*, 7 (2), pp. 131-156.

Campos, Paul F. (2015). "The Real Reason College Tuition Cost So Much", *The New York Times, Saturday Review*, 4 April 2015.

Crosier, David & Parveva, Teodora (2013). *The Bologna process: its impact on higher education development in Europe and beyond*. UNESCO International Institute for Educational Planning, Paris.

Economist, The (2015). "The Whole World is Going to University: Is it Worth It?" Special Report, *The Economist*, 28 March 2015.

Etzkowitz, H. (2008). The Triple Helix: University-Industry-Government Innovation in Action, Routledge, London.

Etzkowitz, H. (2014). "The Entrepreneurial University Wave: from ivory tower to global economic engine", *Industry and Higher Education*, 28 (4), pp. 223-232.

European Commission (2011). A New Agenda for the Modernisation of Europe's Higher Education Systems, European Commission, Brussels.

European Council (2007). *Lisbon Treaty*, European Council, Brussels http://europa.eu/Lisbon_treaty/index_en.htm.

Fukuyama, Francis (1992). *The End of History and the Last Man*, Free Press, New York.

Gibbons, M., Limoges, C., Nowotny, H., Schwartzman, S., Scott, P. & Trow, M. (1994). *The New Production of Knowledge; The Dynamics of Science and Research in Contemporary Societies*, Sage, London.

Marginson, S. (2014). "Social Science and University Rankings", *European Journal of Education*, Vol. 49, No. 1.

Marope, M., Wells, P. & Halzelkorn, E., eds. (2013). *Ranking and Accountability in Higher Education: Uses and Misuses*, UNESCO Publishing. Paris.

National Center for Education Statistics/Institute for Educational Sciences (2012). *Fast Facts: What Are The Trends In The Cost Of College Education?*, Washington. http://nces.ed.gov.

Nowotny, H., Scott, P. & Gibbons, M. (2001). *Re-Thinking Science: Knowledge and the Public in an Age of Uncertainty*, Polity Press, Cambridge.

Nowotny, H., Scott, P. & Gibbons M. (2003). "'Mode 2' Revisited: the New Production of Knowledge", *Minerva* 41, pp. 179-194.

Olsen, Johan & Maassen, Peter (2007). "European Debates on the Knowledge Institution: The Modernization of the University at European Level", in Maassen, P. & Olsen, J. eds. *University Dynamics and European Integration*, Springer, Dordrecht.

Power, Michael (1997). *The Audit Society: Rituals of Verification*, Oxford University Press.

Rauhvargers, A. (2011). *Global University Rankings and their Impact*, European University Association, Brussels.

Ritzen, Jo (2009). A Chance for European Universities: Or, Avoiding the Looming University Crisis in Europe, Amsterdam University Press.

Scott, Peter (2012). "Going Beyond Bologna: Issues and Themes", in *European Higher Education at the Crossroads: Between the Bologna Process and National Reforms*, Curaj, A., Scott, P., Vlasceanu, L. & Wilson, L. eds, Springer, Dordrecht.

Smelser, N. (2013). Dynamics of the Contemporary University: Growth, Accretion and Conflict, University of California Press, Berkeley CA.

Wilsdon, J. et al. (2015). The Metric Tide: Report of the Independent Review of the Role of Metrics in Research Assessment and Management, Higher Education Funding Council for England, Bristol.

PART I

The Role and Responsibility of Research Universities

CHAPTER 2

Global Diversity in Higher Education Systems: The Divergent Fortunes of USA, Europe and Asia

Howard Newby

INTRODUCTION

A persistent theme of the Glion Colloquium, almost since inception, has been the impact of globalization on higher education worldwide. Indeed the sixth colloquium, which took place in 2007, was devoted to this topic. (Weber & Duderstadt, 2008). It was at that colloquium that Bob Zemsky, quite rightly, reminded us of the distinction between internationalization and globalization (Zemsky, 2008) and cast a sardonic eye over some of the more exaggerated claims that were being made in the United States, based on the popularity of Tom Friedman's book *The World is Flat* (Friedman, 2005), about the potentially transformative impact of globalization on education generally, and higher education in particular.

It is worth reminding ourselves of Zemsky's summary. Two decades into what Friedman has described as the 'global revolution', its list of attributes, Zemsky wrote, could be said 'to apply to few, if any, of the world's leading universities. Most observers outside the academic world would argue, correctly I believe, that universities, both in their operations and their governance, remain opaque, even obtuse, rather than transparent. Few transactions can be said to be instantaneous, while the time necessary to develop new educational programmes has probably lengthened rather than shortened. Student markets have remained decidedly local. Even less global are the mechanisms by which prices are set for university education. The result is an academic world that has become aggressively more international without it fast becoming much more global. Students travel more; faculty wander more broadly; and leaders of international enterprises find themselves spending more time abroad attending the interests and soliciting the support of their increasingly international alumni... Scientific research is the principal exception... [but] most of what higher education does internationally is not global.' (Zemsky, 2008).

In the same volume I presented an analysis of global trends which drew upon the comprehensive study of 24 countries undertaken by the OECD (Newby, 2008). This analysis attempted to demonstrate the commonality of the challenges facing higher education policy makers around the world, whatever their history and level of development. Stated quite simply:

'There is a common move towards expanding the proportion of the population achieving higher education qualifications. This produces a common desire to shift from an 'elite' to a 'mass' higher education system — known in Europe as 'massification'. This is occurring because governments all around the world accept that higher education is a major driver of the knowledge-based economy....In many countries there are also strong social pressures to expand the opportunity to participate in higher education.

Governments all around the world not only wish to expand the sector, they also wish to achieve this expansion without any dilution of quality. Indeed, they wish to enhance quality at the same time as engage in expansion.

And finally, Governments all around the world wish to expand the sector and enhance quality whilst simultaneously reducing... the burden of resources this requires from public finances'. (Newby, 2008, pp. 56-57)

I went on to argue that these three public policy polarities created a kind of force-field which put higher education systems around the world in a state of some considerable tension. Local — i.e. national- political factors often determined where a particular higher education system came to rest between the competing forces of massification, quality enhancement and fiscal prudence.

In the year following these publications, in 2009, UNESCO held its World Conference On Higher Education, having commissioned a trend report which formed the centrepiece of the conference. (Altbach et al., 2009). This report proclaimed that 'an academic revolution' had taken place in higher education in the past half century, marked by 'transformations unprecedented in scope and diversity'. In particular the report focussed on 'the challenge of massification', whose 'logic' is deemed inevitable: greater social mobility, new patterns of funding, increasingly diversified higher education systems and an overall lowering of academic standards. Globalization, it is suggested, 'has already profoundly influenced higher education'. The report calculated that between 2000 and 2007, the percentage of the age cohort enrolled in tertiary education grew from 19% to 26%, with the most dramatic gains taking place in the most affluent countries. The report estimated that there were some 150.6 million tertiary students globally, roughly a 53% increase since 2000 alone. In addition, more that 2.5 million students were studying outside their home countries, even though cost remained a major barrier to all but the most affluent (see also IAU, 2014). Two main flows were discerned. The first consisted of students from Asia to North America, Western Europe and Australia, principally — although not exclusively — to Anglophone countries. The second was largely state-sponsored — the growth of student mobility within the European Union, through such programmes as Erasmus, etc.

And then came the global financial crisis, the consequences of which remain with us.

THE FORTUNES OF HIGHER EDUCATION SYSTEMS

So what happened next? The main purpose of this paper is to reflect on what has occurred in higher education systems across the world (viewed inevitably in a very generalized and macro sense) since the above observations were written and to assess how far the global economic crisis has produced a convergence, or a diversity, of response.

Statistics on global trends in higher education are often less than reliable and take a long time to compile. Perhaps the most authoritative recent survey was the report by the British Council, "The Shape of Things to Come, Higher Education, Global Trends and Emerging opportunities to 2020". (British Council, 2012). It analyses the prevailing trends that are shaping higher education globally, covering both teaching and research.

On the basis of the latest data available global tertiary enrolments (undergraduates and post-graduates) were estimated at 170 million in 2009. It should be noted, however, that a more recent estimate by Euromonitor international (Lennard, 2014) has put the total number at 199 million in 2013 with, significantly, more female than male students now participating (98.6 million females; 95.1 million males). This growth seems primarily to be driven by increasing literacy and participation in schools education. Despite growing demand for science and engineering students globally, the number of arts and non-science students continues to grow. The most popular subjects are social sciences, business and law (33.4%) well ahead of science (8.7%) and engineering (11.8%). Four countries alone — China, India, the USA and Russia — account for 45% of the global total, but there are emerging countries which now contain significant number of tertiary enrolments — Brazil (6.4 million), Indonesia (4.9 million), Iran (3.4 million), South Korea (3.3 million) and Turkey (3.0 million).

International student mobility continues to rise in absolute terms, heading towards 6.5 million by 2020. But proportionately, this is only keeping pace with the growth of higher education students more generally. Outbound mobility ratios vary enormously — from 50% in some African and Caribbean countries to less than 1% in the UK, USA and Australia. As is well known the distribution of destination countries is highly concentrated in the USA, UK, Australia, France, Germany, Russia, Japan and Canada. Together these countries account for 60% of total international students. But there are many countries with significant inbound flows at the regional level — South Africa, Singapore, Hong Kong, Malaysia and South Korea. As the report observes, somewhat laconically, 'while bilateral flows to China are not yet likely to rival the above in volume terms, they could have profound implications in future for tertiary institutions across the globe'. (p6). Indeed they could.

The report also notes that international student flows are highly correlated with international trade flows (statistically this accounts for 70% of the variance). It also notes the impact of demographic change: by 2020 just four countries — India, China, the USA and Indonesia — will account for over half of the world's 18-22 year olds, with a further 25% coming from Pakistan, Nigeria, Brazil, Bangladesh, Ethiopia, Philippines, Mexico, Egypt and Vietnam. However, it is India and China which dominate global growth in tertiary enrolments, with nearly half of the global growth in these two countries alone. Nevertheless, looking forward, diverging demographic trends mean that while China's rate of growth is likely to decline, that in India will continue to grow. For this reason, international student flows into the Gulf States are likely to rise considerably, especially given the level of investment in higher education infrastructure taking place there. These trends are summarised in Table 1.

The report also notes that the volume of global research output is dominated by a few large countries including the USA, Germany, Japan, China and the UK. Although smaller niche players such as Switzerland and the Netherlands flourish via extensive collaborations, volume dictates that the majority of future reach collaboration opportunities will continue to come from major players such as the USA and China. As is widely recognized, researchers with international experience create the most widely-cited research articles, but the countries generating the highest average citation impact is somewhat different — Switzerland, the Netherlands, the Nordic Countries, the UK and the USA. So smaller countries which excel in niche technological growth markets can continue to sustain a globally-competitive research base. But overall, as the report concludes, the global tertiary education sector is starting to move east, but at this stage less so south (see Table 2).

Table 1: Summary of future higher education opportunities for global engagement (2020)

International tertiary education opportunity	Future opportunities[4]
International student mobility	• **Largest outbound mobile student flows by origin (2020):** China (585k), India (296k), South Korea (134k), Germany (100k), Turkey (84k), Malaysia (82k), Nigeria (67k) • **Fastest growing (absolute) outbound mobile student flows (next decade):** India (71k), Nigeria (30k), Malaysia (22k), Nepal (17k), Pakistan (17k), Saudi Arabia (16k), Turkey (13k) • **Largest inbound mobile student flows by destination (2020):** US (582k), UK (331k), Australia (277k), Canada (176k), Germany (155k) – China and Malaysia are also likely to feature here • **Fastest growing (absolute) inbound mobile student flows (next decade):** Australia (51k), UK (28k), US (27k), Canada (23k) – again China will surely feature here • **Major bilateral mobile student flows (2020):** India to US (118k), China to US (101k), China to Australia (93k), South Korea to US (81k), China to Japan (64k), India to UK (59k) – flows to China, and possibly India also • **Fastest growing (absolute) bilateral mobile student flows (next decade):** India to UK (20k), India to US (19k), China to Australia (17k), Nigeria to UK (14k), India to Australia (11k) – flows to China, and possibly India also • **Fastest declining (absolute) bilateral mobile student flows (next decade):** China to Japan (-14k), Japan to US (-8k), China to US (-8k), China to UK (-7k), Kazakhstan to Russia (-5k), Greece to UK (-4k) – the impact of China's aggressive pursuit of international students could well lead to some well-established bilateral flows declining
Size and growth of domestic tertiary education systems	• **Largest tertiary enrolment levels (2020):** China (37.4m), India (27.8m), US (20.0m), Brazil (9.2m), Indonesia (7.7m), Russia (6.3m), Japan (3.8m), Turkey (3.8m), Iran (3.8m), Nigeria (3.6m) • **Fastest growing (absolute) tertiary enrolment growth (next decade):** India (7.1m), China (5.1m), Brazil (2.6m), Indonesia (2.3m), Nigeria (1.4m), Philippines (0.7m), Bangladesh (0.7m), Turkey (0.7m), Ethiopia (0.6m) – growth in certain markets could be larger still if ambitious international student recruitment targets are met • **Largest falls in outbound mobile students (next decade):** Japan (-10k), Greece (-10k), Poland (-8k), Singapore (-6k), Russia (-6k), Germany (-2k) – China is one to watch here given its demographic outlook and ambitious domestic tertiary sector expansion plans
TNE	• **Dual and joint degrees:** China, US, France, India, Germany • **Franchising and validation:** Asia, Latin America, possibly Africa (Nigeria) • **Branch campuses:** Far East, possibly Middle East • **Online:** Gulf countries, Asia, possibly Scandinavia
Academic international research collaboration	• **Largest growth in research output:** Volume growth to be driven by collaborations involving US and Chinese institutions • **Highest collaboration rates:** Research collaboration rates are higher in many smaller countries, such as Switzerland and Belgium (50-70%); they are lower in China (around 15%). Overall opportunity for collaboration depends on both the volume of research and propensity to collaborate • **Highest average citation impacts:** Switzerland, Netherlands, Denmark and US – collaborating with these countries in theory should help to maintain and increase research average citation impacts • **Three core opportunity groups:** Specifically for the UK, future growth in collaborations likely to be with (i) the US and other established high volume research leaders (Germany, France, Italy, Canada, Australia); (ii) high average citation impact leaders (also Switzerland, Netherlands, Denmark) and niche opportunities in smaller, technology-intensive countries such as the Nordic countries, Switzerland and Israel; and (iii) a chance to tap into rapid research output growth in key emerging markets, most notably China but also Malaysia, Iran, Saudi Arabia, India and Qatar
Business international research collaboration	• **Large companies:** Growth in collaboration opportunities with multinationals; large US, European, Chinese, and Latin American companies; niche opportunities in research and technology-intensive countries e.g. Israel, Switzerland, learn from approach in Nordic countries, Netherlands. Opportunities in countries with high tertiary sector-large firm innovation collaboration rates (e.g. Finland, Sweden) and unexploited opportunities in countries with low tertiary sector-large firm innovation collaboration rates (e.g. Brazil, UK, Spain, Italy) • **Smaller companies:** Further growth opportunities in small and medium enterprises (SME) collaboration rates for research and development (R and D), focused on niche, high-value technology areas and/or links to multinational supply chains. Opportunities in countries with high tertiary sector-SME innovation collaboration rates (e.g. Finland, Belgium, UK) and unexploited opportunities in countries with low tertiary sector-SME innovation collaboration rates (e.g. Brazil, Italy) • **Leading countries in internationally-filed patent application:** Japan, US, South Korea and in volume terms, China and India • **Innovation:** Continuing promotion of open innovation models, with fluid collaboration between business and the higher education sector

Source: The British Council (2012). The Shape of Things to Come: Higher Education Global Trends and Emerging Opportunities to 2020, p. 7.

Table 2: Summary of future higher education opportunities for global engagement — top country listings (2020)

Rank	Domestic tertiary education system		International student mobility – outbound		International student mobility – inbound	
	Size 2020	Growth Next decade	Size 2020	Growth Next decade	Size 2020	Growth Next decade
1	China	India	China	India	US	Australia
2	India	China	India	Nigeria	UK	UK
3	US	Brazil	South Korea	Malaysia	Australia	US
4	Brazil	Indonesia	Germany	Nepal	Canada	Canada
5	Indonesia	Nigeria	Turkey	Pakistan	Germany	
6	Russia	Philippines	Malaysia	Saudi Arabia	France	
7	Japan	Bangladesh	Nigeria	Turkey	Japan	
8	Turkey	Turkey	Kazakhstan	Iraq	Russia	
9	Iran	Ethiopia	France	Zimbabwe		
10	Nigeria	Mexico	US	Angola	See point a	See point b

Note: Asian countries shaded in grey

a China, Malaysia and India will be amongst the top ten host countries by 2020. Due to the data issues discussed in this report the exact position of these host countries is difficult to forecast with certainty although China has potential to be one of the top three hosts of international students.

b China, Malaysia, Singapore and India will be in the top ten fastest growing hosts of internationally mobile students.

Source: The British Council (2012). The Shape of Things to Come: Higher Education Global Trends and Emerging Opportunities p. 9.

BENEATH THE GLOBAL TRENDS

In Europe it has often been noted that the greatest impact of the global financial crisis has been on inter-generational equity. Rates of youth unemployment, for example, are far greater — alarmingly so in some countries — than the rate for the population of over-25's. The increasing participation of females in the labour force outside the home has also produced a steep decline in birth-rates in most European countries and in high income countries elsewhere, such as Japan. Meanwhile it has been estimated that Asia, Africa and Latin America will contribute 97% of the world's population growth between now and 2030. So the trend is towards higher birth-rates, larger populations, low affordability and a lack of higher education capacity in the world's fastest growing countries; and declining birth rates, stable or even declining populations and hence ample higher education capacity in high income countries, which in turn suffer from chronic graduate-level skills shortages in some sectors. International student flows have bridged these divergent trends. Mobility assists in mitigating the challenges of excess demand in fast-growing countries (notwithstanding the attendant risks of 'brain drain'), whilst international student recruitment and migration are seen as part of the solution to skills shortages in high income countries in relative or absolute demographic decline.

There are, however, two major inherent risks, viewed from a European perspective. The first concerns political trends in Europe. A generally ageing population has, under the impact of recession, increasingly resisted mobility across national boundaries — even within Europe, let alone from outside. Anti-immigration parties have made major electoral gains right across Europe in the last decade and increasing controls on immigration, including student immigration, are on the rise. An ageing population has also put increasing pressure on other public services — most notably health and welfare — which has in turn had implications for the support for increasing public funding for higher education.

The second risk follows on from this. As the public funding of higher education has declined, at least in real terms, in many European countries, so universities have sought to recruit more international students as a lucrative source of fee income (where this exists) and/or to prop up demand in some strategically important subjects with low indigenous demand (principally the physical sciences, mathematics and engineering). A few countries, and several universities, have now become dependent on international students for their short-term sustainability. In Europe the UK is probably the most prominent example of this; elsewhere in the world it is probably Australia. The proportion of non-EU undergraduate students in British universities now approaches 25%. In London it is much higher — closer to 40% — London being a particularly favourite destination for overseas students. For post-graduate students these percentages are higher still (especially for STEM subjects) and the taught postgraduate market (Masters) hugely so, in part due to the impact of the introduction of undergraduate fees for domestic students, who now graduate with significant loan debt. If overseas students feel that the political and social climate is more and more unreceptive to them, they will go elsewhere. Last year the number of students arriving from India to the UK fell for the first time in living memory, following well-publicized visa restrictions on student entrants. The embryonic emergence of China as a destination country, which is likely to grow in significance as its sector matures, may have serious repercussions.

The global financial crisis has had one further impact on European universities. It hardly needs to be stated that the crisis has had a much deeper impact on countries in southern and eastern Europe than in the north and the west (Ireland excepted). Budgetary cuts in countries like Greece, Spain, Portugal and Italy have directly affected university funding, bringing the sector in these countries to the brink of collapse. It has been estimated that 1.5 million Italians with professional qualifications have migrated abroad in the last decade. A diaspora of academic faculty from southern Europe has moved out of their collapsing university systems, mostly to northern Europe, North American and Australia. This illustrates that inter-regional trends across the world often mask significant intra-regional divergences which have had huge impacts on the present younger generation's accessibility to higher education, the quality of the student experience for those who do enrol and declining employability on graduation. In some European countries, therefore, massification is no longer affordable and teaching quality has suffered. But elsewhere in Europe, enrolments continue to grow and public funds continue to sustain improvements in teaching quality and the overall student experience. The impact of the global financial crisis has thus been greater within Europe than between Europe and the rest of the world.

This is not to say, however, that the sources of university funding have remained unchanged, even in the less-affected countries in Europe. There has been a notable trend for governments to explore, within what is electorally acceptable, the possibility of pushing more of the cost of higher education onto the users (student fees) and institutions (private providers). This has also been accompanied by the widespread adoption of performance management in the higher education sector, both in teaching and research, as governments seek to make universities more efficient as well as more effective.

The classic case of this in Europe has been the UK, with its troubled recent history of placing the bulk of the cost (approximately 85%) of undergraduate tuition on the students (technically, the graduates through a loan scheme) themselves. As a social experiment it has been closely watched in neighbouring countries, following on from their adoption in many cases of an earlier, and equally contentious UK innovation, the Research Assessment Exercise, which related block grant research funding in universities to an evaluation of its quality. The introduction of fees has had some not entirely predictable consequences. Student demand, contrary to most expectations, has increased and the proportion of students from poor socio-economic groups has also risen, assisted by scholarship and bursary schemes funded out of other students' fee income. University finances have been granted a new lease of life ('awash with cash' is a frequently heard phrase), though capital developments now have to be funded almost entirely out of income-generated surpluses. Still, during a period when many public services have suffered considerable cuts, higher education sometimes looks like an oasis of public sector prosperity. It has not, however, saved the government very much money in the short term as it must finance the student loan debt (some of it already sold off to the private sector at a considerable discount) and certainly the government continues to act as if it controls university finances even though in reality government funding now constitutes quite a small proportion with some small specialist teaching-only institutions receiving no government funding at all. Fee-paying students have, however, become much more sensitive to issues of employability and so changes in demand for certain subjects have become very volatile, especially in the arts and humanities subjects.

In the USA, these trends have been apparent for longer. A recent report from the respected Boston Consulting Group, Five Forces are Re-Shaping Higher Education (BGC, 2015) painted a challenging picture. Revenue from key sources is continuing to fall across the University sector, 'putting many institutions at severe financial risk'. Enrolment at public universities is flat or in decline. The age cohort, moreover, peaked in 2011 and is predicted to continue falling or stay the same until 2024. State appropriations have been in precipitous decline and now amount as little as 1% at the University of Colorado, Boulder, though the mean contribution is around 18%. More of the cost has been placed on tuition fees and these have escalated to a point where tuition costs are now a political issue in the USA with a real prospect that fees will no longer be affordable for vast swathes of the population. The annual rate of increase is currently 5.2%. The average fee per annum at a four-year public university was $9,000 in 2013 and more than $30,000 for a private non-profit institution.

If this were not bad enough absolute unemployment levels have remained stubbornly high for college graduates. And student debt loads have grown 8% annually since the financial crisis began. The debt default rate now stands at 15%, double the rate of 2008. One result of all of this is that greater transparency about student learning outcomes is becoming the norm. In many states the legislatures are relating university funding to completion rates. Some of this is familiar in Europe, but other aspects less so: many colleges are providing detailed report cards to justify the cost of an education and to demonstrate the outcomes of specific programmes and study. A few are even making guarantees of employment after graduation and more are certifying the knowledge and skills of their graduates: shades here of a European-style qualifications framework linked to learning outcomes.

The Rise and Rise of Private Provision

The recent experience of the UK and the USA demonstrates that 'affordable massification' has been a fraught process under the impact of recessionary economic conditions. But this has been in nations where, by comparison with some parts of the world, demand has been rising only modestly. However, in Latin American, Asia and even (from a low base) Africa, the growth in demand for higher education has been exponential and socially unstoppable. Socially to be a university graduate is seen as a badge of modernity and an entry visa to an aspirational lifestyle. Economically it is regarded as a passport to higher-paid employment and career progression. In most emerging economies there is no way that this burgeoning demand can be met solely from public resources. So the choice for students and their parents has been not so much between a public university and a private university, as between a private university and no university. The private sector has stepped in to fill this gap.

This is where the USA is an exception when viewed internationally. In the USA the elite Universities are predominantly private (they do, of course, receive substantial public funds, especially for research); whereas the public universities provide an alternative for those unable to gain access to the elite colleges. Elsewhere in the world the reverse is usually the case: the elite universities are publically funded and the alternative is a private provider. The latter also focus on what might be termed 'vocational' higher education, often disdained by the elite institutions, but where there is huge, and often unmet, demand. Worldwide it is the private sector which is growing the most rapidly, assisted rather than hindered by the recessionary climate, and it is this part of the sector which has been in the forefront of educational innovation with on-line learning and the use of other technology-led pedagogies a particular focus.

The sales and marketing of the private sector plays to and feeds off an understandable anxiety about the cost and return on investment of enrolling in higher education. This has been exacerbated by the recession and has affected the perceptions of publically-funded higher education, too. As students bear more of the costs they behave more like customers and demand value for money. They increasingly regard higher education as a means to an end — employment in a 'graduate job' — rather than an end in itself. Employability trumps teaching quality. A common critique of private providers, especially for-profit institutions, is that they represent poor quality. And sometimes this is true, especially in countries with weak or non-existent regulatory regimes. But quality sells and behind the accusations of poor quality there is usually a more atavistic fear — that higher education is no longer higher and has become a form of vocational training, a utilitarian activity, a means to an end.

The search for affordable massification shifts the balance between public and private, but it also shifts the balance between vocational and professional provision. It is not as clear as it once was how far higher education is a public or a private good and while we all know that it is both, the balance between public and private funding has not been derived from any assessment of public and private returns. It is a result more of economic necessity produced by political choices.

The Rise of Asia

The old cliché, that Europe is the past, America is the present and Asia the future, has some resonance in the world of higher education. Education, including higher education, has been regarded across Asia as a *sine qua non* of economic and social development, reflecting in part the high valuation placed on education in virtually all Asian cultures. While Europe and North America have faltered during the recession, Asia has continued to forge ahead. The position of Asian universities in global (predominantly research-based) rankings continues to improve — and who, a generation ago, would have believed that an invention of a Deputy Dean in a Shanghai University would have such a profound influence in North America, Europe and the rest of the world on the direction of national higher education research policies?

As indicated earlier in this paper, as Asian university systems mature, recently-established patterns of international student mobility are quite likely to change, with severe implications for some older-established systems. In the meantime, the governments of China, Singapore, Malaysia, Hong Kong, South Korea and the Gulf States all have ambitions to be regional hubs for education and research. They also have associated ambitions to create, or increase, a cohort of 'world-class universities' which will give these aspirations a degree of credibility. This is clearly a long-term strategy which requires a long-term political commitment and some very deep pockets. But, unlike in the West where the recession has produced a wobble in the public estimation of higher education (see below), there are no significant signs that this long-term commitment is weakening. Asian higher education is on the up and both governments and the wider public know it. A highly aspirational Asian middle class continues to regard participation for their children in higher education as their most important familial objective, one for which they are still prepared to make enormous personal sacrifices.

If the rise of Asian higher education falters, it is unlikely to be a result, then, of either a lack of financial commitment or public support. Other, softer, issues, represent greater risks. The promotion of national and regional ambitions in both research and teaching, has proceeded by building stronger relations with the West, from which they have sought to learn the ingredients of building 'world class' university institutions. Initially student mobility was at the centre of this, graduates returning (usually) to their home countries to participate in their embryonic professional activities, including university teaching. Later, these same teacher returned and were supplemented by others to undertake PhDs in the West and thereby raise the quality and standards of their home institutions. The most recent phase has been characterized by a number of Asian countries co-operating with elite foreign universities as part of their regional hub strategy, up to and including the establishment of local campuses by overseas universities. Where these have not been successful it has not usually been due to a lack of resources but to what might be broadly described as cultural issues. These include definitions of academic freedom, civil rights, the treatment of female students and staff and broader quality of life issues which have, from time to time, conspired to make it difficult to recruit and retain top quality international staff and students.

For every success there are several which have left a trail of disappointed expectations. Unfortunately there is no culturally-neutral template for a word-class university and money alone is not the complete answer.

Is It Worth It?

In the post-war period higher education was regarded in the USA as a key component of equality of opportunity and upward social mobility. 'College' is part of the American Dream. In the more traditional ambience of Europe, opinion was more ambivalent. University education was more of a positional good and therefore access was more selective and socially exclusive. In the words of the English novelist and former academic, Kingsley Amis, as far as higher education was concerned 'more means worse'. Mass higher education would inevitably lead to lower standards as students of lower scholastic ability were able to gain access.

In Britain today, perhaps uniquely in the world, this statement continues to hover in the ether. When the Blair Government set a target of a 50% participation rate, large parts of the press and public met this with incredulity and hostility. Rather than welcoming an expansion in opportunity, the sentiment of many was to echo Amis's nostrum. Ever since, a large part of the British press has waged what amounts to a campaign against the expansion of university education, deploying a toxic mix of promoting status anxiety among affluent parents over universities' admissions policies favouring students from poor backgrounds to questioning the standards of many degree programmes — 'Mickey Mouse' degrees' in the words of a (Labour Higher Education) Minister.

Today this hostility has shifted somewhat. The status anxieties still remain, so that parents continue to pay school fees which are much higher than university fees in order to try to ensure that their children will be admitted to 'good' universities. But contemporary rhetoric questions the value of a university education in terms of a crude cost-benefit analysis — does the lifetime return on earnings from obtaining a degree outweigh the cost in the first place? (The answer, by the way, is resoundingly yes.) A persistent theme is to ask, why bother going to university and pay fees when you could be earning money and/or take sub-degree vocational qualifications, especially those that are based in the workplace, such as apprenticeships.

Unlike 'more means worse' this is not a uniquely British argument. Echoes of it appear elsewhere in Europe and in North America. Clearly this is in part a consequence of students meeting more of the costs: a degree is no longer a 'free good'. But in part it is also a product of the global crisis: graduate starting salaries, terms and conditions of employment and even career prospects are not perceived to be what they once were. Moreover, it is seen as essential not just to obtain any degree in any subject from any university. As higher education has expanded so the sector has differentiated. To be competitive in the labour market a graduate must now obtain a 'good' degree from an elite university in a subject for which there is high demand. Wellesley and Harvard continue to guarantee success; Apache Creek College, Iowa (a fictional example I must add) less so.

In this sense higher education has become, to repeat a common critique of recent trends, a commodity, to be bought and sold like other expensive items, such as a house or car, and to be appraised accordingly. It is clear to me that the disaffected and somewhat disenfranchised generation which has suffered disproportionately from the effects of the global financial crisis, now assesses higher education in this utilitarian fashion far more than their predecessors. 'Is it worth it?' a recent edition of *The Economist* asked. When the Glion Colloquium was founded this question was unthinkable. But it is now. Anti-intellectualism is on the rise. Perhaps this is the greatest challenge which the global financial crisis has bequeathed to us.

REFERENCES

Altbach, P.G., Reisburg L., Rumbley L.E. (2009). Trends in Global Higher Education: Tracking an Academic Revolution, Paris: UNESCO.

Boston Consultancy Group (2015). "Five Trends to Watch in Higher Education", Boston: BCG.

British Council (2012). The Shape of Things to Come: Higher Education Global Trends and Emerging Opportunities to 2020, London: British Council.

IAU (2014). Fourth Global Survey on Internationalisation in High Education, Paris: International Association of Universities.

Economist, The (2015). "Is your Degree Worth it?". London, *The Economist*, 14 March, 2015.

Friedman, T. (2005). The World is Flat: A Brief History of the Twenty-First Century New York: Farrar, Strauss and Giroux.

Lennard, C. (2014). "The Top Five Trends in Higher Education Globally", Euromonitor International, [blog.euromonitor.com].

Newby, H. (2008). "The Challenge to European Universities in the Emerging Global Marketplace", in Weber & Duderstadt (eds.) (2008), pp. 55-64.

Weber, L. E. & Duderstadt, J. J., (eds.) (2008). *The Globalization of Higher Education*, London: Economica Ltd.

Zemsky, R. (2008). "Has Our Reach Exceeded Our Grasp? Taking a Second Look at Higher Education as a Global Enterprise", in Weber & Duderstadt (eds.) (2008) pp. 251-258.

CHAPTER 3

The Future of Universities — Academic Freedom, the Autonomy of Universities and Competition in Academia revisited

Bernd Huber

INTRODUCTION: UNIVERSITIES UNDER ATTACK

Over the last 50 years, universities and tertiary education have experienced a remarkable, unprecedented expansion. Europe, the continent with the oldest universities, provides a case in point: Before World War II, only around 150,000 students were enrolled altogether in the U.K., France and Germany (Hobsbawm, 2013, p. 2). Nowadays, the area of London alone has more than 360,000 students ("How many students are there", 2013/2014).

A key characteristic of (most) universities is a strong commitment to research and, in particular, basic research as a defining core activity. In this sense, the modern university follows Humboldt's ideal of unifying educating and researching. Further characteristics which I will discuss in more detail in part II are (i) that academics enjoy a large degree of "academic freedom", (ii) that universities are autonomous institutions in many respects, and (iii) that competition and peer review are key elements of the research process.

The current university can be and is often seen as an outstanding success story of an institutional development. However, recently, universities and the university system face a worldwide wave of criticism and attack. Some critics, like Barber, Donnelly and Rizvi (2013), even argue that the university as we know it may not survive in the future (p. 9). In my contribution, I will deal with this criticism and the demands for change at universities, concentrating on those which concern research activities at universities.

The following examples from all over the world illustrate the criticism of the research activities and research performance of universities:

- In October 2013, *The Economist* ran a cover story on "How science goes wrong", providing various arguments which indicate that the quality of research in science is flawed (p. 11; p. 21ff). According to the article, "there are errors in a lot more of the scientific papers being published, written about and acted on than anyone would normally suppose, or like to think" (p. 21). Concerning biomedical research, the article even concludes that the (public) research process at universities (and, for that purpose, non-university research institutions) "seems to have failed" (p. 21).
- The Research Excellence Framework (REF) in the United Kingdom, the successor to the former Research Assessment Exercise (RAE), uses — as one criterion to assess the quality of research at U.K. higher education institutions — the impact arising from excellent research: Impact concerns "any social, economic or cultural impact or benefit *beyond academia* (emphasis added)" ("Decisions on assessing", 2011). The assessment of impact will enter at a 20% weight in funding decisions for U.K. universities, beginning in 2014 ("Decisions on assessing", 2011). The REF approach to assess research performance on the basis of impact beyond academia has been severely criticized, not surprisingly, by academics in particular (Oswald, 2009, para. 1f.).
- In March 2013, the U.S. Senate passed an amendment which prohibits "the use of funds to carry out the functions of the Political Science Program (. . .) of the National Science Foundation" (Consolidated and Further Continuing Appropriations Act, 2013, amend. 65). The only exceptions are research projects that "the Director of the National Science Foundation certifies as promoting national security or the economic interests of the United States" (Consolidated and Further Continuing Appropriations Act, 2013, amend. 65). This so-called Coburn amendment drew strong criticism from many academics, especially from the American Political Science Association (Stratford, 2014, para. 7). It is interesting to note that the Coburn Amendment only applied to the 2013 NSF budget, but is no longer

part of the 2014 spending bill that the U.S. Congress passed in January 2014 (Mervis, 2014, para. 5). In a similar vein, House Representative Lamar Smith has frequently criticized the funding policy of the NSF (Mervis, 2015, para. 1f.). Again, this has given rise to a heated public debate about research funding policy in the U.S.
- In December 2013, the American Studies Association (ASA) endorsed a resolution to boycott Israeli academic institutions. The boycott is understood as "a refusal on the part of the ASA in its official capacities to enter into formal collaborations with Israeli academic institutions" ("What does the boycott", n.d., para. 4). The decision of the ASA has drawn massive criticism by many academics, university presidents and academic organizations (Schmidt, 2014).
- In Canada, scientists protested against the government in autumn of 2014, blaming Prime Minister Stephen Harper for leading what has been labelled a "war on science" (Macdonald, 2014), as federally employed scientists are laid off and funds are cut or programs cancelled that interfere with the government's position on environmental issues. In addition, the allocation of funds is questioned by academics who observe that a decreasing number of members of the scientific community are part of the bodies who decide on funding — and thus political instead of scientific reasons being the driver in these decisions (Macdonald, 2014, para. 7).

These examples represent various strands of criticism of research activities at universities. In particular, they concern the assessment of research ideas and research projects, the quality of research, research topics, the sources of research funding, and international collaboration in research.

Of course, some of the criticism can easily be dismissed as purely political in nature or as an attempt to politicize the universities' policies. But, nonetheless, the extent and the breadth of this critique indicate a (novel) scepticism and mistrust concerning the performance and activities of and at universities.

In what follows, I will analyse why this scepticism has arisen. In part II, I will first discuss the particular merits of the modern university system and then turn, in part III, to potential reasons for critique.

THE MODEL OF THE MODERN UNIVERSITY

The current university system entails certain stylized features; most importantly:
- Academics at universities (professors and to a lesser extent, junior staff or other academic staff members) enjoy a large degree of independence in terms of the research topics they pursue, the academic views they

express, and the way they teach. This is often referred to as "academic freedom", although the exact meaning of this term is subject to debate. But it is clear that the idea of academic freedom of the individual academic is at the heart of the idea of the modern university.

- Universities are autonomous in their decisions, to a large extent. For example, universities independently appoint new members of faculty or, at least, exert strong influence on appointment decisions. Universities also have, at least to a certain degree, discretion over the range of academic subjects taught at their institution. In addition, the modern university system is also characterized by a large degree of independence concerning the day-to-day management of academic and non-academic issues.

- A large part of the research funding is granted on a competitive base where the expected scientific outcomes of a research project are the key criterion for the funding decision. Peer review is the main instrument to make these funding decisions.

- Universities compete with each other in many respects, e.g. for funding, students and academic staff. For instance, one feature of the university system is that a university hires, often at considerable cost, a professor from another university to strengthen its academic performance. It is interesting to note that, from a national (or social) point of view, the movement of an academic to another academic institution may only create a minor net benefit. But this highlights that competition, even if it involves considerable cost, is a key pillar of the university system. This holds true even in pure public university systems, as, for example, in continental Europe. I will return to this below.

Reflecting on these characteristics, it is important to bear one caveat in mind. While the universities in many countries, especially in North America and Europe, have much in common along the lines discussed above, there exists, of course, a lot of variation across countries and institutions which deserves some comment. For instance, the autonomy of universities significantly differs between private and public universities. Even among public universities, the degree of autonomy can be very divergent. Public universities face very different regulations of their activities concerning, for example, salary levels for faculty, property investment, student admission and the choice of academic subjects. It is also interesting to note that governance structures within universities show remarkable variation. For example, the distribution of powers can be quite different resulting in highly-decentralized or centralized decision-making processes. A study by the European Universities Association (EUA) further analyses university autonomy at European universities (Estermann & Nokkala, 2009).

Most importantly, the degree of academic freedom is often significantly endangered or even non-existent. A particularly worrying case arises when academic freedom is de iure granted, but de facto suppressed.

With these reservations in mind, I would nevertheless argue that the considerations mentioned above capture, in an admittedly very stylized way, some key features of the current university system which has evolved over the last 100 years, with much of the significant expansion arising after World War II.

Let me now turn to the question why the university system has developed in this particular way. And what are the perspectives for the future? How should the universities respond to the global challenges and criticisms mentioned in part I?

I will try to sketch an answer to these questions which puts particular emphasis on the role of competition. Of course, this approach reflects my *déformation professionelle* as an economist, and many of the arguments I will develop have been elaborated on, in particular, by economists like Aghion, Dewatripont, Hoxby, Mas-Colell and Sapir (2008). Let me begin with what can be seen as conventional wisdom: Research at universities is a key driver for innovation and growth, though it should be noted that this conventional wisdom has not gone undisputed. For further reference, see also R. E. Lucas (2008). In this view, the results and insights of basic research — inventions in Schumpeterian terms — while offering little direct economic benefit, form the base for — again Schumpeterian — innovations of new products and new processes. From a somewhat idealizing perspective, the university system can be seen as a mechanism to generate new inventions, new scientific ideas and results. This mechanism is based on competition and peer review. Researchers (or a team of researchers) with new ideas can apply for funding to further explore these research ideas. In a competitive peer review process, those projects are picked out and will be granted funding which have the potential to be the scientifically most promising and interesting prospects. The results of research are then published, often again on a competitive base with peer review, and thus become available to the scientific community and the general public. There is an ongoing academic debate at conferences and in journals which continually evaluates and assesses the scientific impact and quality of scientific results. In this way, particularly important scientific results are identified and the path and direction of future research are shaped.

Before discussing the potential flaws of this idealized setting, it is interesting to note that, from an economic perspective, the university system provides an ingenuous solution to an inherently public goods problem. Invention, scientific ideas and the results of basic research offer little direct economic benefit for the inventor. Therefore, no private company, no investor will — in general — finance inventive activities and basic research. However, the results of basic research offer potentially large benefits, sometimes in the far-distant future when inventions are taken up and transformed into new products, processes and other innovations. Thus, inventions and basic research are a prototype example of what economists call a (pure) public good. A (pure) public good has two basic features: First, additional users cannot be excluded from using the good and, second and more importantly, additional users can use the good at zero (marginal) cost (Oakland, 1987). Like other public goods, basic research and inventive activity require public funding. It is a matter of ongoing debate whether this (necessarily) implies (exclusive) funding by the government (Oakland, 1987). The crucial aspect, however, is that the university system generates research und invention in a competitive way such that efficiency is enhanced and the cost of the research process to society are minimized. Note that this competitive element of the university system is a unique advantage in the provision of the public good basic research. For many other public goods, like roads, public transport, or national defence, the efficiency of the provision often suffers from the lack of competition. To sum up, one can say that the university system offers a particularly efficient solution of creating inventions and progress in research to society.

But what is the specific role of universities in this context? Of course, a key role of universities and their academics lies in higher education. But universities also provide and supplement the framework for competition in research in important respects: Universities offer employment opportunities for academics who can advance their academic careers by their academic performance. Thus, it provides an additional incentive for successful research activities. Furthermore, as was mentioned above, universities compete for academic staff. The "arms race" between universities trying to attract the best academics worldwide is often complained about, but it adds an important dimension of competitive pressure improving the overall performance of the higher education system. The competition between universities, for example, in terms of rankings and funding adds another element of competition.

Another interesting aspect to consider is the idea of the comprehensive university covering as diverse subjects as humanities, science, medicine and social sciences. One rationale for a comprehensive university is, of course, to fully use the potential for interdisciplinary collaboration between different academic subjects. But, from an economic perspective, another effect of a comprehensive university is to introduce competition within the university, where departments, different academic subjects and fields compete for funding and support by the university. The competitive pressure to further improve the academic performance of, for example, a department is thereby further strengthened.

Moreover, one may ask: What is the role of humanities (and, to a large degree, social sciences as well) in this competitive framework? Of course, humanities as a discipline play a crucial role in improving our understanding of society, history and culture. The contribution of humanities is, thus, best understood as a direct benefit to society which, of course, also represents a public good and requires public provision. Again, the university system provides a framework to nurture the academic debate in the humanities in a competitive and efficient way.

Finally, one may note that academic freedom — at least in the sense that academics enjoy a large degree of independence in pursuing their research — and the autonomy of universities are key elements of the competitive mechanisms provided by the university system. Academic freedom and the autonomy of universities are often seen as privileges granted to universities and their academics. However, from the perspective developed in the previous paragraphs, these privileges are not granted per se, and, in this sense, are not privileges at all, but are based on a clear rationale: Academic freedom and the autonomy of universities are key pillars of the competitive mechanism to enhance the productivity of the research process in society.

So far, I have drawn a rather bright picture of the current university system. It is now important to add some caveats and to discuss potential points of critique. To begin with, the idea that competition and autonomy are well suited to organize the research process in society, and thus, to provide the public good inventions is based on an analogy to the efficiency enhancing mechanisms of competition in markets for private goods. While an analogy may offer attractive and, at face value, plausible implications, it is only a mere sketch and does not substitute for a rigorous analysis. While empirical evidence shows that competition and autonomy improve the performance of the university system, it is nonetheless possible, at least in theory, that there may exist other mechanisms with better outcomes (Aghion, Dewatripont, Hoxby, Mas-Colell & Sapir, 2009). To my knowledge, this issue has not been comprehensively analysed yet, only certain aspects of it; Aghion, Dewatripont and Stein (2005), for example, demonstrate the efficiency-enhancing effects of academic freedom.

Second, it is useful to note that the university system involves quite significant cost to society. For example, the "arms race" between universities in filling academic positions is costly, while the net benefit to society may be quite small. Even more importantly, the peer review mechanism to allocate research funds can be very expensive and can produce significant transaction costs in terms of the overall efficiency of the research process. These transaction costs reduce the net benefit for society from basic research; and the higher they are, the less attractive is a mechanism where the research process is based on peer review.

Another important caveat arises from the impact of new developments on institutional settings. New technologies, fundamental changes in the nature of the research process, and new ways to communicate may render the current system of universities outdated or may require significant changes. The recent debate on MOOCs provides another example in the field of higher education for the potentially far-reaching consequences of such changes. Below, I will discuss the problem of the "burden of knowledge" (Jones, 2010, p. 1) and increasing globalization as specific examples of a significant change in the research landscape.

Bearing these admonitions in mind, I would nonetheless argue that the current university system with its key features — academic freedom, autonomy of universities, competition and peer review — has provided a highly successful model to organize (basic) research and higher education. While there may be theoretically and conceptually better models, the current system at least deserves the benefit of the doubt. Therefore, one is surprised by the above-mentioned global wave of criticism and mistrust universities face today. I will now turn to the question how one can explain this criticism, where the critics may be wrong and where they may be right, and how universities should respond to it.

WHY HAVE UNIVERSITIES COME UNDER ATTACK?

There are several ways to explain and to understand the current global wave of criticism of universities. First, one can see it as just one particular point in the regular ups and downs of public perception of universities. From this perspective, there is little to worry about, and one only has to wait for the next wave in the news cycle which will normalize the public debate. Another, more serious approach is to analyse each specific piece of criticism in detail and to try to assess its significance and its potential consequences for the designs of the university system.

In this paper, I will explore a third route: The university system as we know it has certain weaknesses and faces significant challenges in the future. Much of the criticism of universities mentioned in part I can be understood and appropriately analysed in terms of these weaknesses and challenges. This approach also allows identifying potential remedies and reforms.

I begin with the following issue: At the heart of the current university system is the idea that basic research and innovations at (research) universities are a key driver of innovation and growth. It is a matter of debate whether this view holds true for the past, as Phelps (2013) critically assesses. However, several empirical studies show a quite significant contribution of basic research to economic growth and productivity. For example, a recent study by Goodridge, Haskel, Hughes, and Wallis (2015) estimates for the U.K. the social rate of return of basic research at 20% (p. 5f.) However, even if basic research has made a significant contribution to economic well-being in the past, it is not clear that this will continue to be true in the future. The eminent economist

Robert Gordon (2012) has recently argued to the contrary. In his view, (highly-developed) economies like the United States can expect only little growth and few benefits from inventions in the future (Gordon, 2012). His conclusion is based on three key observations: First, in historical terms, (per capita) economic growth is not the rule, but the exception. From 1300 to 1850, economic growth was very low and almost close to zero (p. 4). Second, growth significantly picked up after 1850, reflecting, according to Gordon, the impact of the industrial revolution (p. 7ff). However, and this is his most important point, growth in the U.S. started to continually decline in the middle of the last century (Gordon, 2012). Gordon's interpretation of these facts is that many innovations enhancing growth in the past represent a unique type of progress which cannot be repeated in the future. One example is the development of travel speed. While travel speed has significantly increased due to the invention of trains, then of cars, and finally of airplanes in the last century, it has stagnated (or even fallen) in the past decades (Gordon, 2012, p. 11).

Thus, Gordon's (2012) analysis suggests that, in the future, inventions and innovations will do little to increase economic growth. His views have, not surprisingly, been criticized on various grounds. A lively summary of this debate can be found in *The Economist* ("Growth"; "Has the idea machine", 12 January 2013). Furthermore, the MIT Committee to Evaluate the Innovation Deficit (2015) provides an analysis of several examples for potentially high benefits of future basic research ranging from Alzheimer's disease to batteries. One argument of the critics is the difficulty to predict the path of future innovations; the notorious example of the Roosevelt Commission represents a case in point (Boulton & C. Lucas, 2008, p. 8). Concerning the benefits of basic research and inventions, one also has to take into account that, even if the impact on growth and job creation is small, basic research may yield important benefits for the well-being of the society. For example, progress in medical treatments may have little consequences for growth, but may significantly improve the welfare of patients.

But Gordon's analysis highlights an important point: Some of the recent debate on the contribution of research projects to society's welfare can be understood as a demand of the public to better understand the (potential) benefits of basic research. These demands become more urgent (and more understandable) if the prospects of basic research become more uncertain and more difficult to identify. Universities, the academic and scientific community, and research policy, therefore, have to face the task to better explain the role of basic research to a public which, simultaneously, is asked to provide a huge amount of resources for that purpose.

A second challenge for the university system arises from the breath-taking expansion of research activity and research output. In the 1950s, less than 50,000 journal articles were annually published worldwide across all fields of science, engineering and social sciences (Jones, 2010, p. 2). In 2013, the number of published articles amounts to more than 1.4 million ("Trouble", 19 October 2013, p. 23). This raises several issues. The huge expansion in the stock and the new production of research results creates the phenomenon of the "burden of knowledge" (Jones, 2010, p. 1). Each potential researcher has to spend considerably more time on learning and taking stock of the existing results of previous research. This tends to negatively affect the incentives to take up a scientific career in important respects. A related point is that the expansion of the knowledge frontier and of worldwide research activity requires an increasing specialization of the individual researcher. However, increasing specialization makes the decision to enter a career as researcher more hazardous. Increased specialization is also one key driver for the significant increase in team production in research: The mean number of authors in science and engineering papers has continuously grown from around two in the 1960s to more than four in the new millennium (Jones, 2010).

All these developments raise important issues for research policy. But one particularly important aspect is how the rapid expansion of research affects the quality of research. The above-mentioned article in *The Economist* ("Trouble", 19 October) reports some alarming facts: According to sources quoted in this article, it is probably "hard to reproduce at least three quarters of all published bio-medical findings" (p. 21). Another worrying item of information is that one third of the clinical trials financed by the National Institute of Health (NIH) did not result in any publication within more than four years after completion ("Trouble", 19 October, p. 24). In addition, the article quotes evidence which indicates that a large part of published papers have serious statistical flaws (p. 21ff.).

One much discussed recent example of errors in an academic project concerns the work of Carmen Reinhart and Kenneth Rogoff. In their paper "Growth in a Time of Debt" (2010), they identified a critical threshold level of public debt of 90% of the GDP (p. 7). If a country's debt level is higher than this threshold level, economic growth is significantly negatively affected (Reinhart & Rogoff, 2010, p. 2). This result has been referred to in many policy debates in Europe and the United States. However, the conclusion of this paper has been severely criticized by economists from the University of Massachusetts Amherst who claim that the Reinhart & Rogoff paper contains several flaws and errors (Herndon, Ash & Pollin, 2013, p. 14f).

These criticisms of the quality of current scientific research require careful consideration because they can seriously undermine trust in research policy and research at universities. The critique clearly indicates the need to improve the peer review process both at research funding institutions and at academic journals. As *The Economist* acknowledges, several measures have already been taken on: For example, programs now exist to support studies which try to replicate results of existing studies ("Trouble", 19 October, p. 24). Similarly, scientific journals increasingly try to improve the standards, for example, in terms of availability of research data ("Trouble", 19 October, p. 24). But there may be considerable room for further improvement. For example, Jones (2010) suggests that the increase in teamwork in research should be accompanied by the introduction or intensification of the use of teamwork in the evaluation of research ideas for, e.g., research funding (p. 29). He also highlights the complexity arising from evaluating research ideas along these lines: While evaluation teams should be highly specialized in the field of consideration, initial evaluators defining and approaching these teams have to be generalists with far-reaching expertise (Jones, 2010, p. 4f.).

But improvements in the quality of research may not only require changing review processes, but also altering incentives for researchers. For example, Jones (2010) argues that, due to the growing significance of teamwork in research, prizes and awards like the Nobel Prize or the Fields Medal honouring individual researchers should be transformed into awards honouring teams of researchers (p. 25f.) Furthermore, the quality of research may be enhanced if advances in academic careers depend on the fact that researchers also undertake a significant number of replication studies (Jones, 2010, p. 25f.). To stimulate original, novel research, the design of research grants is also crucially important (Jones, 2010, p. 21). For instance, empirical evidence suggests that grants with rather long-term funding and few strings attached enhance creative research outcomes (Azoulay & Graff-Zivin, 2012, p. 8f.).

To sum up, the huge expansion of research activity and research output requires increasing efforts of universities, research funders and research policy to maintain and improve research quality. This represents an important challenge since the future of the current university and research system critically depends on the credibility of, and the public's trust in, the quality of the research process.

I will now turn to another aspect concerning the huge increase in research activity and research output: Basic research (and higher education as well) today is a global activity. The same is true for the modern university. Among the top 100 or 200 in global university rankings such as the Times Higher Education World University Rankings 2014-2015, the Times Higher Education World Reputation Rankings 2015, and the Academic Ranking of World Universities 2014, there are very often many universities from North America, but from Asia, Europe and Australia as well. Nowadays, academics (and students) move globally from one country to another and across continents. Similarly, the competition for new ideas and new results in research goes on at global level.

The benefits of basic research accrue globally, as well. Thus, the insights of basic research or, more generally, new knowledge, represent what is called a global public good (Stiglitz, 1999, p. 308). The global character of the public good basic research raises several issues. A global public good requires an international coordination of research policies if an efficient provision is to be achieved. Purely national research policies will lead to an inefficient outcome since, at the national level, only the national benefit and cost are accounted for, while the impact of a nation's basic research on other countries tends to be ignored (Stiglitz, 1999).

The foundation of the European Research Council (ERC) can be seen as one important step of coordinating research policies at the European level. Another step represents the recent activities of networks of research universities like the League of European Research Universities (LERU) to improve cooperation and the exchange of ideas ("International Collaboration", n.d.). But further progress is needed to fully take account of the global nature of basic research.

One worrying aspect is that some of the recent criticisms of universities can be seen as an attempt to shape research activities at universities in terms of specific national interests, opposed to a truly global perspective. For example, if research projects have to calculate the potential contribution to social benefit in a funding proposal (Norrie, 2012, para. 1; 3), one can expect national funding agencies to prefer projects with a high national benefit and not necessarily those which offer a high global return. From a global perspective, this induces a serious distortion of research activities.

Similarly, national interests may dictate research policies to define particular research areas like life sciences or "great challenges" like ageing on which research funding is concentrated. Again, this may divert from a truly global evaluation of the benefit and cost of research activities.

To sum up, basic research as a global public good requires an improvement in the international cooperation in research policy. Understanding the truly global nature of academia is, in my view, far more important than attempting to calculate the economic or social impact of research activities at the national level.

REFERENCES

The Academic Ranking of World Universities (2014, August). Retrieved from http://www.shanghairanking.com/de/ARWU2014.html.

Aghion, P., Dewatripont, M., Hoxby, C. M., Mas-Colell, A. & Sapir, A. (2007, September). "Why reform Europe's universities?" Bruegel Policy Brief 2007/04. Retrieved from http://www.bruegel.org/publications/publication-detail/publication/ 34-why-reform-europes-universities/.

Aghion, P., Dewatripont, M., Hoxby, C. M., Mas-Colell, A. & Sapir, A. (2008, June). *Higher aspirations: An agenda for reforming European universities.* Bruegel Blueprint

Series V. Retrieved from http://www.bruegel.org/publications/publication-detail/publication/1-higher-aspirations-an-agenda-for-reforming-european-universities/.

Aghion, P., Dewatripont, M., Hoxby, C. M., Mas-Colell, A. & Sapir, A. (2009, April). "The Governance and Performance of Research Universities: Evidence from Europe and the U.S." NBER Working Paper Series Number 14851. Retrieved from http://www.nber.org/papers/w14851.

Aghion, P., Dewatripont, M. & Stein, J.C. (2005, August). "Academic Freedom, Private-Sector Focus, and the Process of Innovation". NBER Working Paper Series Number 14851. Retrieved from http://www.nber.org/papers/w11542.

Azoulay, P. & Graff-Zivin, J. (2012). "The Production of Scientific Ideas". NBER Reporter Number 3. Retrieved from http://pazoulay.scripts.mit.edu/docs/nber_reporter.pdf.

Barber, M., Donnelly, K. & Rizvi, S. (2013). *An Avalanche is coming. Higher Education and the Revolution Ahead*. London: Institute for Public Policy Research.

Boulton, G. & Lucas, C. (2008). *What are Universities for?* Leuven: LERU.

Consolidated and Further Continuing Appropriations Act 2013, H.R.933, amend. 65, 113th Cong. (2013). Retrieved from https://www.congress.gov/amendment/113th-congress/senate-amendment/65/text.

Decisions on assessing research impact. (2011, March). "Research Excellence Framework". Retrieved from http://www.ref.ac.uk/pubs/2011-01/.

Estermann, T. & Nokkala, T. (2009). *University Autonomy in Europe I. Exploratory Study*. Retrieved from http://www.eua.be/eua-work-and-policy-area/governance-autonomy-and-funding/projects/university-autonomy-in-europe/.

Goodridge, P., Haskel, J., Hughes, A. & Wallis, G. (2015). "The contribution of public and private R&D to UK productivity growth." Retrieved from https://spiral.imperial.ac.uk/handle/10044/1/21171.

Gordon, R. J. (2012, August). "Is U.S. economic growth over? Faltering innovation confronts the six headwinds". NBER Working Paper Series Number 18315. Retrieved from http://www.nber.org/papers/w18315.

Growth: The great innovation debate. (2013, 12 January). *The Economist*, p. 9.

Has the idea machine broken down? (2013, 12 January). *The Economist*, pp. 19-22.

Herndon, T., Ash, M. & Pollin, R. (2013). "Does High Public Debt Consistently Stifle Economic Growth? A Critique of Reinhart and Rogoff." Working Paper Series Number 322. Retrieved from http://www.hesa.ac.uk/content/view/1897/239/.

Hobsbawm, E. J. (2013). Fractured Times: Culture and Society in the Twentieth Century. New Press, New York.

How many students are there in my region? (2013/2014). Higher Education Statistics Agency. Retrieved from https://www.hesa.ac.uk/stats.

How science goes wrong. (2013, 19 October). *The Economist*, p. 11.

International Collaboration. (n.d.). League of European Research Universities. Retrieved from http://www.leru.org/index.php/public/global-network/.

Jones, B. (2010, May). "As Science evolves, how can Science Policy?" NBER Working Paper Series Number 16002. Retrieved from http://www.nber.org/papers/w16002.

Lucas, R. E. Jr. (2008, June). "Ideas and Growth". NBER Working Paper Series Number 14133. Retrieved from http://www.nber.org/papers/w14133.

Macdonald, C. (2014, November 20). "Canada and the 'war on science'." *Times Higher Education*. Retrieved from http://www.timeshighereducation.co.uk/news/canada-and-the-war-on-science/2016985.article.

Mervis, J. (2015, 23 February). "Malware and search engines: Lamar Smith goes far afield in his latest hit list of NSF grants". *Science*. Retrieved from http://news.sciencemag.org/funding/2015/02/malware-and-search-engines-lamar-smith-goes-far-afield-his-latest-hit-list-nsf.

Mervis, J. (2014, 23 January). "U.S. Political Scientists Relieved That Coburn Language Is Gone". *Science*. Retrieved from http://news.sciencemag.org/funding/2014/01/u.s.-political-scientists-relieved-coburn-language-gone.

MIT Committee to Evaluate the Innovation Deficit (2015). "The Future Postponed. Why Declining Investment in Basic Research Threatens a U.S. Innovation Deficit." Retrieved from http://dc.mit.edu/innovation-deficit.

Norrie, J. (2012, 5 June). "Universities to explain benefit of research to 'end users'." The Conversation. Retrieved from http://theconversation.com/universities-to-explain-benefit-of-research-to-end-users-7478.

Oakland, W. H. (1987). "Theory of Public Goods". In Auerbach, A. & Feldstein, M. Eds., *Handbook of Public Economics* (Chapter 9, pp. 485-535). North Holland, Amsterdam

Oswald, A. (2009, 9 November). "REF should stay out of the game." *The Independent*. Retrieved from http://www.independent.co.uk/news/education/higher/andrew-oswald-ref-should-stay-out-of-the-game-1827306.html.

Phelps, E. (2013). Mass Flourishing. How Grassroots Innovation Created Jobs, Challenge, and Change. Princeton University Press. Princeton and Oxford.

Reinhart, C. M. & Rogoff, K. S. (2010, January). "Growth in a Time of Debt". NBER Working Paper Series Number 15639. Retrieved from http://www.nber.org/papers/w15639.

Schmidt, P. (2014, 5 January). "Backlash Against Israel Boycott Throws Academic Association on Defensive". *The Chronicle of Higher Education*. Retrieved from http://www.nytimes.com/2014/01/06/us/backlash-against-israel-boycott-throws-academic-association-on-defensive.html?_r=0.

Schumpeter, J. A. (1950). *Kapitalismus, Sozialismus und Demokratie* (Sechste Auflage). Wilhelm Fink Verlag, Munich.

Stiglitz, J. E (1999). "Knowledge as a Global Public Good". In Kaul I., Grunberg I. & Stern, M.A. (Eds.), *Global Public Goods. International Cooperation in the 21st Century*. Oxford University Press, pp. 308-325.

Stratford, M. (2014). "Poli Sci Victory, For Now". 24 January. Retrieved from https://www.insidehighered.com/news/2014/01/24/wake-coburn-amendment-repeal-social-science-groups-plot-path-forward.

The Times Higher Education World University Rankings. (2014-2015). Retrieved from http://www.timeshighereducation.co.uk/world-university-rankings/2014-15/world-ranking.

The Times Higher Education World Reputation Rankings. (2015). March 2015. Retrieved from http://www.timeshighereducation.co.uk/world-university-rankings/2015/reputation-ranking.

Trouble at the Lab. (2013). *The Economist*, 19 October, pp. 21-24.
"What does the Boycott of Israeli Academic Institutions mean for the ASA?" (n.d.). American Studies Association. Retrieved from http://www.theasa.net/what_does_the_academic_boycott_mean_for_the_asa/.

CHAPTER 4

The Role of the University in Economic Development

Rebecca M. Blank

INTRODUCTION

Any top-rated research university has two core missions, namely, education and scholarly research. The primary focus of the institution must be on maintaining quality in these two areas, since the external reputation of the university depends upon its ability to serve students well and on the research reputation of its faculty.

But universities are frequently asked to address other societal needs. This is particularly true of state public universities in the U.S., which were often created with the expectation that they would serve the commonwealth. Public universities typically face a host of additional demands such as providing an education that is affordable to all state citizens or translating research into practical applications for agriculture and industry. As a result, many state public universities also pursue outreach and service to the state. For instance, at the University of Wisconsin-Madison (UW), we regularly talk about our three-fold mission of "education, research and outreach".

This paper focuses on one particular aspect of outreach, namely, the demand that universities contribute to the economic growth and development of their region. In many ways, such an expectation has been present since the founding of public universities; indeed, as the U.S. expanded geographically in the 1800s and created new states, establishing a state university was considered essential to building the educated citizenry needed for the state to grow. With the economic slowdown of the past decade, however, state legislators and local political leaders have increasingly come to expect that universities should take part in a host of economic development activities that often go beyond the traditional mission of the university. This can include everything from helping to attract new businesses into the region, creating training programs that cater to local industry needs, forming shared research partnerships with local companies, encouraging and supporting new business start-ups, or actively facilitating technology transfer to existing businesses.

Such demands are not limited to states or regions. The U.S., like many other countries, also encourages universities to engage in joint work with industry on immediate technological challenges. For instance, the U.S. government has recently launched several Institutes for Manufacturing Innovation (IMI), as part of its National Networks for Manufacturing Innovation (NNMI) program (2013). Each IMI is focused on a key technology issue in manufacturing, from digital design, to new materials, to 3-D printing. IMIs are selected for federal funding by a competitive bidding process. In order to bid, a combined group of universities, community colleges, businesses and government entities come together to propose how they will work collaboratively to train individuals and advance knowledge in this area. The universities involved are explicitly asked to put teams of their researchers together with industry people to address specific technological questions with high commercial value.

Whether at the national level or through economic development activities at a regional and state level, these efforts all pull the university into more direct involvement with industry and with public sector economic development activities. They also push the University into putting more of its resources into applied research questions, as well as providing more directed training in areas defined as high value to industry.

THE TRADITIONAL ROLE OF THE UNIVERSITY IN ECONOMIC GROWTH

There is nothing controversial about expecting a university to play a role in economic growth. Indeed, the two central functions of any university — education and research — are also central to economic growth.

Universities provide training to some of the most highly skilled individuals in society. Economists have long discussed the impact of higher education on economic growth. Goldin and Katz (2008) indicate that the founding of state public universities in the U.S., providing broad access to all citizens, helped the U.S. build its economic strength. Post World War II, the U.S. expanded higher education faster than almost any other country; this provided a competitive edge with a higher share of skilled employees in the workforce. In more recent decades, as the share of college-educated workers in the population has grown in other countries (now exceeding the share in the U.S. for many developed nations), these other countries have seen their economic strength rise as well.

Economists often try to decompose economic growth into different factors. Within the U.S., growing worker skills has been a steady component of growth. Between 1980 and 2014, a little more than one-tenth of economic growth was due to skill increases in the labour force. (These growth calculations are based on data from Fernald [2014].) It is worth noting that in recent U.S. history, growth in the sheer number of workers has mattered more than skill growth. Major growth in women's labour force participation since the 1960s and substantial immigration since the 1980s have increased the size of the U.S. labour force, adding almost 20% to economic growth since 1980.

The role of universities in fostering research is also central to economic growth. Much of the research done by universities is basic research, that is, it is not focused on a specific applied problem, but is designed to expand the boundaries of knowledge in a particular field. Such work is often highly theoretical and motivated by intellectually interesting questions as defined by disciplinary frameworks. Much of this work has no immediate or obvious application. But today's basic research is the basis for tomorrow's innovation in industry. Basic research done in the 1950s and 1960s in engineering, electronics, early computers and material sciences, often with no obvious instrumental value, over time produced an explosion of new technologies that have transformed our world, including such items as personal computers, mobile phones and GPS systems. At the same time, basic biological research from past decades is now leading to a revolution in medical and biological science with individually targeted treatments based on personal genomic information. None of these new technologies would have been possible without the basic and often highly-theoretical work done at universities in the past.

Recent work on the citations to past work included in patent applications suggests that many current patents are based on published ideas from more than a decade ago. Fully 25% of patents cite work that is more than 20 years old. In addition, it is not uncommon for patents to cite work far outside the field in which the patent is registered (Jaffe & Trajtenberg, 2005).

Hence university research is central to economic innovation. Scientific advances can lead to new products that improve well-being and create new markets. Or, often just as important, they can lead to new processes that produce goods more efficiently or at a higher quality level or that deliver services more effectively. For instance, think of the just-in-time inventory systems that allow retail firms to track goods and meet consumer demand more effectively at a lower cost, all based on software systems and silicon.

Innovation is even more important to economic growth than labour quality. Since 1980, innovation (making better products or products that are produced or delivered more efficiently) accounts for 68% of U.S. economic growth. Not all of this can be ascribed to universities, of course. The actual translation of existing research into new products and new processes often occurs in applied research within industry. But the initial basic research — much of it done in universities — is crucial for businesses that stay competitive by adapting new technologies to transform existing products or to create new products.

Most industrialized countries recognize the value of this basic research by funding it through public dollars. It is not by accident that public funding of research has risen sharply in many of the most globally-competitive nations. Indeed, just as the U.S. has lost its top-ranked position as a country with one of the highest share of college-educated workers, it has also lost its top-ranked position as a country with one of the highest investments of public dollars into research (Atkinson & Stewart, 2011). U.S. funding of basic research (largely going to universities) has declined in the past decade (Association of American Universities, 2015).

In short, by pursuing their core mission, universities are central to economic growth. But that has not prevented a rising demand for universities to participate even more directly in efforts at economic development.

ANALYSING MORE DIRECT ROLES FOR THE UNIVERSITY IN ECONOMIC DEVELOPMENT

There is little disagreement about the importance of universities in making sure that societies have access to educated citizens and to new research developments. But what about the more applied demands for universities to be directly involved in an economic development agenda? This section discusses and evaluates some of those demands.

Meeting training needs

Universities might be asked to develop curriculums that directly meet local employer needs. It is common for community colleges or professional programs to establish partnerships with industry to provide workers with specific skills, to certify skill levels or to retrain individuals in new skills, but it less common for universities to undertake such specific educational partnerships. In part, the educational program in universities is often more general than applied. It is designed to prepare students for a career, not a specific job, teaching them cognitive and communication skills that can be used in a wide variety of jobs.

That said, many universities already offer courses that cater to specific industry needs. In locations where a substantial number of students are hired by one or two major industries, it's not uncommon to see classes that provide in-depth instruction in issues relevant to those industries. Professional schools that are affiliated with universities frequently run training or retraining programs for industry.

Ideally, such programs make sense if they can both meet local industry needs and provide broadly useful skills for other students as well. For instance, at UW-Madison, we have initiated a computer science (CS) certificate for undergraduate students who are majoring in other areas. One reason to do this is a very large local employer who is interested in computer science majors but can't find enough to fill all the required jobs. This employer is willing to hire smart undergraduates and train them, but wants to know if an English or Chemistry major has some basic CS knowledge. This certificate will provide useful information to their hiring process. But we were willing to offer this certificate at UW because we thought it would be broadly useful to students far beyond the needs of this specific employer, allowing students to expand important skills and identify themselves as computer-literate regardless of major.

Assisting in technology transfer

Second, universities might be asked to step up their efforts to increase technology transfer from research into commercial applications, as a way to stimulate economic growth and business development in the region. There are two quite different ways of accomplishing this. On the one hand, universities can be pushed to build more and stronger industry collaborations with existing businesses. On the other hand, universities can be pushed to help develop potentially commercializable ideas from within the university community. Let me talk briefly about each of these.

University/industry partnerships have long existed, but regularly raise difficult questions. This is particularly true of partnerships aimed at collaborations between University researchers and industry product developers. As firms have become less vertically integrated in recent decades, they have often shed basic research functions and looked instead for partnerships with research institutions. In many cases, they propose to provide additional funding for certain research areas at a University, in exchange for close access to the results that emerge.

University faculty often worry that such partnerships can contaminate the research process. For instance, it might focus researchers on more limited (and more commercializable) research than they might otherwise undertake. In the worst case, universities worry that the credibility of university-based research results may be tainted by funding from interested parties who desire certain outcomes. For these reasons, there are often clear agreements signed in such partnerships indicating the expectations of both parties and establishing limits to what industry can request in exchange for funding. Among other things, such agreements almost always make it clear that faculty research is owned first by the faculty member and/or the university, and faculty have the right to publish results, whatever they may show. The ownership of any patents or licences is typically agreed upon ahead of time.

These issues can make university/industry partnerships complex. But such partnerships can also provide great benefits to both parties. They provide a business with early access to research results that can give a competitive edge in developing new products. They provide the university with funding support for researchers and graduate students; they can help university faculty understand better what research questions might have the most value to those outside the university; and they often provide hiring opportunities for students who are involved with the research. Effective collaborations typically exist when both sides have well-defined and congruent expectations about how they will operate together, with the university receiving the independence necessary to pursue and publish research without interference.

An alternative to working with existing businesses to transfer research results into products is to work directly with university researchers, helping them identify and develop potentially commercializable ideas, creating new business start-ups or selling technology to interested parties. For instance, many universities have structures in place to help faculty receive and develop patents or to support other promising ideas.

Helping to support tech transfer directly from the university into new start-ups is attractive for several reasons. If universities support the start-up of new businesses, they may be able to capture some of the revenues through ownership rights as the company grows. If they are able to sell a patent that is used in a successful product, they will capture the patent revenue over time. If successful new businesses emerge from technologies created at a university, this can have multiple favourable effects. It can attract new faculty and students to the university who believe this is a place where they can be entrepreneurial. It can create jobs for graduating students in a company run by people closely connected to the university. It can lead to successful future donors. And it builds community and political support for the university as a contributor to job and business growth in the area.

The biggest problem with these efforts is that there are few models of how to do this in a way that guarantees a high likelihood of success. For instance, UW is one of the universities that has been highly successful in pursuing patents on faculty inventions. We have an independent organization, the Wisconsin Alumni Research Foundation (WARF), founded in 1925, which has built a substantial endowment based on patent income, the returns from which are invested in UW research. Only a few other universities can claim similar levels of financial success in patenting. Yet, even WARF will tell you that patents are a very uncertain thing. There is no guarantee that any patent will make money... and many reasons why it won't. While WARF has a long history of identifying promising patents, the vast majority of their patents have not produced financial returns. Their financial success is due to a limited number of patents which came out at the right moment and were utilized in the right way. In short, there's a strong element of luck in making money through patenting faculty inventions.

Similarly, lots of universities are experimenting with ways to help faculty start companies based on their ideas and inventions. But there is no clearly-agreed upon model of how to do this successfully. Faculty often have little interest or training in running a business. Hence, the university needs to create a structure of support that identifies ideas with high commercial potential (and faculty are rarely the best judge of this); that links faculty up with the legal and business expertise needed to develop their idea into a potentially saleable product; and that provides the early start-up funding needed to do this. Like many other universities, we're experimenting with this at UW, trying to develop the expertise and the funds to move more ideas from the university into the commercial world. But this is still a work in process, at our university and elsewhere.

Developing entrepreneurship

Universities are increasingly being asked to encourage entrepreneurship, among both their students and their faculty. The technology transfer initiatives discussed above are one way to reward and develop faculty entrepreneurship. Let me focus this discussion on student entrepreneurship.

The success of Silicon Valley has resulted in efforts around the world to recreate such success locally. The importance of entrepreneurs to the explosion of rapidly growing and successful companies in Silicon Valley has meant that everybody wants to create their own group of local entrepreneurs. Communities are creating spaces for people engaged in new business start-ups to gather and work together and are working to attract the venture capital and angel investors necessary for new start-ups to launch. These communities expect universities to turn out graduates who want to be involved in this work, full of ideas and ready to launch a dozen companies.

There remains a lively debate about whether entrepreneurs are born or made. Research suggests that there are clear differences in people's risk-taking behaviour, and that entrepreneurs have a higher tolerance for taking risks. But entrepreneurship also requires encouragement and knowledge about how to nurture an idea into a successful product.

Many universities have increased their efforts to provide entrepreneurship training... and not just in business schools, where courses on entrepreneurship have long been common. For instance, at UW, we now have an undergraduate entrepreneurship certificate, available as an add-on to any major on campus. Over 220 students are currently in this certificate program, from majors that range from psychology to arts to retailing to economics. We also have a certificate program for Ph.D. students in entrepreneurship, so those who think that they may put their disciplinary training to use by developing new ideas can gain insight into the business and legal issues in which they will also need expertise.

It's hard to evaluate the impact of entrepreneurship training programs. Since the students who enter such programs are already interested in business development, it's not surprising that a higher share of students in these programs try to start their own business at some point in the future. Student interest in entrepreneurship training is strong right now. Just as universities add courses in other areas of student demand, so adding courses in entrepreneurship is a reasonable response to shifting student interests.

Regional marketing

Those who run economic development organizations are actively involved in courting new businesses to persuade them to settle locally or in working with existing businesses to persuade them to expand locally rather than elsewhere. Public universities are particularly likely to be asked to participate in such efforts at local marketing.

For instance, at UW we are regularly asked to host site selection groups who come to the region, to tell them something about UW, our students and our research activities. Upon occasion, I and others have been asked to talk with senior officials in companies that are considering locating their next facility in the south Wisconsin region. I consider taking part in these requests part of the responsibility we have to the state as a public university.

UNIVERSITIES AS DRIVERS OF ECONOMIC GROWTH: SHOULD THIS BE A RECOGNIZED MISSION?

Through their core missions of education and research, universities are centrally involved in the economic development agenda. But the demand for them to do more is not likely to go away soon. Should universities respond to these demands to make curricular and programmatic choices in order to directly benefit the local economy?

Major involvement in economic development efforts can affect the scope of university activities. Such programs tend to emphasize the training that has immediate job rewards and the research that has obvious industrial applications. While doing some of this is important and probably necessary at any university, it does not recognize the full sweep of a university's responsibility. Such efforts de-emphasize the importance of fields of study without immediately apparent economic benefits, such as philosophy, astronomy or the arts. A university thrives because of its scope across the fields of knowledge; in the long run, a weaker arts or philosophy program can also make for a weaker university and a less effective set of science programs. For instance, the opportunity for scientists to interact those who study the philosophy of science or the ability of social scientists to understand the role of arts in society is important.

Similarly troubling, economic development efforts often emphasize the value of applied versus basic work. Basic research is absolutely essential to the long-term development of new commercial products. Taking too many resources from basic research directly weakens one of the core missions of the university. Few other institutions see basic research as a core function, and its long-term value to the economy is immense. Ironically, too much of an immediate emphasis on economic development can lead to long-term economic weakness.

But these drawbacks simply indicate that such efforts need to be wisely selected and pursued. When done well, programs that facilitate economic development can reinforce and create synergies with the educational and basic research missions of the university. Effective technology transfer programs can help faculty think about how their ideas can be applied. Industry partnerships can open up new areas of inquiry. Entrepreneurship programs can enrich the college curriculum.

This suggests that programs which involve the university in direct economic development will be useful efforts when they mesh with the central goals of the university. For instance, creating an entrepreneurship certificate expands the curriculum, and can serve students from across the university. It meets the demands of students, who are clients of the university much more directly than any local economic development agency. But providing a narrowly-defined training program for a local business is less clearly advantageous. If one of the programs within the university has expertise on this, and/or if the local business is willing to pay a price that makes this a net money-maker, then there may be reasons to set up such a program. But providing narrowly-focused training may be better done by another educational institution than the research university.

Similarly, industry partnerships can be highly beneficial to certain research groups on campus, but they also have the potential for controversy and arguments over appropriate roles and ownership of results. A university that says "yes" to every collaborative proposal with industry is probably not being discriminating enough; a university that says "no" to every industry proposal is probably not being creative enough in thinking about the gains from such partnerships. The appropriate balance will vary across universities.

The easy decisions are those where it's clear up front that a new partnership or new program will benefit the university. But in many cases, it's just not possible to evaluate new programs without some experimentation and learning over time. This is particularly true of many of the tech transfer efforts, as well as some industry partnerships. Universities need to be nimble enough to regularly reevaluate what they are doing and decide if the design of their current programs is working or needs to be tweaked in some way.

Demands that universities be actively engaged in activities that promote current economic development efforts will continue. And universities will continue to find benefits to participating in some of these efforts. But this is not a core mission. Faced with these demands, universities should first communicate all the ways in which they already make key contributions to economic growth through education and research. If there is a willingness and the resources to do even more, then these additional efforts should reinforce and build upon the things a university is already doing. In the end, direct involvement in economic development should be in the portfolio of a university's activities (particularly a public university), but should be done in a way that adds to its other activities rather than diverting resources. And, like all things that universities undertake, the effectiveness of these programs should be evaluated regularly. Universities can do more for long-term economic growth through excellent education and top-quality research than through many other activities.

REFERENCES

Association of American Universities (2015). "Basic Scientific and Engineering Research at U.S. Universities". AAU Data and Policy Brief. AAU, Washington, DC. February, No 1. Available at: http://www.aau.edu/WorkArea/DownloadAsset.aspx?id=15974

Atkinson, R. & Stewart, L. (2011). "University Research Funding: The United States is Behind and Falling". Washington, DC: Information Technology and Innovation Foundation. May. Available at: http://www.itif.org/files/2011-university-research-funding.pdf

Fernald, J. (2014). A *Quarterly, Utilization-Adjusted Series on Total Factor Productivity.* Working Paper 2012-19. March. Federal Research Bank of San Francisco, San Francisco, CA. Available at: http://www.frbsf.org/economic-research/files/wp12-19bk.pdf. Data from this paper are available at http://www.frbsf.org/economics/economists/jfernald/quarterly_tfp.xls

Goldin, C. & Katz, L. (2008). *The Race Between Education and Technology.* Belknap Press of Harvard University Press. Cambridge, MA.

Jaffe, A. & Trajtenberg, M. (2005). *Patents, Citations and Innovations: A Window on the Knowledge Economy.* MIT Press, Cambridge, MA.

NNMI (2013). For more information on this program, see http://www.manufacturing.gov/nnmi.html.

CHAPTER 5

The social and political Responsibilities of research-intensive Universities: University Policies or Politics for Universities?

Alain Beretz

INTRODUCTION

This paper attempts to come up with possible answers to the question: "What do universities consider to be their most important priorities and responsibilities in 1) addressing the challenges facing their institutions; and 2) expectations arising from their societies at the local, regional or global level?" Specifically, I wish to address some possible inconsistencies between a university's strategy and external societal and political constraints.

During a recent visit by French university presidents to the Weizmann Institute, its president, Professor Daniel Zajfman, started his speech with a provocative sentence: *"We have no scientific strategy!"* Then he explained how, in their quest for excellence, he does not fix quotas, or abide to top-down plans. Of course, this is a strategy in itself, and a quite successful one. What he probably meant through this witticism is: "Our strategy is pragmatic and cannot be fixed top-down by external stakeholders." It points out that the way academics conceive basic science and related education, and the way our governments or research organizations see it, are sometimes conflicting.

This paper will try to analyse some aspects of this gap between academic basic values and the way politicians and other external stakeholders consider them, or try to influence them, but also propose some tools and strategies that could bridge the gap.

THE DIVERSITY OF UNIVERSITIES: CHALLENGE OR ASSET?

My first assumption is that the answer to the basic question of this paper is highly dependent on the type of university. Universities are diverse by nature; this should be considered as an advantage, and one can speak about an academic ecosystem, even if this biological metaphor might be riskier than it seems. But is this diversity well known to external stakeholders, and is it perceived as an advantage when lobbying government, industry or philanthropists for academic interests?

I will thus concentrate here on the specific characteristics and responsibilities of the research-intensive university, and not attempt to generalize to other types of higher education institutions.

Universities are diverse by nature, but university-directed regulations are not

The public of the Glion Colloquium will find this assumption that universities are diverse as rather commonplace. However the politicians very often do not consider these differences as relevant. We thus have to remind them that universities will differ by many parameters such as the place and level of research, the importance of graduate education, the level of graduation, national and regulatory specificities, etc.

Unfortunately, in France, recent legislative changes concerning universities still have a uniform range, targeting the wide diversity of situations with only a single set of measures. For example, the budget allocated to universities is based on a single algorithm, whatever the specific profile of the university. The additional costs induced by research in research-intensive universities are not well taken into account. Even the basic notion of "research university" (see below) is seen as not acceptable by some unions or civil servants, precisely because it introduces diversity into the system.

The French strategy of pushing forward 10 world-level campuses through the "Excellence initiative" is probably the right one. However there was a major flaw in this national policy. It led to "forcing" small universities, engineering schools or other *grandes écoles* to join these federations under a single model, without having the courage to redefine their roles, their goals or their assets.

Decision-makers lack information and cultural knowledge about universities

National or international policies that affect directly the life of universities are sometimes designed or supervised by people that do not have the clear answer to some basic questions such as: What is a university? What types of universities exist? And, even more obviously: what are universities for? In France, this is in part caused by the fact that high-level civil servants have for the most part *not* been trained in universities! Also, the French government counts only about 50% university graduates (the others are from *grandes écoles*), and not one single Ph.D!

Science advisors or advisory boards could provide this information to decision-makers (for a recent review, see Wilsdon & Doubleday, 2015). They can play a key role in improving policy-making in relation to science and research, by contributing independent expert advice. They exist in many countries (U.K., Scotland, U.S., India…). European academics have sometimes looked with envy at the U.S. situation, beginning in 1933 with President Franklin D. Roosevelt's Science Advisory Board, where each U.S. President has established an advisory committee of scientists, engineers and health professionals. But Pielke and Klein (2009) have regretted "a long-term decline of the influence of the president's science advisor, while, at the same time, the importance of expertise to government has increased tremendously". This is exemplary of the general opinion considering that the issue is now too important to be left to a single advisor.

On the other hand, the position of science advisor is only theoretical in France. Academics have been present in the cabinet of most French ministers, but their number has recently gone down.

The recent debate on this subject within the European Commission also illustrates the complexity and importance of this issue. Jean-Claude Juncker had first abolished the position of Chief Scientific Advisor to the President of the European Commission. This had sparked a vast movement of protest in the academic community. Finally, the Commission proposed to create a new "Scientific Advice Mechanism" (SAM), aiming for an integrated approach to science-based E.U. policy-making (Wilsdon & Doubleday, 2015).

Clearly, stakeholders have to drive the agenda, and we have to design efficient strategies to embed science into the democratic process.

Can research-intensive universities speak globally in defence of universities?

Lacroix and Maheu (2015) have recently reviewed some criteria, especially those of the Carnegie Foundation, that define research universities:
- offer a broad and rich array of undergraduate studies. These form the base of their diversified pyramid of teaching programs,

- show a peak of their teaching pyramid that reflects the weight they assign to teaching at the upper graduate level,
- award a certain number of Ph.D.s every year,
- carry a large amount of basic research, and are able to secure for that activity significant amounts of research grants.

It is clear that most universities in the world are *not* research universities. Thus we should question the fact that they are sometimes (including by us) seen as the gold standard, towards which all universities have to aim. This is a major mistake that has a strong negative impact on academic policies, but also national policies. The research university is essential in a national academic network, but this model is *not* a universal paradigm. We require political strategies that give more consideration to the rich variety of the universities in a given country.

The Glion Colloquium is mainly concerned with research-intensive universities, which have a specific approach to these matters. Precisely because of their widespread interests and capacities, research universities also have a leading role for the global academic community. They should stand up as leaders in the defence and promotion of academic values, of university diversity, and of the global role of universities in our society. Along these lines, the League of European Research Universities (LERU) has always advocated global academic values, instead of just lobbying for its own members.

THE POLITICAL DEFENCE OF UNIVERSITIES

Philanthropy

Leszek Borysiewicz (2015) addresses this point in detail during this meeting. My purpose here is just to underline the political and even strategic role of philanthropy, which can complement, or even sometimes replace, a flawed political system. This has been summarized by Rohe and Hausmann (2015): "As forces of a pluralistic democratic society, foundations are able to introduce subjects to the political agenda that require treatment and yet may be familiar to only a few experts, or are perhaps ignored because they are politically inconvenient". This is precisely one of the points raised by Borysiewicz: "Funders (…) can afford to engage in a relationship driven less by financial calculations or time pressures, and more by a shared sense of purpose".

Many of the top U.S. universities were founded through philanthropy, such as the University of Chicago in 1890 by John D. Rockefeller, Stanford University in 1890 by Leland Stanford and Carnegie Mellon University in 1900 by Andrew Carnegie. On the other hand, most of our European universities are public, and do not (yet?) rely on philanthropy to provide their core resources. In such a situation, philanthropy cannot (and should not) substitute for public funding, but it can help universities to be ambitious about what they want to achieve (LERU, 2014).

Thus philanthropy is not just a question of money; it was historically based on strong beliefs by the donors that they were doing something essential for the future of their country. In present times, the level of philanthropy also reflects quite accurately how issues and values carried by universities are shared by the general public, and is a good indicator of the public's and stakeholders' general interest in universities.

The level and acceptance of philanthropy are not equivalent in different countries. French universities certainly have a long way to go, when you consider that the University of Strasbourg is proud to lead the pack with a record four-year first campaign that raised 22.5 million euros, with a third as endowment. These figures are of course very far away from those achieved in many European and, of course, American universities. But we are mostly proud of the new and wider relationship this campaign has created with the public, a benefit that goes far beyond the amounts that were raised. This will be certainly a major benefit of this campaign.

Are universities a political issue or should they be?

The study "Research Universities and the Future of America" (National Research Council, 2012) highlights some threats to the future of top U.S. research universities and to the prosperity and security of society. The basic line of this paper is to reaffirm the central role of research universities. It starts with a very direct statement: *"Our nation's primary source of both new knowledge and graduates with advanced skills continues to be our research universities. However, these institutions now face an array of challenges (…). It is essential that we as a nation reaffirm and revitalize the unique partnership that has long existed among research universities, the federal government, the states, and philanthropy, and strengthen its links with business and industry."* It supports, in part, the idea that the high level of excellence attained by U.S. research universities is the result of national policies, which can indeed profoundly and durably shape the academic landscape: *"America's research universities, through education and basic research, have emerged as a major asset (…). This did not happen by accident; it is the result of prescient and deliberate federal and state policies that have powerfully shaped these institutions".*

In this situation, the role of the academic community is essential (through reports, lobbying etc.), in order to provide inspiration to decision-makers, and suggest directions for action. But we rely also on the personal beliefs and commitment of first-rank politicians.

Our colleague James Duderstadt has just been awarded the prestigious Vannevar Bush Award from National Science Board (NSB) (2015).

Duderstadt said: "*It is a great honour to receive this award named for Vannevar Bush, who defined the role of the American university in serving the needs of this nation through science and technology(...)*". Vannevar Bush indeed helped establish federal funding for science and engineering as a national priority, and played a pivotal role in the creation of the National Science Foundation. It is not in my capacity to comment on Bush's detailed proposals and plans. As a European academic, I am clearly not familiar with his legacy; I could, however, say that France, and maybe even Europe, has not often had the chance to benefit from a similar political vision.

The state of Israel was founded in 1948, which is much later than some of its main research-intensive academic institutions such as the Technion (1912), the Hebrew University (1918) or the Weizmann Institute (1934). This is not to say that science or technology necessarily determine history and the creation and destiny of nations; it is just to underline that pioneers such as Haim Weizmann or Albert Einstein wanted research universities to be the cornerstone of the new nation. And apparently they succeeded, at least on academic matters. For example, Israeli institutions lead the pack in their ability to secure competitive European research funds such as the ERC.

Which leads us to Europe. One could think that the old Europe, where universities were born, where the widespread model of the Humboldtian university originated, would be built upon the same basic values and the same visionary spirit that Haim Weizmann or Vannevar Bush had for their country. However we know that the European Union was first built from a major political idea (bring permanent peace after two bloody wars), but upon an economical platform ("coal and steel community"). It created a "common market" aimed at economic expansion, growth of employment and a rising standard of living, not a "common campus". More than 60 years later, the founding values are still valid, but we know that neither steel nor coal can be pointed as Europe's assets. Europe is now pushing for the establishment of a European research area (ERA). But support for universities and research has not really replaced coal and steel as a first-row goal for the European Commission.

Europe is, on this subject, at a crossroads. We do have a Commissioner for research, Carlos Moedas, who is indeed very supportive of the cause of a major role of universities in the construction and wealth of Europe. But he has no role for the supervision of higher education, which is under the dependence of another official, the commissioner for education. Moreover, the commissioner is under political control of the Vice-President for Jobs, Growth, Investment and Competitiveness. With some exaggeration, this could be interpreted as: "Higher education and research are here to serve economic growth and competitiveness, but they are not a primary objective".

One recent episode supports this point of view. One of the main projects of the Commission is EFSI (European Fund for Strategic Investments), a major investment plan designed to boost European economy (so called "Juncker plan"). It is a very ambitious plan that could foster jobs, growth and innovation, but which requires significant contributions from many parts of the European budget. Cuts of 2.7 billion € from the Horizon 2020 budget were therefore decided, including contributions from major and valuable research tools such as the European Research Council (ERC) and the Marie Skłodowska-Curie system, which are exemplary funding mechanisms for basic science. The European Commission or the national finance ministers saw nothing to say to this, while it clearly meant that long-term support for basic science could be sacrificed for the benefit of more short-term economical development. Thanks to continuous action of many stakeholder organizations, the European Research Council and the Marie Skłodowska-Curie scheme have finally been safeguarded, but it remains clear, as LERU communicated to the press, that *"it is a bad and wrong signal, one year after the launch of Horizon 2020, that 2.2 billion € is plundered from its budget. The daily rhetoric about investments in research and innovation has a very cynical ring to it."* (LERU, 2015a).

Universities as political actors?

If we want the university to remain (become?) a major political issue, we should stimulate academic personnel to participate widely in the public debate and not remain in the "ivory tower". As stated by Boulton and Lucas (2008) in the LERU paper "What are universities for?": *"It is timely that this aspect of university capacity should be better cherished and rewarded by the universities themselves and recognized and supported by government. The increasing priority for 'evidence-based' public policies depends on access to a wide range of specialists, many based in universities, and the willingness of academics to be called upon for advice and involvement in the policy process."*

We see, for example, that, at the University of Strasbourg, the creation of the position of Vice-President in charge of "Science and society" has been very productive in creating new types of dialogue with external stakeholders, private, institutional or corporate.

THE ROLE OF RESEARCH-INTENSIVE UNIVERSITIES IN THE INNOVATION/TECHNOLOGY TRANSFER SCENE

Universities and economy: a complicated relationship

The present European situation shows too well that universities are now expected to deliver, in a short-term time frame, economics goods, employment and innovation. For some politicians, this role on the innovation-technology transfer scene is now considered as our major (only?) task and duty for the society. In this sense universities are sometimes just seen as "innoversities" (Lucey, 2014).

Of course we do not reject this responsibility. We all know that universities have a major duty in the economic field. Economic achievements by research-intensive universities have been numerous. But, precisely, it is the success of these endeavours that now puts us at risk of seeing our basic goals and duties being neglected by political authorities. As was stated by Boulton and Lucas (2008): *"Universities are not just supermarkets for a variety of public and private goods that are currently in demand and whose value is defined by their perceived aggregate financial value. We assert that they have a deeper, fundamental role that permits them to adapt and respond to the changing values and needs of successive generations, and from which the outputs cherished by governments are but secondary derivatives. To define the university enterprise by these specific outputs, and to fund it only through metrics that measure them, is to misunderstand the nature of the enterprise and its potential to deliver social benefit."*

It is not the purpose of this paper to analyse in detail how research-intensive universities have a direct and positive influence on the economy. Other speakers will have a more detailed and documented view on this matter. But we can ask ourselves why this goal is now so much overrated, and if there are some solutions.

First we have to look at our own flaws. It is true, especially in France, that some academic circles have treated with great contempt the possibility that their intellectual production could, or should, have any effect on the national or global economy. They showed the same contempt for any demand about the effect of the education they provide on the future professional status of their students. The French situation on this matter is even made worse by the existence of the *Grandes écoles*, engineering schools that train most of the top executives of major French companies, and that consider the field of the economy as their own preserve (*"chasse gardée"*). This has also led to the fact that the managers and government officials have sometimes looked down on the societal role of universities, thinking that they are a necessary evil, train only teachers, are a source of civil trouble, but certainly not an asset for society outside the service to universities themselves.

Return on investment: do we have the data?

We all feel, more or less spontaneously, that allocating resources to higher education and research delivers a high return on investment to society. We need strong messages such as the one delivered recently by Drew Faust, president of Harvard University, at the World Economic Forum: *"Higher education is essential for a thriving society: it is the strongest, sturdiest ladder to increased socio-economic mobility."* (Faust, 2015).

But strong messages are not enough, we also need data! We suspect, or at least wish, that the economic return of universities is several fold the value of the public funds allocated, since universities produce much of the human and intellectual capital that is the source of indigenous economic growth.

There are many sources of economic impact of universities, but politicians seem to narrow their attention to only a few, such as the number of spin-off companies, hoping for their own Silicon valley. There are many other fields for this economic return, such as graduate productivity benefits, or shorter term impacts such as spending by staff and students in the local economy and support for other sectors (such as tourism and construction). Some long-term benefits are often overlooked, because the politician wants results for the next election. The positive image that a major research-intensive university casts upon its local community is also very valuable and can yield significant indirect economical returns.

But this discourse should be based on evidence, rather than anecdotes. Therefore, to defend our case, we should rely on scientific data, not just on opinion papers, even if issued by a group of distinguished university presidents! This is not an easy task. Actual methodological approaches of impact studies may have many pitfalls, as pointed by Siegfried et al. (2006): *"If these economic impact studies were conducted at the level of accuracy most institutions require of faculty research, their claims of local economic benefits would not be so preposterous, and, as a result, trust in and respect for higher education officials would be enhanced."* This is why we need to increase the number of studies of the impact of research universities on our society, such as Star Metrics, a U.S. project to create a repository of data and tools that will be useful to assess the impact of federal R&D investments (Lane & Bertuzzi, 2011).

LERU has recently commissioned a study of the economical impact of its members. Briefly, the study estimates that in 2014 the 21 LERU Universities generated a total economic value of €71.2 billion in GVA and 900,065 jobs across Europe. For each €1 in GVA directly generated by the LERU Universities, there was a total contribution of almost €6 to the European economy and every job directly created by the LERU Universities supported almost six jobs in the European economy (LERU, 2015b). Even if we are not totally confident about these figures, this is the type of data we need to convince external stakeholders that universities are not an expense, but an investment.

INNOVATIVE TOOLS FOR STRATEGIC LEVERAGE

Because of their prominent role, universities are now confronted with demands from the society and decision-makers that do not always fit with their values and strategies. Research-intensive universities are, for the most, considered to be able to respond to global or national issues, while vocational institutions would have a stronger local importance. However, as was mentioned by Lacroix and Maheu (2015): *"When government regulation is joined with preponderant, even quasi-exclusive, public funding of universities, its influence is much more constraining and ubiquitous, with serious strategic fallout"*. To be able to resist to this "top-down" pressure, universities can rely on their fundamental values, but also make optimal use of innovative tools.

These innovative tools, designed by governments, can indeed represent major cornerstones for the development of the role of universities and research in our society, by providing a unique platform for strategy development. I will only cite two examples.

Excellence funding schemes, focused on the development of wider institutional strategies, have been implemented in many European countries (Bennetot-Pruvot & Estermann, 2015). For example, the "excellence initiative" program in France has been designed to allow both a competitive research strategy *and* new cutting-edge research. This program is exemplary of possible complementary approaches of national and university policies. For the university of Strasbourg, it is one of our main tools to fulfil our external responsibilities. There are two "magic ingredients" in this program: long-term financing through a public endowment mechanism, and a great degree of freedom for strategic choices.

The European Research Council (ERC), which provides generous individual grants for basic research, is another example of these innovative tools. One of its main qualities is that it is open to any topic, and remains light on bureaucracy. *"The ERC has become a recognised success of the 7th Framework programme, having established itself as an indispensable component of the European Research Area with a high reputation for the quality and efficiency of its operations"* (ERC, 2011). This is certainly why the scientific community was recently so active in lobbying against the planned budget cuts on this program.

It is interesting that Jean-Pierre Bourguignon, president of ERC, is now speaking about the idea of transforming the ERC into an endowment-based agency, precisely to be less dependent on political variables, and to secure its financing over the long time frame that is intrinsic in the ERC's goal and duties.

What those two examples stress is that top-down policies for research-intensive universities can be successful only if they use trust as a basic value, building on the autonomy that universities should all be granted. Money without trust and autonomy will not reach the goal. A striking example is that the flux of governmental funding and strong top-down incentives are still not enough for Chinese universities to reach the top level, because, as pointed out by Rhoads *et al.* (2014): *"(…) limitations in the area of academic freedom posed one of the most significant barriers to the nation's leading universities joining the elite of the world"*. These authors also point out to the problem of *"(…) imposing a research culture from above and not at the same time growing it from below"*.

CONCLUSION: PLAYING THE GAME WITH RULES AND STYLE

The second Glion declaration summarized the social compact of universities, which is discussed in this paper: "Universities must reaffirm and continue to fulfil their role in the unwritten social compact by providing new knowledge, educated leaders, informed citizens, expert professional practitioners, services and training, as well as individual certification and accreditation in these fields. In exchange for the responsible and effective provision of these services, society supports higher education, contributes to its finance, accepts its professional judgment and scholarly certification, and grants it a unique degree of institutional autonomy and scholarly freedom" (Rhodes, 2009).

This declaration of principles, to which all can adhere, is too often questioned by universities and governments alike; both sides can show a tendency to put their own interest and priorities forward, and try to force the other party to abide to them. To avoid this situation, universities have to go forward and explain their positions to external stakeholders, staying away from the academic arrogance that is sometimes so common (Weber, 2015). This positive attitude could use some of the tools and arguments described in this paper, and summarized in Table 1.

Universities have apparently nothing to do with football. However this metaphor may reveal a parallel between both worlds. Heldin (2008) had written that ERC (one of the tools described in this paper) *"will create a 'Champion's League' for Europe's scientists"*. This prediction came true; but one should remember that those teams playing the Champion's League also have a responsibility to set an example, so that smaller clubs play the game with pleasure, while respecting the rules.

Professional football, with its extraordinary commercial stakes, should still rely on basic human values, just like universities. Arsène Wenger, manager of Arsenal football club in London, is an alumnus of the University of Strasbourg, where he graduated in economics. He said in recent a interview on BBC: *"I believe that our sport has moved forward a lot on the technical side, on the physical side, on the tactical side but as well we must not forget the values that our sport carries through the generations… I believe big clubs have a responsibility to win, but to win with style."* (Wenger, 2015). Probably, research universities have the same responsibility.

Table 3: Summary/recommendations

1. Universities are diverse by nature, this should be considered as an asset. A national university policy aimed at "one for all" model is doomed to failure, as would be the ambition of all universities in a country to become world academic leaders.
2. No national university system can develop without a stable core of ambitious research universities, carrying innovative strategies.
3. Economical and societal impact of universities are not just political issues, they are part of academic duty. It is our responsibility to sponsor research and teaching on economical and societal impact of universities.
4. The future of European research universities stands clearly in ambitious, specific European policies, designed at making those universities one of the major assets of the continent
5. Science/academic advisors or advisory committees should counsel decision-makers. Academics should show high motivation to participate in theses activities.
6. A national, and even more a European policy should be based on two major complementary ingredients: trust and autonomy.

REFERENCES

Abbott, A. (2015). "European Commission unveils long-awaited science advice plans". Nature Breaking News, Available from: http://www.nature.com.scd-rproxy.u-strasbg.fr/news/european-commission-unveils-long-awaited-science-advice-plans-1.17557 [Accessed: 19 August 2015]

Bennetot-Pruvot, E. & Estermann, T. (2015). "Define Thematic Report: Funding For Excellence" [Online] Available from: http://www.eua.be/Libraries/Publication/DEFINE_Funding_for_Excellence.sflb.ashx [Accessed: 19 August 2015]

Borysiewicz, L. (2015). "The importance of philanthropy", in: Weber, L. E. & Duderstadt, J. J. (eds) Glion colloquium Series No 9. London, Paris and Geneva (this book.)

Boulton, G. & Lucas, C. (2008). "What are universities for?" (LERU paper). Available from: http://www.leru.org/files/general/•What%20are%20universities%20for%20(September%202008).pdf [Accessed: 19 August 2015]

ERC (2011). European Research Council Task Force. Final report. [Online] Available from: http://erc.europa.eu/sites/default/files/document/file/erc_taskforce_report_2011.pdf [Accessed: 19 August 2015].

Faust, D.G. (2015). 3 forces shaping the university of the future. World Economic Forum [Online] Available from: https://agenda.weforum.org/2015/01/three-forces-shaping-the-university-of-the-future/?utm_content=buffer011b7&utm_medium=social&utm_source=twitter.com&utm_campaign=buffer [Accessed: 19 August]

Heldin, C. H. (2008). The European Research Council — a new opportunity for European science. *Nature Reviews Molecular Cell Biology* 9, 417-420.

Lacroix, R. & Maheu, L. (2015). *Leading research universities in a competitive world*. McGill-Queens University Press.

Lane, J.I. & Bertuzzi, S. (2011) Measuring the results of science investments. *Science* 331 pp. 678-680.

LERU (2014). Philanthropy at research-intensive universities. Available from: http://www.leru.org/files/publications/LERU_note_Philanthropy_at_research-intensive_universities.pdf [Accessed: 19 August 2015]

LERU (2015a). *Press release. EFSI: Stalemate avoided, time to get down to business* [Online] Available from: http://www.leru.org/index.php/public/news/efsi-stalemate-avoided-time-to-get-down-to-business/ [Accessed: 19 August 2015]

LERU (2015b). Press release The economic impact of LERU universities [Online] To be published 7 Sept, 2015

Lucey, B. M. (2014). "Why the rush to replace Universities with Innoversities…?" [Online] Available from: http://brianmlucey.wordpress.com/2014/07/12/why-the-rush-to-replace-universities-with-innoversities [Accessed: 19 August 2015]

National Research Council (2012). Research Universities and the Future of America: Ten Breakthrough Actions Vital to Our Nation's Prosperity and Security. The National Academies Press, Available from: http://www.nap.edu/catalog.php?record_id=13299 [Accessed: 19 August 2015]

National Science Board (2015). *Press Release 15-050 James Duderstadt is NSB's 2015 Vannevar Bush awardee* [Online] Available from: http://www.nsf.gov/nsb/news/news_summ.jsp?cntn_id=134981 [Accessed: 19 August 2015]

Pielke, R. & Klein, R. (2009). The Rise and Fall of the Science Advisor to the President of the United State. *Minerva* (47) pp. 7-29 (2009).

Rhoads, R. A, Wang, X., Shi, X. & Chang, Y. (2014). *China's Rising Research Universities*, Johns Hopkins University Press, Baltimore.

Rhodes, F. (2009). The second Glion declaration [Online] Available from: http://www.glion.org/?p=736 [Accessed: 19 August 2015].

Rohe, W. & Hausmann J. (2015). "The role of foundations at the science — policy interface" in: Wilsdon, J. & Doubleday, R. (eds.) (2015), *Future Directions for Scientific Advice in Europe*. Centre for Science and Policy, University of Cambridge, Available from: http://www.csap.cam.ac.uk/projects/future-directions-scientific-advice-europe/ [Accessed: 19 August 2015]

Siegfried, J., Sanderson, A. & McHenry, P. (2006). The Economic Impact of Colleges and Universities; Department of Economics, Vanderbilt University Working Paper No. 06-W12, [Online] Available from: http://as.vanderbilt.edu/econ/wparchive/workpaper/vu06-w12.pdf [Accessed: 19 August 2015]

Weber, L. (2015) *L'université au XXIème siècle*. Economica, Paris, pp. 104-105.

Wenger, A. (2015), Interview on BBC's World At One, [Online] Available from: http://www.goal.com/en-gb/news/2896/premier-league/2015/05/28/12165592/big-clubs-have-a-responsibility-to-win-with-style-wenger and http://www.bbc.co.uk/programmes/p02s7w79 [Accessed: 19 August 2015]

Wilsdon, J. & Doubleday, R. (eds.) (2015). "Future Directions for Scientific Advice in Europe". Centre for Science and Policy, University of Cambridge, Available from: http://www.csap.cam.ac.uk/projects/future-directions-scientific-advice-europe/ [Accessed: 19 August 2015]

CHAPTER 6

Learning to Think Critically

Lino Guzzella and Gerd Folkers

Learning without thought is labour lost; thought without learning is perilous.
(Confucian Analects, Wei zheng [Ho Peng Yoke, 2012])

INTRODUCTION

Confucius explains to his students and scholars his ideas about how to gain knowledge. In doing so, he continues, "… shall I teach you what knowledge is? When you know a thing, to hold that you know it; and when you do not know a thing to allow that you do not know it — this is knowledge." (Ho Peng Yoke, 2012)

These ideas seem entirely reasonable. So, why should the acquisition and reflection of knowledge be questioned or even endangered?

Confucius taught in the 6th century BC, at the same time when classical Greek philosophy arose in Europe, times of elitist education where the transfer of wisdom was to only a few scholars in an "inner circle". Since then, higher education has completely changed, becoming a mass enterprise of knowledge transfer. Small discussion groups have been replaced within the modern (still Humboldtonian?) university with more and more face-to-face lectures, programmed doctoral studies and the (in)famous Bologna Process. The acquisition of credit points within the latter may serve as a metaphor for the establishment of tailored structures in higher education as a consequence of the "massification of scientific enterprise" (Trajtenberg, 2013). The resulting functional behaviour of students and professors, and the economic motivation of political institutions trying to manage the cost of higher education may lead to a utilitarian attitude based on a simplified paradigm of a knowledge-based economy. Is there a need to counter-act? Can it be done without falling back into traditional or even revisionist attitudes? The Critical

Thinking Initiative at ETH Zurich, the Swiss Federal Institute of Technology in Zurich, is an ambitious project that started in 2014 to analyse and, at the same time, to gather the criticism that weighs on current academic life.

ECONOMIZATION OF SCIENCE

Currently, on a global perspective, we find nearly 6 million people who claim to be scientists defined by their ability to publish in peer-reviewed journals. While this sounds like a modest number, it represents about 1 person out of every 1,200 of the global population making it a quite remarkable quantity. Never before in history has the world seen so many scientists. Roughly one million of them have emerged from the developing countries within the last decade. The scientific community produces approximately one million publications annually and, on average, for each paper accepted for publication at least one is rejected. Each manuscript requires two reviews as a prerequisite for publication, such that at least four million reviews are written annually. Bibliometrics indicate that more than 50% of the published papers may never actually be read. This is the output of some 25,000 peer-reviewed journals fed by scientists from 22,000 universities worldwide. In 1665, the first issue of the Royal Society's *Philosophical Transactions* appeared. Since then, the scientific community has produced some 50 million publications, (Trajtenberg, 2013; Folkers, 2013); the vast majority of which saw the light of the day after 1950. (Jinha, 2010)

Academic career success and, to a certain extent, promotions in science-based companies bear a direct correlation to the scientist's reputation — a value measured predominantly by the volume rather than the quality of a scientist's publications. This raises the question of whether or not the growth rate of "real talent," i.e., the future "Einsteins", is accurately reflected in the measured output. One of the most important tasks of leading universities is to provide a space to develop and foster talent for the benefit of society, but how can universities detect such talent in the vast "noise" generated by the publication frenzy?

THE POSSIBLE CONSEQUENCES OF THE ECONOMIZATION PROCESS

Career promotions and position appointments have always been a question of a signal-to-noise ratio. If an individual catches the attention of the community and/or decision-makers, his/her promotion or advancement is most assuredly on (tenure) track. The enormous expansion of players, however, has considerably sharpened the fight for attention. In order to get rid of the "old boy's networks" and render a more objective system of advancement, we have, for more than three decades, applied various types of rating and ranking systems, commonly known as bibliometrics. Consequently, such metrics correlate scientific reputation with paper output. For a deep analysis, it may be worthwhile to consult the musings of the Vienna-based architect Georg Franck, whom we quote here as follows, "*Scientific information is measured in terms of the attention it earns. Since scientists demand scientific information as a means of production, the attention that a theory attracts is a measure of its value as a capital good. On the other hand, the attention a scientist earns is capitalized into the asset called reputation*" (Franck, 2002). If an individual career is a function of the H-index (citation, impact-factor, etc.) and if the growth curve of the publication ratio becomes even steeper, it is quite comprehensible that scientists at all levels of advancement jump on the Scientific Bandwagon (Caulfield, 2012). What are the consequences of this behaviour?

Get More Specialized

The increasing specialization and segregation of disciplines seem to follow a natural trend. Drilling very deep holes generally requires a narrowing of the diameter. This is simply due to the nature of the scientific method. It yields the advantage for the individual scientist that he or she is eventually alone in his field and by that reduces competition. In the best case, the newly drilled hole can be established as a new area of research and promote the scientist as "first-in-class". Given this to be the desired outcome of an individual scientific endeavour, the question remains whether enough time and space are granted to the individual scientist to step back and reflect the new findings in respect to the neighbouring fields, to the discipline as a whole, and how to incorporate the novelties into the scientific system. Individual ambition may be different, though. Seduced by the fight for attention, the novelties may be used to establish hype and to advance the individual career.

Get More Efficient and Increase Your Output Qualitatively

Drilling deep holes is not a problem *per se*. It depends on the material, the method and the nature of the ground. When choosing soft ground, even not-so-sharp drill bits may yield quick results, (i.e., high publication frequencies). This is known as reaching for the low-hanging fruit in science. If "only" the number of novel findings and not their weight in terms of the knowledge already established is valued in gaining reputation, then there is a great temptation to act along these lines. This may result in an increasingly observed "publication bias", where broader reflection is avoided in favour of reporting single observations. Especially in the field of life sciences, where Ph.D. students are often obliged to finish their doctoral thesis with one or more "accepted" papers, the pressure exerted leads to the attitude of trade-offs such as, "Don't look beyond your own nose, but focus and publish." The same pressure is on the faculty. Funding related to annual reports of "always better" scientific achievements triggers a novelty-publication spiral and increases the pressure for productivity. Is this the right approach? Is detecting novelties relevant for the knowledge system? Some institutional leaders think that is not relevant, *"For some of our projects, we need people who aren't concerned about getting a publication out in two years to get a job because we're trying to work on a more challenging problem."* (Rubin, 2006a).

'Move the Food'

Leaders in higher education generally face a dilemma in terms of resource allocation when developing relevant strategies. Even the wealthiest universities cannot afford to do everything and the shotgun principle does not accumulate enough resources for costly research in particle physics, imaging technologies, genomics or clinical research. If, on the other hand, only hypothesis or curiosity-driven research following an idealistic model is the focus of a university, (Schleiermacher, 1808):

- Freedom of teaching and learning, radical break with any form of set curriculum
- The unity of teaching and research, learning as a collaborative enterprise (of students and professors)
- The unity of science and scholarship, co-equal status of sciences and humanities
- The primacy of "pure" science, over specialized professional training (Ash, 2008)

It will never cope with the challenges of modern higher education as a mass enterprise. It will struggle to compete with "entrepreneurial" and "research" universities for students and other resources from the state or the private sector.

Consider a mixed model where managers in higher education organize a university-wide or nationwide competition in special research areas considered important for society, the economic welfare of a nation or for knowledge procurement. In a competitive context, peer-review mechanisms would select appropriate topics. Generous research grants, awarded to the competition winners, provide the motivation for doctoral students to produce results, publish papers, increase attention for their work and elevate their reputation. A competitive model, like this one, may prompt scientists to think carefully — even critically — about their proposals before leaving the comfort of their traditional area of research. Ultimately, brains and talent follow money. With the competition at the front door, only a model that provides both excellent funding and infrastructure will attract the most promising young researchers.

The Chinese National Academy recently gave up on bibliometrics for the evaluation of their member institutes — noted around the globe as a remarkable and unexpected decision. The Chinese National Academy has introduced instead a "One-Three-Five System", where every institute has to come up with ONE research topic, within which THREE expected breakthroughs should be realized within a FIVE-year period. In such a system, the lack of research diversity will surely harm the institutes. How to evaluate "breakthroughs" remains open, but the manner in which the money is distributed seems clear: *Chinese scientists should do things that are useful for China first of all...* (Huang Kun, 2015).

In general, allocating resources or "moving the food" is a heavy load of responsibility on the shoulders of university managers. They have to fight two battles at the same time. The first, with scientists who feel their field is underfunded; and the second with those who provide funding — whether from the government or private sector — they come with their own perspectives, agendas, and incentives for moving the food (Folkers, 2012).

Put Disciplines at Stake

Discipline ranking precedes establishing incentives for research and creating competitions. The large project may be "interdisciplinary", but at the local level academic institutions, often only one research group, garner the money and the reputation. This may start a "chain reaction" going back to the last century known as "accumulated advantage". In science it is commonly called "The Matthew Effect". The term, first coined by sociologist Robert K. Merton in 1968, takes its name from a verse in the biblical Gospel of Matthew that pertains to Jesus' parable of the talents:

For unto every one that hath shall be given, and he shall have abundance: but from him that hath not shall be taken even that which he hath. (Matthew 25: 29, King James Version.)

Academic administrators aim to distribute research funds — especially funding that comes from taxpayers — in a manner that poses the least risk and offers the highest potential for output. Risk avoidance creates a "winner takes all" strategy that contradicts basic economic logic that purports there are no gains without risk. However, in terms of the leverage philosophy in finance that aims to multiply gains (and losses), the attitude makes sense and partitions the "successful" research fields in a university from the less successful ones.

Teaching

Second only to "attention", "time" is among a scientist's most scarce capital good. When academic reputation is based solely on research output, teaching falls behind. Scientists restrict their "teaching load", keeping it to a minimum for the sake of efficiency, having deemed the ideal, "*the unity of teaching and research*" unattainable. The semantics of the term "teaching load" already reflects the general attitude. Not surprisingly, many universities offer a reduced teaching load in contractual negotiations to attract desired candidates. Hiring strategists at some universities even correlate a reduced teaching load with success in seeking external funding. This development leaves us with a somewhat unprincipled scenario.

If, in the present paradigm, the aim is for an academic education is to create insight, conceptual understanding and motivation in young scientists, then shouldn't the best scientist focus on teaching rather than knowledge transfer? This idea, however, runs counter to the current framing of a successful career in science. If follows that this dilemma may be solved by reintegrating teaching as a primary function of faculty members. This is the point where the ideal of Humboldtonian Education breaks down. In the real world, however, such ideals do not simply implode. At the beginning of the last century, many eminent German scientists — researchers of mainly basic science — found their main occupation at the Kaiser Wilhelm Institutes. The institutes provided an innovative research atmosphere leaving universities unaffected and thus, the Humboldtonian constitution of universities became a myth, at least for the sciences (Ash, 2008). This paper is not about re-introducing Humboldt, but rather it is about finding solutions that follow our deep convictions to provide the best education for young scientists and future leaders.

CRITICAL THINKING

Further critical reflection and creative thinking at all levels and in all units, as envisioned and initiated by the ETH Zurich leadership, may provide an onset for the future improvement of academic education and research. The overall objective must be to minimize the restraints imposed by the economical paradigm that prevents us from achieving our desired goals. (e.g., Quack, 2014; Spelsberg, 2015).

Three serious and tightly interwoven arguments are in favour of the initiative:
- Responsibility
- Sustainability
- Economy

Responsibility

Critical reflection of our own work is the cornerstone of the academic endeavour. Referring to Confucius, "*Learning without thought is labour lost;*

thought without learning is perilous", achievements, whether they be new findings, theories, teaching, or lab methodologies, should be: a) Continually scrutinized to align with the aims of sound and rigorous reasoning; and b) Placed in a larger context that demonstrates relevance. In principle, the scientific process provides the means to achieve this endeavour. Global conferences, publications, research proposals, lectures, lab meetings and bilateral discussions, as well as platforms for interdisciplinary exchange, are opportunities that could guarantee the reflection process, provided time and space are allocated.

If scientists take the process of critical reflection seriously and take time to focus on the most difficult challenges, rather than seek the low-hanging fruit that lead to the next incremental research publication, perhaps the process might inspire different or more relevant research questions. Both curiosity-driven basic researchers and problem-driven applied researchers are invited to pursue a reflective approach in order to avoid quick "symptomatic" problem-solving and, instead, foster a process that generates fundamental and even controversial new ideas. Positive examples may be found intrinsically in interdisciplinary fields such as brain research, material sciences or computational sciences.

Since career, publication and communication rituals vary tremendously among academic disciplines, a "one size fits all" strategy is neither possible nor necessary. The Critical Thinking Initiative strives for a more intense reflection in each discipline, taking into account the pecularities in each and every field of research. The success of the initiative relies upon the willingness of all stakeholders in an academic institution encompassing faculty, students, post-doctoral researchers, senior researchers, administrators and managers.

The overall goal is to have more fun, take calculated risks, show courage and ultimately achieve an increasingly higher standard of research and a greater sense of satisfaction in academic life.

The "three commandments" declared at the foundation of Janelia Farm, Howard Hughes Medical Institute's pioneering research centre in neuroscience, outline the expectations of this process in a nutshell:

1. The ability to define and the willingness to tackle difficult and important problems;
2. Originality, creativity, and diligence in the pursuit of solutions to those problems; and
3. Contributions to the overall intellectual life of the campus by offering constructive criticism, mentoring, technical advice and in some cases, collaborations with colleagues and visiting scientists. Such criteria are not readily assessed by simply looking at someone's resume or publication record. (Rubin, 2006b)

Sustainability

At the turn of the century many leading academic institutions initiated sustainability strategies. When one takes a closer look at these strategies, they seem to consist of a maze of projects and initiatives in sustainability research that seek quantitative rather than qualitative growth. Sustainability in research and teaching has to consider: "Why, what, how and who" (McGill, 2015). In serious sustainability, research and problem-oriented practice address these questions, but here, the main focus is on environmental topics, agriculture, waste management, food and general development. While the latter topics immediately relate to "serving society", we think that sustainability will also find its merits in basic sciences and humanities. In addition, research and teaching are all about the respectful use of resources. The well-established scientific approach requires one to think first and perform the experiments later. Often human behaviour acts differently. Daniel Kahneman points out this fact in his bestselling book, *Thinking, Fast and Slow* (Kahneman, 2011). Kahneman's key observations (the following reformulated from excerpts of his book) emerge from behavioural economics and psychology and among many others relate to: *planning fallacies, overconfidence, availability heuristic, sunk cost fallacies and loss aversion.*

In *planning fallacies*, benefits are consistently overestimated, while costs are underestimated. *Overconfidence* lacks sustainability by only taking into account the "Known Knowns" and forgetting about the "Unknown Knowns". Even worse, *Overconfidence* leads one to underestimate the complexity of a problem — the "Unknown Unknowns" — by seeking simple answers to complicated problems or superficially interpreting the results to align with the expectations. The *availability heuristic* is a mental bias that judges the probability of events with anecdotal knowledge of some examples. *Sunk cost fallacies* describe the tendency to continue to invest more funding in projects that exhibit poor results and have already consumed significant resources — a frequent practice seen in incremental research. The *loss aversion* finally stands for the psychological phenomenon that we fear the losses much more than we value the gains. Raising awareness and sensitivity for these attitudes may considerably improve the quality of research, increase relevance and reduce the publication frenzy. Qualitative growth rather than quantitative growth, in the long run, is more efficient and effective.

Economy

Evidence suggests that there are economic consequences for many of the aspects addressed in this paper for example: reducing incremental research publications, addressing scarce resources in terms of laboratory space and increased teaching time all bear an economic impact. In theory, one must remember that, at least for the moment, neither the internal character of academia nor external pressures of the economy favour change. Academic networks force universities to compete globally; therefore, "ivory tower" behaviour without accountability to the needs of society will certainly have an effect a university's ability to compete in an international market.

The economic reality of the status quo is that researchers will continue to face the inevitable uneven distribution of resources. The vast majority of grants and budgets, as well as individual promotions, are currently dependent on "counting papers", ratings and rankings. "Hype" projects and those with a sharp disciplinary focus will be favoured over unruly rebelliousness in the current epistemic. Change is not only necessary, it is inevitable.

THE QUEST FOR A NEW FORM OF QUALITY ASSESSMENT

It is a commonly accepted perception that citation frequency directly relates to the importance and the relevance of a scientific publication. The more provocative question is whether or not truly important papers are reliably recognized, as such, by peers? One may consider the *annus mirabilis* 1905, seeing three fundamental papers of Albert Einstein as a positive example, but he stood at the end of the era of classical physics, where many contemporaries had paved the ground for a transition for new and revolutionary concepts. We live in an era where the scientific community rarely questions the prevailing paradigm. Under these conditions, will the peer-review be able to recognize the relevance of a conceptual (not methodological) breakthrough?

The following editorial in one of the leading science journals may shed some light on the situation:

The most cited Nature *paper from 2002-03 was the mouse genome, published in December 2002. That paper represents the culmination of a great enterprise, but is inevitably an important point of reference rather than an expression of unusually deep mechanistic insight. So far it has received more than 1,000 citations. Within the measurement year of 2004 alone, it received 522 citations. Our next most cited paper from 2002-03 (concerning the functional organization of the yeast proteome) received 351 citations that year. Only 50 out of the roughly 1,800 citable items published in those two years received more than 100 citations in 2004. The great majority of our papers received fewer than 20 citations.*

None of this would really matter very much, were it not for the unhealthy reliance on impact factors by administrators and researchers' employers worldwide to assess the scientific quality of nations and institutions, and often even to judge individuals. There is no doubt that impact factors are here to stay. But these figures illustrate why they should be handled with caution. (Nature, 2005)

When valuing publications and their citations as a correlate for quality, exercise care ensuring an objective assessment of both the field of research and the individual cited. Reading a specific paper may help. Discussing it and explaining it to non-specialists may further clarify the quality and relevance of the citation. This raises another hot issue prompting the question: "Is the contemporary peer-review system still adequate?" In neuroscience, for example, several journals in the field have established a peer-review alliance that is striving to speed up the review process and grant a higher degree of "fairness" to the authors. This may address some initial issues of the peer-review review system, but does not answer the underlying problem. The heart of the problem does not lie in the creation of new structures or a change in administration, but rather the responsibility rests with reviewers and authors. The immediate response to the citation issue emphasized the responsibility as follows: "*Shoddy authorship, editorship or peer-review review pollute the scientific record, cause colleagues to waste time and money trying to replicate findings, and can do serious damage to public trust of science.*" (*Nature*, 2009). Since there is currently no better solution than peer-review review and given the fact that science cannot survive without self-government, scientists must avoid all of the "Kahneman fallacies" mentioned earlier in this paper. Peer-review requires time. Should scientists who choose to take the time to contribute careful, helpful (for the authors) and honest reviews merit the same credit for the review as for other publications? By initiating an ongoing (intramural) discussion, the Critical Thinking Initiative strives to raise awareness and positively contribute to the improvement of the peer-review system.

Hiring at all academic levels is a matter of quality judgment and, therefore, closely related to the arguments related to peer-review and citations. A rigorous quality assessment process with transparent methods and standards may add to the reputation and attractiveness of a university. Indeed, such standards and processes may attract the scientists who possess the types of qualities and character a university desires (i.e, highly motivated, innovative and independent-minded).

SPACES FOR EXPERIMENTATION

The Critical Thinking Initiative considers not only processes, but also how best to address infrastructure. Classical university settings with half-day, face-to-face lectures may need to give way to more innovative teaching formats in order to foster creative and constructive learning. Flipped classrooms, peer learning, cross-curricular seminars and service learning models support inter- and transdisciplinarity transfer of theory into practice. Massive Open Online Courses (MOOCs) and Small Private Online Courses (SPOCs) may tap the potential offered Information and Communication Technology (ICT) developments allowing for blended teaching and learning opportunities.

In the coming decade, the university will need to address the challenge of the overall cost of maintenance on the existing facilities and the scarcity of land. The rate of transformation and growth challenges university managers and campus architects. While new buildings at ETH Zurich have already adapted to the emerging challenges, the redesigning of existing buildings remains a huge task that looms on the horizon. Securing financing for an ambitious plan to expand and develop available space still remains a challenge. Therefore, an efficient use of scarce surface areas will be a necessity making flexible, multi-use and well-scheduled space allocation attractive considerations. The planned "Student Project House" at ETH Zurich may serve as an example of how to satisfy many of these requirements.

Last, but not least, time is at stake. Assuming that time management is a matter of individual preference, it is evident that scientists prefer choices that optimize their opportunities to build reputation. In simple terms, if the number of publications is the measure of reputation, it is not surprising that scientists favour research over other responsibilities such as: teaching, reviewing, public science, managing technology transfer and university administration. Therefore, a careful examination of both the scope of a scientist's activities, as well as the system for awarding reputation, may be necessary to create space for experimentation.

SETTING OFF ON A JOURNEY TO NEW FRONTIERS

In spring 2015, the management board of ETH Zurich met 200 invited faculty members to discuss three important topics to further develop the strategy of the university: Defining quality; finding, attracting and fostering talent; and minimizing the publication "frenzy". It is no surprise that the participants, from all disciplines of ETH Zurich, found themselves engaged in a fierce debate that revealed the urgency of these strategic topics. From the concerns raised during the meetings, a consensus emerged that fundamental changes are necessary and that scientists need to bear some of the responsibility for such changes. The meeting concluded with participants offering full support for the initiatives of the management board and yielded some visionary recommendations.

One of the most challenging gaps to bridge is the need to accommodate the individual trajectories of scientists, without losing the relationship to the ETH Zurich community. It became evident that students, faculty and staff at all levels and units need time and space to establish a common discussion culture, to continually improve the curricula, and to make room for experimentation in teaching and research.

As the community implements the Critical Thinking Initiative, a change has started to take place in the first phase that focuses on teaching. Various measures have been set in motion to initiate the processes of a more interdisciplinary and collaborative working culture at ETH Zurich. The following are examples of some of the concrete projects initiated:

- The Spring 2015 term saw a new course that paralleled the lectures in basic physics with physicists and philosophers teaching joint lectures and applying flipped classroom techniques (Schiltz, 2015).
- The Autumn 2015 term offered a large choice of educational training courses, seminars and lectures gathered under the umbrella of the Critical Thinking Initiative. All the departments contributed in setting up special student lectures, events to promote interdisciplinarity, and workshops to foster new teaching methods (Critical Thinking annual program, 2015).
- ETH Zurich organized for the very first time the ETH Week in autumn bringing together some 150 Bachelor and Master students from all departments with faculty members and external experts to jointly work on a topic of high societal relevance (ETH Week, 2015).
- It is projected that in 2018 the "Student Project House" will be realized. In the meantime, a core group of students, faculty and staff launched a pilot phase to gain experience with novel thinking, making, showing and connecting spaces. Ultimately, the university will establish a spacious laboratory for student projects in a former heating plant located near the ETH Zurich main building in the centre of Zurich. ETH Zurich envisions an interdisciplinary space in a collaborative "workshop-like atmosphere". More self-organized student projects have arisen along the way with the start of the initiative: "getBriefed" — a Zurich-based event series bringing together curious students, doctoral students and researchers from all disciplines to explore, share and revive the unconventional. "getBriefed" is both a community and source of inspiration and discovery. (*getBriefed*, 2015).

This is just the beginning. Fundamental change takes time and has to go much deeper in order to be effective. In addition to teaching, the Critical Thinking Initiative hopes to influence and transform other major fields of activities at ETH Zurich. The ultimate goal is to pursue the noblest quest of every university: to empower the community of students and faculty and enable them to gain new and deep insights, to teach and to learn to think creatively and critically.

CONCLUSIONS

This paper explores the challenges of recognizing and developing talent within the current status quo where scientific reputation directly correlates to paper output. The pressure to build a successful academic career often tempts faculty to specialize in areas where there is less competition and to reach for the "low-hanging fruit" in order to build a reputation measured by the number rather than the value of research publications. The consequences are that broader or perhaps an interdisciplinary reflection is avoided in favour of reporting single observations and teaching is marginalized to allow time for research and publication.

Leaders in higher education face similar dilemmas in how to assess value when making budget allocations. Such dilemmas challenge leaders to think critically about the "publish or perish" model and whether such a model is effective in assessing and rewarding faculty and whether it serves our ultimate goals for teaching and learning. If, at the extremes, universities and their stakeholders retire into a "splendid isolation" or dwell in an arbitrary state, further academic education and research may be absorbed by a knowledge-based economy, resulting in either utilitarianism or ideological idealism, which reins those institutions.

ETH Zurich's Critical Thinking Initiative prepares the ground for a paradigm shift in academia — one that allows for space and time for experimentation. One consideration is a mixed model where managers in higher education organize a competition in special, even multi-disciplinary research areas considered important for society, the economic welfare of a nation, or for knowledge procurement.

Three arguments for the foundation to move forward: responsibility, sustainability and economy require a reflective approach. It was concluded that achievements need to be continually scrutinized in order to align with the aims of sound and rigorous reasoning that adopting a reflective approach avoids quick "symptomatic" problem solving ultimately leading to fundamental and even controversial new ideas. Sustainability research and teaching refer to the respectful use of resources requiring one to first think critically. Economic consequences of the peer-review system necessitate the question: "Is the contemporary peer-review system still adequate?"

The Critical Thinking Initiative strives to guarantee the future achievements of science for the increase of knowledge and ultimately the benefit of society. Inherent to change and true to the nature of academia, such ideas will most certainly spur controversial debate. Such discussions are welcome as they signify a community that is not only open to change, but to becoming leaders in the academic world.

REFERENCES

Ash, Mitchell G. (2008). "From Humboldt to Bologna: History as discourse in higher education reform debates in German-speaking Europe". In: Jessop, R., Fairclough, N. & Wodak, R. (Eds.), *Education and the Knowledge-Based Economy in Europe*, SENSE Publishers, Rotterdam. pp. 41-62.

Caulfield, T. & Condit, C. (2012). "Science and the Sources of Hype". *Public Health Genomics*, 15, pp. 209-217.

Critical Thinking annual programme (2015). https://www.ethz.ch/intranet/en/teaching/critical-thinking-initiative/ct-annual-programme.html

ETH Week (2015). https://www.ethz.ch/de/die-eth-zuerich/nachhaltigkeit/ETHweek.html

Folkers, Gerd (2012). "Wissenschaft in Gefahr: Den Fressnapf der Forscher verschoben". *Spiegel*-online, 10 October. (http://www.spiegel.de/wissenschaft/medizin/forschung-warum-der-utilitarismus-die-freiheit-der-forschung-bedroht-a-860141.html)

Folkers, Gerd (2013). "'Economization' in Science and of Science Itself: Changes to the Game". SSTC Report 4/2013, pp. 42-44.

Franck, Georg (2002). "The scientific economy of attention: A novel approach to the collective rationality of science". *Scientometrics*, 55, pp. 3-26.

getBriefed (2015). http://www.getbriefed.org/

Ho Peng Yoke (2012). "Did Confucianism Hinder the Development of Science in China?" In: Wong Sin Kiong, *Confucianism, Chinese History and Society*. Singapore, p. 55.

Huang Kun (2015). "Moving away from metrics". *Nature* 520, pp. 18-20.

Jinha, Arif E. (2010). "Article 50 million: an estimate of the number of scholarly articles in existence." *Learned Publishing* 23, 3 pp. 258-263.

Kahneman, Daniel (2011). *Thinking Fast and Slow*. Farrar, Straus and Giroux, New York.

LEE (2015). https://www.ethz.ch/en/news-and-events/eth-news/news/2014/10/LEE_Eroeffnung.html.

McGill (2015). https://www.mcgill.ca/sustainability/vision-2020-sustainability-strategy/research.

Merton, Robert K. (1988). The Matthew Effect in Science, II: Cumulative advantage and the symbolism of intellectual property. ISIS 79, 606-623.

Nature (2005). "Not-so-deep impact". Editorial, *Nature* 435, 1003-1004, doi: 10.1038/4351003b.

Nature (2009). "Striving for excellence in peer review". Editorial, *Nature Neuroscience* 12, 1 doi: 10.1038/nn0109-1.

Quack, Martin (2014). Myths, Challenges, Risks and Opportunities in Evaluating and Supporting Scientific Research. In: I. M. Welpe, J. Wollersheim, S. Ringelhan, and M. Osterloh (Eds.). *Incentives and Performance: Governance of Research Organizations*. Springer International Publishing, Cham, Heidelberg, New York, pp. 223-239.

Rubin, Gerald (2006a). In: Beryl Lieff Benderly, *Betting the Farm*. Science Careers, 3, November 2006.
Rubin, Gerald (2006b). "Janelia Farm: An Experiment in Scientific Culture", *Cell*, 125, 2, pp. 209-212.
Schiltz, Guillaume (2015). https://blogs.ethz.ch/deliscope/2015_03_31/critical-thinking-im-flipped-classroom/.
Schleiermacher, Friedrich Daniel Ernst (1808). Gelegentliche Gedanken über Universitäten in deutschem Sinn. Nebst einem Anhang über eine neu zu errichtende. Berlin, Realschulbuchhandlung.
Spelsberg, Angela & Burchardt, Matthias (2015). *Unter dem Joch des Drittmittelfetischs*. Forschung und Lehre, 2, pp. 108-109.
Trajtenberg, Manuel (2013). http://www.swir.ch/de/arbeitsprogramm/weitere-themen

PART II

Intellectual Constraints

CHAPTER 7

Creating Shared Value through Open Innovation[1]

Stefan Catsicas, Anne Roulin and Valerio Nannini

INTRODUCTION

"For a company to be successful over the long term and create value for shareholders, it must also create value for society. At Nestlé, this begins with the creation of superior long-term value for shareholders by offering products and services that help people improve their nutrition, health and wellness." Peter Brabeck-Letmathe, Chairman of the Board, Nestlé.

Any business that has a long-term perspective and follows sound business principles, creates global value for society through its activities — for example, creating jobs for employees, paying taxes to support public services and general economic activity. Creating Shared Value (CSV) goes one step further through consciously identifying areas of focus where shareholders' interests and society's interests strongly intersect, and where value creation can be optimized for both — a perspective articulated well by Porter and Kramer (2011). The choice of focus areas leads to decisions on investment in talent, capital, research and development, where the potential for joint value creation is greatest (Nestlé, 2015).

At Nestlé, we analysed our value chain and determined that the areas of greatest potential for joint value optimization with society are water, rural development and nutrition. These activities are core to our business strategy

---

1. **Acknowledgements:** The authors are grateful to their colleague Sarah Sheppard for reviewing this manuscript.

and vital to the welfare of the people in the countries where we operate. We actively seek engagement and partnerships with stakeholders that optimize positive impact in these areas of focus. Importantly, CSV is not about philanthropy; it is about leveraging core activities and partnerships for the joint benefit of the people in the countries where we operate and for our shareholders. These projects and activities need to be sustainable over time rather than one-off arrangements.

Our ambition to be the leading Nutrition, Health and Wellness Company is at the heart of our corporate strategy and what we live for as a company. We are investing for the future through our network of research centres and expanding the boundaries of nutrition with the Nestlé Institute of Health Sciences and with our two new companies, Nestlé Health Science and Nestlé Skin Health. A deep understanding of nutrition, and access to tastier and healthier food and beverages, is what people demand and what society needs. Our global commitments on research, product reformulation and innovation, nutrition labelling, responsible marketing to children, and promotion of healthy lifestyles help ensure effective implementation. However, as shown below, the complexity of this mission requires leveraging beyond our own footprint and engaging with academics and entrepreneurs.

Creating Shared Value should not be confused with compliance or sustainability. It is built on the foundation of a strong compliance culture and commitment to sustainability, but it goes beyond those and aims to create new and greater value for society and our shareholders within the three areas of focus. In doing so, Nestlé maintains a very long-term perspective on business development and welcomes dialogue with external stakeholders who are committed to principled behaviour and constructive engagement. This includes government and regulatory authorities, intergovernmental organizations,

Figure 1: Creating Shared Value

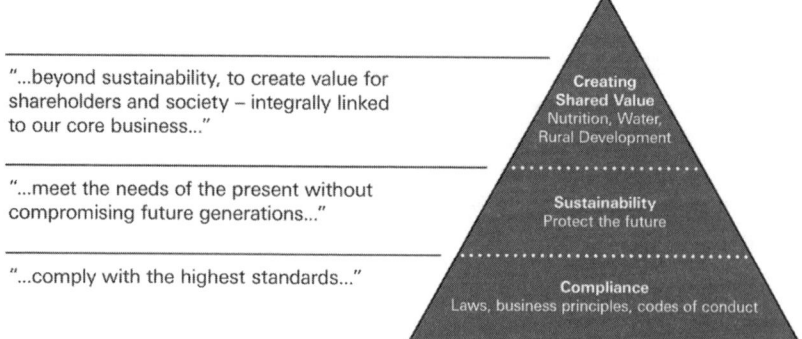

non-governmental organizations (NGOs), academic and professional bodies plus local communities, many of whom we partner with on CSV initiatives.

Water is an essential component of good nutrition and, at the same time, a human right and the linchpin of food security. We actively promote healthy hydration at all ages, while making every effort to reduce water use in our own operations and advocating for inclusion of a specific goal on water in the post-2015 Sustainable Development Goals. Water is an important pillar of our business, an operational challenge and a societal issue that is of deep concern to us all.

Likewise, **rural development** and our work with farmers, combined with our Responsible Sourcing Guidelines, help address the need to build sustainable farming communities, and also to answer our own consumers' concerns to know "where does my food come from?" Our rural development work helps secure the quality and quantity of supply of our key categories, increasing the attractiveness of farming for future generations.

We continue to actively manage our commitments to environmental and social sustainability, necessary for operating our factories and for the sustainable growth and development of the communities and countries where we operate. Our commitment to youth employment, called the Nestlé Needs YOUth Initiative, helps strengthen and develop the skills and employability of young people across Europe. This programme will soon be extended globally.

Our third CSV area, **nutrition**, focuses on the unmet nutritional needs for micronutrients. Here again, while deficits are observed worldwide, the most sensitive populations are found in developing countries and emerging economies.

The following three case studies illustrate different aspects of our engagement in CSV in water, nutrition and rural development, and illustrate the key role of partnerships and innovation in achieving our CSV objectives.

WATER

We have been working to improve the environmental performance of our factories. Over the past 10 years, production volumes have increased by 61%, and yet absolute water consumption has decreased by 16%, greenhouse gas emissions by 14% and total waste for disposal by 51%. This is due to quantitative targets and a strong focus on continual improvement. However, we felt that this was not sufficient, and that a more radical approach was required. We were stimulated by John Elkington, a thought-leader in Sustainability, and his book entitled *The Zeronaughts* (2012). His premise is that to stimulate creativity and devise entirely new solutions and ways of operating, the target should be zero rather than purely continuous improvements. This has led to an approach across our operations and manufacturing activities that we call "Going for Zero": Zero Environmental Impact, Zero Injuries, Zero Defects and Zero Waste.

It was in this context that our Dairy business challenged the organization with the following questions: Why do we need to use an external water supply when we produce milk powder? Why can't we use the water that is already in milk, since the majority of our dairy factories produce powdered milk from incoming liquid milk? Project "ZerEAU" was born with the aim of having a positive water impact with a net discharge of water instead of using ground water supply. A study evaluated priority factories based on the level of water scarcity in the region and production levels. Our factory in Lagos de Moreno, in the water-stressed state of Jalisco, Mexico, was selected as the pilot factory for implementation. Water availability in Mexico has drastically declined over the past 60 years due to population growth. Through close collaboration with our research and development organization and operations, together with the support of a series of technology providers and suppliers, the factory is now saving 1.6 million litres of water a day — enough to meet the average daily consumption of 6,400 people in the surrounding area. The water vapour is generated when evaporated milk is condensed and then treated. Technologies include reverse osmosis, membrane bioreactors and centrifugation to purify the water to the required level for use as potable process water or for cooling or cleaning. The process is being replicated in locations such as South Africa, where our five-year investment plan includes converting our Mossel Bay dairy factory to Zero Water, and technology transfer has already taken

Figure 2: Schematic diagram of the "ZEREau" factory where water is treated, circulated and re-used many times

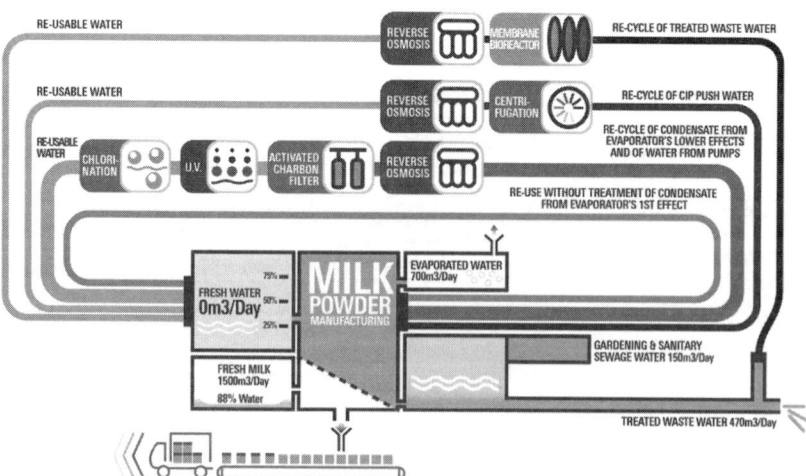

place to reduce water consumption in other stressed areas like the Indian Punjab and Pakistan.

Investments such as these do not always meet the normal internal pay-back criteria since, paradoxically, the price of water is often low in water-stressed regions. For this reason, we have adopted an approach where we calculate a "notional" cost of water — this includes a conversion factor to take into account water availability, and this cost of water is then used to calculate financial pay-back.

NUTRITION

Micronutrients are essential for growth and development. However, deficiencies or inadequate dietary intake remain a challenge for an estimated one-third of the global population. The WHO and FAO (2006) estimate that over 2 billion people around the world, mostly young children and women of child-bearing age, suffer from deficiencies in micronutrients (i.e. essential vitamins and minerals, of which the most prevalent are iron, zinc, iodine and vitamin A). This is commonly termed "Hidden Hunger" (1st International Congress Hidden Hunger, 2013; 2nd International Congress Hidden Hunger, 2015). Nestlé is committed to helping address micronutrient deficiencies, for example, by using information from national and international health authorities to provide fortified, affordable and nutritious foods and beverages in areas with a high risk of deficiencies.

With this objective, Nestlé has been fortifying products with micronutrients for many years, and in 2014, products corresponding to 183 billion such servings were sold (well on track to meet the external public commitment of 200 billion servings by the end of 2016). Many of these products reach low in the socio-economic pyramid and include bouillon cubes, all-family cereals and growing-up milks. However, there are limitations to the direct addition of micronutrients in terms of taste, colour and stability of products. For this reason, a programme was initiated on biofortification, which involves developing and sourcing conventionally-bred staple crops (non-GMO) which are naturally rich in these micronutrients. Agricultural research institutes around the world within the CGIAR organization (a group that unites those engaged in research for a food-secure future) have been very active in developing such new varieties with funding from the Bill and Melinda Gates Foundation through the NGO Harvest Plus. In addition to micronutrients, it is essential that yield and disease resistance are at least as good, if not better, than the varieties currently grown in these regions. Nestlé's research and development unit in Abidjan, Côte d'Ivoire, has been working with the International Institute of Tropical Agriculture in Nigeria to evaluate new varieties of vitamin A-enriched maize that we plan to use in all-family cereals. Biofortification requires detailed study and analysis of the many factors that determine how a crop grows and working closely with the farmers who will harvest it. For example, we are establishing a supply chain for vitamin A-rich maize in north Nigeria, where the average yield of maize is currently only 1-2 tonnes per hectare. Our aim is to significantly improve yield, while at the same time providing the fortified crop for our own supply chain and for direct consumption by the local community to help improve the nutritional status of smallholder farmers and their families.

We are committed, through these means, to continue to intensify efforts to extend our reach to vulnerable populations, notably mothers and children. We pursue scientific research in this area and document the contribution of our products in addressing the burden of micronutrient deficiencies. In doing so, we work in a collaborative manner with NGOs and other relevant partners to further improve people's nutrition and health.

RURAL DEVELOPMENT

Nestlé relies on millions of farmers around the world to supply us with the agricultural raw materials we need for our products. More than 695,000 farmers supply Nestlé either directly or through co-operatives and collection centres. These farmers and farm workers are essential to the on-going success of our business. Through the Farmer Connect program, farmers are assisted with agricultural support and capacity-building programs to increase yields, crop quality and income levels, and to reduce the environmental impact of agricultural activities. A Rural Development Framework has been established to help align business activities with local priorities. Nestlé has also reinforced its responsible sourcing commitments, guidelines, policies and standards, supplier assessments and traceability activities, as well as the Nescafé and Cocoa plans to improve the lives of farmers, the quality of their crops and their social conditions. In 2014, 376,000 farmers were trained through capacity-building programs.

One of the specific means which is used within the rural development context is the RISE methodology (Response-Inducing Sustainability Evaluation) (Grenz et al., 2011; Häni et al., 2003), which is a powerful tool to develop farmers and make sustainable agriculture measurable, communicable and tangible across a number of agricultural raw materials, including milk, coffee, cocoa and vegetables. The RISE tool was developed by the University of Bern in Switzerland and uses 10 indicators (rated from "problematic" to "good") to assess and improve sustainability at a farm level, including the environmental, social and economic aspects. Data collected by Nestlé sourcing staff is analysed for strengths and weaknesses, with scores given for the 10 indicators.

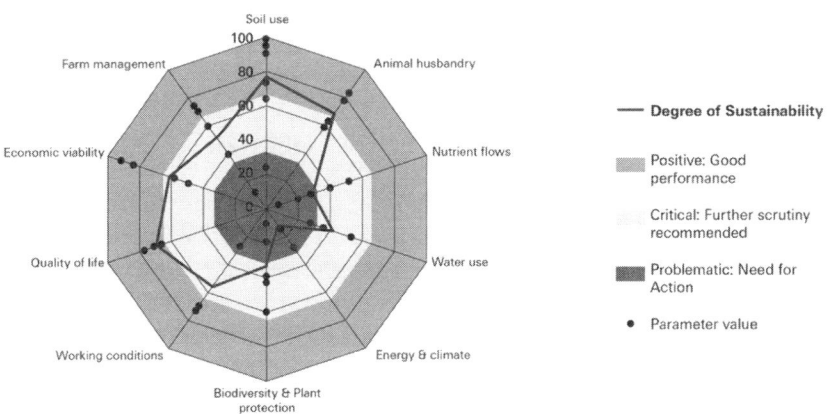

Figure 3: Summary polygon of 22 farms analysed using the RISE methodology in the region of Lagos de Moreno in Mexico

Results are then discussed and potential action plans suggested, in personal meetings with the farmers.

Education and training activities are also targeted specifically towards women farmers, to help empower them and strengthen their role in the supply chain. This may lead to greater yields of higher-quality crops, increased incomes and higher standards of living. For example, in Côte d'Ivoire, cassava is an important part of the local diet, but faces supply chain challenges including disease and pest infestation, insufficient post-harvest processing and low levels of commercialization of the crop. Through an on-going public-private partnership, with Swiss and German organizations working alongside the Ivorian National Agricultural Extension Agency, Nestlé has helped to develop the cassava supply chain, working with 4,000 producers, 78% of whom are women. This has involved using a non-GMO, high-yield, disease-resistant variety with the appropriate properties for commercial starch production, and working with local producers to improve the collection and transportation of raw cassava to our factory.

Making Creating Shared Value a reality and delivering on our 38 external commitments is only possible through a collaborative approach. The case studies included in this paper illustrate diverse examples of open innovation with academia, NGOs, entrepreneurs and major companies in the private sector. This approach is essential to address the issues and opportunities across the entire value chain encompassing agricultural production, the supply chain, processing and production by Nestlé, through to point of sale and final consumption. Nestlé reports annually on the company's CSV progress, with our 2014 CSV document recognized by CR Reporting Awards 2015 as the best corporate responsibility report. Open innovation now extends beyond the boundaries of CSV, and the following sections address our main goals and way forward to better connect with the surrounding science and technology world.

OPEN INNOVATION: A WIN-WIN FOR INDUSTRY AND ACADEMIA THAT SHOULD INCLUDE EMERGING ECONOMIES

No company can be truly innovative by working alone. Open innovation adds synergistic value where internal capabilities cannot match an unmet business need. It opens up the organization to external opportunities by efficiently locating, selecting and delivering the right innovations for the company and effectively leveraging an opportunity. In an R&D-driven organization like Nestlé, it is essential to harness the best knowledge externally with capabilities internally; the capacity to understand and translate science into commercial opportunities is essential for companies to lead in their field.

The foundation of most innovation is laid by visionary scientists. Hence, collaboration with academia is essential for companies like Nestlé, allowing us to scout for the best-in-class science. Working with leading academic institutions enables companies to benchmark and compare current in-house capabilities with global scientific trends.

For example, with Nestlé Health Science, Nestlé has the ambition to champion the role of nutritional therapies which have proven clinical and health economic value, and improve the quality of people's lives. The company focuses on three areas:

- Consumer Care addresses specific health conditions with an emphasis on enhancing "healthy ageing";
- Medical Nutrition supplies hospitals and other healthcare facilities; and
- Novel Therapeutic Nutrition works on new nutritional therapies against specific diseases and conditions.

Nestlé Health Science requires competences that go beyond today's general know-how and existing capabilities. It was for this reason that the Nestlé Institute of Health Sciences was founded on the campus of the École Polytechnique Fédérale de Lausanne, thus leveraging on the presence of experienced scholars and committed students.

Another example for a visionary public-private partnership is the Nestlé research collaboration with the EpiGen Consortium, an international alliance of the world's leading epigenetics researchers from institutions in New Zealand, the United Kingdom and Singapore. Its research programme aims to understand and substantiate optimal nutrition for mothers during pregnancy and for infants, to promote optimal metabolic health throughout life. These objectives will serve mothers across the world, but should have particular relevance in countries where under-nutrition is a serious risk. The experienced network provided by the EpiGen consortium is of paramount importance to achieve our goals in a spirit of open innovation.

Academia should also significantly benefit from long-term collaborations with industry partners. Besides the obvious funding, the relationship should allow academic researchers to understand industry practices and technology goals, and what commercial success looks like. This is important for students who may join industry, and especially relevant in applied research areas such as engineering or biochemistry. For example, by considering all aspects from proof-of-concept to successful production and commercialization, an initial scientific experiment is more tailored towards a final product. A mutual understanding of the long-term timeframe is needed to develop a breakthrough innovation, while the desire of business to commercialize its product is essential for successful innovation.

Overall, industry collaboration can make an academic institution a more attractive place of study for young scientists. Additionally, in today's competitive environment, it allows companies early access to a rich source of state-of-the-art knowledge and an exceptional talent pool for recruitment. This is also true in developing regions of the world, where our CSV approach will contribute and bring benefit to training the next generations of food scientists and engineers.

Recognizing we operate in a fast-paced, volatile world, what is essential for the success of future public-private partnerships between academia and industry?

Open innovation requires an excellent education system. Successful innovation is dependent on the education base of students and employees. This includes not only competences and creativity in science and research, but also production, marketing and sales, as well as new business models to be developed for future innovations. The world-leading institutions in engineering (MIT), management (Harvard), finance (Columbia) and law (Yale), all in one Boston-New York corridor, created a unique cluster and talent pool, traditionally accounting for industry dominance and wealth creation in the region. More clusters are being created around the world, including in emerging markets.

Open innovation requires an eco-system of concomitant industries and academic excellence to generate a cluster effect. An innovative company like Nestlé is dependent on suppliers, industry and academic partners who can deliver best-in-class equipment, services, research and innovative concepts. Infrastructure such as transportation, good living standards and communications are essential to attract qualified workforces and ensure global exchange

Figure 4: World Competitiveness Index, 2014

World Competitiveness Ranking 2014 (selected countries, normalized scale)

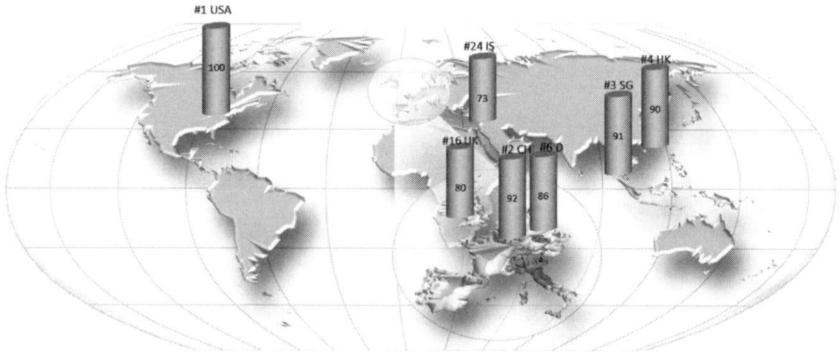

Source: IMD World Competitiveness yearbook 2014

of ideas. Singapore's transition from third world to first in about 30 years is attributed mainly to getting its infrastructure right and its clean governance, leading to international players investing and skilled foreign talent arriving onto its shores. Its focus on public-private partnerships and making it easier to do business has led it to consistently achieve the top rankings in the World Competitiveness Index in recent years (2014 ranking: #1 USA; #2 Switzerland; #3 Singapore; #4 Hong Kong; #6 Germany; #16 U.K.; #24 Israel).

Open innovation requires a sound and stable research and academic environment. Innovative companies conduct proprietary research and product development. However, alone, they can seldom cover all the necessary competencies. Companies focus internal research and development on their strategic business areas. As science and basic research are often commercially not yet viable, it requires public funding to build the necessary foundations for future successful innovations.

Future company growth cannot rely solely on internal efforts and capabilities. Solving the future challenges of society requires physically stepping into innovation clusters to support and build a vibrant innovation eco-system. Academia is essential to drive this development. What needs to be done to foster future entrepreneurship? Focus must be given to educate and train entrepreneurs. Concretely, early stage venture funding is required to encourage young scientists to create their personal spin-offs. Would companies like Google or Facebook exist today without the entrepreneurial spirit of their founders and the risk capital of visionary investors? The sheer number of start-ups out of academia (centred on Stanford, Berkeley and others) and the huge market capitalization created by the thriving venture capital eco-system have resulted in California establishing itself as an economy of its own, with numerous business-friendly governments around the world wanting to copy and create their own version of a Silicon Valley. In the Global Innovation Index 2014, countries have been ranked according to innovation capabilities (based on number of researchers, gross expenditures on R&D, ranking of the top 3 universities) and knowledge and technology output (number of patents and publications, growth rate of GDP, business density, high- and medium-tech output) as follows: #1 Switzerland; #2 U.K.; #3 Sweden; #6 U.S.; #7 Singapore; #15 Israel.

Although early venturing can be high-risk, funding models need to be established jointly with industry to share risk while fostering breakthrough innovation in all science and technology areas. Within such an environment, companies are capable of establishing proprietary incubation hubs with an entrepreneurial mind-set and the necessary funding to enable breakthrough innovation. The most prominent example for Nestlé is Nespresso, which has been kept separate from the main organization to ensure the necessary start-up spirit, which results in today's success.

Universities can and do provide locations and office space, allowing start-ups to build their operations. This needs to be complemented with business plan competitions and business acceleration phases whereby start-ups can meet industry partners, customers, venture funds, business plan consultancies and start-up mentors. Learning from others and building on each other's ideas creates the breakthrough innovations of the future. Industry may use such a set-up to spin off non-core but innovative business ideas in order to ensure return on its research and development investment. These structures can be seen as true incubators, allowing small start-up businesses to grow to a relevant scale, as large companies are often reluctant to cover significant losses in their P&L to build up new business beyond their core competences.

Although several incubation clusters can exist in parallel, it is also important for universities to join forces between each other to achieve a critical mass with respect to the number of meaningful business ideas to be created, and to attract enough venture money for the required early start-up funding. Such clusters should extend beyond the frontiers of technologically advanced countries, in order to foster innovation and entrepreneurship in developing countries and emerging economies.

Driving meaningful innovation is tightly linked to the success of these open incubation clusters and a close collaboration between industries, academia and venture industry. Therefore, Nestlé strongly supports the efforts of the European Union and its Knowledge and Innovation Communities (KICs) (European Institute of Innovation & Technology, 2015) with the expected call for a food and nutrition KIC in 2016. Through these models, companies like Nestlé achieve their innovation ambition to significantly improve the impact of future investments in R&D, and stay ahead of the competition. We

Figure 5: EIT Strategy, 2014-2020

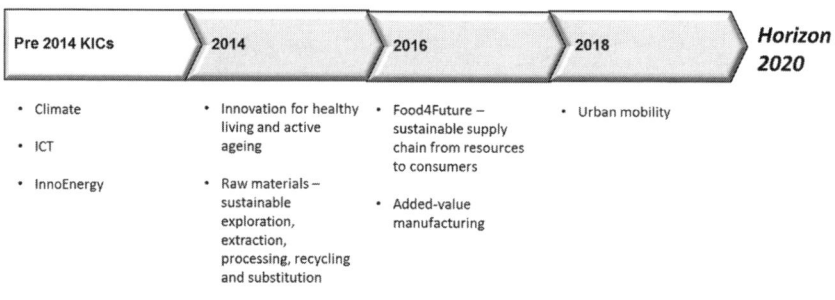

look forward to similar opportunities bridging advanced and developing countries in a joint effort to stimulate shared growth and common values.

In summary, companies must embrace a culture of engagement to be innovative, one of transparency and sharing, inside and outside their organization. In doing so, the results obtained will be greater than the sum of their respective efforts.

CONCLUSION

In modern societies, large companies are often criticized for aiming for sustained global growth that is perceived as being generated at the expense of the local populations where they operate. Worse, as corporations engage further in responsible businesses, they face the increasing risk of being blamed for global societal failures. Consequently, governments may take actions and sanctions that undermine this emerging goodwill, thus creating a negative spiral of corporate disengagement. Nestlé's approach to Creating Shared Value addresses these concerns. By creating value for our shareholders, for the populations in the countries where we operate and for the population of the world as a whole, we generate growth that stimulates and improves people's quality of life in advanced as well as emerging economies.

Historically, open innovation has been established within the eco-systems of developed countries. However, the economic development of emerging countries will result in the expansion of open innovation thinking. Additionally, conventions such as the Nagoya Protocol on biological diversity and access to genetic resources (established in 2010) will result in future collaborations between the food and pharma industry, and national institutions in South America, Africa and South East Asia.

In 2012, the Nestlé Research Center in Lausanne formed a research partnership with the Council for Scientific and Industrial Research (CSIR) in South Africa. It is aimed at contributing to a range of research and development work based on indigenous South African biodiversity to evaluate the potential for nutraceutical and functional foods with proven health benefits. This partnership seeks to promote the reintroduction of highly nutritious — but neglected — native plants back into the community's regular diet, and future collaborations will follow.

In the future, by engaging with additional stakeholders and leveraging our global network to involve major universities in the countries where we operate, we hope to bring the concept of Creating Shared Value to an unprecedented "open innovation-driven" level for the global betterment of societies.

REFERENCES

1st International Congress Hidden Hunger (2013). "From assessment to solutions", 6-9 March, University of Hohenheim, Stuttgart, Germany.

2nd International Congress Hidden Hunger (2015). "Childhood development and long-term prospects for society and economy", 3-6 March, Stuttgart, Germany.

Elkington, J. (2012). The Zeronaughts: Breaking the sustainability barrier, Routledge, London.

European Institute of Innovation & Technology (2015). A body of the European Union. eit.europa.eu.

Grenz, J., Schoch, M., Stämpfli, A. & Thalmann, C. (2011). *RISE 2.0 field manual*, Bern University of Applied Sciences, Zollikofen.

Häni, F. J., Braga, F., Stämpfli, A., Keller, T., Fischer, M. & Porsche, H. (2003). "RISE, a tool for holistic sustainability assessment at the farm level", *IAMA International Food and Agribusiness Management Review* (6), pp. 78-90.

Nestlé (2015). "Nestlé in Society: Creating Shared Value and meeting our commitments", http://www.nestle.com/csv.

Porter, M. & Kramer, M. (2011). "Creating shared value", *Harvard Business Review*, January-February.

The Global Innovation Index (2014). Co-published by INSEAD, Cornell University and WIPO (World Intellectual Property Organisation, an agency of the UN).

The World Competitiveness Index by IMD Switzerland (2014).

WHO and FAO (2006). *Guidelines on food fortification with micronutrients*, eds. Allen, L., de Benoist, B., Dary, O. and Hurrell, R., FAO. http://www.who.int/nutrition/publications/guide_food_fortification_micronutrients.pdf.

CHAPTER 8

The Evolution of globalized Higher Education

Nicholas Dirks and Nils Gilman

INTRODUCTION

This essay is intended to elicit discussion around current thinking about the globalization of higher education (from a U.S. point of view in particular) in the context of proposing a new model we are attempting to develop at the University of California, Berkeley. We begin with a brief narrative of the historical evolution of efforts to internationalize education, from the 17th century to the present day, before providing a schematic outline of efforts to create new models for the global university. It turns out, perhaps not surprisingly, that higher education was global in its origins as well as in its subsequent trajectory. With that said, as in so many other domains, the globalization of higher education has accelerated rapidly over the last quarter century, motivated by a quest for additional revenues (especially in the case of Anglophone universities), a desire for greater international relevance and hence prestige (for all universities, but especially in the case of European and Asian universities), and a desire to provide a foundation for a knowledge economy (especially in the case of Asian universities) (Altbach & Knight, 2007; Wong, Ho & Singh, 2007; Marginson, 2006). This essay will focus on the development of globalization strategies of North American universities — a history that begins with the religious history that drove early educational experiments in the new world that was in more than one way connected to the history of global empires.

PREHISTORY: GLOBAL ENDOWMENTS AND THE COLONIAL PAST

It is well known that many of the early colleges established in colonial America were designed to foster dissenting denominations and to disseminate theological views at odds with what was possible in the mother country (Brubacher & Rudy, 1997; Humphrey, 1972). Less well known, however, is the fact that Yale College — one of the new dissenting colleges — was named after an Anglican, who gave his founding endowment in part to satisfy his (general) missionary zeal, and in part to ensure posterity for his surname after the death of his son David in Madras, where Elihu Yale had been Governor (Viswanathan, 1994). Yale, as was the custom for East India Company Governors during the 17th and 18th centuries, earned his vast fortune through the custom of "private trade", engaging in an activity that ultimately led Edmund Burke to push for the regulation of mercantile capitalism in India (Dirks, 2009). The fruit of global trade — unfortunately in this case the same kind of trade that propelled a new class of "Nabobs" to enter gentry status, acquire huge estates, and buy seats in parliament — played an important role in the foundation of one of America's oldest, and most prestigious, institutions of higher education.

We do not mean to draw perverse analogies between the current push for globalization and this particular history, though admittedly global trade has often been part of the mix for the generation of wealth that continues to be so important for the philanthropic support of higher education. We do mean, however, to suggest that even the most local of educational beginnings were always already quintessentially global. Yet this historical anecdote is not just an isolated example, but also the prelude for thinking through the global relationships of American higher education throughout its history. This history is one that began with England and its role in setting the terms for the fundamental values of higher education, shifting in part to Scotland (and the 18th-century Scottish enlightenment), before migrating across the continent to Germany, which became the most important new influence for U.S. educational institutions in the mid-19th century, especially in the area of research and graduate training. This is also a history that shows how important higher education was for early settlers and then citizens of the new world, while expressing the continued importance of Europe — and its civilizational inheritance — for the emergence of the United States as a new nation. Indeed, education was not just to inculcate religious learning, but also an understanding of and appreciation for the civilizational inheritance that was seen as so critical a base on which the new world was to develop (Marsden, 1994). For much of its early history, American higher education was oriented in relationship to Europe, both as the touchstone and the point of departure.

Europe was also a point of perpetual return. As Edward Gibbon observed in his autobiography, "According to the law of custom, and perhaps with reason, foreign travel completes the education of an English gentleman." (Gibbon, 1900) During the 18th century, "travel became fashionable as a means of finishing the education of youths, as a source of social polish, and as a pleasant and desirable way to spend periods of leisure." (Black, 2003) For English aristocrats, in particular, time spent perusing the (mainly ancient) glories of the continent provided just the right touch of gentlemanly polish (Cohen, 1992). This aristocratic tradition was not lost on settlers in the new world. As students in American colleges studied theology, the classics, and — especially after Jefferson created the University of Virginia — a growing array of new subjects, the Hellenic and Roman worlds remained primary referents, though European civilization as the continuous space for enlightenment was always the ultimate referent. Although sponsoring formal study abroad was beyond the reach of early colleges, the curriculum fed into a desire to replicate the grand tour, if only in theory for most students. Increasingly, however, the new American elite sought to ape the model of the English aristocracy, sending their children not just to college in America, but also to Europe for their own version of the Grand Tour (Rodgers, 1998). (Henry James's fiction, from "Turn of the Screw" to *Portrait of a Lady*, offers a portrait account of what upper-class Americans hoped to achieve by sending their children for a jaunt around Europe — and how often they left disappointed.) Soon this was being institutionalized: by the late 19th century, some American finishing schools for girls began to market themselves in part around the chaperoned travel that they afforded their students — updating the thematic content of the Grand Tour for a new gender dynamic, while also presaging the role that colleges would soon play in funneling new generations to various packaged versions of the Grand Tour, disseminating a patina of refinement to growing numbers of young Americans who coveted cultural capital and, of course, elite status (Ridder-Symoens, 1996).

MODEL I: TRAVELLING

Though collegiate study abroad remained fundamentally a luxury good throughout the Progressive Era, the professionalization of advanced scientific education, particularly in Germany, was spurring fundamental change of a different kind, change that would metamorphose the idea of higher education in the United States. In fact, the first pedagogically serious efforts at international education would begin in the late 19th century, with graduate students from around the world (and particularly the United States) (Ellis, 2013) coming to study at the new breed of German research universities, whose model of scientific training was soon exported back to the United States (and to

Figure 1: The first U.S. foreign study group, sponsored by the University of Delaware, en route to Paris in 1923.

other countries too) (Charle, Schriewer & Wagner, eds, 2004). The desires of students to learn from the best professors in Europe was supported by scholarships designed explicitly to lure top talent from abroad — iconically, the Rhodes Scholarship, which had Oxford hosting foreign students from 1902 on. Up through the Great War, intellectually serious international education remained the province of graduate education.

The idea that American universities would actively encourage their own undergraduate students to study abroad first began to take off after World War I, with American universities (led, curiously enough, by the University of Delaware) for the first time actively encouraging their students to consider spending a semester or a whole year at a European university.

Study abroad suddenly seemed a good idea to U.S. university administrators in the 1920s, not only because such an offering promised students a frisson of continental sophistication that echoed the Grand Tour, but also because the strength of the dollar in the post-war years made educating students in war-ruined Europe a cheap alternative to educating them at home. Study abroad in its modern guise began, in part at least, as a price arbitrage play.

If this original idea made good financial sense, it would soon flower into what until recently was virtually the only (and even today remains the modal) model for international collegiate education, namely the iconic "School Year Abroad." Through the 1920s and 1930s, there was a rapid proliferation of foreign study programs at American universities, both public and private, though the total number of students studying abroad remained relatively small at first.

The idea of the school year abroad really took off in the post-World War II years, as a result of a number of factors. First, transportation linkages between continents intensified with the rise of the long-distance air travel, democratizing international travel to an unprecedented and ever-increasing degree.

Second, the rapid expansion of university systems in the United States, combined with great stratification, led many universities to begin to offer school year abroad programs as a "product differentiator". While these programs were often marketed to the students in terms that would not have been unfamiliar to the grand tourists, travel to Europe began to become a marker not just of elite status, but of a new American middle class. Finally, there was also a distinct Cold War imperative behind the push to internationalize post-war higher education in the United States. As Princeton linguist and USIA consultant Albert Marckwardt (1964) put it in 1964:

"Certainly we can grant without further argument that the position of the United States in the world today demands, on the part of everyone who has a share in the decision-making processes through which the country is governed and moved to action, a heightened and sympathetic reaction to the ways of life, the values, and the problems currently facing other areas of the world. As a democracy, we can no longer tolerate the unhappy spectacle of a thirty- to fifty-year lag between the public state of mind and those who must assume the responsibility for our relationships with the outer world, Western as well as non-Western. In fact, it is urgently necessary that the gap be closed at once. Even if we were not one of the powerful nations, the technological conquests of time and space which have occurred would still demand this of us. In the world we are approaching, not even a third-rate power will be able to afford the easy, retreat of isolationism, either in its political thinking or in its social and ethical outlook. How is such a general broadening of the horizons to be achieved? Direct foreign contact, which is becoming a far more common experience than it used to be, still cannot begin to take care of the situation adequately. Moreover, it takes more than a vacation trip or even a school year abroad to work the changes in thinking and outlook that are necessary; if anything, this is only a beginning. Operating on the scale which seems almost inevitable, we can only put the new experiences and the extension of the personal environment into the educational system in this country. In short, we shall have to bring the non-Western world to the student, since we can send only a limited number of students to the non-Western world."

It was in this context that the semester in London or Paris began to seem a normal if not fundamental ingredient of a college education, at least in many private colleges, and a few of the leading public ones too. It was also in this context that study abroad began to include not just the standard European destinations, but some in the "Third World" as well. Japan, India, Latin America and the Middle East all began to be the sites of new interest, propelled not just by the new Fulbright program and the National Defense Education Act (among other federal government initiatives), but sponsored by some of the leading foundations as well, including Ford, Rockefeller and Carnegie (Brooks, 2015; Bu, 1999). Under these programs, students from the

Global South now came to study in the North as much as the reverse. (Less studied is the Soviet Union's sponsorship of parallel student exchange programs for socialist bloc nations, which would significantly influence the political imaginaries of many postcolonial cadres in the later years of the Cold War (Katsakioris, 2014). Although post-war "Area Studies" were predominantly directed towards graduate training and advanced research, the growth of Area Studies faculty and programs led inexorably to increased attention to study abroad as a genuinely global phenomenon.

MODEL II: EXCHANGING

Study Abroad programs began by being sponsored and organized by colleges and associations in the U.S., but increasingly relied on "host" institutions in Europe and elsewhere. As programs became more dependent on these institutions (and in turn, host institutions began to rely on the regular revenue models that went along with them), new kinds of partnerships were established, in order to formalize the curricular and financial aspects of student exchange (even if students moved more in one direction than another) and to curate a student experience that required regulation, oversight and "*in loco parentis*" in multiple global sites. This model commonly involved two universities collaborating to set up a shared pedagogic and/or research program. In some instances, each university would contribute roughly equal numbers of students, faculty and resources to the venture, with none of the resources flowing off campus, and students simply flowing between the campuses. This model worked well for U.S. liberal arts colleges, but worked less well for the more fixed curricula of most European institutions, which nevertheless valued their role in helping to educate American students. In many instances, U.S. programs would be run through associations or consortia that provided structure, housing and some set of curricular guarantees through relationships with host institutions.

The partnering model became the basis for the proliferation of cross-institutional agreements: the ubiquitous memoranda of understanding that began to create dense global networks, at least in theory. Over time, partner universities began to generate new programs at the graduate level as well, increasingly in professional degree programs (especially MBAs) where international exposure also attained major significance. In recent years, a variety of universities have offered dual degree programs that offer students the chance to spend time at the two campuses, allowing them to broaden their international experience, which is seen as particularly valuable for those intending a career in international business or in a globalized industry. This model began to be used in Asia throughout the 1990s as a number of privately owned institutions provided outlets for students to study for foreign degrees in their home countries (Chen, 2015). These programs were in some ways more precursors for new models of institutional collaboration than the standard study abroad programs of earlier decades.

MODEL III: BRANCHING

Though the first international "branch campus" opened in the 1920s, when Parsons Fashion School in New York launched a location in Paris, the fashion capital of the world (Lane & Kinser, 2015), few universities followed Parsons's suit until the 1990s, when all of a sudden a welter of universities began to consider building full-blown extensions of their home campuses overseas (Wagner & Schnitzer, 1991). Over the last 20 years, few ideas have been more popular with ambitious university administrators: According to the Cross-Border Education Research Team (C-BERT) at SUNY-Albany, as of May 2015, there are a total of 235 international branch campuses in operation worldwide. Universities in 32 different countries have "exported" campuses, including 51 U.S. universities (with a total of 81 branch campuses) and 26 British universities (with a total of 34 branch campuses). Conversely, there are a total of 73 "importing" countries, including United Arab Emirates (with 33 branches), China (28), Singapore (14), Qatar (11), and Malaysia (9) (http://www.globalhighered.org).

The motives behind the establishment of international branch campuses are multifarious, ranging from a desire to unlock new sources of revenue for the university, to offering faculty and students of the home campus with a more comfortable environment for international engagement (Wilkins & Huisman, 2012). While many different models have been attempted, the common idea is to replicate the academic and other experiences of the home campus, while injecting appropriate local flavour into the mix. Sometimes this entails building a stand-alone campus, with NYU-Abu Dhabi as perhaps the most famous example, whereas sometimes it involves building a bilateral joint venture, e.g. Yale-NUS, Technion-Cornell (which bleed into Models IV and V, see below) (Olds, 2007).

Depending on where these campuses are set up, such international branch campus are often bold (and risky) experiments, introducing various American styles of education (including the liberal arts) where they did not previously exist, creating new levels of investment in and collaboration with partner universities, and opening universities to global forces that are fundamentally new and different. Yet they also create a thicket of operational complications for the institutions involved, ranging from financing, to convincing the professors of the home institutions to participate, to ethical questions concerning labour practices and academic freedom (Altbach, 2013). To be successful, the managers of higher education institutions who embark on branch campus ventures need to understand the cultures and business practices of the countries they are entering. The greater the cultural distance between the two countries, most importantly including differences in the institutional understandings of the role and function of higher education, the greater the chances something will go awry. So far, the most successful experiments have been those where partner universities already shared faculty cultures of research and teaching. Exciting though many of these experiments are, however, the downside risks are enormous: even leaving aside losses of prestige or "face" should the venture go awry, financial losses from failed joint ventures have been known to run into the tens of millions of dollars. Despite these risks, for most universities this model remains the state of the art in terms of global institutional ambitions.

MODEL IV: MODULARIZING

Some universities, tempted though they have been to build branch campuses, decided to take a different strategy in developing their global "footprint". At Columbia University in the early 2000s, for example, we decided to build a global network of "consular" offices to provide a limited, yet discrete, physical presence in various global centres. Our thinking was that these offices would be free-standing (that is, not linked to any particular university), enabling the development of partnerships and collaborations with multiple institutions, and yet capable as well of developing links to and programs for faculty, students and their parents, and alumni, while also handling local legal, political and fundraising issues of relevance to the university. We believed that these "centres" or offices (some very small, some larger, depending on local funding and resources), would significantly advance our global activities, encourage faculty and students without significant global experience or expertise to become more global, while minimizing risk and, for that matter, upfront investment (most of the resources were raised from local alumni pleased to have an opportunity to "give back" to their alma mater while doing so locally). Columbia began by opening offices in Beijing, Paris, Amman and Mumbai, soon expanding as well to Istanbul, Nairobi, Rio de Janeiro and Santiago. So far, these centres have steadily established themselves as important resources and generated new activity, from different forms of study abroad, to new faculty research, to the generation of new grants to support research in areas such as global health and environmental policy.

The Columbia model has been followed by a number of other universities, usually with a focus on key areas of the world. Stanford, for example, has opened an impressive new centre in Beijing, and though it has done so on the Peking University campus, it has not restricted the centre's activities to specific collaborations with PKU. Like Columbia (and to some extent deliberately following its example), the University of Chicago has opened a number of global international centres, in Beijing, Hong Kong, New Delhi and Paris. The list of universities that have opened some set of consular office is growing almost exponentially, and this is true for universities all over the world. For example, the Freie Universität of Berlin has seven global centres (New York, São Paolo, Paris, Cairo, Moscow, New Delhi and Beijing), explicitly establishing for itself the model of a global network university. If offering your students the opportunity to study abroad has become table stakes for any major university, the "Consular Office" model remains the most popular for universities with bigger ambitions about "going global".

MODEL V: NETWORKING

While various global centres, most notably Dubai, Abu-Dhabi and Qatar in the Gulf, and a myriad of cities in China (e.g. Souzhou), have established new university research parks, inviting global universities to take advantage of land, proximity to other new research and educational ventures, shared use of infrastructure, the promise of growing and talented student populations, and often major infusions of resources, to date only a few of these research parks have been sponsored by highly ranked research universities themselves. Where top-ranked universities such as Stanford have built research parks, the goal most often has been not to partner with foreign universities, but rather with industrial partners, with the aim of lubricating the process commercializing technology and other intellectual property. This process has typically been kept quite intentionally distinct from the process of partnering with other universities, if only to lessen potential legal and operational complications.

The only important exception in this regard is the National University of Singapore. NUS has made major partnership agreements with a whole slew of foreign universities including Duke, Carnegie-Mellon, Australian National University, University of North Carolina, Cambridge, King's College London, Waseda University, and perhaps most significantly with Yale, providing land and facilities on or near their main campus with the express purpose of developing new kinds of international partnerships to drive innovation and enhanced global collaboration. Each of their educational collaborations has been bilateral, although some research ventures have been multilateral (e.g. CREATE). In both of these areas, NUS has been pioneering a new model for a global university, what might be described in the language of "insourcing."

This is a model we at Berkeley are ourselves developing, especially since we were recently cleared to develop a new campus — 134 acres on the San Francisco Bay formerly known as the Richmond Bay Field Station — less than 15 kilometres to our north. As we have considered different options for extending our global reach and establishing a real global network for ourselves, we have been mindful of the successes (and failures) of other ventures, as also of our public mission, in particular our obligations to the region of northern California and more generally to the state of California itself. We have also been mindful of the fact that while we all have seen how global centres can exert powerful incentives for partnership and collaboration, no U.S. university has initiated a similar kind of "insourcing" strategy as begun by NUS, and indeed (viewed in a wider context) developed by a number of countries in the Middle East and Asia. The most direct example of U.S. "insourcing" might be said to be the initiative undertaken by New York City, at the instance of Mayor Michael Bloomberg, when he invited universities from across the world to compete for money and land with direct access to the myriad of resources represented by an institutional presence in one of the greatest global centres. The winner of this much-heralded competition, of course, was a partnered proposal by Cornell and Technion, an Israeli university, and this new experiment in global collaboration is currently under construction (Kiley, 2011).

At Berkeley has taken and elaborated these ideas and examples to propose a new model, in effect that our new campus be labelled as the Berkeley Global Campus (BGC) at Richmond Bay, separate from but inexorably and deeply connected to the home campus. We are in the process of recruiting international and local partners — universities as well as private corporations, government agencies as well as non-governmental organizations — to join us in designing an integrated global network of activities, programs and enterprises. The goal of this new campus will be to provide our students, faculty and staff with an unparalleled global experience and education, as well as to generate and to sponsor global research and entrepreneurship that will benefit both our campus and the entire region of northern California.

BGC will create a unique global footprint, involving a multilateral consortium of universities from across the world (along with other public and private institutions), who will partner with UC Berkeley in the establishment of a global centre for research, teaching and practical engagement in the East Bay. BGC will bring global resources to bear on the construction of the campus, while at the same time opening up the entire Berkeley community to global opportunities. Building on our strengths in engineering, computing and technology, climate science, global public health, big data, entrepreneurship, law, social science, humanities, the arts and design (as well as leveraging our developing partnerships with UCSF on the other side of the Bay, for example in the field of personalized medicine, as well as the Lawrence Berkeley National Lab, in energy biosciences, computing, etc.), we propose to establish a global campus that will extend out from our Berkeley base while inviting global universities to partner with us in a wide range of activities that align with the university's core academic priorities and take full advantage not just of our resources but of our location in the world's leading centre of innovation.

This bold idea initially emerged as we began to consider and evaluate a wide range of issues and risks associated with a potential UC Berkeley presence in mainland China, either through the establishment of a "consular" office or by setting up joint educational and research ventures. Along with some of the challenges in areas related to academic freedom, there are complicated regulatory and political issues, as well as local concerns about ensuring wide participation across the Berkeley campus for a venture of this kind. While we will proceed on a parallel track with the planning for global centres not just in China, but in critical world locations, we will commence the development of a global strategy by establishing a central node in the form of a new global campus close to the home campus.

The proposal inverts the usual model whereby U.S. universities establish themselves in sites all around the world, and instead proposes to invite the world's leading universities to come to join us at Berkeley. BGC represents a model of educational globalization that is sharply distinct from the "commensalist" models of academic globalizations outlined above. These models of global engagement are all in one way or another premised on the educational analog to a "special economic zone," creating autonomous campuses that purport to be somehow "in" but not "of" the country in question. What Berkeley envisions in BGC, by contrast, is a "mutualist" model: rather that sallying forth to conquer the world, we wish to invite the world not just to partake of the benefits of our campus and region, but to establish a genuinely global network of activities. BGC will be host to the research and educational facilities of a small set of elite partner universities from around the globe, as well as P3 research facilities. All of these facilities will be formed in partnership with specific research initiatives (both ongoing and new) that are taking place at Berkeley and in partner universities. As the BGC grows, we believe it will increasingly draw in the most resources and talents of people from around the world, thus acting as a sort of tractor beam for drawing in the brightest lights from across the world into California.

The real innovation of BGC will be to create a new hierarchical network structure to transnational academic collaboration. This pushes it one step beyond the admirable work that Singapore has done in making multiple bilateral arrangements with foreign universities in order to turn the city-state into an "Educational Hub". In other words, where Singapore has been building a brilliant hub-and-spoke model, what we hope to do is to create a true *network* — a "Star Alliance" for international higher education. To put it somewhat technically: whereas the topology of higher education has always been scale-free, our aim is to formalize the clustering among the world's top educational brands by creating an altogether new global structure.

CONCLUSION: THE GLOBAL PUBLIC AND THE PUBLIC UNIVERSITY

As we embark on this new venture, we will also provide new opportunities for our extraordinarily diverse student body to become not just citizens of California — the original charter of the land grant university — but of the world. We take this challenge quite literally, as we have decided to place at the core of the global campus a College of Advanced Study that will take on issues related to global governance, global ethics, global citizenship and global relationships more broadly. The goal here is two-fold: the first, that universities represent the most successful experiments in global institution building; the second, that if universities work together to build global curricula and global platforms, for research and teaching, they might provide models and ideas that will predicate new ways of engaging — and reimagining — globalization itself.

This mutualist vision of the globalized university is rooted in a fundamental assessment of the inexorable direction of the global future, which is increasingly knitted together not just around a single global research enterprise, but also of the changing social and economic role of a preeminent research university like UC Berkeley in the 21st century. In contrast to the "high modernist" vision of the state university as a machine whose output would be knowledge workers contributing to the state economy — the apotheosis of which was the California Master Plan for Higher Education that Clark Kerr developed during the 1960s — BGC *represents the first-class research university as a focal point for enabling the state and its citizens to engage the world*, connecting Berkeley scholars and local industry with researchers and innovators worldwide, and drawing human and financial capital from across the globe into the state. Rather than the cloistered space envisioned by the traditional inward-looking campuses, BGC will be a site for the flow of ideas, information, money, technology and people — moving not only between Berkeley and foreign universities, but also between the private and public sectors, with increasing velocity as they pass through.

By acknowledging the irreversible force of global trends, the extent to which no local challenge is disconnected from global issues, and the powerful role that our universities — both within the United States and across the world — can play, we seek to establish a new kind of global presence that is fully in concert with our public mission. Berkeley is seeking to enable the renewal of its core ethical and political commitment to remaining an elite institution that enables the best and brightest Californians from all backgrounds to gain access to the highest echelons of research and opportunity. In sum, BGC offers what we hope to be a fundamental reimagining of the role of the state university in the age of globalization, and the role of the public university in an age of privatization.

REFERENCES

Altbach P. G. & Knight, J. (2007). "The Internationalization of Higher Education: Motivations and Realities," *Journal of Studies in International Education* 11: 3-4 (2007): 290-305

Altbach, P.G. (2013). "Is There a Future for Branch Campuses?" *The International Imperative in Higher Education* (SensePublishers, 2013): 101-106.

Black, J. (2003). *Italy and the Grand Tour*, 11-12. See also: Bruce Radford, *Venice and the Grand Tour* (Yale, 1996).

Brooks, C. (2015). "'The Ignorance of the Uneducated': Ford Foundation Philanthropy, the IIE, and the Geographies of Educational Exchange," *Journal of Historical Geography* 48.

Brubacher, J. S. & Rudy, W. (1997) *Higher Education in Transition: A History of American Colleges and Universities* (Transaction Publishers, 1997 [1956]): 14-16;

Bu, L. (1999). "Educational Exchange and Cultural Diplomacy in the Cold War," *Journal of American Studies* 33: 3 (1999).

Charle, C. Schriewer, J. & Wagner, P. (2004). Transnational Intellectual Networks: Forms of Academic Knowledge and the Search for Cultural Identities (Campus Verlag).

Chen, P.-Y. (2015). "Transnational Education: Trend, Modes of Practices and Development," *International Journal of Information and Education Technology* 5: 8 (2015): 634-637.

Cohen, M. (1992). "The Grand Tour: Constructing the English Gentleman," *History of Education* 21: 3 (1992).

Dirks, N. (2009). *The Scandal of Empire: India and the Creation of Imperial Britain*, Harvard University Press.

Ellis, H. (2013). "National and Transnational Spaces: Academic Networks and Scholarly Transfer between Britain and Germany in the Nineteenth Century," in Löhr, Isabella & Wenzlhuemer, Roland, eds. *The Nation State and Beyond: Governing Globalization Processes in the Nineteenth and Early Twentieth Century*, Springer-Verlag.

Gibbon, E. (1900). *Memoirs of the Life of Edward Gibbon.* Aberdeen University Press, 148.

Humphrey, D. C. (1972). "Colonial Colleges and English Dissenting Academies: A Study in Transatlantic Culture," *History of Education Quarterly* 12: 2 (1972).

Katsakioris, C. (2014). "The Soviet-South Encounter: Tensions in the Friendship with Afro-Asian Partners, 1945-1965," in Babiracki, Patryk & Zimmer, Kenyon, eds., *Cold War Crossings: International Travel and Exchange Across the Soviet Bloc, 1940s-1960s*, Texas A&M University Press.

Kiley, K. (2011). "The Lure of the City," *Inside Higher Ed*, 20 December 2011: https://www.insidehighered.com/news/2011/12/20/cornell-and-technions-win-new-york-competition-reflects-desire-grow-urban-ties.

Lane, J. & Kinser, K. (2015). "Is today's university the new multinational corporation?" 5 June: https://theconversation.com/is-todays-university-the-new-multinational-corporation-40681.

Marckwardt, A. H. (1964). "The Humanities and Non-Western Studies," *The ANNALS of the American Academy of Political and Social Science* 356: 1: 46.

Marginson, S. (2006). "Dynamics of national and global competition in higher education," Higher Education 52: 1 (2006): 1-39.

Marsden, G. M. (1994). The Soul of the American University: From Protestant Establishment to Established Nonbelief (Oxford University Press, 1994).

Olds, K. (2007) "Global Assemblage: Singapore, Foreign Universities, and the Construction of a 'Global Education Hub'," *World Development* 35:6 (2007): 959-975.

Ridder-Symoens, de H. (1996). *Universities in Early Modern Europe, 1500-1800* Cambridge. (Earlier, during the Renaissance, Europe had a broad tradition of wandering scholars, with students going to sit at the foot of masters in Paris or Bologna. See Hilde de Ridder-Symoens)

Rodgers, D.T. (1998). Atlantic Crossings: Social Politics in a Progressive Age, Harvard.

Viswanathan, G. (1994). "Yale College and the Culture of British Imperialism," *The Yale Journal of Criticism* 7: 1 (1994).

Wagner, A. & Schnitzer, K. (1991). "Programmes and Policies for Foreign Students and Study Abroad: The Search for Effective Approaches in a New Global Setting," *Higher Education* 21:3 (1991): 275-288.

Wilkins, S. & Huisman, J. (2012). "The International Branch Campus as Transnational Strategy in Higher Education," *Higher Education* 64:5 (2012): 627-645.

Wong, P.-K., Ho, Y.-P. & Singh, A. (2007) "Towards an 'Entrepreneurial University' Model to Support Knowledge-Based Economic Development: The Case of the National University of Singapore," *World Development* 35:6 (2007): 941-958.

CHAPTER 9

University Research comes in many Shapes

Carlos H. de Brito Cruz

In "The Usefulness of Useless Knowledge", written in 1937, (Flexner, 1955) Abraham Flexner described a conversation with George Eastman: *"I ventured to ask him whom he regarded as the most useful worker in science in the world. He replied instantaneously, 'Marconi'. I surprised him by saying: 'Whatever pleasure we derive from the radio or however wireless and the radio may have added to human life, Marconi's share was practically negligible."*

I shall not forget his astonishment on this occasion. He asked me to explain. I replied to him: "Mr. Eastman, Marconi was inevitable. The real credit for everything that has been done in the field of wireless belongs, as far as such fundamental credit can be definitely assigned to anyone, to Professor Clerk Maxwell, who in 1865 carried out certain abstruse and remote calculations in the field of magnetism and electricity. Maxwell reproduced his abstract equations in a treatise published in 1873. Other discoveries supplemented Maxwell's theoretical work during the next 15 years. Finally, in 1887 and 1888, the scientific problem still remaining — the detection and demonstration of the electromagnetic waves which are the carriers of wireless signals — was solved by Heinrich Hertz, a worker in Helmholtz's laboratory in Berlin. Neither Maxwell nor Hertz had any concern about the utility of their work; no such thought ever entered their minds. They had no practical objective. The inventor in the legal sense was of course Marconi, but what did Marconi invent? Merely the last technical detail, the now obsolete receiving device called a coherer, almost universally discarded.' Hertz and Maxwell invented nothing, but it was their apparently useless theoretical work which was seized upon by a clever technician and which has created new means of communication, utility and amusement by which men, whose merits are relatively slight, have obtained fame and earned millions. Who were the fundamentally useful men? Not Marconi, but Clerk

Maxwell and Heinrich Hertz. *Hertz and Maxwell were geniuses without thought of use. Marconi was a clever inventor with no thought but use."*

How knowledge created by science converts into material benefit for society became an explicit and pressing question as the 20th century ended. It is not that before then an expectation that science would create wealth, well-being and power, did not exist. It did, and the perfect testimony to that was Vannevar Bush's "Science: The Endless Frontier" report (Bush, 1945). Somehow, both the public and their representatives, accepted the idea that there is a connection between science and development, and were most of the time happy to see science advance, counting that this would bring benefits to society in the future.

The Bush report is a good starting point to discuss and understand the ways in which research can be classified. He presents a definition for both Basic and Applied research:

Basic and Applied research — **Basic research** is performed without thought of practical ends. It results in general knowledge and an understanding of nature and its laws. This general knowledge provides the means of answering a large number of important practical problems, though it may not give a complete specific answer to any one of them. The function of **applied research** is to provide such complete answers.

Presently NSF (National Science Foundation) has a slightly updated definition, that in addition defines Basic and Applied research independently of each other (NSF, n.d.):

Basic research — systematic study directed toward fuller knowledge or understanding of the fundamental aspects of phenomena and of observable facts without specific applications towards processes or products in mind.

Applied research — systematic study to gain knowledge or understanding necessary to determine the means by which a recognized and specific need may be met.

Universities, governments and funding agencies around the world have been using Bush's definition or the updated NSF definition to classify research activities, and this classification has helped the development of knowledge for many decades. However, its use presents some challenges. One immediate difficulty is the fact that the definition depends on guessing what is in scientists' minds when they decide about the topic they will study. In addition, there are situations in which obtaining *fuller knowledge or understanding of the fundamental aspects of phenomena and of observable facts* might be enough *to determine the means by which a recognized and specific need may be met*, which would make the research in question both Basic and Applied.

Fifty-two years later, Donald Stokes (Stokes, 1997) came to help, bringing a different view. He classified research in a two-dimensional diagram, considering in one axis the relevance of the research to the advancement of

Chapter 9: University Research comes in many Shapes

Figure 2: Stokes' quadrants for classifying research (Stokes, 1997).

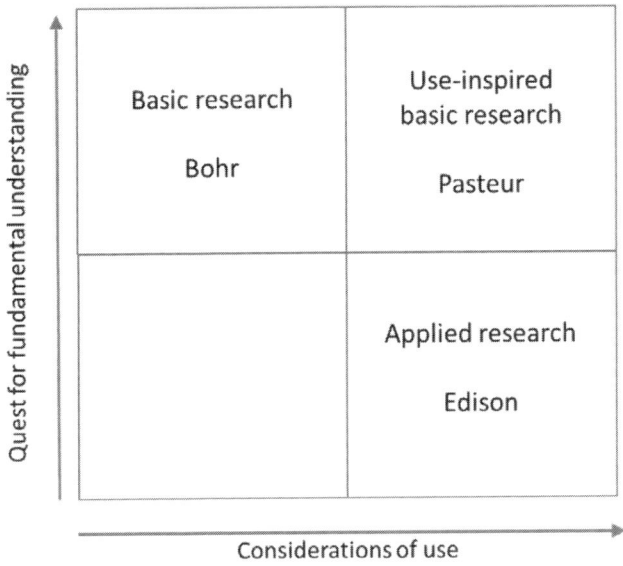

fundamental understanding, and in the other the considerations related to the use of the research results. To help the reader, Stokes classified the quadrants in the resulting diagram, as shown in Figure 1 (being a kind person, he did not name any scientist for the quadrant where there is no fundamental knowledge and the results are not of any use).

To my knowledge, Stokes' was the first formulation that lifted the opposition by definition that existed between Basic and Applied research. Moreover, it came in an interesting epoch, when many knowledge-related organizations in the world were feeling the pressure to produce more useful results, or results with higher and immediate impact.

THE ORGANIZATION OF NATIONAL RESEARCH SYSTEMS

Starting after World War II, many countries took action to build systems to support science, research and higher education. The basic idea was that by enhancing its science base, a nation would create ideas and train people, and these two actions would be determinant in creating development. In many places, the recipe worked for some time, until the economic difficulties at the end of the 1970s started to take a toll on government spending.

Searching for a more effective connection between science and societal needs

Most people would agree that knowledge drives development. Still, the fine mechanics of how knowledge leads to development is a subject of intense debate, more so in recent years, especially after the advent of the IT revolution brought by the invention of the transistor, integrated electronics, the personal computer and, later, the internet and the World Wide Web. Some time around the second half of the 1970s, the life sciences joined the engineering and physical sciences branch of the knowledge revolution. In both branches, the subsequent boom of start-up companies, some of which grew at a fast (or extremely fast, in some cases) pace, made clear to taxpayers and their representatives that there was an opportunity ripe to be exploited: how to create wealth from knowledge at a much faster pace than had been done before.

Governments and society in most countries started an intense debate about the "knowledge-revolution", or the "knowledge-based-economy", searching, in a much more explicit way than had been done before, how to optimize the connections between universities, government and the economy, for the public benefit.

The Bayh-Dole Act of 1980 was especially relevant as it raised the bar for the standards of intensity in university-industry interactions. It had an effect in many countries, as they emulated the U.S. initiatives trying to obtain more impact from university research. In Brazil, an "Innovation Law" was enacted in 2004. On the institutional level, researchers, mostly European, came up with the concept of "National Innovation Systems" (OECD, 1997). A large effort in the measurement, modelling of, and understanding of the institutional interactions ensued, as can be seen in the ever-growing series of OECD reports on Science, Technology and the Economy.

The rising cost of research, increasing the demand on governmental funding agencies and on the taxpayer, also contributed to favour the move towards applications and short-term impact. It must be remembered that members of governments, national congresses or state senates go through the budget tables with the cost of public universities and funding agencies several times each year. However, they seldom find time to pay attention to the news (when it exists) about the benefits of these organizations, which reach the decision-makers in a scattered and non-systematic way throughout the year. On top of this, universities and funding agencies are often not completely effective in transmitting to the public, and to their representatives, the information about its successes.

As a result, the national and regional policies were readjusted, changed or reinvented, to obtain more impact, which usually implied redirecting research to more applied objectives, or altogether to the creation of "innovation".

Themes like university-industry interactions, small-business research support, measuring the impact of research results, and intellectual property protection/licensing, became more and more common in the agenda of funding agencies, universities and research institutions. Among the consequences, there was an intensification of the debate on how research should be organized to bring maximum societal impact.

ORGANIZATION OF RESEARCH IN THE BEGINNING OF THE 21ST CENTURY

Looking for higher impact of the research, funding agencies and universities came up with new ways to classify the research objectives or the way research should be performed. Impact is a broad concept, and it might be useful to think of it along three dimensions: intellectual impact, economic impact and societal impact.

Transformative research

Intellectual impact relates to the way research results will contribute to the advancement of knowledge. The category of Transformative Research, as defined by the National Science Foundation, addresses this dimension (NSF, 2007):

Transformative — *Transformative research involves ideas, discoveries or tools that radically change our understanding of an important existing scientific or engineering concept or educational practice or leads to the creation of a new paradigm or field of science, engineering or education. Such research challenges current understanding or provides pathways to new frontiers.*

Other organizations use different names for activities similar to this category, such as Frontier Research, High-impact and High-reward. Fostering transformative research does not imply abandoning incremental research. The NSF report makes a point on this by starting with:

Science progresses in two fundamental and equally valuable ways. The vast majority of scientific understanding advances incrementally, with new projects building upon the results of previous studies or testing long-standing hypotheses and theories. This progress is evolutionary — it extends or shifts prevailing paradigms over time. The vast majority of research conducted in scientific laboratories around the world fuels this form of innovative scientific progress. Less frequently, scientific understanding advances dramatically, through the application of radically different approaches or interpretations that result in the creation of new paradigms or new scientific fields. This progress is revolutionary, for it transforms science by overthrowing entrenched paradigms and generating new ones. The research that comprises this latter form of scientific progress, here termed transformative research, is the focus of this report.

The challenge here is that transformative research opportunities appear less frequently and, depending on the methods and processes used for the selection of proposals, transformative proposals might find a harder time in a selection process. Transformative research might also be adversely affected by the incentives used for rewarding researchers, as professors involved in transformative projects, that might take longer to show results, might be bypassed in career progression processes.

In Brazil, the São Paulo Research Foundation (FAPESP) has been working to foster high intellectual impact research. This has been done by emphasizing programs for funding long-term projects (5 to 11 years) by fostering international collaborations and long-term industrial cooperation, and by requiring universities to offer institutional support to the Principal Investigators (PIs) and their projects. In Brazil, unlike what happens in most countries, funding agencies contract the projects directly with the PIs. The reasons for this relate to two facts. First, historically, back in the 1960s it was in the interest of the development of a merit-based science system to award funds directly to the investigators to single them out within their institutions bypassing the non-meritocratic power-structure in the universities, thus making sure the funds would get to the right persons. Secondly, due to arcane legislation regulating the use of public funds, contracting with the PIs removes some hurdles. As the values of the contracts increased, the time burden on the PIs also increased. Thus, having institutional support through a Grants Management Office became essential to allow PIs to direct their time to science and training of students.

Translational research

Another category that appeared in the last 20 years is Translational Research, mostly used in the Health Sciences. This one belongs mostly to the economic, and the societal, impact dimensions I outlined above. The definition given by the NIH National Center for Advancing Translational Science specifies Translation and Translational Science as (NIH National Center for Advancing Translational Science, 2015):

1. **Translation** — The process of turning observations in the laboratory, clinic and community into interventions that improve the health of individuals and the public — from diagnostics and therapeutics to medical procedures and behavioural changes.
2. **Translational Science** — The field of investigation focused on understanding the scientific and operational principles underlying each step of the translational process.

In the U.K., the Medical Research Council (MRC) uses a slightly different definition (MRC, 2015):

- **Translation** is the principle of turning fundamental discoveries into improvements in human health and economic benefit. MRC's translational aims — to drive innovation, speed up the transfer of the best ideas into new interventions, and improve the return on investment in fundamental research — and objectives are outlined in the MRC Strategic plan.

In both cases, it is clear that the focus is on applications of science to improve human health. It is striking that both definitions are unidirectional, from fundamental (or laboratory, clinic) discoveries to the patients or the public — from bench-to-bedside is a common buzzword. The possibility of motivating basic research from the needs of the patient/public — or doubling back from the bed-to-the-bench, does not appear emphasized, even though it has been raised by prominent scientists (Ledfort, 2008). That might have happened because the origin of the translational idea seems to have been affected by the consideration that NIH had been lending too much support to Basic Research (Butler, 2008). It should be noted that, regardless of the formal definitions, several research centres around the world are using the concept of "bench-to-bedside-and-back" to redefine the way they connect, bi-directionally, basic research to applications in the health sciences.

Research applied to societal needs

A generalization of the concepts behind Translational Research brings us to "Research applied to societal needs", which would describe the bi-directional connection between Basic research and societal needs. This is an encompassing category that can include any field of knowledge, from Anthropology to Zoology. It includes, of course, Environmental Science and there are several international efforts geared towards connecting the community in the social sciences to the physical and life sciences communities in topics related to global climate change (or global change, in the broader version). Sustainability is also a topic with growing relevance.

Curiosity-driven research

This is a favourite of academic researchers. More important, there is a breadth of works demonstrating how curiosity-driven research brought essential contributions to the stock of knowledge, leading to several instances of innovation and creation of benefits for society. Lasers, semiconductors, atomic physics and nuclear energy, modern biotechnology, are some of the examples that come to mind (Braben, 2004).

Many times, curiosity-driven research is a favourite target of politicians and the public, when they want to criticize universities for being disconnected from the public interest. In many ways, curiosity-driven research is a twin of academic freedom, so important for the advancement of knowledge. Interestingly enough, curiosity-driven is not a quality that implies the uselessness of the research. It assumes only that the investigator chooses the theme or topic. Investigators choose themes and topics today taking into account the chances they have for obtaining the necessary funding to perform the research. At the same time, researchers many times want to create ideas relevant for society that will be recognized as such.

I do not believe anyone would defend the idea that there should be absolutely no support for curiosity-driven research[1]. The trouble comes when deciding about supporting research with taxpayer money, as the decision translates into defining how much societal needs should define research topics and how much should be left for the researchers to choose, according to their qualification and curiosity.

In the heated debate, most times the first line of defence for curiosity-driven research is to argue that discoveries will lead to economic development (or to curing diseases, or making the poor richer) in due time. Flexner used this argument in his exchange with Eastman. It might work sometimes, but this argument leaves out a large and relevant set of knowledge that might never be translated into wealth. Think of what is learned from studying philosophy, the humanities, astrophysics or particle physics. It seems difficult to make an argument that we need (or want) to learn the age of the universe because this knowledge will bring economic development. Some things must be learned just to make humankind wiser, and university research is (also) about this. Some might argue that it should be mostly about this.

HOW THE RESEARCH IS DONE

University-industry collaborative research

The collaboration in research between universities and industry has been recognized for some time as desirable for both organizations and potentially beneficial for the economy. Industry can use university research to mitigate scientific risks, to have access to highly qualified researchers and sophisticated research facilities, and to have privileged access to students and post-doctoral

---

1. There might be exceptions to this. For example, the then Governor of California, Ronald Reagan, famously said in 1967, "There are certain intellectual luxuries that perhaps we could do without"… [Taxpayers] "should not be subsidizing intellectual curiosity." (Bennet, 2015)

fellows that can be hired in the future. Universities look for joint research with industry as it brings research funds and creates a visible contribution to the economy. University researchers often value the scientific challenges they can find in problems brought by industry.

In the North the intensity of interaction can be measured in terms of the relative participation of industry funds in the support of research. In the U.S. this percentage has been between 5% and 7% in recent years. Among OECD countries, the participation of the business sector funds in the total university research expenditure (OECD, n.d.) ranges between 2% and 10%, with Germany being an outlier at 14%.

In the South there is not much information, but recent data for the state of State of São Paulo, Brazil, shows a percentage around 5%. A relevant difficulty in the South is that industry does not have a strong tradition of having internal R&D. In Brazil, for example, for some time, there was an illusion that universities would be the R&D labs that industry did not have. After a few successes and many more failures, the three sides learned that there is R&D that must be performed in industrial R&D labs, there is research that fits well for university labs, and there might be some smaller part that might be performed by both. Recent legislation in Brazil, passed in 2004, created many incentives for joint university-industry research, and facilitated the licensing of IP created with taxpayers' money to the private sector.

University research and start-up companies

Start-up companies are another way in which university research can be translated to economic and social benefits. A few universities in the world are well known for their successes in this endeavour, and many more work hard to facilitate their occurrence, stimulated by the successful examples. In South America start-up creation is more and more frequently mentioned as an important goal, but few universities can display large numbers, either in the quantity of companies, or in the size of the larger ones. An especially successful university in the region is the University of Campinas (Unicamp), one of the three state universities in the State of São Paulo. Unicamp displays a list of 254 start-ups initiated by its students or professors in the last 25 years that sustain more than 16,000 jobs. Some of these became international companies in software, photonics and optical communications. Around the Aeronautics Technology Institute, in São José dos Campos, again in the state of São Paulo, a sizable cluster of airspace and defence companies has developed since the 1960s, the main one being Embraer, which is the third largest aircraft manufacturer in the world today.

SOCIETY EXPECTS MORE ECONOMIC AND SOCIETAL IMPACT FROM UNIVERSITY RESEARCH

The message is clear: society continues to expect intellectual impact from university research, but now society has added to the charge more economic and societal impact. On top of this, it is also fundamental to consider that the value of scientific research includes not only economic and social impact, but also intellectual or cultural (knowledge that makes humankind wiser).

Research in higher education represents an important part of the R&D expenditures in the world (Figure 2) at a value above $PPP 200 billion in 2012.

Universities have been listening to the message and acting accordingly. A major challenge is how to listen and use society's expectations for more and faster impact while avoiding the trap of short-termism for research objectives. Relevant portions of society forget that the technology achievements of today occur because there was a lot of patient and continuous effort towards discovery in the past. This is a point well analysed in Mariana Mazzucato's *The Entrepreneurial State* (Mazzucato, 2013) in a parallel situation: the role of the state in creating or subsidizing the creation of knowledge that involves high enough risk.

In the Northern Hemisphere, it is easy to notice that universities are directing their research strategies towards Pasteur's Quadrant (Figure 1). An important part of the challenge seems to be how to figure out a way to give larger weight to use considerations, while still fostering the curiosity-driven concept or the value of fundamental research. An illustration of this behaviour is the growth in the quantity of new problem-oriented research centres created in universities in the last 10 years, as compared to the previous period.

Figure 3: Dimension of higher education research expenditures in selected regions/countries, as a percentage of regional GDP and in $PPP (values for Latam region estimated by author).

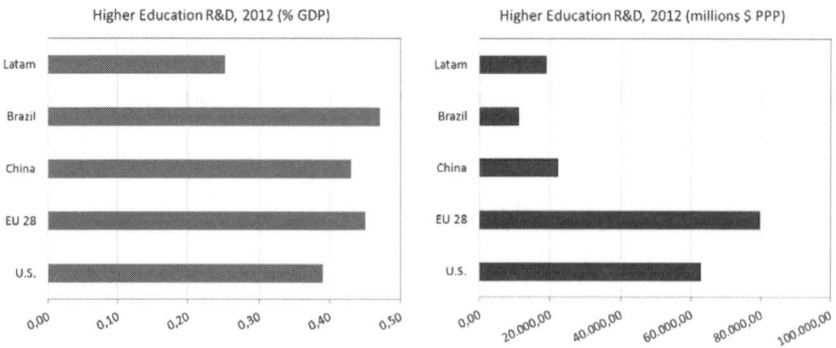

In the South there are some differences worth mentioning. Universities and their communities often lack conviction about their commitment to advancing knowledge and educating students. On the other hand, governments (and society) are quick, especially in times of scarce resources, to reach the conclusion that excellence is a luxury we perhaps can do without, to paraphrase Ronald Reagan. That applies to excellence in education and in research. In Brazil there is an interesting cyclical evolution around the year: when the international university rankings appear, society criticizes universities for not being excellent enough as Brazil appears with few names among the best 200. Then comes the season when the university entrance exams happen, when society criticizes the universities for being too demanding on excellence, requiring high qualifications to approve candidates and leading to the exclusion of those who have not had access to good middle education. Then someone in the media or government will criticize the high expenditure per student in the public universities (which are the ones that have research activities in Brazil). Then, after a few weeks, the same government (but another department) will criticize universities for not graduating enough engineers and other STEM that are necessary to maintain the competitiveness of the aircraft industry, or agriculture production, or energy generation. In doing that, they forget that, to a large extent, the cost of educating internationally competitive professionals is not set by how much money one wants to spend but by an international standard of excellence and quality.

CONCLUSION — THE SEARCH FOR MORE IMPACT AFFECTS AND IS AFFECTED BY FUNDING AGENCIES TOO

Finally, universities can and have been taking action to connect investigator-initiated research to impactful applications and applied research, while striving to maintain their fundamental contribution to increasing the stock of fundamental knowledge. It must be added that the success of the initiatives depends also on having access to research funds provided externally. Achieving all these goals might be impossible if government agencies direct most of their funds to short-term applied research. It must be remembered that the same kind of pressure that afflicts universities in this matter affects government research funders. For this reason, it is essential that research-funding agencies strive to maintain a balanced portfolio of programs that supports (GRC, 2015):

- Basic research and applied research
- Curiosity-driven and mission (or use)-oriented research
- Research executed by individual investigators and centres of excellence
- Non-thematic and priority areas.

REFERENCES

Bennet, Daniel (2015). "The day the Purpose of College Changed." *The Chronicle of Higher Education*, 26 January.

Braben, Donald (2004). *Pioneering Research: a risk worth taking.* John Wiley & Sons, Hoboken, N.J.

Bush, Vannevar (1945) *Science: the Endless Frontier*, A Report to the President by Vannevar Bush, Director of the Office of Scientific Research and Development. Washington, DC. https://www.nsf.gov/od/lpa/nsf50/vbush1945.htm (accessed April 10, 2015).

Butler, Declan (2008). "Crossing the valley of death." *Nature* 453: 840-842.

Flexner, Abraham (1955). "The Usesfulness of Useless Knowledge." *J. Chron. Diseases* 2, no. 3: pp. 241-246.

GRC (2015). "Statement of the Principles for Funding Scientific Breaktrhoughs."

Ledfort, Heidi (2008). "The Full Cycle." *Nature* 453: pp. 843-845.

Mazzucato, Mariana (2013). *The Entrepreneurial State.* Anthem Press, London.

MRC (2015). *Translational research.* http://www.mrc.ac.uk/funding/science-areas/translation/ (accessed 7 June).

NIH National Center for Advancing Translational Science (2015). *Translational Science Spectrum.* 04 13, 2015. https://ncats.nih.gov/translation/spectrum (accessed 7 June).

NSF (n.d.). *Definitions of Research and Development: An Annotated Compilation of Official Sources.* NSF, Arlington, VA. http://www.nsf.gov/statistics/randdef/fedgov.cfm (accessed 14 April 2015).

NSF (2007). *Enhancing Support of Transformative Research at the National Science Foundation.* NSB, Arlington, Va.

OECD (n.d.). *Main Science and Technology Indicators.* http://stats.oecd.org/BrandedView.aspx?oecd_bv_id=strd-data-en&doi=data-00182-en# (accessed 13 April, 2015).

OECD (1997). *National Innovation Systems.* OECD Publications, Paris.

Stokes, Donald E. (1997). *Pasteur's Quadrant.* Brookings Institution Press.

The Economist (2010). "Brazil's agriculture miracle: How to feed the world." *The Economist*, 26 August.

CHAPTER 10

Global Research Questions and Institutional Research Strategies

Patrick J. Prendergast and Martina Hennessy

INTRODUCTION

Two years ago, one of the authors (PJP) was at a conference in Seoul on "The Role and Responsibilities of Research Universities", moderating a session on "Higher Education and Strategic Knowledge Creation". It was an intensive session, with ten papers, in which university presidents and senior academic officers from around the world spoke about research projects and knowledge transfer. In the discussion afterwards, the vice-president of National Tsing Hua University in Taiwan, Da Hsuang Feng, stood up and said: "You know, all these [glittering technologies] are irrelevant"; he continued: "Every single day we are given three grids: water grid, sewage grid and electric grid. Imagine we don't have one of them on any single day. Life would be hell. Then I realized a large percentage of the world of people doesn't have at least one of them, and some don't have three of them… So, as research universities, should we not think about that? … we have a global warming problem. It's real… water shortage is real… Energy shortage… Disease… Finally, human hatred. Shouldn't research universities think about those issues… My gut feeling is that if universities are not going to do it, then nobody will. Governments are not going to do it and corporations are not going to do it." (*International Presidential Forum on Global Research Universities*, 2013, p. 157)

It was a provocative intervention, coming as it did at the end of a celebratory session of academic achievement. It struck a chord. People stood up to say that universities should aim to make a direct contribution to tackling some of the great problems facing our world. Such crucial research may never even get off the ground if university research is driven only by the research priorities of individual academics. But it was the end of a very long day, the session was closing, and the discussion went no further.

Back in Dublin, that passionate intervention continued to echo. Those three grids resonated, perhaps because delivering water, sewage treatment and electricity is part of what engineers do, but also because Da Hsuang Feng is right: without those three grids being available every single day, life for many of us would be impossible.

Today, the greatest challenges facing our globalized world are to protect human rights, overcome poverty, disease and exclusion, and achieve self-determination. But we also face global challenges that previous generations did not have to consider, perhaps most urgently, the need to maintain a liveable planet; other challenges include the migration of populations between continents; the mass collection of data on individuals and how that is used; and the rapid development of technology and our tenuous ability to control it. What is different now is that while our predecessors could justifiably claim a degree of ignorance about the effects of these changes, today the extreme connectedness of our modern world means we can no longer fail to recognize the significance of such global issues for the lives of individuals, or fail to fully appreciate their impact on human dignity.

More to the point, over the last 300 years, a new understanding of health and new technological capabilities and forms of social organization have permitted many countries to attain a massive improvement in living standards characterized by adequate food, shelter, clean water, education, good health and enough income to live with dignity. However, despite all we have achieved, many societies remain mired in extreme poverty and deprivation. At the same time, more economically developed communities are just beginning to understand the implications of diminishing natural resources, and other phenomena allied to technological development such as the ubiquitous availability of personal information.

We need to improve our understanding of "emerging communities" in order to explore the sources and dynamics of their success, as well as to understand the major development challenges they continue to face. Their fast growth raises new questions about the development of nationhood and identity, the relationship between health and poverty, and the promotion of sustainable, equitable and environmentally acceptable growth. Different parts of the world provide vital learning for other parts; universities, with their networks of students and staff, can ensure a better understanding of those regions of the world that will inevitably become the cultural, economic, political and social powerhouses of the 21st century. These are just some of the most important challenges we face; as universities, we have the freedom and the capacity to ask the important global questions that will begin to explore these challenges and point towards solutions. Such questions include:

- What can communities do to attain levels of human well-being that we know are achievable?
- How do we reshape research and education to create an equitable future for all?
- How do we make nature and technology work as one?
- Why does poverty become destiny, and how can that be changed?
- How do we bring emerging societies onto the grid?
- How will we sustain a liveable planet?

The concept of developing global research questions seems at first "topical" or even populist, but this is not the case. Poverty, inequality, disease, hunger and corruption, and the moral dilemmas that underpin their origins have always been with us and perhaps may always remain with us. Nonetheless, down the ages university scholars have used their academic freedom to provide intellectual and ideological leadership in the consideration of these challenges; their efforts have resulted in societal change, improving the ability of people to act in pursuit of their own ends and participate socially and politically.

Trinity College has a tradition of addressing the most important and pressing questions facing society. In 1729, Jonathan Swift, who attended Trinity between 1682 and 1686, wrote *A Modest Proposal* (Swift, 1729), his satirical response to the failure of intellectual elites to address the appalling conditions facing the poor.

Despite the enormous strides that mankind has made in combating war, injustice, hunger and poverty, these horrors remain a significant threat to the integrity of states and emerging societies; the imperative for universities to provide leadership and to work together to make an impact upon these challenges and create solutions to them has never been greater. The great political philosopher and Trinity graduate Edmund Burke said: "No moral questions are ever abstract questions." So we must understand that the global challenges and the questions we must ask to address them are not abstract or slow-burning, but real and urgent, deserving of our *special* attention and efforts. Neither are these challenges ephemeral, being as they are the inevitable consequence of unstoppable globalization.

GLOBAL RESEARCH QUESTIONS AND INSTITUTIONAL STRATEGIC PLANNING

Following the Seoul conference, the authors started work on Trinity College Dublin's Strategic Plan for 2014-2019, which was published last October. We have now inserted into this Plan the objective that Trinity address a Global

Research Question — or a GRQ, as we rather optimistically refer to it, in the hope that the idea of universities addressing global research questions gathers such currency that we can start using acronyms.

Many universities have indeed recognized the importance of addressing global challenges; in this regard other universities are ahead of us, and U.S. universities are leading the way though they have yet to formulate GRQs. For example, Georgetown University has a "Global Futures Initiative" which "involves inviting members of the Georgetown community to undertake innovative teaching, research and dialogue with world leaders in the public sector, business and civil society around pressing global issues" including development, governance and the environment (Georgetown University, 2015). The President of Georgetown, John G. DeGioia, has spoken of universities' "special responsibility to address the global challenges that will shape humanity's future". The Earth Institute in Columbia University focuses on "environmental challenges — from rapid population growth and climate change to extreme poverty and infectious disease" (Columbia University, 2015). While it is too early to speak of a groundswell, there are now enough targeted initiatives to enable us to speak tentatively of a growing movement within universities discussing these issues, engaging in informed advocacy at the highest level in international forums, and setting up targeted collaborations in areas where an impact can be made. Important as these activities are, they have not been mainstreamed into the fundamental work of the academy; they are identifiable because they stand apart from the main thrusts of research questions posed by academics.

In drawing up Trinity's Strategic Plan, we did not identify what our GRQ would be, and we still have not identified it, although we intend to do so within the 2015/16 academic year. It is, we admit frankly, a work in progress. As a university, we wanted to put the idea of a GRQ in the Strategic Plan to get the ball rolling, but we did not, and do not, underestimate the disciplinary and structural challenges facing universities addressing GRQs (Trinity College Dublin, 2014).

Our purpose with this paper is to share some of our current thinking, and to present some ideas that will enable an exchange of views about strategizing for collaborations on GRQs in research-intensive universities.

DEFINING THE GLOBAL RESEARCH QUESTION

Defining what we mean by a global research question is not hard: such a question addresses fundamental challenges that affect the future of the planet. A GRQ addresses an issue that has emerged across the globe, at scale, that cannot be solved by a single discipline or within a single country. Therefore, GRQs are interdisciplinary *and* of global consequence: water shortage, energy provision, climate change, poverty, global warming, migration, inequality, the ageing population, conflict resolution — all these challenges to humanity are the basis for GRQs.

To further particularize, we might ask what areas of research *do not* qualify as GRQs Very little of the research done in universities qualifies as a GRQ. In Trinity we have excellent research institutes in neuroscience, nanotechnology and digital humanities, and we are planning a cancer institute. None of these concentrates on what we mean by a GRQ. Cancer is potentially a tragedy for individuals, particularly if they are young, and it is something we all fear, but cancer research is not a GRQ even though it is utterly essential for individual lives that we find a cure for cancer. However, other diseases have the potential to decimate regions and communities and, if not solved, could wipe them out, eventually affecting the planet itself. This potential to have a global consequence characterizes a GRQ.

THE CHALLENGES OF ADDRESSING GLOBAL RESEARCH QUESTIONS

The disciplinary challenge

Given how crucial GRQs are, why do universities not concentrate on them? Why do we not all have Climate Change Institutes, Migration Institutes, Inequality Institutes? The answer is that when it comes to research areas, universities tend to converge. Trinity College Dublin is not unique in its research institutes: neuroscience, nanotechnology, biosciences, cancer. There are counterparts of these all around the world. There are good reasons for this. These are genuinely important areas — just because they are not GRQs does not mean they do not need our attention. They are exciting areas where new discoveries are being made all the time, and where individual scientists lead active research teams.

This thought prompts another question: are GRQs intrinsically less exciting than subjects such as nanotechnology or digital humanities? Is that why universities avoid them? This is probably not the answer. Universities can only approach research questions that are in their remit to solve — research questions that are, if you like, "sized" appropriately for the resources available.

In addition, topics of research become exciting when communities around the world are concentrating on them. The global support systems built around, say, bioengineering or cancer or Joyce studies, enable researchers to get funding and find collaborators through these networks. Areas of research that already have momentum are attractive for researchers — perhaps this is one constraint holding back the pursuit of GRQs. Thoughts about another constraint are triggered by recalling Winston Churchill's famous remarks in the House of Commons in 1922 on the Northern Irish conflict: "Then came the Great War... Great empires have been overturned. The whole map of Europe has been changed... but as the deluge subsides and the waters fall short, we see the dreary steeples of Fermanagh and Tyrone emerging once again. The integrity of their quarrel is one of the few institutions that has been unaltered in the cataclysm which has swept the world." (Churchill, 1939). When Northern Ireland erupted again, in 1969, after five quiet decades, there was a lot of talk about the "dreary steeples of Fermanagh and Tyrone". This catches something about our attitude to the very problems that lie behind GRQs — they can appear long drawn out, unvarying and intractable.

The GRQs — of conflict, migration, inequality — are topical now, and they have always been topical. Is it for that reason that they may be less intrinsically interesting than the hot topics of the day? Do university researchers and students stay away from these questions because, instead of promising the excitement of discovery, they induce feelings of exhaustion, and even of irritation? In addition, many of these issues are highly political. Research requires donors and funding, and certain types of research will always prove particularly appealing while others fail to attract support.

The structural challenges

When presidents of universities meet and talk about collaborating, they tend to talk about student exchanges and joint programs in teaching. They do not talk so much about research collaborations because they rely on individual faculty members to set up the projects and links that will grow their research. They do not talk about GRQs much either, or about sharing resources and expertise to address the kinds of problems mentioned above.

This is not — we hope — because university presidents do not care. It is because the way that academic research is structured and funded does not facilitate strategic planning and direction from the top; instead, there is a bottom-up approach. Universities create research strengths through the efforts of individual faculty members, and the outputs are those that materially affect the advancement of the individual researcher's career, notably publication of highly-cited journal articles or books with prestigious publishers. Let us look at this in some more detail.

Universities empower individual faculty members. This is institutionalized by individual Principal Investigator (PI) grants. Getting such grants is the *sine qua non* for promotion, and individual PIs build up a track record which is the marker of success. Incentivizing individual effort is the bedrock of the strategy in research-intensive universities, and it is rooted in the academic freedom which is so precious to research universities, including our own (Trinity College Dublin, 2011).

Drawing on this bedrock of individual achievement, how do universities strategize for research? There are some very successful institutions whose strategy is stated as (and we paraphrase): "Hire the best people and let them get on with it." Of course, this statement is a strategy in itself: what is "best"? And what are researchers supposed to "get on with"? Notwithstanding therefore that some universities may not explicitly write out a research strategy, all have strategies.

The universities obliged to write out an institutional research strategy generally proceed in the following way: (i) do an audit of research activities, (ii) identify strengths, (iii) link the strengths together into multidisciplinary themes, (iv) assess the themes based on external peer review, and (v) assign the best themes as strategic priorities for preferential recruitment and philanthropic support. Often these strengths can be structured into research institutes that are funded separately from the budget that supports teaching. This is the bottom-up approach and it is relatively democratic. This approach also has the appeal of supporting individual academic freedoms; indeed, the "strategy-less" approach is individualistic *in extremis*.

However successful these approaches based around individual PIs may be, they are open to criticism as wasteful of the world's intellectual resources in the face of serious and mounting global problems. The individualistic approach atomises research questions into individual packages, and the university then tries to create scale by aggregating individual efforts. There is much to say in this approach's favour: it promotes individual responsibility, and it is the individual who is promoted, rarely a group. It also stimulates output of the kind measured by rankings and is therefore the bedrock of research universities, including our own. However, the approach results in the strikingly similar research prioritizations already mentioned — the fact that many of our universities have cancer institutes, nanotechnology and neuroscience institutes, and so on, is evidence of this.

Indeed, there is strength in numbers, and it is a great thing for Trinity researchers that they can find peers around the world to collaborate with. But, while much research in the same field is complementary, much is also — and let's be frank here — duplicated. That is what might appear to be wasteful. In an ideal world, if our research were genuinely global, there would be greater complementarity and less of a herd instinct when it comes to defining research questions.

SOLUTIONS: A FOUR-PRONGED APPROACH

What do we do? The bottom-up approach to research strategizing based on individual researcher priorities does not facilitate GRQs; research coming bottom-up tends to flow along existing grooves (there is a reason why we talk about funding "streams"). Creating new grooves is no easy task, and could prove disadvantageous to successful universities. Why then take the risk to change if already in a strong position?

We don't have all the answers. But we suggest a four-pronged approach:

Get agreement on the necessity for GRQs

As research universities we employ the vast majority of the world's researchers across a diverse array of fields; we should reach an agreement that, without some degree of coordinated response, it will be difficult to come together to collaborate to address GRQs. This agreement may not be easy to achieve. Some universities may prefer to stay within the status quo, which is working for them. We need to test the appetite for GRQs. We are hoping that it is strong, because this is not an area where a single university can go it alone. It is encouraging that Columbia has an Earth Institute, and Georgetown has a Global Futures Initiative, and Trinity has a Global Research Question (though it has yet to be specified). These do raise the profile of global challenges, but a single institution is unlikely to have the breadth of activities or the global presence to marshal the academic resources needed to solve a GRQ on its own. If we are dealing with global issues, requiring coordinated inter-disciplinary, inter-institutional and international responses, then all the world's leading universities should engage.

Redefine what 'exciting' means when it comes to research

Academics do the research they are personally interested in, and so they should. But what is considered exciting can be subject to change. One of the most exciting, certainly the most headline-making, books published in the last few years is, of course, Thomas Piketty's *Capital in the Twenty-First Century*. It deals with inequality, and he has created huge excitement around this area — an excitement which universities could harness. The people who try to solve some of the world's more intractable global challenges are mostly outside academia, whether it be in conflict resolution, climate change or inequality. At some point during the many years these individuals give to these issues they may grow weary, but when breakthroughs are made their efforts are rewarded manyfold. We are inclined to admire noble, inspirational leaders. That admiration could be harnessed by universities to encourage researchers to solve these global challenges by formulating GRQs that are amenable to collaborative research within the academy.

Accelerate inter-disciplinarity and extend 'translational' research

We have been concentrating on the structural set-ups that work against GRQs, but there are also benefits to the way universities and funding have developed, which could facilitate GRQs. We are thinking first of all of the move towards inter-disciplinarity. Universities now routinely offer programmes in areas such as creative studies, entrepreneurship, multimedia and innovation which demand an interdisciplinary approach and which were not being offered a generation ago. And new interdisciplinary fields, such as bioengineering, neuroscience or deaf studies, continue to be synthesized from older disciplines.

Universities have also succeeded in pioneering translational research, which has been led by Academic Medical Centres. Such translational research is often said to be "from bench to bedside". If we extend this thinking across other fields, then research questions may be formulated around matters that link up with fundamental science at one end of the spectrum and with actual practice at the other. This extends the idea of what complex research actually is. Certainly it is arguable that there may be matters that are more pressing if not more important than fundamental research. In a paper entitled "The Post-Scientific Society", Christopher T. Hill (2007) argued that we are moving away from a focus on "fundamental research in the natural sciences and engineering [towards] world-leading mastery of the creative powers of, and the basic sciences of, human beings, their societies and their cultures". As a result, we could become a society in which successful research depends not on the ability to specialize but rather on the ability to synthesize and design. We cannot address GRQs without inter-disciplinarity and a "translational" attitude to research.

Incentivize an extended range of university activities

Universities such as our own are clear about their mission in education and research, with research-led teaching being an unbreakable link between the two activities. However, in addition to teaching and research, universities now have an extended range of "tools" at their disposal, for example, company incubation, provision of creative spaces such as arts venues; alumni networks, and so on; it is clear that these activities help to address GRQs. Since GRQs are global, we need to go beyond the merely national frameworks currently in place; a global dimension to funding would further help to prioritize global issues. This is happening with global foundations, but public funding is also required and this too is starting to be granted. One example is the European Institute for Innovation and Technology, the EIT. The EIT has created pan-European groups called Knowledge and Innovation Communities, or KICs, which coordinate partners from three sectors: higher education, research and business. There are five KICs currently under way:

- Climate
- ICT
- InnoEnergy

- Raw Materials, and
- Healthy Living and Active Ageing.

Climate and Energy are GRQs, as is Active Ageing — the European Parliament made a deliberate choice to concentrate on these areas of significance to the future of humankind, where entrepreunerial solutions needed to be boosted. The first three KICs — Climate, ICT and InnoEnergy — have already delivered impressive results in terms of start-ups (205), new and improved products/services (280), knowledge transfers (558), and graduates (1028) (Prendergast, 2015). All this is very promising because the way that universities will help to address global challenges in the 21st century is precisely through extending the range of university activities to spin-out companies and the not-for-profit sector.

One of the authors (PJP) is on the EIT board and is delighted to be associated with an institute which is taking seriously the challenge of addressing complex issues not usually seen as suitable topics for university research activities. Without making huge claims for the EIT, the incentive it provides — a very well-funded one — is greatly to be welcomed. The EIT also uses public funding to kick-start activities that may, after this public investment, attract the interest of entrepreneurs and the business community. Without the ultimate interest of private organizations, GRQs will not be solved.

Over the next few years, much will happen in any event as global challenges are too important to be ignored, so that addressing them — whether by formulating GRQs or not — is inevitable. However, we should not wait until the incongruity of research universities not playing a visible part in addressing global challenges becomes apparent. We should help to move towards a situation where GRQs are considered the routine activity of any leading university.

DISCUSSION AND CONCLUSION

It is understandable that universities avoid defining a single GRQ which would be too big, intractable and unanswerable. Such a GRQ would be a constraint for individual researchers and would present too major a change in objectives for established research institutions: how would it be measured and funded? Instead, we formulate multiple questions and sub-questions and objectives, each relevant in its own way but also easily aligned with stated research priorities, themes and sub-themes of research funders. There is something in there for everyone, each step incrementally measureable in terms of achieving critical mass, output and metrics.

This is the long-established, predictable and sensible ground-up approach imposed upon the university system by good sense, economic direction, funding constraints and rankings. We are not suggesting that we abandon it, but we are suggesting that if we still believe that universities can actually change the world, then we must move beyond the conventional approach as our only way of finding answers to the most important issues of our time.

Global challenges and their effects cannot be addressed merely by hoping that they somehow enter the provenance of individual academic interest; rather, putting GRQs on the agenda needs our explicit support if the questions are to become the focus of teams of academic researchers working smoothly across many disciplines in the arts, sciences, law, social sciences, technology and the health sciences. A new kind of global interdisciplinary collaboration needs to be promoted.

In preparing this paper, we read the second Glion declaration published in 2009. The declaration reflected upon the impending second decade of the millennium. It stated:

"It is… clear that 'business as usual', a casual continuation of our present patterns and current practices, is not sustainable in the longer term, at least, not without growing hunger, disruption and social dislocation." (Glion Colloquium, 2009).

That declaration was a call to action, for research universities to adopt new approaches of such boldness that they would be "disruptive of much conventional thinking and many established practices". It would seem that as we enter the second half of that decade, hunger, poverty and social isolation continue unabated and the need for research universities to take up the most pressing challenges and find new ways to address them has never been greater. If the universities will not take up the challenge who will? As leaders of research universities have often said, it is within these institutions that the leaders and intellectuals of the next generations are shaped, the frontiers of knowledge crossed and partnerships that can achieve greater than the sum of parts created. We have the opportunity, the ability and the academic responsibility to define the most important global research questions of our time. We must grasp that chance so that we can identify the inventions, the art and the actions that will forge a collective and equitable future. We think we have an obligation to do this; although obligation can be a rather off-putting concept, we also think that ultimately universities will derive great inspiration from meeting the challenge.

REFERENCES

Churchill, W. S. (1939). *The World Crisis: The Aftermath*, London.
Columbia University (2015). www.earth.columbia.edu
Georgetown University (2015). www.global.georgetown.edu/futures
Glion Colloquium (2009). http://www.glion.org/?p=833

Hill, C. T. (2007). www.tcd.ie/about/policies/academic-freedom.php

International Presidential Forum on Global Research Universities (2013). *The Role and Responsibility of Research Universities: Knowledge creation, Technology Transfer and Entrepreneurship*, Sung-Mo 'Steve' Kang & Chang Dong Yoo, eds., KAIST Press, Yuseong-gu, Daejeon, South Korea, p. 157.

Prendergast, P. J. (2015). "The European Approach to Universities Supporting Innovation", European Institute in Washington, 1 June 2015, www.tcd.ie/provost/addresses/2015-06-01-european-institute-washington.php

Swift, J. (1729). *A Modest Proposal*, Dublin.

Trinity College Dublin (2011). www.tcd.ie/about/policies/academic-freedom.php

Trinity College Dublin (2014). www.tcd.ie/strategy/research-impact/#b63

PART III

Financial Constraints

CHAPTER 11

A Business Model for the 21st Century European University

Patrick Aebischer and Gérard Escher

MOVING IN THE AMERICAN DIRECTION

"The world is moving in the American direction. More universities in more countries are charging students tuition fees," says *The Economist* (2015). Of course, there is more to the American university model than merely tuition. Many of us have benefitted from the opportunities of great American research universities. Some of us have further implemented their spirit within a European university by instituting, for example, tenure track positions, professional deans, competition for funds, doctoral schools and a president devoted to fundraising.

However, the reported — and confirmed — crisis of student debt in the U.S. has shed doubts on the role model of the American university. Can we avoid throwing away the baby with the bathwater? We take up the challenge that we should continue to move towards the American model of research universities while maintaining our European values.

Universities are known for their resilience and stoic resistance to change. "Once I identified 85 institutions that had been in existence since 1520 and were still largely unchanged. Seventy of them were universities," wrote U.C. Berkeley's first chancellor, Clark Kerr (Kerr, 2001). Europe invented several university models, not just one (Sam & van der Sijde, 2014). The **Humboldtian** model unites research and teaching, where teaching of *new* knowledge is the fundamental mission, in total academic freedom, but with a centralized governance. The **Napoleonic** model focuses on high-level vocational and technical training, or professional education, also within a centralized system. The **Anglo-Saxon** model emphasizes a "liberal education," giving students the flexibility to develop personally, with institutional autonomy and self-governing institutions. Finally, there is the **(Anglo-)American** model. It has all the (somewhat contradictory) features of European models integrated by the U.S. (and later spread back to Europe). This model has far more students, a decentralized system of governance, autonomous institutions and an entrepreneurial model of higher education, whereby universities play a critical role in the economic development of their region or nation.

Implementing the American model is not easy. According to Swiss Nobel Prize winner Richard Ernst (Herbst, 2009), "[...] we follow a kind of hybrid system that is situated somewhere between the German institutional system (with few professors) and the U.S. American system with a high number of professors heading small teams but without workers on permanent contracts. [...] We try to combine the advantages of both systems but tend to ignore the fundamental incompatibility of the two systems. We think we have vanquished the German system, but we are still a long way from the American one. [...] There is no middle way."

IS THE AMERICAN MODEL BROKEN?

In 2008, the net cost (tuition, room and board, subtracting financial aid) for one year in a four-year public university in the U.S. was equivalent to one quarter (25%) of the median family income (Zumeta et al., 2012). Alarmingly, the net costs have increased by about one percentage point per year for the past decade. Net costs, in fact, might not be very different from those in many European countries; tuition costs, however, are. Tuition absorbs an ever-higher proportion of family income: for private four-year university courses, tuition was 16% of the median income in the 1970s and is 30% today. "Tuition hikes are addictive" (Bowen, 2013), but for universities, tuition revenue is the only readily available source of income to compensate for declining state appropriations. Accordingly, as a percentage of total educational revenue in public higher education, net tuition rose from 23% in 1986 to 43% in 2011 (Bowen, 2013).

As a result, the number of students (or parents) who borrow money for university education is steadily increasing, at a rate of roughly 7% per year (reaching close to 40 million borrowers in 2012). The amount borrowed increases at the same rate. Why bother to borrow for college? Because college still pays. The private return on investment of a college education is significant, both during and after economic downturns.

Despite these statistics, it's important to note that the looming student debt crisis is NOT due to the great research universities — even with their impressive levels of tuition.

In July 2012, the U.S. Senate Committee on Health, Education, Labor and Pensions published an 800-page report, (Collini, 2013) which was the culmination of a two-year investigation into "for-profit" higher education institutions. The senators found that many from the least advantaged sections of society are stuck with massive student debts after having enrolled in, and quickly withdrawn from, courses that were never suitable for them. ("Subprime degrees, like subprime mortgages, are sold to communities relatively unfamiliar with the product.") (Collini, 2013). Indeed, a tsunami of substandard private universities hit the American market in the last decade. These for-profit schools are overwhelmingly dependent on revenue from tuition. One player, Laureate, already has more than 150 campuses in North America, Latin America, Europe and Asia and operates 15 medical schools and well-regarded hotel management schools in Switzerland and Spain (Wildavsky, 2012). The biggest player in this market is the University of Phoenix, with a claim of 600,000 students and annual revenue of more than $4 billion in 2010 (Collini, 2013). The Senate investigation showed that 60% of these students dropped out within two years. Among those who completed their degrees, 21% defaulted on student loan payments within three years of finishing (Collini, 2013).

In contrast, most elite schools currently have policies whereby middle-income families do not have to pay *any* tuition fees. Bloomberg Business (Otani, 2015) analyses ten of them. For example, Stanford University announced at the end of March 2015 that, starting this fall, students whose families make less than $125,000 a year will not pay any tuition fees. Previously, the school had set the bar at $100,000. Students with a family income above $65,000 a year still have to cover room and board. And Stanford is not alone in this. Brown University's (tuition for 2015 is $48,272) policy is that families making less than $60,000 don't pay tuition, room or board. Princeton, Cornell, Duke, Harvard, Yale and MIT all have similar policies.

TUITION IN EUROPE (NOT THE AMERICAN WAY)

European countries have three models of tuition and student aid in higher education systems (OECD, 2013). In Model 1, high tuition fees are combined with a well-developed student-support system; the Netherlands and the United Kingdom use this "American" model. The systems in these countries present potentially large financial obstacles to entry into university education, but they also offer substantial public support to students. The average entry rate for this group of countries is significantly above the OECD average of 60%. In Model 2, there are no or low tuition fees alongside generous student support systems. This group is composed of the Nordic countries (Denmark, Finland, Iceland, Norway and Sweden). The average entry rate into a tertiary-type education for this group is also significantly above the OECD average. These high entry rates may also reflect the attractiveness of highly-developed student financial support systems, not just the absence of tuition. For instance, in these countries, more than 55% of students benefit from public grants, public loans or a combination of the two. In a third model — which includes all other European countries for which data is available — low tuition fees are combined with a less-developed student-support system. All of these countries charge moderate tuition fees. A fourth model — countries with high tuition fees but less-developed student support systems — is not present in Europe, but is typical in Asia.

Student numbers are growing faster than global GDP (*The Economist*, 2015). The global tertiary enrolment ratio increased from 14% to 32% in the last 20 years. The number of countries with a tertiary enrolment ratio of more than 50% went up from five to 54 in that period. As an example of this tertiary explosion, "in the decade to 2009, Chinese universities hired nearly 900,000 new full-time faculty members" (*The Economist*, 2015). The OECD estimates the number of international students to have grown from 2.1 million to 4.3 million in the past decade alone. This potential financial resource has not gone unnoticed by European universities. In some countries, such as the U.K., extra-European students already make up a near majority of international students, and these students can be targeted with higher tuitions fees (within E.U. regulations). In other countries, the topic is hotly debated, less for reasons of tuition and more regarding a broader discussion on migration and job permits. Nevertheless, for a few select countries and renowned universities, the financial stream from international students will become a valuable resource.

THE AMERICAN WAY: THE ENTREPRENEURIAL UNIVERSITY

What is new is that universities have become much more relevant to economic growth and social *bien-être* (see, for example, the "Knowledge for Growth" report of the European Union [2008]). Many academic scientists no longer believe in the necessity of an isolated "ivory tower" for scientific discovery. "This reflects a genuine sense that the process of scientific exploration has become a much more collaborative process, requiring input and stimulation from a wide variety of sources," says former president of Harvard University Derek Bok (Bok, 2003).

There is indeed rapid growth in "money-making opportunities" for research universities provided by a technologically sophisticated, knowledge-based economy. "Now that scientific discovery and continuing education are valued so highly," writes Bok (2003), "pressures have arisen from every quarter to have universities make their services available to those who need them. State officials ask campuses to speed innovation, job creation and economic growth by cooperating more closely with industry. Businesses urge universities to do more to train their executives and collaborate scientifically in ways that will lead to valuable new products. Citizens everywhere look for courses of study that will help them qualify for better jobs and promising careers. These growing demands allow universities and their faculties to profit from academic work in more ways than ever before."

An entrepreneurial university, therefore, is not just one that actively seeks to innovate how it conducts business. It also undertakes "entrepreneurial activities with the objective of improving regional or national economic performance as well as the university's financial advantage and that of its faculty" (Sam & van der Sijde, 2014).

FUNDING OF EUROPEAN UNIVERSITIES

In a nutshell: the more generous public funding of universities in Europe still does not reach the heights of the total (private + public) funding of tertiary education in the U.S. The average total expenditure for higher education within industrialized countries is 1.7% of GDP, while the U.S. invests a full 2.7% of their GDP into higher education (OECD, 2013). About two-thirds of the total expenditure in the U.S. is private (i.e. personal or family); in Europe, the private, personal and family contribution is only half that. When ranking countries by private expenditure on universities, the U.K. is surprisingly ahead of the United States, and Switzerland is dead last (alongside Luxembourg). The U.S. also dominates expenditure per student, standing a solid 20% over the expected expenditure on OECD's wealthy countries' regression curve. The dominance of U.S. universities in all rankings (especially at the top) is in keeping with this impressive investment.

For OECD countries there has been a slow erosion over time in the share of public funding at the tertiary level. This percentage decreased from 78% in 1995 to 69% in 2007 and, since then, has stabilized at around 70%. After the 2008 economic downturn, U.S. states reportedly slashed their tertiary education appropriations. However, nearly all European countries — though also in recession — maintained or increased their public spending on tertiary education (even Greece). Then later, in 2011, almost half of the 28 countries for which data was available ultimately did reduce their budgets for tertiary and adult education.

It's time for European universities to wake up.

EUROPEAN UNIVERSITY FUNDING: 70% PUBLIC

Reliable comparative numbers for university funding in Europe are not easy to obtain. A 2011 report by the European Commission (De Dominicis et al., 2011) based on 200 European research universities showed that the government continues to be the main funding source for European universities, at 70% of total funding. An investigation by the European Association of Universities with voluntary participation (Estermann & Pruvot, 2011) produced similar numbers, with 72.8% of university income attributable to national and regional funding.

Core Versus Competitive National Public Funding

This public support is further split into two main parts: national core funding and national competitive funding (typical of Research Councils and National Science Foundations). Thus, on average the 70% public national funding is further split into 57% for core funds and 13% for "national competitive funds." When comparing different European practices regarding this split, no clear message emerges. Top universities are found with both high and low proportions of national competitive funds. A preliminary comparison between a few excellent universities shows considerable variation. National core funding makes up 74% of total national public funding at EPFL, and 78% at our sister university ETH. For our friendly competitors, national core funding is 63% (TU Delft) and 55% (TUM) of total national funding.

Core funding — the Swiss way

When the Swiss parliament adopted (at the beginning of this century) "core" funding for federal universities, this global budget was accompanied by a parliament-approved "performance mandate". This budgeting mode was politically driven and "resonated well in a nation characterized by a traditionally strong governmental role in the steering of higher education" (Herbst, 2009). An intermediate body (the ETH Board) was installed between politics and academia, formally charged with controlling implementation. This intermediate body, very different from a "Board of Trustees," is continuously under pressure to micro-manage the implementation of the performance mandate.

Zooming in on a real budget (EPFL)

In 2014, core funding from the federal government amounted to 64.3% of our total expenditure (of around 900 million CHF). A mere 15 years ago, this core funding was at 80%. This implies that, in 2014, 35.7% (or more than 300 million CHF) had to be obtained through competitive research funds, private sponsoring, negotiations with regional governments and public-private partnerships. Internal income (notably student fees and interest from our endowment) makes up one-tenth (3%) of this effort.

The growth over the past 15 years of our budget is due, in good part, to our success in competitive research funding and sponsorships. Securing competitive research funds, both national and international, has contributed most to the growth of our budget. Sadly their often-insufficient overhead "punishes" a successful research university. Sponsoring was not even recognized as a source of funding before 2005; today it constitutes 12.9% of external funding.

If the trend continues, core funding will be below the 50% barrier by 2030, with consequent implications on the governance and autonomy of our university.

FINDING NEW INCOME STREAMS

As said, on average, (continental) European universities still benefit from a solid and comfortable level of public (national) funding, at around 70% of total income. In the U.S., when it became increasingly apparent — in the 1990s — that the share of state support devoted to higher education was not likely to return to 1960s levels, universities aggressively sought other revenues, including higher tuition, increased private fundraising and more aggressive endowment investment strategies (Zumeta et al., 2012).

As we saw above, with slowly declining public support, it may now be wake-up time in Europe. World-class universities (on this, the Russell Group [Russell Group, 2012] and the World Bank agree) do not depend solely on finances for their success. They need 1) a critical mass of talent which includes both faculty and students; 2) favourable governance that allows and encourages autonomy, strategic vision, innovation, efficient resource management and flexibility; and 3) sufficient resources to provide an extensive, comprehensive learning environment and a rich environment for advanced research. This paper concentrates on this last point.

As in the U.S., pressures on public budgets and threats of budget cuts drive the diversification of income, and risk mitigation is a powerful driver for the strategic pursuit of new funding sources. While a definitive and comprehensive view of the different "funding streams" for European universities is still out of reach, both the E.U. Commission and the European University Association have offered first glimpses into these income streams.

In the analysis by the E.U. Commission (Fig. 1, left) (De Dominicis et al., 2011), industry sources represent approximately 6% of total income; 3% comes from the non-profit sector, and 2% are (international) European funds; 19% of these extra-incomes are classified as "other", another indication that university accounting is far from standardized. In the analysis by the E.U.A.

Figure 1: Average distribution of different income streams for European universities. Left: E.U. Commission (JRC). Right: E.U.A.

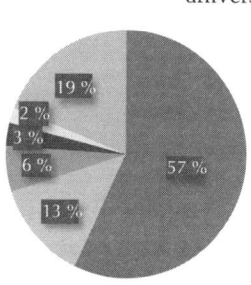
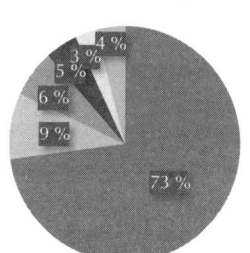

- National Public Core
- National Public Competitive
- Industry
- Non Profit
- EU and Abroad
- Other

- Public Funding (National and Regional)
- Student Contribution
- Funding from contracts with business sector
- Philanthropic funding
- International public funding
- Service-related income

(Fig. 1, right) (Estermann & Pruvot, 2011), 6.5% of total income comes from contracts with the business sector, 4.5% is from philanthropic funding and 3% from European funds. Altogether, philanthropic funding, collaboration with industry, non-national (European) funding and service-related services represent, on average, between 12% to 18% of the total income of European universities.

In the case of EPFL, total national funding (core and competitive) declined from a high of 91.1% of total income in 2000 to 85.2% of total income in 2014, reflecting an increased pressure on national finances. Had national funding remained stable, EPFL would receive 90 million CHF more than it received in 2014. These "missing millions" are covered by revenue from sponsoring, philanthropy and, especially for EPFL, a very successful drive for E.U. funds (after the creation of the E.R.C).

Below is a review of the principal "money-making" streams outside national funding and tuition, as detailed by the E.U.A (Estermann & Pruvot, 2011).

Philanthropy

Philanthropic sources are a potentially vital source of income for universities. Philanthropy is not nearly as well developed in Europe as it is in the U.S. In fact, a recent collection exercise by the E.U.A. showed that only half of the universities in the sample were able to provide reliable data on this income stream (De Dominicis et al., 2011). Philanthropic sources today are typically 3%-4% of university income in Europe. The underdevelopment of philanthropy has cultural roots. For instance, alumni in continental Europe are reportedly reluctant to "pay twice," i.e. to donate to the university after having paid for their education (Estermann & Pruvot, 2011). Also, there is no "culture of asking" from the side of most universities. There are furthermore structural insufficiencies; the capacity to attract philanthropic funding is related to the ability of the institution to found other legal entities (foundations) and build up reserves. Most importantly, philanthropy must be identified as a priority by the university and especially by the university president.

Endowment

Nowhere is the chasm greater between U.S. and E.U. universities than in endowments. In 2014 (NABUCO, 2015) data gathered from 832 U.S. colleges and universities show that these institutions' endowments (totalling **$516 billion** in assets) returned an average of 15.5% for the 2014 fiscal year. On average, annual endowment funds accounted for 9.2% of institutions' total operating budgets. Not only the yearly returns (15%) but also the size of the endowments is impressive.

This mode of fundraising was pioneered in Europe by the University of Cambridge, which raised an impressive £1.2 billion. If philanthropic endowments are to play a bigger role in the future of European universities, a workforce dedicated to operating them will have to exist. Again, the U.K. is leading in Europe (see the Pearce Report, [HEFCE, 2012]). At EPFL, we have likewise set up a Development Office for this purpose.

Charities

Philanthropic funding of research projects and chairs is on the rise. In Europe, these sources now supply, on average, 6.5% of competitive research funding: 3%-4% in most European countries and almost 10% in the United Kingdom (Aebischer, 2012). At EPFL, private sponsorship has tripled, from 3% to 9% of research income over the past 10 years, funding numerous new chairs primarily tenure-track assistant professors. Full-fledged research centres are also made possible through this funding source, as for our Wyss Center for Bio- and Neuro-engineering in Geneva, financed by a single donor.

We have elsewhere (Aebischer, 2012) drawn attention to the risk of philanthropic funding if charities refuse to cover a university's overhead costs. This leads to institutions with many privately funded projects being punished, in a sense, for their success. Universities may drain resources from education to meet the higher costs of research infrastructure. Private bodies should not hijack university resources. They should contribute a fair share to the expenses of a sustained research enterprise. To make it easier for them to do so, universities should better identify the full cost of research activities and share that information. Because most charities operate internationally, these overheads should be aligned worldwide.

Collaboration with Industry

Despite a lot of hoopla regarding the threat of commodification to universities, industrial funding makes up a mere 6%, on average, of the total income of European universities. Interestingly, while corporate support has grown, it still makes up less than 10% of all university research — even in the U.S. (Bok, 2003).

In today's knowledge society, a better connection between universities and industry is profitable for both universities and society. This happens through stronger networking arrangements, collaborative funding of research programs, better exploitation of ideas, professional management of intellectual property and investment in "spin-off" and "start-up" companies (David & Metcalfe, 2007). Technology is a "mixed" good, containing both private and public elements. This "mixed good" model (Baycan & Stough, 2013) holds great potential to better serve society through a knowledge transfer system that encourages interactions between universities and industry. Thus, the "public good" model is not dying. We are witnessing a gradual convergence between academic and commercial culture toward "open science" and "open innovation."

From the perspective of universities, engaging in knowledge commercialization activities is more than a money-making scheme. It also gives access to jobs for students and Ph.D.s, adds inspiration for researchers and leads to new ideas (PriceWaterhouseCooper, 2007, cited in Baycan & Stough, 2013).

Tech-transfer and revenue from patents

Science lore has it that the two U.S. Nobelists who invented DNA sequencing (Herbert Boyer and Stanley Cohen) patented their work, thereby making Stanford and UCSF rich(er), while the two European Nobelists who discovered monoclonal antibody-producing hybridoma cells (Cesar Milstein and Georg Kohler) did not.

In fact, European countries were quick to adopt legislation akin to the U.S. Bayh-Dole Act, and, as in the U.S., a financial windfall from patents does not (or rarely) occur. EPFL, like many other universities, is increasingly successful with patenting and licensing; however, financial returns are unconnected. The fact that these discoveries have led to the creation of numerous start-ups (250 to date) is far more precious and valuable for society, and the regional impact, in direct and indirect employment, is substantial. Interestingly, the higher economic impact of the United Kingdom's entrepreneurial universities is also explained by entrepreneurial spin-offs, rather than revenue from patents (Russell Group, 2012).

Attracting Companies

Another important consequence of industry collaboration is that it attracts existing companies to campus to build sustainable partnerships. The U.K., in particular, has been highly successful with attracting commercial investment in research and development (R&D) from overseas (Stromquist, 2007). Inviting bigger companies — especially international ones — to campus has been an ongoing and, thus far, successful strategy at EPFL. While direct financial benefits for the university are modest, over the long term the economic impact on the region and jobs for graduates pays off handsomely through a renewed interest of government and parliament for universities. World-class universities are able to form high-tech innovation clusters of knowledge-intensive activity. R&D companies and venture-backed companies tend to settle near top universities, and research-intensive universities are one of the main driving forces behind the development of high-tech clusters (Russell Group, 2012).

Service-related income

Revenue generating services comprise the management of conference facilities, catering and accommodation (including student residences). In Europe, some universities do generate revenue from these services, but in general institutions seek to cover running and lifecycle costs of these services. In other words, making a profit is not the primary aim. This is the case at EPFL, where student residences, hotels and a conference centre were built by the university in a public-private partnership (rent-to-own scheme), without government aid or investment — a first in Switzerland.

International Public (EU) Funding

This income stream makes up, on average, less than 2% of the total revenue of European universities. However, some schools that are firmly integrated into the European Research Area, such as EPFL, score very highly in European research funding. We recommend the vigorous and sustainable development of ERC-type funding, which gives a unique and competitive playing field for all universities. Coverage of total cost is a point of contention, since insufficient coverage of indirect costs punishes successful universities.

In addition to such a funding scheme that favours the best universities, networks of universities could be sustained through a healthy use of structural funds (as with, for example, the Teaming partnerships in Horizon 2020).

ERC-grant successes delineate European hot-spots for leading universities. Paris, London, Munich, Cambridge, Oxford, Zurich, Barcelona, Amsterdam, Lausanne and Madrid comprise the top ten (European Research Council, 2015).

Extension Schools and MOOCs

At a previous conference, we pledged the rebirth of world-class European universities through MOOCs (Aebischer & Escher, 2013): "If we play our strengths right and engage the IT revolution cleverly, European world-class universities will once again be among the best." Two years later we now know that, unlike the perspective of American universities, we do not have to think of MOOCs primarily as a cost-saving teaching technology. MOOCs per se seem irrelevant in a discussion about diversification of income streams. However, we also know that most of our MOOC students already have university degrees and are using MOOCs for professional development; they also wish to be certified (see e.g. Escher et al., 2014). This creates an opportunity for a new financial stream. How important that stream will become remains to be seen.

Reduce Costs?

We have focused our discussion on additional financial income for European universities and have said nothing about reducing costs and improving productivity. As long as our customers — i.e. students — are not a decisive financial resource, raising completion rates and lowering time-to-degree, while highly commendable, will not bear significant financial impacts. Generally, efficiency is not a helpful guide in discussing the financial set-up of great universities. As one president of Harvard used to say: "To encourage real creativity, you need to have a good deal of slack" (Bok, 2003). Interestingly, our cursory analysis of some great universities in Europe shows that the cost per student at a great university is around $80,000 per year (and roughly $100,000 at Harvard), regardless of the underlying financial streams or conditions. Thus, we know the cost of necessary "slack".

CONCLUSION ON DIVERSIFICATION

World-class universities require adequate investments for teaching and research from a broad range of sources (Russell Group, 2012), and research-intensive universities draw on a complex mix of public and private income sources. All these funding streams — endowments, charitable income, business partnerships, expansion of international activities, income from international (extra-European) students — offer crucial funding opportunities. However, ultimately our great universities owe their success and financial stability to public support. Moreover, public support will remain high given the societal relevance of universities, as politicians and the public understand that the knowledge economy requires top-flight research and world-class universities.

Cities that are lucky enough to host great European universities will increasingly be inclined to contribute to these lively campuses and the substantial economic impact they produce.

REFERENCES

Aebischer, P. (2012). "Philanthropy: The price of charity". *Nature*, *481*(7381), 260-260. doi: 10.1038/481260a

Aebischer P. & Escher G. (2013). "Can the IT revolution lead to a rebirth of world-class European universities?" In: *Preparing Universities for an Era of Change*, Weber, L. & Duderstadt, J. (Eds), *Economica*, pp. 87-99.

Baycan, T. & Stough, R. R. (2013). "Bridging knowledge to commercialization: The good, the bad, and the challenging." *Annals of Regional Science*, *50*(2), pp. 367-405. doi: 10.1007/s00168-012-0510-8

Bok, D. (2003). Universities in the Marketplace: The Commercialization of Higher Education. Princeton University Press.

Bowen, W. (2013). *Higher Education in the Digital Age*. Princeton University Press.

Collini, S. (2013). "Sold out". *London Review of Books*, *35*(20), pp. 3-12. doi: 10.1016/S0026-0657(03)01109-3

David, P. & Metcalfe, S. (2007). Knowledge Economists' Policy Brief n° 2. "Universities must contribute to enhancing Europe 's innovative performance". *Technology*, (October), pp. 2-6.

De Dominicis, L., Pérez, S. E. & Fernández-Zubieta, A. (2011). *European university funding and financial autonomy*. doi: 10.2791/55199

Escher, G., Noukakis D. & Aebischer P. (2014). "Boosting Higher Education in Africa through Shared Massive Open Online Courses (MOOCs)" in *Education, Learning, Training: Critical Issues for Development*, International Development Policy series No. 5, Geneva: Graduate Institute Publications, Brill-Nijhoff. Boston; pp. 195-214.

Estermann, T., & Pruvot, E. B. (2011). Financially Sustainable Universities II European universities diversifying income streams. EUA.

European Commission. (2008). "Knowledge for Growth" Report.

European Commission/EACEA/Eurydice. (2013). Funding of Education in Europe 2000-2012: The Impact of the Economic Crisis. doi: 10.2797/50340

European Research Council. (2015). Annual Report on the ERC activities and achievements in 2014. doi: 10.2828/18398

HEFCE (2012). "Review of philanthropy in UK higher education: 2012 status report and challenges for the next decade". ("The Pearce Report"). Report to HEFCE by More Partnership, September 2012.

Herbst, M. (2009). Financing public universities — the case of performance funding. Springer.

Kerr, C. (2001). *The Uses of the University*, 5th edition. Harvard University Press. Cambridge.

NABUCO. (2015). 2014 NACUBO-Commonfund Study of Endowments (Final Data).

OECD. (2013). Education at a glance.

Otani, A. (2015). "Ten Elite Schools Where Middle-Class Kids Don't Pay Tuition". *BloombergBusiness*, (April 1), 63-66. doi: http://www.bloomberg.com/news/articles/2015-04-01/ten-elite-schools-where-middle-class-kids-don-t-pay-tuition

PriceWaterhouseCooper. (2007). Schretlen, J.-H., Dervojeda, K., Warmenhoven, B. "Staying in control while unlocking the knowledge", The Hague.

Russell Group. (2012). Jewels in the crown: The importance and characteristics of the UK's world-class universities, (4), 52.

Sam, C., & van der Sijde, P. (2014). Understanding the concept of the entrepreneurial university from the perspective of higher education models. *Higher Education*, 891-908. doi: 10.1007/s10734-014-9750-0

Stromquist, N. P. (2007). Internationalization as a response to globalization: Radical shifts in university environments. *Higher Education*, 53(1), 81-105. doi: 10.1007/s10734-005-1975-5

The Economist. (2015). The world is going to university. *The Economist* Newspaper Limited, March 28, 2015.

Wildavsky, B. (2012). The Great Brain Race: How Global Universities Are Reshaping the World. Princeton University Press.

Zumeta, W., Breneman, D., Callan, P. & Finney, J. (2012). *Financing American Higher Education in the Era of Globalization*. Harvard Education Press, Cambridge.

CHAPTER 12

The Importance of Philanthropy

Leszek Borysiewicz

INTRODUCTION

The research universities represented by the Glion Colloquium have been responsible for many of the greatest discoveries and intellectual breakthroughs in history. I am proud to lead one of these universities. For the last 800 years in Cambridge, new discoveries have been forged to transform the way we live and understand our world. Yesterday's discoveries here — gravity, evolution, DNA — are the foundations for our current understanding of the world. And today, thousands of world-class researchers at Cambridge are seeking equally transformative answers to the greatest challenges now facing mankind.

My responsibility as Vice-Chancellor — and the responsibility of all university leaders — is to create an environment that enables this research to thrive. But, as the world has changed, so too has the environment in which we operate. In this paper, I argue that philanthropy, while always important, is now vital if we are to secure the future of research universities and fulfil our critical mission in society.

The heritage of philanthropy is everywhere in Cambridge. And it is not just in the physical spaces, the Colleges, museums and libraries where our academics and students work. Our earliest recorded donation was in 1284, when the University's scholars accepted a gift of 50 marks from King Edward I for the support of poor students. Today more than £10 million a year is available for student scholarships, bursaries, travel and other costs, including support for disadvantaged students.

Gifts such as these, both large and small, help sustain the fabric of the university, its teaching and research to this day. With such a heritage, why should we be concerned? I believe there are three key reasons, which I would like to explore in this paper.

The first is that philanthropy is the vital seed investment in intellectual breakthroughs and innovation. Public finances are increasingly burdened with debt, low growth and ageing populations, as well as the limiting factor of the political cycle. Yet research universities need the freedom to take the long-term view. As the issues facing humanity grow ever more complex and interconnected, a bolder approach is needed — one that encourages curiosity, promotes new thinking and accepts, or even encourages, failure. Such an approach requires funders who can afford to engage in a relationship driven less by financial calculations or time pressures, and more by a shared sense of purpose. Where else, then, is this investment in the transformative change our society needs going to come from? Philanthropy allows universities the freedom to engage in the sustained pursuit of applied intellectual curiosity.

The second is that we are learning from our success and building on momentum. Institutions in the United States have a long tradition of raising funds from alumni and major donors. Cambridge and Oxford have pioneered philanthropic fund raising in the U.K., and can point to numerous examples where academics supported by philanthropy have achieved major discoveries. Often these successes have been unpredictable: an initial idea or project had looked promising, but led to a breakthrough elsewhere. The critical element has been the relationship and trust between academics and donors: a shared sense of purpose and discovery that has led to a sustained relationship over many years.

The final reason that philanthropy must be taken more seriously is that it is hard to do. It involves not just seeking funds and building fundraising teams. It involves creating a new culture, developing new capabilities and perspectives across institutions that have been focused, understandably, on national and public sources of funds. It involves a change in approach from transaction to partnership. And it requires a commitment to demonstrate — both internally and externally — the value of philanthropy. All of these challenges are difficult for institutions rightly focused on teaching and research, and with cultures established over decades or even centuries. Yet, in a world where global competition for talent is ever fiercer, forging these new skills has never been more vital.

THE ENABLING POWER OF PHILANTHROPY

Prominent benefactors founded and funded the Colleges of Oxford and Cambridge, and our buildings, students and faculties are still supported by their legacy. Public subscription helped to establish the great civic universities of 20th-century Britain and charitable trusts have funded some of the most far-reaching innovations to emerge from academia.

That tradition continues today. At the heart of Cambridge, the University is building a new Conservation Campus, bringing together researchers, leading conservation organizations and the Museum of Zoology. In an exciting, innovative and green building, only made possible by the support and belief of donors, the Cambridge Conservation Initiative (CCI) will house over 500 academics, practitioners and students from the University and its CCI partner organizations.

And new treatments for diseases such as Alzheimer's and Parkinson's are one step closer thanks to philanthropists who have supported research in Cambridge to pinpoint the trigger for dementia-related diseases, opening up possibilities for earlier diagnosis and a new generation of targeted drugs.

A university must maintain a diversity of funding sources if it is not to be beholden to any single stakeholder — whether central government, funding councils, industry or alumni. Philanthropic donation can be a potent guarantor of that autonomy.

Autonomy is important at two levels: for individual researchers, who must have the freedom to follow their intellectual curiosity, unfettered by political or commercial considerations and for the institution itself as an independent intellectual authority.

This freedom is to be valued not for its own sake, but because it permits the university to fulfil its mission to society and take a disinterested, long-term perspective. A short-term, utilitarian and instrumentalist approach cannot resolve the great global challenges that face us today. We can direct our resources to the best of our ability, but we cannot predict where and how the great breakthroughs will be made. And wherever there is a lack of financial stability and predictability, a university's autonomy is inevitably compromised, affecting its ability to pursue this approach.

In the 1970s, researchers at the University of Cambridge discovered monoclonal antibodies and set to work on adapting them to medical use. In the past two years, this research reached fruition with two new drugs receiving regulatory approval: Alemtuzumab, a treatment for multiple sclerosis, and the anti-cancer agent Lynparza.

I believe it is worth restating two points that I made at the conference on "Global Universities and their Regional Impact" earlier this year, marking the University of Vienna's 650th anniversary. Firstly, these timescales do not fit into government-backed or commercial timescales; but it is incontestable that the investment of time, money and trust in these research teams has made a valuable contribution to society. Secondly, it is often the cumulative effect of fundamental research that produces such breakthroughs: the ongoing development of new knowledge and insight, which is not easily quantifiable and does not fit into funding cycles.

Research universities are unique in their ability to take this approach. Given the imperatives of the market, very few private-sector enterprises have the ability to look decades into the future. Likewise, the long-term planning of governments is always limited by shorter-term political expediencies. Universities have the responsibility to look further ahead; it is the only way that they can find solutions to the most important societal challenges.

However, it is the case at the University of Cambridge, as it is elsewhere, that resources are insufficient without philanthropy: the money received for research does not cover its full cost. If the University's research program is to be expanded — something the University has identified as an imperative — this deficit can only increase. Put simply, philanthropy produces discoveries that would not otherwise be made.

I could cite many more examples, all of equal merit. There is the Wellcome Trust Centre for Stem Cell Research, where human stem cells are used to create new models of disease which, in turn, permit the development of new drugs. Private donors have supplied it with funding for fellowships, studentships, capital projects and equipment. Then there is the Centre of Governance and Human Rights, a cross-disciplinary research hub. It brings together expertise in a vast array of disciplines, from international studies and politics to law, computer science and geography, to tackle the big questions of global justice and good governance. Without a generous benefaction, it would not exist. The list goes on, and not just at the University of Cambridge.

Yet it is not only in supporting transformational research that philanthropy adds value. As the Pearce Report of 2012 (HEFCE, 2012b) said: "Philanthropic investment is not an alien intrusion to the campus... but an organic part of achieving institutional clarity and of building effective relationships and partnerships."

The support of donors can be a progressive force: through bursaries and scholarships, it can enable students who would not otherwise be able to attend university to benefit from the life-changing power of higher education. Each year the Cambridge Bursary Scheme spends around £6 million on means-tested bursaries. And it enables outreach activities to take place, carrying the name of the university into society at large, and bringing in those who will benefit most from it. A donation from a former student has allowed the University of Cambridge and its Colleges to work with state schools and colleges around the U.K. to encourage more academically-able students to make competitive applications to top universities.

Where else are universities to find the funds for such far-reaching aims? Public finances are increasingly burdened with debt, low growth and the implications of an ageing population. Austerity remains the main bill of fare across Europe, despite efforts to soften the blow. Efforts to boost Europe's economies are focused on areas such as jobs, health and infrastructure — not higher education. Yet, even if they were, it would not replace philanthropy. As the League of European Research Universities (LERU) said last year: "Philanthropy is not, and never should be, a substitute for public funding. It could, however, be the crucial key to unlocking every last drop of potential from our research-intensive universities." (LERU, 2014)

BUILDING MOMENTUM

Across different parts of the world, there are vast differences in levels of philanthropy to the university sector. The culture of philanthropic giving in the United States continues to be held up as the gold standard, and justifiably so. The majority of universities in the United States have been able to rely upon a significant income from private donation. Many started taking fundraising activities seriously in the 1970s and 1980s; in some cases, sophisticated operations had been inaugurated decades earlier. Until recently, no similar apparatus had been developed in United Kingdom. Philanthropy benefited only a small number of well-known universities, and the number of benefactors was small. (HEFCE, 2014)

For the most part, there is a similarly underdeveloped culture of giving to universities across other European nations. A recent study of philanthropy across universities in the European Union made the bald assessment that "philanthropic fundraising is not, on the whole, taken seriously in European universities. Only a very small number of institutions are raising significant sums of money from this source, and even fewer are accessing philanthropic funding to pay for research and research-related activities." (EC, 2011)

One reason for the difference in the culture of giving to universities in the U.S. and U.K. is that giving in Europe is historically focused on charitable causes. The U.K. population has a long history of giving to charitable causes and over half the U.K. population gives to charity each year. Yet, only 1.2% of U.K. alumni currently give to their university compared to ~10% of U.S. public universities (HEFCE, 2012b).

There is much ground to make up — even though the overall participation rate of charitable giving in the U.K. places it fourth in the world, ahead of the U.S.'s ninth position (Charities Aid Foundation, 2014a), there is clearly a huge potential for growth in European university philanthropy. We need to engage supporters and convey the understanding of the charitable impact that universities deliver.

British universities are now in a transitional stage with regard to building philanthropy. In the U.K., the government first made a serious and welcome attempt to engage with the issue of university philanthropy by commissioning the Thomas Report in 2004. This took as its starting point that universities function best when given increased control over their own destiny.

Indeed, figures from the past decade suggest that the level of financial support from benefactors to universities is gathering upward momentum in the U.K. There have been a number of major fundraising campaigns in Britain since the beginning of the 21st century — two of which have become the first outside the U.S. to pass the £1billion mark in income received. Universities remain by far the most popular beneficiaries of large donations, accounting for 64% of the total value gifted in £1 million-plus donations during 2013 (Coutts, 2014). What's more, the most recent data from the annual Ross-CASE Survey — the most reliable indicator of philanthropy in British universities — showed total funds received in 2013-14 rose significantly to £807 million, exceeding the previous highest comparable total of £753 million in 2011-12.

There is still very large variation in income from philanthropy between different higher-education establishments. This is one thing that differentiates the U.K. and European picture from that of North America, where disparities exist, but almost all universities can rely upon at least some income from philanthropy. Within the U.K., the largest and most established universities continue to attract by far the greatest amount of philanthropic funding. In the latest figures, Oxford and Cambridge accounted for 40% of new funds secured in 2013-14; and other members of the Russell Group of research-intensive universities (excluding Oxford and Cambridge) received the next 38%.

This has led some commentators to cite a "Matthew effect" after the Biblical quote that "to all those who have, more will be given" (Matthew 25: 29). But, while it is true that elite U.K. universities currently receive far greater funds (as do universities carrying out medical or related research), scrutiny of the trends suggests that all higher-education institutions can benefit from investment in philanthropy. The Pearce Report noted that a number of universities formed after 1992 had achieved impressive results with imaginative and well-run development programs. The spread of large donations is also encouragingly diverse. A total of 53 universities received seven-figure gifts in 2013-4, and 16 higher-education institutions received eight-figure sums. (Ross-CASE, 2014)

Despite minor fluctuations, the headline figures and trends for giving in the U.K. are encouraging. If momentum is maintained, the rewards for universities could be rich indeed. If the growth trajectory of giving is maintained until 2022, there is potential to reach a total of £2 billion per annum. (HEFCE, 2012b)

Major campaigns have proved an extremely effective construct to generate enthusiasm, build momentum and create urgency. They have been embedded in the North American higher education landscape for generations. More recently, a significant number of universities in the U.K., mainland Europe and Australia have launched their own U.S.-style campaigns.

This mode of fundraising was pioneered in Europe by the University of Cambridge's 800th Anniversary Campaign, *Transforming Tomorrow*, which reached completion in 2011 after 10 years. A total of £1.2 billion was raised for the University and its constituent Colleges, and this marked the first time a university outside the United States had managed to pass the £1 billion mark.

The success of this campaign was not measured merely in the amount of money raised, but in opening our eyes to the enabling power of philanthropy. At the campaign's conclusion, more than 30 professorships had been supported by donations, and the value of the University's endowment was 35% higher in 2011 than it would otherwise have been. In addition, donations contributed around a third of the cost of major building projects at the University during the campaign's lifetime — a total of £225 million. Contributions to the University endowment reached £241 million.

This campaign demonstrated that if we engaged with philanthropy in a sustained and professional manner, we were able to achieve far more than we had previously imagined. With the benefit of this experience, we were able to set even greater targets for ourselves academically and philanthropically. Since the close of the campaign, we have continued to invest in building our philanthropic apparatus and maintain philanthropic support at an elevated level.

A raft of further high-profile programs with ambitious financial goals have been seen in recent years. Launched in 2008, the *Oxford Thinking* campaign at the University of Oxford became the second in the U.K. to pass the £1 billion figure in 2010-11 and is now aiming at a sum of £3 billion. Like the Cambridge appeal, it makes available opportunities at all levels of giving. While student support, academic posts and programs, and buildings and infrastructure have been identified as priorities for fundraising, *Oxford Thinking* also facilitates giving for donors who would prefer to see their money spent on specific College prizes, scholarships or bursaries.

In passing, it is worth noting that a hallmark of the most promising recent campaigns is that their branding is very much results-oriented, demonstrating the difference that universities — and thus their donors — can make in the wider world, as well as on campus. King's College London, for example, has branded its £600 million campaign *World Questions, King's Answers*; the University of Leeds has *Making a World of Difference*; and Sussex has *Making the Future*. The aims of the campaign and the desired impacts are clearly stated. Alumni and others are invited literally to buy into the university's mission. It represents a significant move onward from the model of simply instituting an opaque "annual fund" and expecting donors to contribute on the basis that the university knows best what to do with their money.

But what speaks most strongly of a nascent cultural change in philanthropy outside North America is the number of higher-education institutions mounting their first-ever campaigns, notably including some of the longest-established universities. Though founded in 1850, the University of Sydney had not run a major fundraising initiative until it inaugurated INSPIRED in 2008, with the aim of securing A$600 million (£310 million) from 50,000 supporters. In the same year, France's École Polytechnique — established during the French Revolution in 1794 — launched its own campaign. Its target figure is €35 million (£25.3 million) which it plans to raise exclusively from alumni. (Jackson, 2014)

TAKING PHILANTHROPY SERIOUSLY

What successful initiatives have in common is clear goals — and a well-defined statement of what the funding will be used to support — as well as a gearing up of investment and a corresponding increase in development activity for the duration of the campaign.

But fundraising needs to be sustained, consistent and oriented to the long term if it is to maintain momentum, to continue to engage existing donors and to succeed in enlisting new ones. This not only requires appropriate investment but also, as the European Commission's 2011 report made clear, it requires a cultural readiness among senior academic leaders and other research staff to commit time and effort to fundraising efforts.

Philanthropy can be encouraged by the removal of fiscal and regulatory barriers to universities accepting donations, as well as encouraging matched funding schemes. For example, HEFCE's matched-funding scheme, which operated for three years from August 2008, made available £148 million in Government funding to match philanthropic donations to English universities. (HEFCE, 2012a)

And universities that have success at fundraising recognize the importance of — and provide long-term resources to — fundraising, alumni relations and communications teams.

Yet such practical changes can only be the first steps to success in philanthropy. Success can only come from a university-wide culture that involves senior leadership, academics and administrators. As LERU's paper says: "Successful fundraising is nearly always the result of collaboration."

Potential benefactors want close contact with those leading the projects they support. And they want to feel part of the community of enquiry they are fostering, accompanying researchers in the trials as well as the successes of discovery.

There may be some resistance from those who believe that a *cordon sanitaire* must be maintained between research and the outside world. But this approach is not only outmoded, it is unrealistic in an academic world where grant applications, administration and audits already absorb vast amounts of time and collaboration between different partners.

Philanthropy is a partnership. It is built on sustained and sustainable relationships. Take, for example, Sir James Dyson, who began by supporting research students at one of our Colleges — but then became inspired by the cutting edge science in the Department of Engineering. He established a professorship and research programs. Seeing the impact of this philanthropy and how effectively these donations were used by the University to leverage more funding and attract the best minds, he has made a further investment in Cambridge to put up a new Engineering Building.

It is worth returning again to the Pearce Report, and an affirmation of the value of philanthropy that is not easily bettered in its incisiveness: "At its best, philanthropic support not only adds financial resources to an institution, but also brings the intellectual and emotional engagement of the donor. Philanthropists are attracted by innovation, excellence and energy; their gifts also help to drive these qualities… It is notable how often interactions between donors and the projects, academics and students they support generate optimism and enthusiasm. This is a virtuous circle." (HEFCE, 2012b)

In the U.K. and Europe, it is not simply a case of emulating the successful model of North American universities. The European Commission report coined the phrase "accumulative advantage" to explain the need to build on pre-existing fundraising performance, as well as the cultural and practical realities of what a university is, what it does and where it is located.

"Accumulative advantages accrue more easily to some institutions than others — such as those that have had centuries to develop links with donors, and that have long-standing reputations for excellence — but it is not true, or helpful, to view accumulative advantage as a structural force over which an institution has no control. The task is to find ways to create and grow such advantages for themselves." (European Commission, 2011)

The Pearce Report also offers valuable guidance to universities in the practicalities of implementing an effective development operation (HEFCE, 2012b; HEFCE 2014; Universities U.K., 2014). But models may vary from country to country, and institution to institution.

What is not optional is the drive to harness the power of philanthropy for the good of the higher education sector. We must take philanthropy seriously. Cambridge's mission statement is succinct. It is "to contribute to society through the pursuit of education, learning, and research at the highest international levels of excellence." Such a mission — which is our charitable purpose — cannot be achieved without philanthropy.

CONCLUSION

In conclusion, research universities can take encouragement from the success of Cambridge and similar institutions in attracting funding on a scale unprecedented outside North America. But every type of higher education establishment can — and indeed should — seek philanthropic support for its activities.

Philanthropy is the critical element that enables ongoing academic autonomy and long-term research. It is the keystone of alumni relations, and the driving force behind the recruitment of new stakeholders into the mission of the university. It is the catalyst for discovery at a time of unparalleled financial challenge.

Moreover, philanthropic support has a value beyond the financial. The association between donor and university is a two-way partnership, benefiting both. It gives donors an active role in the mission of the university to serve society and a presence in discovery, education and intellectual progress. It grants alumni the opportunity to engage with their *alma mater*, share in its ambitions and profit from a lifelong association. It binds the university into wider society, and prevents academic communities from becoming insular and self-regarding by demanding that they clearly explain the nature and value of their work. Enabling philanthropy is not just a bonus. It is an obligation for universities if they are to fulfil their mission.

REFERENCES

1994 Group (2010). "Developing the Future: Successful university fundraising that enables philanthropy to grow." November 2010.

Beney, Adrian (2014). "Ross-CASE Survey 2012-13: Reading between the data" More Partnership, 16 May 2014. http://www.morepartnership.com/blog/ross-case-survey-2012-slash-13-reading-between-the-data

Cabinet Office and Paymaster General (2011). "Giving White Paper", May 2011.

CASE (2014). "Enhancing Fundraising Practices of the University of California, California State University and California Private Universities". (Prepared by Kent J Karsevar) February 2014.

Charities Aid Foundation (2014a). "World Giving Index".

Charities Aid Foundation (2014b). "Philanthropy: A Gift or Investment?"

Charities Aid Foundation (2015). "UK Giving 2014".

Coutts (2014). "Million Pound Donors Report". http://philanthropy.coutts.com/en/reports/2014/united-kingdom/findings.html

DfES (2004). "Increasing voluntary giving to higher education: Task Force report to Government". ("The Thomas Report"). May 2004.

European Commission (EC) (2011). "Giving in evidence: fundraising from philanthropy in European universities".

Fitzpatrick, Dan (2014). "Harvard endowment earns 15.4% return for fiscal 2014". *Wall Street Journal*, 23 September 2014. http://www.wsj.com/articles/harvard-endowment-earns-15-4-return-for-fiscal-2014-1411506002

Havergal, Chris (2014). "Overall value of big donations to universities falls", *Times Higher Education*, November 3, 2014. http://www.timeshighereducation.co.uk/news/overall-value-of-big-donations-to-universities-falls/2016756.article

HEFCE (2012a). "Matched funding scheme for voluntary giving: 2008-2011 outcomes". Circular letter from HEFCE to vice-chancellors/senior management, 6 June 2012. http://www.hefce.ac.uk/media/hefce/content/pubs/2012/CL,201214/Matched%20funding%20outcomes.pdf

HEFCE (2012b). "Review of philanthropy in UK higher education: 2012 status report and challenges for the next decade". ("The Pearce Report"). Report to HEFCE by More Partnership, September 2012.

HEFCE (2014). "An emerging profession: the higher education philanthropy workforce". Report to HEFCE by More Partnership and Richmond Associates, April 2014.

Hunter, Kate (2013). "Philanthropic giving to UK universities: a case of onwards and upwards". *The Guardian*, 16 April 2013.

Jackson, Nancy Mann (2014). "Everything you need to know about campaigns". *CURRENTS*, November/December 2014. http://www.case.org/Publications_and_Products/2014/NovemberDecember_2014/Everything_You_Need_to_Know_About_Campaigns.html

Jervis, Joe (2012). "15 tips to increase charitable giving in higher education". *The Guardian*, 27 April 2012. http://www.theguardian.com/higher-education-network/blog/2012/apr/27/15-tips-charitable-giving-higher-education

League of European Research Universities (LERU) (2014). "Philanthropy at research-intensive universities," June 2014. http://www.leru.org/files/publications/LERU_note_Philanthropy_at_research-intensive_universities.pdf

Motion, Joanna (2010). "What UK universities can do to win million pound donations." *The Guardian*, 22 November 2010. http://www.theguardian.com/education/2010/nov/22/universities-fundraising-philanthropy-donations

Motion, Joanna (2013). "Ross-CASE is out! So what does the data really tell us?" More Partnership, 16 April 2013. http://www.morepartnership.com/blog/ross-case-survey-deconstructed

Motion, Joanna (2014). "Make it appealing". (Originally in *Research Fortnight*). More Partnership/Richmond Associates, 9 May 2014. http://www.morepartnership.com/blog/make-it-appealing

Ross-CASE (2014). "Giving to Excellence: Generating Philanthropic Support for UK Higher Education 2012-13. Ross-CASE Survey Report". NatCen, May 2014.

Universities U.K. (2014). "Strategic Fundraising". (Professor Sir Christopher Snowden).

Young-Powell, Abby & Allen, Michael (2014) "Universities receive record number of donations". *The Guardian*, 16 May 2014. http://www.theguardian.com/higher-education-network/2014/may/16/universities-receive-record-number-donations-fall-total-new-funds

CHAPTER

Converging Paths: Public and Private Research Universities in the 21st Century

Ronald J. Daniels and Phillip Spector[1]

INTRODUCTION

The American research university has been celebrated as "the greatest system of knowledge production and higher learning that the world has ever known" (Cole, 2009). As measured by any number of factors — international rankings, Nobel Laureates, publications in peer review journals, or impact on industrial innovation — the American research university has had a disproportionate impact on national and international welfare. The success of the American research university has led other countries, with varying degrees of success, to emulate the model.

Jonathan Cole, one of the leading experts on the American research university, has traced its preeminence to several factors, including its singular fusion of research, education and service; the premium it places on free inquiry and discovery; and the high levels of research funding that the federal government provides to faculty on a competitive and meritocratic basis (Cole, 2009). But surely another distinctive feature that explains the success

---

1. We would like to thank Michelle Crosby-Nagy and Ki Hoon Hur for their research contributions, and Robert J. Birgeneau, Robert M. Berdahl, Jonathan R. Cole, Mary Sue Coleman, Nicholas B. Dirks, James Duderstadt, Edward Iacobucci, Donald Kettl, Hunter Rawlings, Morton Schapiro, Mark S. Schlissel, Shirley M. Tilghman, George Triantis and Michael Trebilcock for helpful comments on earlier drafts.

of the American research university is its institutional heterogeneity. Unlike in most OECD nations, where state-owned research universities have constituted the dominant (although not exclusive) organizational structure, the U.S. system is more diverse, with private and public universities populating the landscape. This diversity in organizational forms undoubtedly has helped to fuel the innovative and responsive character of the American system.

However, as many have observed, America's public research universities now find themselves under enormous strain. Far and away the principal source of this stress has been a substantial withdrawal of state financial support. Between 2008 and 2013, state support for public higher education per student declined by 26.3% in constant dollars at the median public research university (AAAS, 2015a). Public research universities have responded by raising tuition, identifying alternate sources of revenue, and contracting educational programs and support services. And these responses have taken a predictable toll on the mission and the standing of the public university. For instance, there were eight public universities ranked in the top 25 in the U.S. News and World Report Rankings in the late 1980s, but today there are only two. The events of recent years have led a wide range of commentators to lament the privatization of public higher education in the United States, and to question whether — and how — the American public university can survive in its present form (Duderstadt, 2011; Lyall & Sell, 2006; Priest & St. John, 2006).

Although the privatization of the public university is a much discussed phenomenon, less appreciated is the opposite but equally significant trend in the United States — the "publicization" of private universities. In response to a variety of external forces, American private research universities have come to take on many new roles and responsibilities long associated with the mission of public research universities: enhanced socioeconomic diversity, local social policy goals, regional industrial policy, and, most recently, mass online education. Taken together, the privatization of the public research university and the publicization of the private research university suggest a marked convergence of these institutions. Indeed, we argue that there is now ample evidence of movement toward a single model of higher education in the United States that blends elements of two previously distinct institutions: a model that one might call the public-regarding private ("PRP").

The convergence among public and private research universities has been driven by a confluence of forces that exert a powerful effect on the competitive landscape of American higher education. These include: the expansion of the federal role in funding universities, the emergence of the innovation economy, the rise of third-party intermediaries that monitor university performance, and, finally, shifting societal expectations respecting the role and responsibilities of elite institutions. These forces have contributed to the integration of the distinct markets in which public and private research universities have traditionally operated. Significantly, as markets have integrated, the level of competition between public and private universities for faculty, students and research dollars has increased.

But, while private research universities governed by not-for-profit stakeholder boards have been able to respond to these forces with relative ease, the same cannot be said of public research universities. Over the last decade, public research universities have confronted significant opposition to their efforts to preserve and enhance their academic mission in the face of dwindling financial resources and growing competition. In extreme cases, public research universities have been embroiled in wrenching and destructive governance conflicts that have pitted university boards aligned with state political overseers against university leaders. They have also been forced to contend with obtrusive and anachronistic bureaucratic regimes that have impaired their ability to adapt to emerging challenges.

Given the number of areas in which private non-profit research universities have shown themselves to be capable of vindicating public goals and interests with a much less burdensome governance model, the question for policy-makers is whether they are capable of conferring greater scope on public research universities to adopt aspects of the governance and regulatory regime adopted by private universities, which would enhance their capacity to compete on a more level playing field with privates. We will focus our attention on the public and private research universities that are members of the Association of American Universities (AAU), as the convergence has been the greatest among these institutions, and as the AAU publics are in the strongest financial position to persevere through forward-leaning structural reforms.

DEFINING THE PUBLIC OR PRIVATE UNIVERSITY

Although public and private universities are often discussed in the popular press, they are rarely defined. What does it mean precisely for a university to be public or private in the United States, especially as those lines have increasingly blurred? Although the precise nature and purpose of the public and private university have changed over time, one can point at the same time to a distinct set of *structures* and *missions* that define the public university. We will consider both categories of traits, as we chart the convergence of public and private research universities in this Chapter.

Structure

We start with the defining structural features that traditionally have distinguished the public university from the private not-for-profit university in the

United States. Robert Lowry has identified four such features, which we summarize briefly below (Lowry, 2009):

Ownership. The assets of a public university are owned by a state agency or publicly chartered corporation. By contrast, the private not-for-profit university is a private corporation, which owns all of its land and buildings.

Funding. Public and private research universities alike rely on revenue from a range of sources, including tuition dollars, philanthropy, federal research funding and state and local government. What distinguishes public and private universities is the mix of these categories, with public research universities having received a larger percentage of their funding from state and local sources, and private research universities relying to a greater degree over the years on private philanthropy, tuition, and auxiliary enterprises (Delta Cost Project).

Discretion. Public research universities traditionally are subject to a comprehensive system of state laws and regulations that specifically shape its conduct, as well as an array of other restrictions that apply to all state entities, such as freedom of information or sunshine laws and procurement rules. By contrast, the private university usually operates under laws of general applicability.

Governance. Public and private universities can also be distinguished in the design of their governing boards. The public university board is usually elected or appointed by political officials. The private not-for-profit university, on the other hand, is most often governed by boards that are self-perpetuating or elected by alumni — organizational theorists have described how such boards, aligned with various constituencies affected by the conduct of the institution, are essential in ensuring fidelity to the mission of the private not-for-profit institution and preventing erosion of quality of services.

It is important to emphasize that public and private universities do not operate in a world of absolutes, and the above categories are not necessarily binary. For example, with regard to *discretion*, some public research universities have obtained a greater degree of flexibility from state control in a variety of ways, and private universities are often subject to extensive regulatory oversight as a condition of funding. Even so, these four categories provide a useful construct for evaluating what it means for a university to be structured as a public or private institution.

Mission

At the same time, such a construct is not entirely complete. Traditionally, at least, public research universities have embodied not only a distinct organizational form, but also a particular set of civic-oriented objectives that they were understood to be in a unique position to advance.

One could distil that singular mission into four separate goals: First, public universities provide a guarantee of *affordability*, delivering education to those who would otherwise find it beyond their means. Second, public universities have been committed to the goal of *accessibility*, or making the benefits of higher education available broadly, especially to underrepresented populations. Third, these universities have been singularly mindful of *community*, with their public character making them attentive and devoted to the particular economic and social needs of the citizens of their state. And finally, it has been argued that public universities enjoy greater *independence* than private universities from the distortions and biases that can be introduced by outside interests, and therefore that they are specially positioned to maintain a high commitment to the academic process and the common good.

Of course, notwithstanding these differences, public and private research universities have shared many of the same objectives over the years. Both have made it their mission to transfer knowledge to the next generation through education, to create entirely new knowledge through research and discovery, to inspire creative thinking and a love of learning among students, and to serve as a sanctuary for independent scholarship and thought. And yet, the celebrated position that the public research university has occupied in American society is due in no small measure to its success in achieving the distinct set of goals discussed above through much of its history.

CONVERGING TRAJECTORIES

Although private and public universities arose in response to different imperatives and followed different paths, their trajectories have started to converge in recent years. In this Part, we discuss this convergence through two lenses: the privatization of public universities and the publicization of private universities.

The Privatization of the Publics

The single most important catalyst of transformation in the public research university in the last several decades has been a profound decline in state funding. Between 2002 and 2010, state funding per student at major public research universities in the United States declined by 20% in constant dollars, reaching a 30-year low (NSF, 2012; Jackson, 2012). From 1992 to 2010, the percentage of public research universities' total revenue from state funding dropped from 38% to 23% (NSF, 2012). A number of large public research universities now receive less than 10% of their revenue from state funds (UW, 2011; AAAS, 2015b). The Great Recession was an especially harmful episode in this regard, one from which public universities have not fully recovered: Between 2008 and 2013, state support for public higher education per student declined by 26.3% at the median public research university (AAAS, 2015a).

As of 2014, 49 states were spending less money per student on higher education than before the recession, and more than half of states were spending more than 25% less (Hiltonsmith & Draut, 2014).

This decline in state funding has produced a number of consequences for public research universities, each marking a retreat from the traditional distinctive *mission* of a public university — providing an *affordable* education that is *available* broadly to the populace, tailored to the needs of the *community*, and *independent* from influence.

First, the withdrawal of state support has compelled public research universities to increase tuition. From 2001 to 2011 alone, tuition as a proportion of total operating revenue at public research universities has risen from 16% to 23% (Delta Cost Project, 2014). Those universities have tried to limit the impact of the withdrawal of state funds on the neediest students, seeking to support investments in financial aid through a renewed emphasis on philanthropic support and on auxiliary enterprises such as academic medical centres. Nonetheless, the decline of state funds has produced a considerable impact on the *affordability* mission of public universities. Average net tuition at four-year public universities — that is, the average price to those students on financial aid after removing the amount of aid their received — has risen by more than 93% in constant dollars since 2002 (College Board, 2015).

Indeed, when one considers that these price increases were imposed at a time when families were reacting to other economic shocks — unemployment, a real estate meltdown and a stock market correction, it is not surprising that many have highlighted the affordability issue as one of the principal areas in which public universities have seen their public character diminish. The cost of attendance for a public four-year institution, including tuition, fees, and room and board, increased from 32% of a state resident's disposable income in 2000 to 40% in 2009 (NSF, 2012). And although net tuition at most public research universities is still lower than at their private peers, that is no longer always the case: it is now more expensive to attend certain elite public research universities (such as the University of Pittsburgh or the University of Colorado, even as an in-state student) than it is to attend some of the elite private peers (such as Duke University or Stanford University).

Predictably, the decline in state funding has also affected the *accessibility* of higher education. Higher net prices are placing a public research university education out of reach for underprivileged populations. The share of financial aid received by low-income students at public colleges and universities has dropped from 34% in 1996 to 25% in 2012, while the share received by higher income students has risen from 16% to 23% (Wang, 2013). Beset by budget shortfalls, more than half of four-year public doctoral universities in one recent survey have said that they are actively taking steps to attract students who will pay the full tuition. And at other public research universities, the enrolment of underrepresented minorities has fallen in recent years, sometimes by 10% or more (Kiley, 2013).

If one looks at students who received Pell grants (direct federal grants to students from low-income families), public research universities in California such as the University of California-Los Angeles (39% of the student body) or the University of California-Berkeley (35%) enrol far more of these students than private research universities in the state such as Stanford University (15%) or the California Institute of Technology (11%). However, many other public research universities now hover alongside their private peers: in recent years, publics such as the University of Virginia and the University of Wisconsin-Madison, and privates such as Northwestern University and Duke University, have all enrolled 13 to 15% of their student body as Pell recipients.

Another repercussion of the withdrawal of state funding for public research universities has been a shift in the composition of incoming classes from in-state to out-of-state students. Impeded by state regulations from raising in-state tuition, public universities have looked to increase the number of out-of-state students (to whom they can charge higher prices) and international students (who are often excluded from university financial aid policies altogether) in a bid for tuition dollars. According to one analysis, the average public research university increased its nonresident freshmen enrolment from 20.4% in 2002-03 to 24.7% in 2012-13 (Jaquette, 2015). This is yet another way in which public research universities have been compelled to drift away from an objective that traditionally had distinguished them from their private peers — here, providing an education that is targeted to the particular *community* in which they live.

There is one final aspect in which public research universities have come to lose their distinctively public character, and once again it is connected to the recent withdrawal of state funding. While a reliance on public funding might once have been seen as affording public universities greater *independence* from undue private or market influence, it has become apparent that public support is a double-edged sword. The decline in state revenues during the economic downturn has contributed to a climate in which public universities are the subject of ever greater political debate, scrutiny and intervention by public actors (or their agents). This in turn has led in recent years to a number of combustible, high-profile clashes between state political leaders and university leadership on a wide range of topics, including not only their budgets but also the day-to-day operation and even the academic decisions of their universities. Quite simply, there is no parallel among private research universities to this pattern of intervention into the core academic mission of these universities.

A few recent examples of the nature and magnitude of these incidents in the case of public research universities are illustrative:

- *Wisconsin.* Governor Scott Walker of Wisconsin this year proposed cutting $300 million in state funds for public universities, and introduced legislation to make changes to faculty tenure protections and shared governance rules. Faculty members in the University of Wisconsin system rallied against the proposal, stressing that its passage would lead to a number of deleterious outcomes including a lower quality of education and a chilling effect on speech.

- *Texas.* The University of Texas has been embroiled in a years-long feud between the President of the university and the Governor and the Board of Regents over a range of topics including admissions policy, academic research, and the university's curriculum. The state legislature backed the president and initiated impeachment proceedings against a member of the Board of Regents who had attacked him. The faculty council for the university also came to the President's defense. Ultimately, the dispute led to a plan for the President to step down from his post this year.
- *North Carolina.* The President of the University of North Carolina recently came under withering criticism from lawmakers and others over academic programs and financial aid. These clashes ultimately led to the ouster of the president by the university Board of Governors, most of whom had been newly appointed by a legislature that had changed political parties since the president had taken office.

Whatever else might be said for these disputes, it is far more difficult to say that public universities find themselves free to pursue their mission independent of outside pressure or influence. Moreover, as the number and intensity of these conflicts have increased, so too has the frequency of senior executive turnover, which itself can compromise institutional effectiveness. One analysis of executive turnover at American Association of University research institutions revealed that 14% of member public research university presidents are replaced each year, compared to only 6% of their private counterparts.

This discussion should not be taken as a criticism of public research universities, which continue to play a critical role in higher education, research and service in the United States, even in the face of extensive budgetary and political pressures. We intend only to depict how the trajectory of public research universities has shifted over time in response to those pressures, and in particular how these institutions have been pushed away from their distinctive public mission in a number of significant ways.

Publicization of the Private Universities

At the same time that public research universities have seen their public mission compromised, private (non-profit) research universities have been becoming more public in nature. The capacity of non-profit organizations to show fidelity to the public interest should not be surprising — it is, in fact, hard-wired into their stakeholder model of governance. What is striking, however, is how non-profit privates have moved to subsume so many of the distinct goals that were previously regarded as the unique preserve of the publics. As we shall argue below, the fact that non-profit privates are capable of demonstrating fidelity to these goals, but without many of the burdens associated with public universities, calls into question whether a strong normative case in favour of the traditional public model still exists today.

One area in which private research universities have moved towards once distinctively public goals is *affordability*. Over the last 15 years, private research universities have raised philanthropy, tapped their endowments and otherwise made a new institutional commitment to financial aid. According to one study, the average discount rate at private research universities — that is, institutional grant aid as a percentage of tuition and fees — rose from 32% to 43% from 2000 to 2012 (NACUBO, 2013). As a result, tuition and fees net of financial aid declined by nearly 10% at private non-profit universities in constant dollars from 2002-03 to 2014-15, compared to an increase of over 90% at public four-year universities during the same period (College Board, 2014). According to the American Association of Universities, the percentage of students graduating with no debt from AAU private research universities rose from 51 to 54% from 2003 to 2009, a figure that is higher than that for students at AAU public research universities (49%) or all universities (42%) (AAU, 2012).

Next, private research universities have acted to augment the *accessibility* of higher education in recent years, by entering the domain of mass education. Clearly, most public research universities enrol far more students than their private counterparts, and in point of fact, mass education has not traditionally been a strength of private research universities (Delta Cost Project). But the revolution in technology in higher education and a willingness to make their courses available more broadly to the public have carried these institutions into engagements with non-traditional constituencies. For example, private research universities are now among the major investors and participants in leading MOOC platforms such as Coursera and EdX. As of 2013, seven of the top ten courses on Coursera by lifetime enrolment were offered by faculty at private research universities in the United States, and each of those courses had reached more than 100,000 students These courses often are reaching students who might not otherwise have realistic access to education at an American research university: About one-third of their students are from the developing world.

It was also a private research university (MIT) that launched OpenCourseWare, an initiative to make course materials free and available widely around the world — 2,180 courses are now available online. And as of 2012, more than 18% of students at four-year private nonprofit colleges and universities took at least some courses online, a number only slightly less than that at public universities (22%) (IES, 2014). Of course, there is still considerable uncertainty about the role that digital technologies will play in the future of higher education. And yet, it is notable that at least in these early days, private universities are embracing rather than shying away from the ways in which new digital media can expand the reach of education — another sign that they are assuming a role that was once the reserve of their public peers.

Finally, private research universities have also demonstrated a greater fidelity to traditionally public objectives through a renewed commitment to the welfare of the *communities* in which they live. Judith Rodin's *The University and Urban Renewal* describes the University of Pennsylvania's recent groundbreaking investment in comprehensive reforms to support the revitalization of its West Philadelphia neighbourhood, including employee housing programs, commercial development efforts and a local purchasing initiative through which they increased spending in the area from $2 million to over $90 million across 20 years. Other private universities have taken up similar efforts in recent years, including the University of Chicago's programs to transform surrounding neighbourhoods through workforce, commercial and residential development and an initiative to support businesses and residents in the city's South Side, and Johns Hopkins's commitment of more than $60 million to two separate areas surrounding its campuses, including the opening of the first new school in East Baltimore in 25 years. These initiatives vary in scope and impact, but they tend to emerge in common from a dawning sense that their fate is inseparable from that of the communities in which they are rooted.

Quite apart from efforts in community building, private universities have also paid far greater heed in recent years to licensing and entrepreneurial activities, which can have a salutary impact of their own on the surrounding region. With few exceptions, private research universities have not traditionally been seen as engines of regional economic development. And yet, in recent years, these universities have assumed a far more active role as licensors of technologies and therapeutics to existing companies, as well as incubators for new start-ups based on faculty research. Of the 20 universities with the most revenue from the licensing of research in 2013, a majority are private research universities. These activities have not only delivered a variety of new therapeutics and technologies to the world, but also contributed to significant economic development and job growth, with universities at the centre of clusters of economic activity in emerging industries.

One representative study concluded that the increase in university connections to industry in the last three decades produced a rapid growth in long-term employment and earnings per worker in areas surrounding universities, and the impact of these activities increased in geographic proximity to the university (Hausman, 2012). A separate study examined 11 regions abundant with the talent and resources that might have led to a thriving regional ecosystem in the life sciences. Although firms in the biomedical sector were once scattered around the nation, today roughly half of these firms have gravitated to only three of these regions (the San Francisco Bay Area, Cambridge-Boston and North San Diego County). What explains the emergence of these three areas as life sciences clusters? Although there is no single cause, the authors did underscore that each of the regions had benefited from the presence of research universities and academic medical centres that had served as incubators and conduits for the intellectual capital that can pollinate these new economies.

Drivers of Convergence

The convergence discussed in this Part has been driven by powerful market, social and political forces in recent years, which have unmoored public and private research universities from the traditional roles they have occupied in the landscape of higher education in the United States. We take note of five such drivers briefly here. The first is the contraction of state funding for higher education, in favour of investment in other more politically urgent priorities such as Medicaid. The second is the expansion of federal funding for higher education, in particular in the form of research funding and financial aid, both of which have contributed to the creation of a single, integrated national market of research universities. The third is the rise of third-party intermediaries that facilitate the flow of information between prospective students and public and private research universities alike, inevitably drawing these universities in closer alignment.

The fourth is the rise of the knowledge-based economy and the move by the federal government in the Bayh-Dole Act of 1980 to imbue research universities with clear ownership rights over the intellectual property related to federally sponsored research conducted within these institutions, which have served as important catalysts of the emerging role of universities as central to urban policy and economic development efforts. And the fifth and final factor is the evolution in societal expectations surrounding the cost of higher education, and in particular the surge in political and media attention to the issue with regard to private research universities about a decade ago that spurred these institutions into action on this issue. Taken together, these outside pressures have propelled public and private research universities in the direction of convergence, and contributed to an increasingly competitive emerging landscape of higher education.

BARRIERS TO ADAPTATION

And yet, even as public and private research universities have converged, they have not been identically situated to adapt effectively to this emerging landscape. Rather, the legacy of state ownership and significant regulatory control over public universities has left these institutions vulnerable as they seek to compete alongside their private peers in this newly integrated environment (Duderstadt & Womack, 2003). We discuss several of these barriers to adaptation in this section.

One of the leading obstacles facing public universities has been discussed already: the profound decline in state funding over the last decade. Of course, the withdrawal of state funding subverts the traditional academic mission of the research university. But it also has the collateral consequence of weakening the ability of these universities to pursue other public goals (such as investment in regional social and economic goals) because of a lack of available funds. Also, wholly apart from reductions in the amount of state funding, the vagaries of this funding — due to the unreliability of the state appropriations process, the rise and fall of state tax revenues, and the sometimes convulsive shifts in political control from one party to another — further undermine the academic mission. For instance, the difficulty of predicting the amount of even the next year's funding from the state — let alone the amount several years later — frustrates the ability of public universities to engage in the strategic planning that is essential to advancing their mission.

A number of other encumbrances affect the work of public research universities. For one, these universities are burdened by a "tight web of state government rules, regulations and bureaucracy." (Duderstadt & Womack, 2003). This regulatory regime extends to areas as far reaching as contracting, tuition setting, admissions standards and teaching assignments, to name only a few. Many states "still require prior approval for purchasing, dictate line-item funding in silos, and maintain fund management requirements that perpetuate bad habits such as year-end spending sprees rather than building prudent contingency reserves" (Wellman & Reed, 2011). In all of these areas, the state bureaucratic process can slow the activity, distort the decision-making, and "erode... the authority" of academic leadership in ways that simply are not felt by their private peers (Duderstadt & Womack, 2003).

Next, there are the political entanglements that accompany state ownership of universities. As U.S. politics has become more ideologically polarized, and the salience of concerns over the future of higher education has become more acute, the propensity of state politicians to focus their energies on highly symbolic (and we would argue, unproductive) attacks on the conduct and mission of state universities has increased markedly. This phenomenon is reflected in the litany of high-profile political clashes and crises involving public research universities, the rapid turnover in the presidents of these institutions, and the swings in public policy directly affecting state universities in recent years. The role played by the governing boards of public research universities — principally appointed by state elected officials — in exposing state universities to political influence or external agendas cannot be overstated, and it is another way in which public universities are disadvantaged relative to their private peers (*ibid*).

Finally, public universities are burdened by the time and energy that leadership must commit to government relations and lobbying activities directed at state political officials. When public universities enjoyed high levels of financial support (relative to their operating budgets) and protection from competition with other institutions, the costs of managerial investment in these activities were frustrating but tolerable. But with increased competition, these activities come at a much greater cost to the institution. Leadership is forced to commit increasing amounts of time at the state capitol currying favour with public officials and their representatives and taking defensive actions aimed at forestalling unwarranted and dysfunctional state interference in their activities or protecting an ever-shrinking allocation of the state budget — rather than on forward-looking academic strategies designed to strengthen their research, education, and service contributions. Again, this distinguishes public research university presidents from private research university presidents: One recent study found that 77% of presidents of public doctoral universities named legislators and policymakers as one of three constituent groups who pose the greatest challenge to their operation of the university, compared to 30% of presidents of private doctoral universities. And 23% of presidents of public doctoral universities identified government relations as one of their three most time-consuming duties, while only 3% of presidents of private doctoral universities said the same (Song & Hartley, 2012).

These problems should not come as a surprise. Organizational theory tells us that public ownership can be vulnerable to substantial accountability issues, rent-seeking and politicization. This is not an argument for public bodies to remove themselves from involvement in higher education. Indeed, government intervention in the market for higher education is justified by factors as varied as the presence of human capital market failures, information asymmetries and externalities related to investments in basic research and education. It is only to say that the choice of how the government should intervene in a particular industry — through ownership, investment or regulation, and the particulars of how to advance each — demands a careful weighing of considerations, and that the ownership problem is especially susceptible to much that we have seen play out in recent years in higher education.

To be certain, several public research universities have succeeded in securing a greater degree of structural independence from the state. For example, some institutions such as the University of Michigan and the University of California enjoy substantial autonomy as a matter of the state constitution (Duderstadt & Womack, 2003). Others such as the University of Virginia and the University of Florida have struck deals that allow them to operate with fewer restrictions on tuition and related decisions, often in exchange for funding cuts or an agreement to meet various performance targets. However, even these universities are still subject to ongoing state influence and interference in areas such as appropriations, auditing, and health and safety (UW, 2011). As a result, the disparities between private research universities and even the most independent public research universities continue to grow in areas such as faculty pay or expenditures per enrolled students (Duderstadt & Womack, 2003).

A PATH FORWARD

We began this Chapter by sketching the characteristics that define a public or private research university, and divided them into two categories: *structural* attributes such as ownership, discretion, governance and funding, and *mission*-oriented attributes such as affordability, accessibility, community focus and independence. One way of viewing the analysis that followed is that there has been a substantial convergence in the *mission* of public and private research universities, without an accompanying convergence in the *structural* attributes. Specifically, Parts I and II discussed the ways in which public universities have lost some of their public orientation when it comes to *mission*, and how private universities have gained much of that same character. And Part III addressed how the *structural* attributes of public research universities nonetheless persist, in ways that are detrimental to their functioning in a converging world.

One might very well conclude from the convergence in mission of these two institutions that there has been a natural evolution under way towards a new form for U.S. higher education. We could call this form the public-regarding private ("PRP"), a university that combines the uniquely civic-minded mission that was traditionally associated with the public research university and the not-for-profit structure of the private counterpart. And one might go farther yet, and argue that policy-makers should take action to speed our public research universities on their way to this new model, and end entirely the public ownership, funding, governance and operation of public research universities. The premise of this view would be that the non-profit governance model — coupled perhaps with light-handed regulation and earmarked state subsidies for students and research — has proven to be a superior approach to the present mix of ever expanding state interference and ever shrinking state funding now endured by public research universities.

Although we are struck by the capacity of the PRP to vindicate the public goals of higher education, we are not at the point of arguing for across-the-board privatization of public research universities for a number of different reasons. First, as noted earlier, the heterogeneity of our system of higher education has been one of its great and abiding strengths, allowing privates and publics the freedom to compete and influence each other even as they innovated and adapted in different directions within their separate organizational forms. This feature of the U.S. system is not one that should be discarded lightly. Second, as discussed earlier in this Chapter, public universities were created for very important reasons, they have provided unique contributions over time, and they are deeply embedded in the economic and cultural fabric of their states, and policymakers should take care before denuding them of this historic status.

Third, although there has been a remarkable convergence to date in mission between public and private research universities, that convergence is not complete — we are still at a moment where public institutions continue to occupy a distinct role in the landscape of higher education. For instance, with regard to the goal of accessibility, although private research universities have expanded their reach considerably, their reliance on online media is still in its infancy, and public research universities continue to enrol nearly four times as many students as their private counterparts (Delta Cost Project). The same can be said for affordability: Although there has been a meaningful narrowing of the gap on average between publics and privates, public research universities still maintain a significant price advantage. These enduring features of the public research university still demand protection. And finally, even those who do favour the privatization of public research universities would do well to advocate for an orderly transition to that world, one that phases those changes incrementally over time to mitigate the impact on key stakeholders, test the assumptions behind the change, and modulate the final end state as needed over time (Trebilcock, 2014).

For all of these reasons, we do not believe that the optimal result is to usher in a complete convergence of private and public research universities. Our argument instead is that just as there has been a substantial convergence over time in the *mission* of the public and private research universities, so too should there be a substantial convergence in the *structure* of these universities, one that provides the public research universities with the autonomy and flexibility to adapt to this newly competitive environment alongside their private peers. Specifically, we are advocating for a sustained period of focused and thoughtful experimentation with the structure of their public research universities, to identify over time the right combination of structural changes that will empower them to advance their distinctively public mission in the coming years.

There are a number of mechanisms available to a state that would seek to unshackle public universities in this fashion. One option is to shift the governance boards of public universities to the not-for-profit model, in which members are selected largely outside of political channels and the effectiveness of the board is seen as a key criterion of institutional accreditation. Another set of reforms involves new modes of providing public research universities with greater autonomy in areas such as tuition-setting, personnel, capital construction and purchasing, in exchange for agreements to reach certain benchmarks. As noted earlier, these initiatives have been adopted in certain states, and the challenge is to refine these efforts to ensure that the structural changes provide independent not only in form, but in practice. A third area of reform would be for states to provide guarantees of multi-year funding, in an effort to provide their public universities a modicum of the stability and predictability now enjoyed by their private peers (Duderstadt & Womack, 2003; Lyall & Sell, 2006).

A more aggressive option yet would seek to create a financial exit ramp for interested public research universities from the current path of ever-shrinking state support and expanding state politicization. One example of this approach is provided by the University of Oregon, which several years ago proposed that the state could use its roughly $65 million annual appropriation to the university to finance $800 million in new bonds over the next 30 years. The university would then match the bond with its own fundraising to create a new $1.6 billion endowment, payouts from which it estimated would soon exceed the expected state appropriation to the university, and possibly rise to as much as $235 million per year. The need for state support would then end entirely after the payments ended on the bond. The proposal ultimately failed for reasons far more political than substantive. And although the precise model proposed by the University of Oregon may not be feasible for every public research university — the philanthropic component in particular would be a challenge for bigger universities with larger state funding allocations — it is a creative option that could provide public universities with an exit ramp from a status quo of declining and unstable funding, one worthy of additional exploration.

Indeed, we underscore that the argument for a greater structural convergence between public and private universities should not be understood to abrogate the responsibility of state governments (and, equally, the federal government) to invest in public higher education. As discussed earlier, both levels of government have a clear and compelling responsibility founded on a range of rationales to support higher education. That role can and should manifest itself in part through financial support. Assistance in building an endowment as in the Oregon plan is certainly one possible approach, but no matter the specifics, states should take steps to ensure that public research universities have the financial capacity to advance their public mission. Put differently, the dramatic decline in state funding of recent years should not be seen as one element of the structural convergence of privates and publics. A true convergence in this regard would require action on the part of states to provide public research universities with the same sort of financial independence and sustainability that are enjoyed by their private counterparts.

One final note is that — for a number of reasons — we would recommend that the most substantial structural reforms be confined in the first instance to the public research universities in the Association of American University. These are the schools where the convergence with private universities already tends to be the greatest. They are the schools with the most similar portfolios of funding sources and research activities, and in particular the schools with the greatest capacity to sustain themselves through a period of structural change with their own sources of external funding. Moreover, our public colleges and universities represent over 70% of the students enrolled in institutions of higher education in this country, but the public research universities in the AAU represent a small subset of those (less than 6%) (Delta Cost Project; Crow & Dabars, 2015). An attempt to steer public universities away from the current model should start modestly, to avoid any unintended harm to the capacity of our public institutions to meet the needs of students in their state. A collateral benefit of this approach is that if a path to financial independence for flagship universities is successful, it could free states over time to shift support to the financial and other needs of the remaining public colleges and universities.

CONCLUSION

The convergence described in this Chapter presents untold opportunities for public research universities in the United States, which are well-positioned to excel in the evolving landscape of higher education if given the structural freedom to act. However, they will need assistance to play this role, and the sin of inaction here is a grave one. There is every reason to believe that in the absence of corrective steps, the prospects for public research universities will be grim: they will continue to be buffeted by declining financial support and increased political entanglement, all while suffering the disadvantages of state regulation, at a moment when the competitive environment is heightened due to convergence towards the PRP model. We urge swift reforms to provide our public research universities with the structural independence, flexibility, and sustainability they need to continue to advance their emphatically public missions.

REFERENCES

American Academy of Arts & Sciences (2015a). Public Research Universities: Changes in State Funding.
American Academy of Arts & Sciences (2015b). Public Research Universities: Why They Matter.

American Association of Universities (2012). Looking More Closely at Student Debt.
Cole, Jonathan (2009). The Great American University: Its Rise to Preeminence, Its Indispensable National Role, Why It Must Be Protected. PublicAffairs, New York.
College Board (2014). Trends in College Pricing 2014. Trends in Higher Education.
College Board (2015). "Average Net Price over Time for Full-Time Students at Private Nonprofit Four-Year Institutions" Trends in Higher Education.
Crow, Michael M. & Dabars, William B. (2015). "A New Model for the American Research University." Issues in Science and Technology. 31(3).
Delta Cost Project. Trends in College Spending Online. Available at: http://tcs-online.org/Home.aspx.
Delta Cost Project (2014). Trends in College Spending: 2001-2011: A Delta Data Update.
Duderstadt, James J. (2011). Creating the Future: The Promise of Public Research Universities for America. Prepared for APLU Volume Celebrating the 150th Anniversary of Morrill Act.
Duderstadt, James J. & Womack, Farris W. (2003). The Future of the Public University in America: Beyond the Crossroads. The Johns Hopkins University Press, Baltimore, MD.
Hausman, Naomi (2012). University Innovation, Local Economic Growth and Entrepreneurship.
Heller, Donald E. (2011a). "Affordability, Access, and Accountability in Twenty-first Century Public Higher Education," In The States and Public Higher Education Policy: Affordability, Access, and Accountability, Heller, D. ed.
Hiltonsmith, Robert & Draut, Tamara (2014). "The Great Cost Shift Continues." Demos, 21 March 2014. Demos.org.
Horn, Murray J. (1995). The Political Economy of Public Administration: Institutional choice in the Public Sector. Cambridge University Press, Cambridge.
Institute of Education Sciences (2014). "Enrollment in Distance Education Courses, by State: Fall 2012." National Center for Education Statistics. US Department of Education. June 2014.
Jackson, Robert L. (2012). The American Public Comprehensive University: An Exploratory Study of the President's Role in Fundraising. Western Kentucky University.
Jaquette, Ozan (2015). "Tuition Rich, Mission Poor: Nonresident Enrollment Growth and the Socioeconomic and Racial Composition of Public Research Universities." The Journal of Higher Education. Forthcoming.
Kiley, Kevin (2013). "Crowded Out." Inside Higher Ed. 30 April 2013.
Lowry, Robert C. (2009). "Incomplete Contracts and the Political Economy of Privatization." In Privatizing the Public University: Perspectives Across the Academy, Morphew & Eckel, eds.
Lyall, Katherine C. & Sell, Kathleen R (2006). The True Genius of American at Risk: Are We Losing Our Public Universities to De Facto Privatization. American Council on Education.

National Association of College and University Business Officers (2014). 2013 Tuition Discounting Study.
National Science Foundation (2012). Diminishing Funding and Rising Expectations: Trends and Challenges for Public Research Universities.
Priest, Douglas M. & St. John, Edward P., eds. (2006). Privatization and Public Universities, Indiana University Press, Bloomington, IN.
Song, Wei & Hartley III, Harold V. (2012). A Study of Presidents of Independent Colleges and Universities. The Council of Independent Colleges.
Trebilcock, Michael J. (2014). Dealing with Losers: the Political Economy of Policy Transitions. Oxford University Press.
University of Washington (2011). "Planning & Budgeting Brief."
Wang, Marian (2013). "Public Universities Ramp Up Aid for the Wealthy, Leaving the Poor Behind." ProPublica. 11 September 2013.
Wellman, Jane & Reed, Charles (2011). "Mend, Don't End, State Systems." Inside Higher Ed. 28 Mar. 2011.

CHAPTER 14

The University in the 21st Century[1]

Luc E. Weber

UNIVERSITIES AND THEIR ENVIRONMENT

The resilient University

The University is one of the greatest inventions of the second millennium (Rhodes, 1998). Europe can be particularly proud of this, given that the University is first and foremost a European institution which — while keeping its essential characteristics — has since spread worldwide (Rüegg, 1992). Universities have shown themselves to be particularly resilient organizations: created up to 900 years ago, they have survived the many vagaries of history and scholarship, as well as of politics and economics. Even today, the university's dynamic nature is clearly evident. It has shown that it can and does adapt to changes in its environment.

University teachers regularly adapt the content of their teaching, while keeping themselves abreast of latest developments in their field thanks to an innate curiosity for discovery and the sharing of knowledge, which can be labelled the "genetic code" of the university scholar.

However the context for the University has now changed. For centuries, universities had only a few, sometimes only one, professor in each discipline. The simultaneous broadening of knowledge fields across all disciplines,

---

[1]. This chapter summarizes the main arguments of the book I have recently published in French: *L'Université au XXI siècle, innovante, internationale et volontaire*, Economica, Paris, 2015.

together with the massive increases in student numbers during the second half of the 20th century, has resulted in the specialization of knowledge and a large increase in the numbers of university teachers and researchers. Departments and other subdivisions were created to replace professorial chairs for the organization of teaching, often along with research networks linking a group of disciplines, with decisions in these new structures being taken on the basis of collegiality. Furthermore, councils have been created to ensure that the university administration and technical staff, non-tenured teaching and research staff (assistants, etc.), as well as students, can be involved in certain decision-making processes, notably in the organization of teaching and learning.

These necessary developments have proved to have a very positive effect, since they place a large degree of responsibility with university teachers and researchers, and with other stakeholders in the life of an academic faculty or department. This shows clearly that universities have both the human and institutional resources to adapt to the challenges of a changing world, and that they are already doing this in a number of ways. Having said this, it should also be recognized that universities often react under pressure, without which they would be less inclined to change. While some of these changes are positive, others are less so.

The University under challenge

This short reminder of the University's long history and its proven capacity to adapt to changes might give the impression that it can be affected by nothing and that it is guaranteed to continue to exist, in a very similar format, for several more centuries. The rather shorter history of industrial companies and services shows, however, that there is no guarantee. Furthermore, the somewhat longer history of nations also shows that no civilization or country is immune to change.

The real question is to know whether universities will be able to adapt to the new world that is opening up, and whether they will be able to do this quickly enough, in order to preserve the quasi-monopoly which they enjoy in terms of higher education and basic research. We should remind ourselves of a number of the fundamental changes that have taken place recently, especially those which are likely to have the most impact on society in general and, more particularly, on higher education and research.

From the perspective of the universities, they become apparent in four interdependent ways, all of which change the context in which the universities must operate. Some challenges are **universal**, that is they impact on universities wherever they are located:

- **Internationalization.** Globalization means that universities have to think and act internationally, even globally: every aspect of the

university will face the challenge of internationalization, from its students, faculty and staff, to its missions of teaching, research and service, and to its funding, administration and campus life.
- **Competition.** Increasing levels of competition are particularly significant for universities, since they must remain attractive to students, teachers and research staff, and must also obtain the core funding, capital investment and research funding that they need to develop.
- **Increasing pace of scientific and technical progress.** While, to a large degree, a result of the universities' own efforts, scientific and technical progress is somewhat paradoxically a challenge for universities, given their essential capacity to make new discoveries, without which their reason to exist would be significantly weakened. In addition, this progress means that universities and their teaching staff need to keep the range of their study programs updated, including their content and teaching methods.
- **Emergence of the knowledge economy.** In order to meet today's development challenges, all countries — whether they are developed nations or still developing — need, more than ever before, to innovate and to rely on educated citizens and a qualified workforce, capable of undertaking challenging tasks that change frequently and become increasingly complex. Thanks to their long tradition, universities and the tertiary education sector generally are best placed to meet these needs. They must therefore adapt their teaching and research in order to remain attractive and to fulfil this responsibility.

Other challenges are **specific** and/or **regional**.
- Demographics and the higher education participation rate, which determine the number of students at university, differ enormously from continent to continent. In the western world and in Japan, the university student population is in the process of stabilizing at a high level, or is even beginning to decrease. The situation is completely different in continents with a much younger population, including both Africa and the Indian subcontinent where the population is still growing fast. In these regions, however, the university participation rate is comparatively low, or very low, but is increasing.
- The situation regarding the financing of higher education and research is likewise very different from one region to another. This difference can be seen in two areas (OECD, 2012). First, the share of public and private expenditure for higher education and for research compared to Gross National Product differs greatly from one country to the other. Second, the same is true for the share of the public budget dedicated to Higher Education. Moreover, public funding in the western world and

in Japan is in serious difficulty, especially since the 2008 economic crisis. In Europe (Estermann & Pruvot, 2011) a number of countries experienced large or very large budgetary reductions (notably in Eastern and Southern Europe), while only a few countries increased their budgets, notably Germany and France, thanks to their so-called "excellence initiatives", which aim to finance advanced innovative institutional projects or in the fields of research and teaching. It is worth noting that in Europe the university sector has been relatively more affected by national financial difficulties, given that the State plays such an important role in the continent. At the same time, increasing the State's share in GNP is difficult without having negative consequences on the private sector. The size of the State has effectively already become a problem in itself. Public funding is also very tight in the United States where, even if the overall context is improving after five years of austerity, there are ongoing announcements of large budget cuts imposed mainly by individual states. This situation has driven many universities to increase tuition fees much faster than the underlying increase in the cost of living, which in turn creates a number of problems, in particular regarding access to universities for talented applicants on low family incomes. The deteriorating financial situation for universities and for research in the United States has encouraged many higher education stakeholders to raise the alarm (National Research Council of the National Academies, 2012; and American Academy of Arts and Sciences, 2014). One of the aims of these warnings is to press home the message that scientific and technical advances are absolutely fundamental for the prosperity, health and security of the country. As a result of ongoing economic stagnation in Europe and Japan, and the increasing investment requirements in other areas where the State plays an important role, for example, health, security and transport, it is difficult to see how public funding for higher education can improve in the short term. Moreover, universities are at a disadvantage, since the results that they are promising cannot be demonstrated immediately, only at some time in the future.

The burning question

Universities, in particular research-intensive universities, have indeed shown themselves to be especially resilient, able to adapt themselves to all sorts of favourable and less favourable environments. However, the situation which universities now face is much more challenging than 20 or 30 years ago.

- On the one hand, increasingly rapid scientific advances, ground-breaking innovations and the competitive environment all require universities to reform faster and more profoundly, in order to maintain their quasi-monopoly on teaching and their dominance in terms of research. They have in particular to innovate in the way they fulfil their traditional and basic missions, i.e. teaching, research and service to society. In addition, they need to internationalize all aspects of their activity, from students, faculty and staff to missions of teaching, research and service, and to funding, administration and campus life, through internationalizing their human resources, their academic staff and their students. They also need to pay much more attention than they have traditionally done to the quality of all that they do and to their governance.

- On the other hand, in the western world and Japan, most governments find themselves in serious financial difficulties and are increasingly called upon to provide increased funding for other public priorities. The situation is dramatically different from the generous, post-Second World War period when university budgets grew very rapidly, while scientific and technical progress then was not as rapid or even revolutionary as it is today. This period of rapid expansion, driven mainly by an increase in student numbers, also allowed for considerable growth in the numbers of disciplines and specialization covered, which in turn allowed universities to broaden their areas of expertise and research, and at the same time to provide more diverse and richer study programs. As a result, this period allowed universities to adapt to their changing environment, thanks to the additional resources received for absorbing the increasing number of students.

Today, universities are under pressures from two different directions, as if they were facing a pincer movement. On one hand, they have to innovate faster than ever before to respond to the needs of a rapidly changing labour market, take into account new knowledge, be more international, recruit excellent teachers, researchers and students from abroad, to pay more attention to quality, to be accountable, and so on. On the other hand, these huge efforts to maintain their leadership in higher education and basic research have to be done in a context of ever-tighter public budgets. This condemns universities to search for the necessary financial needs necessary to cover the additional expenditures induced by these efforts.

In the following two sections, we shall first examine the possible strategies for universities to raise the necessary funds to cover the additional expenditures. We shall then argue that universities will have to reform themselves all the more deeply and rapidly because they have difficulties raising more resources which implies an improvement of their governance system and strong leadership.

FINANCING THE NEW UNIVERSITY

Raising the necessary additional funds has become more crucial than ever for the development of universities. The fact that the number of students tends to stabilize or even decrease deprives universities of a strong argument in favour of increased public engagement, in contrast to the situation that prevailed in the second part of the 20th century. Moreover, most of the necessary innovations generate additional expenditures. Financing a proactive university that is striving for excellence has become a great challenge for many institutions.

Basically, this raises three questions: a) the degree of state support, b) the right or optimal financial participation of students (and/or their families) and c) the best ways to engage the private sector.

Governmental support. The support given by governments to universities has basically two dimensions. First, traditional state support which differs widely from one country to the other, from 90% in Scandinavian countries and Belgium to less than 35% in countries like South Korea, Chile, the U.S. and Japan and, second, its trend over the years. Considering that the degree of involvement is deeply rooted in the political culture and strongly anchored historically, it is very unlikely that universities can influence this in the short or medium terms. However, particularly in a period of tight or even decreasing public support, university leaders should never stop explaining to the public authorities, to politicians and to society as a whole that higher education and research are crucial in the knowledge society and that it takes many years before results become visible — and that the damage from a lack of support for the sector takes many years to repair. University leaders should also constantly explain and repeat that the optimal teaching and learning environment aims at preparing people to think, to be innovative and critical, and to learn how to learn, more than simply to train individuals to occupy a particular job. Similarly, it should be stressed that research results cannot be planned; new discoveries entail an important element of chance. This engagement of university leaders in favour of strong public support is all the more important in countries where the share of public financing is relatively large, but should not be neglected in countries which have a strong tradition of alternative sources of financing: all potential sources of financing have to be exploited to respond to the challenges of innovation and internationalization.

Optimal financial participation of students and families: It is difficult to imagine that, in some countries and universities, students are paying fees superior to US$50,000 per annum, whereas in other countries higher education is almost free of charge! We believe that both these extremes should be avoided.

- Very high fees are not optimal for three reasons. First, they completely neglect the fact that the personal investment made by the university students is not only beneficial to them, but to the whole population, as it is better to live in a well-educated society than in a non-educated one. The effort of studying made by a proportion of the population generates external benefits for the entire population (spillover effect). Secondly, the public sector has a responsibility to promote and support higher education because it contributes positively to the immaterial welfare of the entire population, which depends also on values like freedom, security, justice, tolerance and the respect of human rights. Graduates have a return on their investment in getting a more interesting, promising and better-paid job and in being less vulnerable to long-term unemployment; however, they have no immediate return for the improved immaterial welfare to which they contribute. It is therefore unfair and wrong to let them participate to the payment for that through high fees. Third, the higher the fees, the more difficult it is to ensure the fees do not become a serious barrier to access to universities for potentially good students who do not have sufficient financial means.

- On the other hand, it is also unfair not to levy any fee. Studying in a university is a profitable investment for students who, on average, can expect a better professional life and a higher income throughout their working lives. Consequently, it is just and fair that they contribute to this important advantage, particularly as the opportunity to attend university is not equally spread over the entire society: despite all the efforts made, the proportion of students from working class families remains much smaller. The consequence is that in a system without student fees or very low fees, everyone is funding higher education through taxes, even though only privileged sections of society have a reasonable chance of getting a university grade. In addition to this equity argument, reasonable fees have an efficiency advantage: they make both students and institutions and their staff sensitive to the fact that higher education is costly and must therefore be used efficiently.
- These theoretical developments are certainly useful when deciding the approximate level of fees, but insufficient to fix them precisely. They can nevertheless help to persuade continental Europe, which is traditionally opposed to any level of fees, that they could tap into this unexploited source of financial resources and, at the same time, improve the fairness and the efficiency of the system. However, one should never forget the risk of creating new barriers to access. The introduction or increase of fees should be accompanied by financial measures for students (or families) who could not afford to pay them and would therefore be excluded.

Fees paid by households (students and their families) are by no means the only source of private financing. Philanthropy is also extremely important in countries where public engagement is modest. Raising money from rich individuals and from firms with a lot of cash, with no or only acceptable strings attached, is an important responsibility of the leadership of the institution and in particular of the president or leader of the institution. The U.S. has a strong record of philanthropic funding for the university sector, while Europe, in particular continental Europe, has access to an ocean of unexploited resources. However, there must be limits to possible enthusiasm about potential funding. Developing philanthropy requires a major cultural change, which has to be done in both "camps", the potential donors and the requesting institutions. This effort, which requires putting in place a professional organization and requires the determined engagement of university leaders, is worth making as there is a real potential for levying additional resources.

The private sector also contributes to the financing of universities and research though different forms of partnerships (contracts, joint projects, royalties…) Here again, the U.S. is an example Europe should follow. There is good potential for increased income, although strict rules should be implemented to prevent contracts and partnership restricting academic freedom and, even worse, influencing research results.

In summary, European universities that are particularly suffering from the financial difficulties of the governments supporting them — and which have in the past provided a relatively large proportion of their revenues — should engage much more in raising additional resources from the private sector (philanthropy and partnership) and households. This is the only way for them to find the necessary means to finance a determined policy of modernization, internationalization and quality improvement in search for excellence.

GOVERNING AND LEADING THE NEW UNIVERSITY

As we have seen, the University in the 21st century faces two big challenges. On the one hand, universities have to adapt to a rapidly changing environment, which requires them to change what they are offering and how they act. On the other hand, they have to secure additional resources to finance their modernization and development in a period of tight or decreasing public budgets, without forcing students to pay for the benefits of higher education which accrue to society at large.

The facts are that the situation is much more challenging than the situation in the 1960s: the changes are more rapid and the budget is not forthcoming. This is a completely new situation for university governance and leadership which concerns all universities in Northern America and, particularly, in

Europe and Japan. The situation in other continents is in general quite different, but this is not the object of this chapter.

This raises two questions: first, are universities changing rapidly enough to retain their position as the leading institution for the creation of new knowledge and of knowledge transfer? Secondly, is the system of shared governance, where most decisions are the fruit of individual initiatives and collegial decisions, adapted to implement the deep changes required?

My conviction is that it is not the case and that universities have to streamline and reinforce the decision-making process.

Improving this process is a delicate undertaking as it is important not to destroy what works well in the present system. Universities are unique organizations because in no other organization is there so much competence at the base of the hierarchy, that is the scholars, researchers, Ph.D. students and other advanced students. Professionally, they know in principle more than the head of their department, dean or member of the presidency, and they are best placed to know what should be done to be up-to-date. They are well aware of this and therefore do not easily accept instructions from the hierarchy, all the more so as they tend to apply strictly the principle of academic freedom that they enjoy. However, it is easy to demonstrate that it is inefficient and unfair to keep all decisions decentralized and to make the president a mere master of ceremonies.

Thousands of decisions are made every day in universities. Most of them concern students (admission, examination, evaluation of work done, etc.). But others are more strategic, like the creation or adaptation of a study program, the nomination of a professor, the decision to build and equip a new laboratory, the decision to merge two departments, etc. It is of the utmost importance to determine who should be responsible for the final decision and how the decision should be prepared. Universities being different from a public administration or a business, it is necessary to find a model of organization adapted to this particular type of institution. I suggest that the federal model helps greatly to determine in a university which type of decision should be taken at which level. The model is based on three principles. First, the principle of subsidiarity, which specifies that decisions should be taken as close as possible to those concerned by the decision. Second, the existence of spillover (or external cost or benefits) which highlights that some decisions (or non-decisions) generate a benefit or a cost not only at the level of the individual or subdivision that has taken it, but also at a higher level in the institution. For example, an excellent department contributes to the reputation of the whole institution, but is unable to develop as much as it should if strategic decisions are taken at its level. Third, the principle of treating equals equally depends on the preferences within the institution: if the equal treatment of equals is considered important, decisions have to be more centralized than if it is not considered important.

These criteria are very helpful to determine the ideal level of decision-making. Basically, decisions can be decentralized as long as the spillovers are insignificant and there is a low preference for an equal treatment of equals. But, if the spillovers are important and if people attach great importance to an equivalent treatment of equals, decisions should be made at a higher level. I am furthermore arguing that the new environment is increasing the spillover of many decisions and the degree of preference for equal treatment of equals. The importance of the changes which have to be made to ensure that the institution remains competitive is reducing the possibility for subdivisions to make the necessary changes on their own. For example, the development of MOOCs or the internationalization of the institution requires a strategy at the level of the university. Decisions should therefore be made at a higher level. This does not mean that the implementation cannot be left to the responsibility of the subdivisions.

The tight financial situation reinforces strongly the need for increased decision-making power at the level of faculties or of the presidency, depending on the object. Convincing the State to do more, introducing or increasing student fees and developing philanthropy are all strategies that have mainly to be decided and implemented at the level of the presidency. The power of the president and/or presidency to decide is all the more important in cases where the decisions to be made are controversial within the institution, in particular because there are winners and losers.

The easiest decision to be made and policy to implement is to convince governments to do more. Everyone within the university agrees. The situation gets much more delicate if these efforts fail and government does not financially support the endeavour of universities to modernize. In the case of stable or even decreasing public budgets, the university leadership is invited to act more decisively. The two strategies which are, as we have seen, open to the leadership of universities are more delicate or difficult politically. One strategy consists in finding alternative sources of financing, which means taking a politically difficult decision to increase fees or to search much more aggressively for alternative additional resources through a campaign of fund-raising and nurturing other sources of income. These policies, like lobbying for increased public allocations, do not produce losers within the institution, but generate nevertheless the opposition of all those who are against students fees for social and political reasons or think that the danger that private money corrupts the independence of the institution is too great to be undertaken.

The situation gets really difficult for institutions that, for whatever reason, fail to increase their financial resources: they do not have another way to find the resources necessary to innovate other than using existing resources differently. In this case, the university should revise its missions, objectives and strategies, and identify activities which are now obsolete, less important or whose quality is mediocre. Then, the university should have the power to act, in particular in closing them or transferring them to another institution in order to liberate the financial means necessary to finance the newly prioritized activities. This cannot be done by the subdivisions alone. The whole institution is clearly concerned, which means that the presidency should be fully involved.

CONCLUSION

The message we have tried to develop in this contribution is straightforward, but challenging for many universities in the "old world", and in particular in Europe and in Japan. Universities have indeed been extremely resilient to change for up to nine centuries thanks to the "genetic code" of the university scholar and to a well-developed system of shared governance. Two parallel developments over the last 25 years are threatening this: today the world is transforming itself much faster than ever before and the financial environment is very different. In the 1960s and after, the world was not changing as rapidly, but a strong increase in student numbers justified — and supported — at the same a rapid increase in pubic budgets, whereas today the world is changing extremely rapidly in a time when public support is stagnating or even decreasing.

Universities face a double challenge. First, innovate, modernize and restructure to keep the quasi-monopoly for discovering new knowledge and transmitting it. Second, be capable of doing this with stagnant or decreasing public budgets. This situation is very challenging for the governance and leadership of the institution. If universities fail to persuade public authorities to increase their contribution to universities to cover the cost of the necessary adaptation, they have to fight aggressively to find new resources with households and the private sector (students fees, philanthropy, different forms of partnerships). And, if this strategy also fails, they have to reallocate existing resources to finance priority projects while closing or terminating older, less important projects.

REFERENCES

American Academy of Arts and Sciences (2014). *Restoring the Foundation: The Vital Role of Research in Preserving the American Dream*, Cambridge, MA.
Estermann, T. & Pruvot, E. B. (2011). *Financially Sustainable Universities II*, EUA Publications.

National Research Council of the National Academies (2012). *Research Universities and the Future of America, Ten Breakthrough Action Vital to Our Nations' Prosperity and Security*, The National Academies Press, Washington.

OECD (2012). *Education at a Glance 2012, OECD Indicators*, OECD Publishing, Paris.

Rhodes, F. (1998). *The Glion Declaration: The University at the Millennium*, Glion Colloquium, Geneva.

Rüegg, W. (ed.) (1992). *A History of the University in Europe, Vol. I, Universities in the Middle ages*, Cambridge University Press.

PART IV

Structural Constraints

CHAPTER 15

The Impact of China's Economic Rise on Global Higher Education

Tony F. Chan

INTRODUCTION

China's continuous economic rise in the last three decades has been one of the most dramatic events in world history. In addition to lifting hundreds of millions people out of poverty, creating a huge middle class with increasing disposable income and modernizing China's economic structure, this rise has also affected the rest of the world in many ways. This paper focuses on the impact on global higher education, from a personal perspective, specifically in terms of competition for talents (both faculty and students), university governance, science and technology research, and entrepreneurship/innovation culture. My observation is based on being the president for the last six years of a public university in Hong Kong, which in itself is governed by the "One Country, Two Systems" framework, and which has afforded me a front-row seat to observe this impact from both inside and outside perspectives.

CHINA'S ECONOMIC RISE

Surging Global Position of China

With the world's largest foreign reserve of US$3.9 trillion and the second-largest economy by GDP, China has achieved an unprecedented breakthrough in economy over the past three decades. While establishing an innovation-driven economy, China has re-oriented the world economy to the East and is on its way to overtaking the U.S. as the world's biggest national economy, as projected by the International Monetary Fund.

The Chinese government has set a goal of forming a comprehensive and moderately prosperous society with a well-established middle class, to be achieved by the 100th anniversary of the Communist Party of China in 2021. General Secretary Xi Jinping reiterated the sentiments of the country and the determination to rewrite its destiny with an elevated ambition — the "China Dream": national rejuvenation, improvement of people's livelihoods, prosperity, construction of a better society and military strengthening.

Higher education is a vital element of this national plan. China's government realizes that developing a modern and effective higher education system is essential to drive the country's economic advancement based on development of human capital, investment in research, cultivating an entrepreneurial culture and building a new economy based on innovation rather than low-cost labour.

As one of the world's largest higher education systems, China has close to 2,500 accredited universities and colleges, with a total student enrolment of 35 million (Ministry of Education in China, 2014) and 7.2 million graduates in one single year.

Hong Kong: One Country, Two Systems

Hong Kong has been in a unique position during China's economic rise. After over 150 years as a British colony, Hong Kong has developed a very British, indeed Western, way of life and business. The population is mainly Chinese, but with a significant expatriate population, some of whose families have been in Hong Kong for generations. Since 1997, Hong Kong has been "handed back" to China and is now governed under a "One Country, Two Systems" framework. Essentially, except for national defence and foreign affairs, Hong Kong is governed under "Two Systems". It has its own legal system, currency and passport, and its residents pay no tax to the Central government. In particular, its education system is separate from the Mainland's and most of its universities are modeled after Western ones, mostly British and American. The national examination and university admission systems are different, the use of instructional language is different, with Hong Kong using mainly English, and, perhaps most importantly, the university governance systems are different.

Yet, because of "One Country" and geographic proximity, as well as cultural affinity, there is frequent interaction between universities in Hong Kong with our counterparts in the Mainland. This takes place at all levels: student and faculty exchanges, faculty research collaboration, joint research proposals and annual meetings of university presidents.

Thus "One Country, Two Systems", as applied to higher education, gives Hong Kong universities a unique vantage point to observe the rapid change in the Mainland's higher education system. For HKUST (Hong Kong University of Science and Technology) in particular, with our vision of developing into a leading international research university with a strategic position in China, this special situation gives me as its president a front-row seat, but relatively objective, view of the impact of the rapid changes of China's higher education system on the rest of the world.

GLOBAL COMPETITION FOR TALENTS: FACULTY

Brain Reclaim

In its quest to develop rapidly a modern university system on China's scale, one of the scarcest resources is faculty. Because China's higher education system suffered a major setback and disruption during the Cultural Revolution, it simply has not yet developed either the capacity or the quality of the huge demand for qualified faculty members of its rapidly expanding universities. Thus China has turned to attracting talents from overseas, in particular its huge diaspora of talented students who had gone overseas for university studies and graduate education starting in the early 1980s, many of whom are now established faculty members at major universities in the West, some at the most prestigious ones. Deng Xiaoping has famously said, when asked why China allowed so many of its brightest students to study overseas, causing a "brain drain", that China has many talents that it can afford a small fraction to leave, and he predicted some of them will return one day. Well, it appears that now is the time!

China's Double-Edged Sword

One reason for these "returning sea turtles" is the fact that the material conditions in China, both living and academic, have dramatically improved in the last decade. Anybody who has recently visited major Chinese cities should have seen the rapid development of high-rise apartments with modern amenities, a world-class highway system and increasing middle-class car ownership (with huge environmental impact), abundant availability of consumer goods (most domestically made, but also global luxury goods) and the large number of international schools for children of expatriates and returnees. The Chinese government has also created special schemes, such as the famous "Thousand Talent Scheme" to attract returnees with Western-level salaries, housing benefits and other perks. Enhanced internet communication and air travel have also shortened physical distances and allowed the returnees to retain contact with their professional networks worldwide. The Western, especially American, university system of long and frequent university teaching breaks during Christmas, winter and summer allows these academics to take frequent visits to China without affecting their duties at the home institution.

Another motivating factor to return is rising research spending. Many Asian countries offer international talents generous research funding, lab space and other resources often superior to those available in Western countries, in addition to the capacity to explore new and unexamined topics. At the same time, research labs from western science and technology (S&T) corporations, built recently in China to tap into the huge market and talent pool, provide industrial research support and internship opportunities for students. Considering the impact aggravated by external factors in some Western countries post the recent financial crisis, resulting in cutbacks in public university and national research budgets, the attraction is enhanced even more.

A related development which has added to the demand for faculty is the recent rise of branch campuses of Western universities in China, with motivation ranging from spreading the educational vision of the home campus, to tapping into the huge student talent pool, to profit generation. Examples include the University of Nottingham in Ningbo, University of Liverpool in Suzhou, NYU in Shanghai, Duke University in Kunshan, the Technion Guangdong Institute of Technology and the University of Melbourne's graduate school in Shanghai. In addition, China itself is starting new universities, many aimed at a high international level, all needing top-quality faculty members. Examples include the ShanghaiTech University and the Southern University of Science and Technology of China in Shenzhen.

All of the developments above generate a huge demand for quality faculty and will continue to have significant impact on higher education systems worldwide. I would venture to say that most of the top academic faculty in Western universities who are part of this Chinese diaspora have already been approached by Chinese universities, often their alma mater, to take up either short-term visiting positions or full-time positions. How to reconcile this big draw from China with the home university's own governance and policy poses a big challenge for many universities in the developed world.

But China's plan to recruit top faculty is not without challenges — in fact it is well known and documented that schemes such as the Thousand Talent Scheme are not working as effectively as the government had hoped. There are many possible reasons. Senior faculty, especially those well established in prestigious institutions in the West, are often reluctant to give up their secure, tenured positions to return full-time to China. They are glad to accept part-time positions, taking advantage of the flexible academic calendar in their home institutions, to travel to China as often as their academic duties and family obligations allow. There are many potential benefits: they can recruit top graduate students directly, apply for research grants, and make use of major research facilities available in China. They can also visit their parents and close family members more often and get personal satisfaction in partaking in the rapid development of China, helping their home country. But an academic department cannot be built based on just a few part-time academic stars. Their much higher salaries and other perks often cause resentment among "domestic" colleagues. Younger faculty face a different reality. They are less established professionally and thus much more susceptible to internal politics in an unfamiliar academic department and research funding system. Even though they may have completed undergraduate degrees in China, they received their doctoral training, and some have begun careers, in the West, making them more familiar and more at home in a Western academic setting than in China. Coupled with scepticism about the pace of academic reform in China and their perception of the difficulty of returning to the West if things do not work out, these younger academics are often hesitant about returning. For them, the professional risk of returning is much higher than for an established academic. Finally, for any academic with young families, environmental concerns, such as air pollution and food safety, are often additional deterrents.

Impact on Hong Kong and Beyond

Interestingly, Hong Kong has benefited from the above considerations and been successful in recruiting some top talents from this Chinese diaspora over the last two decades. In a real sense, Hong Kong has the best of both worlds. On one hand, Hong Kong is an international city, its academic system is Western and thus familiar to members of the Chinese academic diaspora, the salary level is internationally competitive, academic freedom is enshrined in employment contracts, like at HKUST, information, including Facebook, Google and YouTube, flows freely, and basic academic support is more than adequate. On the other hand, Hong Kong is now part of China, culturally familiar, geographically close to parents and other family members, and Hong Kong academics have access to China's abundant academic resources in human talents and research funding. Of course, this relative advantage may not last forever, as China continues to develop and reform its higher education system, but for now Hong Kong continues to benefit from this "arbitrage".

The emergence of China's huge demand for quality faculty has already had, and will continue to have, a big impact on the global higher education system. Any university with top-quality faculty from the Chinese diaspora potentially faces losing some of its stars, either full-time or part-time, to China. More generally, beyond the Chinese diaspora, there will be more competition for faculty in the marketplace, making it more difficult to attract talents. There may be more requests from existing faculty for split-time positions with Chinese universities and new university policies may be needed to accommodate such requests. Denying them may run the risk of losing these faculty members. On the other hand, having faculty who can serve as a bridge to China may actually be beneficial to the home university. Each university will have to develop its own strategy that aligns with its international vision and competitive position.

GLOBAL COMPETITION FOR TALENTS: STUDENTS

New International Student Ecosystem in Motion

The competition for students has also become more intense due to China's emergence in higher education. Only a decade ago, the flow of university students was mostly from the East to the West. The best students sought study at the West's venerable institutions, with quality and tradition that was simply not available at home. Other students simply sought university education, which often was not available at home due to an inadequately developed and under-capacity higher education system. More recently, as countries in the East develop their economies, they are expanding their higher education systems, realizing that continuing economic growth depends on investment in education. As the quality and capacity of these higher education institutions increase, they are offering increased opportunities not only for domestic students, but also increasingly for some students from the West, who are drawn to these developing countries because of the economic and cultural prospects they offer. Thus the playing field of international student flow is now a bit more level.

On one hand, Asian universities have recorded a significant growth of 45% over five years in enrolling international students. China alone has seen a six-fold increase since 1998, reaching 240,000 in 2009 (Sharma, 2012) and is expecting to reach 500,000 by 2020, with 150,000 in higher education (China's National Plan for Medium and Long-term Education Reform and Development, 2010-2020).

On the other hand, with a rising middle-class in Asia, many families can now afford to send their children overseas for university studies, often paying full tuition. Amidst the enlarged scale with increasing demand from the emerging markets and the East, the number of internationally mobile students doubled over 10 years (2000-11), with Asian students making up more than 50% of all students studying abroad worldwide. The largest numbers of international students are from China, India and Korea, with almost 4.5 million tertiary students enrolled outside their country of citizenship today (Education at a Glance, OECD, 2014). While there has been continuous growth in the number of international students in higher education in the U.S. for seven consecutive years, most of the growth is driven by China, accounting for 31% of all international students in the U.S. (Clayton & Witherell, 2014).

How sustainable and stable is this new international student eco-system? Of course, no one knows for sure, but there are some danger signs and challenges. With the increasing number of Chinese students studying in foreign universities, mostly those in the U.S. and Commonwealth nations, most paying full tuition, these universities are increasingly dependent on international student tuition as an important source of income. For public universities, they run the danger of a taxpayer backlash as these international students often displace domestic students in flagship campuses with a limited enrolment. Over-relying on one source of income is also risky, as the flow of international students can notoriously change quickly, due to economic and political forces beyond the control of the higher education sector. The Australian university sector, which ranks third among the country's economic sectors by revenue, has recently faced crisis caused by factors involving Indian and Chinese students. Another uncertainty is that as the quality of the higher education system in developing countries increases rapidly, they offer an attractive, often at a much lower cost, alternative to studying overseas. Improving economic opportunities at home also give incentives for students to choose to study domestically, with the added advantage of building a personal network that will be useful for career advancement. Finally, it has been widely reported recently that a surprisingly large percentage of this new wave of Chinese students abroad, who are in most cases the only child in the family under China's long-standing One Child per Family policy, have difficulty adapting to the new academic and cultural environment, leading to high dropout rates. If this condition persists, then it would discourage more students from studying overseas.

Institutional Implications: Case of HKUST

HKUST has benefited from this recent more balanced two-way flow of East and West students. On one hand, Mainland Chinese students are attracted to study at our university because of our high academic standards and global rankings, proximity to home, all-English instruction, relatively low tuition (our non-local tuition is about the same as University of California's in-state tuition), and a very safe living environment. Hong Kong also has a very liberal immigration policy, requiring only seven years of legal residency (including as a full-time student) leading to permanent resident status. Students can also legally seek employment in Hong Kong after graduation and a not insignificant fraction of our Mainland students choose to work in Hong Kong after graduation. Both local and international employers like these cream-of-the-crop students who speak fluent English, Putonghua and Cantonese, and understand the cultures of Hong Kong and Mainland China, augmented by a global perspective and experience (e.g. over 40% of our undergraduates have exchanged overseas for at least one semester before they graduate.) For the period 2011-2014, the number of Mainland applicants to our undergraduate program averages about 6,000, all with Gaokao (China's national high school graduate examination) scores that would admit them to the top 10 universities in the Mainland. From this large number of applicants, we admitted on average about 180 — a very fierce competition indeed!

On the other hand, our university has been very attractive to international students as well, for mostly the same reasons as for Mainland students, but with proximity to home replaced by gaining a study experience in China but in a Western system that they are familiar with. For the same period of 2011-2014, we admitted on average 193 international students with close to 3,000 applications received in 2014. The top home countries are Korea, Indonesia, Malaysia, India and Pakistan, but also increasing applications from Europe.

These two cohorts of Mainland and international students, together with a large number of international exchange students, have greatly increased the cultural diversity of our student body, benefiting our local students with a global perspective even if they choose to stay home. Hong Kong has been rated as the 7th-best city globally for students (2nd in Asia) and has the largest number of top-ranked universities normalized by GDP in the world, according to a survey by QS.

What are the implications of the rapidly rising number of Chinese students flooding the global higher education market? Each university will have to decide whether to catch this wave and increase the percentage of Chinese students in its student body. Doing so may bring an immediate financial windfall, but also runs the risk of political pushback from existing constituents and potential financial instability by over-relying on one source of income. Not doing so runs the risk of missing out on opportunities presented by one of the biggest historical shifts in international student mobility.

REFORM

China's Higher Education: From Late Starter to International Spotlight

The full impact of China's economic rise in global higher education is difficult to fully assess because China has embarked on a series of major reforms of its higher education system, the full impact of which is still evolving.

China's higher education system has had a relatively late start. The oldest universities, such as Peking University (Beida), are just over 100 years ago. Some of them, like Tsinghua, were modelled after Western universities. This late start was further disrupted by major historical events. During WWII, whole universities, e.g. Zhejiang University, were uprooted and moved from coastal regions to further inland to avoid the Japanese invasion. During the Cultural Revolution, the Gaokao was suspended and university education was essentially stopped. The restart of higher education only began in earnest in the early 1980s. At that time, for example, only a very small number of professors nationally were allowed to be Ph.D. thesis advisors. Since then, the higher education system has ridden the economic wave of the country and has gone through many stages of reform and self-improvement. As an example of the dramatic change that has taken place, who would have predicted even as recently as a decade ago that a Chinese university would publish an Academic Ranking of World Universities, as the Shanghai Jiao Tong University (SJTU) does, that exerts enormous influence on higher education globally, including in developed Western countries?

Several reform plans have been initiated in the past two decades. Project 211 is the Chinese government's new endeavour aimed at strengthening about 100 institutions of higher education and key disciplinary areas as a national priority for the 21st century. Project 985, started in May 1998, is a constructive project for founding world-class universities in the 21st century. A huge increase in university funding was invested by the central government, with a corresponding rapid upgrading of campus infrastructure, as well as in research spending. In 2012 alone, more than RMB700b. was spent by the Central government on higher education. New universities are being formed, the most recent ones include the ShanghaiTech University as à la Caltech, University of Science and Technology of China (USTC) as part of the Chinese Academy of Sciences, Southern University of Science & Technology of China in Shenzhen, also an investment by the city of Shenzhen, partially-modelled after HKUST, with its first President Zhu Qingshi, former President of USTC, and current President Chen Shiyi, former Vice-President of Beida. These new universities represent attempts to build a new kind of university to compete with the best around the world and supply the elite graduates who will lead the continuing economic growth of the country. Most of the top universities in China are now true research universities in the von Humboldt sense. A new generation of university presidents is in place, most educated post-Cultural Revolution and with extended overseas experience, some with foreign-earned doctoral degrees. Thus the seeds have already been planted for sustaining this continuing reform.

One area of reform is the structure and role of higher education institutions. After WWII, China adopted the Soviet system of higher education.

Research was done at specialized research institutes and national academies, whereas teaching was done at large, state-run universities. Moreover, universities themselves were specialized into specific disciplines, e.g. universities of medicine, communication, petroleum, mining, etc. The von Humboldt model of a research university, where teaching and research are both conducted while complementing each other, was not adopted. The situation has changed and China has moved towards a more Western model, but the process is still not complete by any means, and probably will never be an exact copy of any particular Western model. The C9 universities, i.e. China's nine elite universities, are more similar to their American counterparts, with some being comprehensive universities, such as Beida, and others more specialized, typically only in S&T like USTC. Several have gone beyond their perceived and more specialized roles and transformed themselves into more comprehensive universities, like Tsinghua and SJTU. Some others have introduced a tenure system for faculty, and more generally different career tracks in teaching, research and tenured.

They are also turning increasingly global, in terms of attracting faculty from overseas, in sending their own students overseas for exchanges, in seeking strategic partners across the world, and generally in increasing their global profiles and branding, e.g. joining members of global alliances such as the Association of Pacific Rim Universities (APRU) and the Association of East Asian Research Universities (AEARU) — HKUST is a member of both. Some have started to offer more courses in English, with an eye towards attracting more international students. Some have started special colleges within their larger university, such as the Yuan Pei College in Beida, as an initiative to reform its undergraduate education by strengthening liberal studies. Other initiatives are designed to encourage cross-disciplinary studies, encouraging creativity rather than rote learning.

A relatively new development is the building of branch campuses of foreign universities in China. Examples are Nottingham-Ningbo, Liverpool-XJTU, NYU-Shanghai, Duke-Kunshan, Technion Guangdong Institute of Technology in Shantou, and Melbourne-Shanghai. These new universities all aim to bring the DNA of the educational culture of their home campuses to China. Some are also planned to be part of a global network of campuses based on the home campus. The Central government requires a domestic partner in all these new ventures and heavily subsidizes some of them, but also keeps a close eye on them, while all claim to have full academic autonomy. Hong Kong is not foreign, but falls under the same rules. As of now, only the Chinese University of Hong Kong has started such a joint venture — a new university in Shenzhen partnering with the University of Shenzhen. Many of these joint ventures are relatively new and it remains to be seen whether they will be successful.

Reciprocally, we may start seeing a trend for Chinese universities to open "branches" overseas. In June 2015, it was announced that Tsinghua University is partnering with the University of Washington to create the Global Innovation Exchange (GIX), a new institute to be built in Seattle to facilitate academic and corporate integration for technological innovations, partially funded by US$40m. from Microsoft. Tsinghua is expected to send faculty members to teach at GIX and also to help recruit Chinese students, providing an important global aspect. This will be the first time a Chinese university has a physical presence in the U.S.

Challenges Ahead

Despite these on-going reforms of China's higher education system, there are serious challenges and roadblocks. First, is the top-down, centrally-controlled system of higher education governance which compromises academic autonomy, at least in the normally understood meaning in the West. As is well known, every university in Mainland China has a Party Secretary, in addition to the President; how well a university can move forward to realize its academic plans depends on the working relationship between these two people. Both are appointed directly from the Central government — there is no counterpart to a "Board" or "Council" that governs Western universities. Student numbers and degrees at universities are also controlled centrally. For example, universities need central approval and an allocated quota before they can start a Ph.D. program. Occasionally, the Central government does issue "guidelines" to universities which in the West would be viewed as interfering with academic autonomy, although this sometimes does not prevent politicians in the West from interfering anyway. In 2013, there were unconfirmed media reports about a confidential internal directive widely circulated within high-level government departments, *Concerning the Situation in the Ideological Sphere*, prohibiting discussion of seven topics. Included on the list of prohibited topics were: western constitutional democracy, universal values of human rights, western conceptions of media independence and civil society, pro-market neo-liberalism and "Nihilist" criticisms of past errors of the party. Earlier this year, the Minister of Education publicly called for a ban on textbooks that promote Western values. Such edicts from the government are seen in the West as infringing on academic freedom, but one also has to understand that this system is designed for China's specific needs and constraints. Given China's history of university student-led unrest and the government's desire to promote societal harmony, I do not believe that the system will change in the near term. It may yet prove to be successful in the long run, but during the process there is an unavoidable tradeoff between public accountability and institutional autonomy.

A second challenge is the fact that sometimes Chinese regulations can have unintended consequences which may adversely affect universities. Recently, China released a draft law on Foreign/Overseas Non-Governmental Organizations (NGOs) Management, under which foreign NGOs (which most interpret to include universities) are required to seek approval of an official government sponsor and registration with the Ministry of Public Security before engaging in any local activities, including raising local funds. The proposed law is regarded by some (including Harvard University and New York University, which have openly commented on this) as potentially impeding transnational faculty and student collaborations, and undermining the ability of foreign universities to operate in China according to principles of academic freedom.

A third challenge is the fact that too many resources in too short a time can actually distort academic value and culture, leading to over-emphasis of faculty on publishing without due consideration for quality, sometimes even resorting to faking data and multiple submissions of the same work to different journals, as widely reported.

Finally, there are also expectations and challenges. With the rapid increase in the number of university graduates in recent years, the job market does not quite match the job expectation of the graduates, who expect to have high-level, white-collar jobs waiting for them upon graduation. The Central government has recently announced plans to convert some universities to polytechnics and vocational training schools.

What impact will these reforms and challenges have for universities outside China? Certainly, the modernization (or Westernization) and globalization of Chinese universities should open up many opportunities for universities from other countries who are interested to be more engaged with this emerging world power. Their students and faculty can potentially benefit tremendously. The huge amount of financial resources invested in Chinese universities can potentially benefit their international partners, in both research and education. On the other hand, foreign universities will have to realize that the Chinese university system is fundamentally different from theirs and they will have to adjust their expectations, as well as operational procedures, if they do decide to engage with Chinese universities.

SCIENCE, TECHNOLOGY AND RESEARCH

Unprecedented Infrastructural Strides

In addition to higher education, China has also been investing heavily in S&T development, seeing both as key to its future economic growth. These two efforts are also complementary, as much of the research is done at universities. China is shifting its economy from low-cost manufacturing and export-based to high-value added advanced manufacturing, design and global brand-building, and domestic-based. In May this year, China's cabinet said it would seek to boost automation in Chinese manufacturing, innovation and environmental sustainability, as well as upgrade railway equipment, engineering machinery and internet-connected factories.

In terms of technological infrastructure, China has been making historically unprecedented strides in a very short time, basically within the last decade. Examples are: the world's largest highway system — bigger than the U.S. — and high-speed rail network — larger than the E.U. — and the world's biggest internet usage and mobile phone penetration with 1.2 billion cellphone users.

Earlier this year, China announced its "One Belt, One Road" (the New Silk Road Economic Belt and 21st-Century Maritime Silk Road) initiative, aiming to strengthen ties between Asia and Europe and develop trade and infrastructure in the region. More recently, China persuaded many Western countries, with the notable exception of the U.S. and Japan, to join its Asian Infrastructure Investment Bank to provide finance to infrastructure projects in the Asia region. In S&T development, China now ranks the 2nd-highest after the U.S. in the world in government research and development (R&D) spending of US$258b. in 2013. In its current National 12th five-year Plan, R&D spending is being increased to 2.2% of GDP by 2015. The prediction is that China's R&D spending could surpass that by the U.S. by 2020. China now has one of the world's largest numbers of "science parks", the most famous is probably Zhongguancun outside Beida and Tsinghua in Beijing. Three of the world's largest five internet companies are Chinese, including Alibaba, Baidu and Tencent, and the world's biggest telecommunication company is Chinese — Huawei.

Chinese Investment in Big Science

China is also making a major investment in Big Science, and taking a page out of the U.S. playbook: supporting basic science leads to technological leadership, as well as attracting the brightest minds to pursue S&T fields. Some examples are:

- Deep-Sea Research: Jiaolong is one of the most advanced manned research vehicles in the world, which can dive to a depth of over 7,000m;
- Supercomputing: Tianhe 2 has been the fastest in the world for over a year;
- Human Space Exploration: Shenzhou, Tiangong-1 and Chinese Lunar Exploration Program are in full development, and a Mars program is being planned;

- Next-generation Super Collider: Higgs Factory; US$3b., 52km circumference by 2028, which would overtake that of the European Organization for Nuclear Research of 27km;
- Super Telescope: The 500m Aperture Spherical Telescope in Guizhou Province; the world's largest and most sensitive; three times more sensitive than the "Arecibo";
- Magnetic Confinement Plasma Physics: China is one of the seven members in constructing the "International Thermonuclear Experimental Reactor";
- Building 1st China Spallation Neutron Source in Dongguan; targeted to operate in 2018, it will be one of only four such facilities in the world;
- Next-generation Gravitational-wave detector will be one of the world's three high-frequency detectors;
- Experimental Advanced Superconducting Tokomak will be world's first fully superconducting experimental Tokomak fusion device ever put into operation;
- The energy emission of SH Synchrotron Radiation Facility is ranked 4th in the world;
- Daya Bay Reactor Neutrino Experiment: Top 10 Breakthroughs of 2012 (*Science*, June 2013).

Of course, making an investment in S&T research and infrastructure, even as large as China's, does not guarantee technological leadership, or a proportionate return on investment in the economy. In China, everyone knows well the "X.S. Qian question" (Qian was the Caltech aerospace professor who was famously prosecuted by Joe McCarthy and left the U.S. to return to China, subsequently becoming the leader in China's space program): will China ever produce its genuinely "home-grown" Nobel Laureate? Much criticism, as well as self-doubt, has been laid at the ability, or the lack of it, to innovate and be creative and lead. China is trying very hard to address this issue. Whether it will succeed eventually is one of the biggest questions in the scientific "race of the nations".

What are the implications of China's rapid advance and huge investment in S&T R&D for the rest of the world? Certainly, to the extent that advances in basic science benefit all humankind, China's contribution should be welcome. There will be an element of competition and national pride — but some competition can also be beneficial to all. S&T journals will see a dramatic increase in paper submission from China, with widely-varying quality level, stressing the refereeing system. But I predict that the high-quality papers coming from Chinese institutions will increase rapidly in both quantity and quality in the near future. Boosted by rapidly increasing research funding, the global rankings of Chinese universities will surely increase dramatically in the near future. Finally, it is not too far-fetched to predict that in the not-too-distant future, Western scientists may travel to China to make use of its major, world-leading scientific facilities, just as scientists all over the world now go to the U.S. and Europe for the same purpose.

INNOVATION AND ENTREPRENEURSHIP

From Counterfeiting to Innovation Giant

Universities today are expected to return to society the results of the public's investment. Technology transfer has become a pivotal key performance indicator for universities. Innovation and entrepreneurship have become key components of strategies adopted by many universities to achieve this mandate. Thus most countries with any ambition in S&T want to build their own Silicon Valleys, and most research universities want to imitate Stanford and UC Berkeley. If only matters were that simple!

Like most countries, China certainly wants to foster innovation and entrepreneurship. It is in a good position to do so: huge talent pool, financial resources and domestic market, as well as increasingly excellent educational institutions and technological infrastructures. Some of its most successful technological companies are indeed global leaders. So what's the challenge? One is the criticism that Chinese, indeed Asian, culture is not conducive to innovation and entrepreneurship, with its Confucius values of exam-centric, risk-averse, group-focused and high value placed on social harmony. So even though many Chinese have succeeded well when they moved to the U.S. to study or start their business, there have been relatively few domestically originated and globally recognized entrepreneurs. Even the big three of Alibaba, Baidu and Tencent have been criticized as following the pioneering trail set by eBay, Google and Twitter/WhatsApp.

My own thinking is more optimistic for China. First, sheer scale helps. With so many talents and such a huge domestic market, the opportunity for budding entrepreneurs with innovative ideas is enormous. Second, China's domestic market is not just huge but also has its own peculiarity and special culture, and out of this mix something innovative is bound to emerge. Third, the business of innovation is global and money goes where good ideas and people are. Increasingly, such opportunities are to be found in China and smart money, including that in Silicon Valley, has been making its way to China. Sir Michael Moritz, Chair of Sequoia Capital, told me that he thinks Shenzhen is the Silicon Valley of China, and Sequoia has been investing in China for over a decade. Wen Hsieh, a partner of Kleiner, Perkins, Caulfield and Byers, told me recently that he thinks the prospect for good investment in Shenzhen is even better than that in Silicon Valley. Finally, even the Confucius cultural barrier is succumbing to enormously successful entrepreneurial role models, not just Jack Ma, Robin Li and Pony Ma, but also HKUST alumnus Frank Wang, whose drone company Dajiang Innovations (DJI) is a true technological innovator and leader, also being one of China's first, and owns 70% of the worldwide market. With Wang as a new kind of role model, more young people will follow and some of them will be successful.

Trends and Responses: Case of HKUST

HKUST has benefited from our proximity to Shenzhen, and we are in fact part of the broader surrounding region known as the Pearl River Delta, which includes Guangzhou, the capital of Guangdong province. We were among the first Hong Kong universities to set up an "Industry, Education and Research" (IER) base in Shenzhen more than a decade ago and now we have built a second IER building in Shenzhen. DJI in fact was headquartered in this newer building a few years ago when it was still relatively small. We also have a larger suburban research base in Nansha, which is a district of Guangzhou, and which now is designated as one of six national developmental zones, while Pudong in Shanghai was similarly designated two decades ago.

Hong Kong itself has recently seen a surge of entrepreneurial activities. The government is trying to set up a new Innovation and Technology Bureau. There has been a mushrooming of private co-working spaces (over 30 now) where entrepreneurs can pay modest rental fees for "startup space". A number of large Mainland technology companies have set up R&D labs in Hong Kong, taking advantage of Hong Kong's advantages of low tax, excellent intellectual property rights protection, and attraction to international talents and excellent local universities. At HKUST, we are working hard in creating an enhanced entrepreneurial environment for our students and faculty. We just completed our 5th annual HK$1m. Entrepreneurship Competition. We run a "Build your own Business" seminar series. We are completing an on-campus space devoted to student entrepreneurship activities, to be run by students. And we have introduced an entrepreneurship minor for all majors. We hope to produce more Frank Wangs and DJIs!

CONCLUSION

In this paper, I have given my personal view of the impact of China's economic rise on the Chinese higher education system, and, in turn, on higher education systems in the rest of the world. I emphasize again that I only have a front-row seat, but I am not part of Mainland China's higher education system and I do not pretend, or have the authority, to speak on behalf of the Chinese official government position. My view is that this recent rapid change in the Chinese higher education system is not only good for Chinese citizens, but also presents tremendous opportunities for universities worldwide. Whether China will succeed in the ambitious reform of its higher education system is anybody's guess, but there is also no doubt that China is determined to pursue its goal. The whole world should welcome this development and will also benefit indirectly from it.

REFERENCES

Altbach, P. G., Reisberg, L. & Rumbley, L. E. (2009). *Trends in global higher education: Tracking an academic revolution*, UNESCO, Paris.

Clayton, E. & Witherell, S. (2014). *Open Doors 2014: International Students in the United States and Study Abroad by American Students are at All-Time High*. [Online] Available from: http://www.iie.org/Who-We-Are/News-and-Events/Press-Center/Press-Releases/2014/2014-11-17-Open-Doors-Data [Accessed: 31 July 2015].

Education at a Glance 2014, © OECD (2014). p. 344, [Online] Available from: http://www.oecd.org/edu/Education-at-a-Glance-2014.pdf [Accessed: 31 July 2015].

IAU (International Association of Universities) (2012). "Affirming Academic Values in Internationalization of Higher Education: A Call for Action" IAU. [Online] Available from: http://www.iau-aiu.net/sites/all/files/Affirming_Academic_Values_in_Internationalization_of_Higher_Education.pdf [Accessed: 2 May 2015].

International Monetary Fund (2008). "Globalization: A Brief Overview" [Online] Available from: http://www.imf.org/external/np/exr/ib/2008/053008.htm [Accessed: 2 May 2015].

Ministry of Education of People's Republic of China. (2014) [Online] Available from: http://www.moe.edu.cn/publicfiles/business/htmlfiles/moe/moe_1168/201501/182851.html [Accessed: 31 December 2014].

Peterson, P. M. (2012). "Liberal-Arts Education: Has the Global Migration Stalled?" [Online] Available from: http://chronicle.com/article/Liberal-Arts-Education-Has/132327/ [Accessed: 2 May 2015].

Rizvi, G. & Horn, P. S. (2010). "Reinventing higher education in a global society: a perspective from abroad" in Johnstone, D. B. (ed.) *Higher education in a global society*. Elgar, Cheltenham.

Sharma, Y. (2012). *Foreign students are part of 'soft power', but targets are ambitious*. [Online] Available from: http://www.universityworldnews.com/article.php?story=20120814135723490 [Accessed: 31 July 2015]

The Central People's Government of the People's Republic of China (2010). "Specific Sectors Defined by Outline for National Medium & Long-term Program for Talent Development (2010-2020)" [Online] Available from: http://www.gov.cn/jrzg/2010-06/06/content_1621777.htm [Accessed: 2 May 2015].

The International Center for Not-for-Profit Law (2015). "NGO Law Monitor: China" [Online] Available from: http://www.icnl.org/research/monitor/china.html [Accessed: 22 June 2015].

Tsinghua University News on Education Reform (2014). [Online] Available from: http://news.tsinghua.edu.cn/publish/news/4204/2014/20141102085929880474580/20141102085929880474580_.html [Accessed: 2 November 2014]

UW Today (2015). "UW and Tsinghua University create groundbreaking partnership with launch of the Global Innovation Exchange" [Online] Available from: http://www.washington.edu/news/2015/06/18/uw-and-tsinghua-university-create-groundbreaking-partnership-with-launch-of-the-global-innovation-exchange [Accessed: 22 June 2015].

Xi, J. P. (2014). "23rd National Conference on Party Establishment of Higher Education Sector" [Online] Available from: http://www.shmec.gov.cn/html/article/201412/78074.php [Accessed: 2 May 2015].

Zhang, J. (2014). "Developing excellence: Chinese university reform in three steps" [Online] Available from: http://www.nature.com/news/developing-excellence-chinese-university-reform-in-three-steps-1.16128 [Accessed: 15 October 2014].

CHAPTER 16

Cities, Research Universities and the Economic Geography of Innovation

Meric S. Gertler

INTRODUCTION

Within the past decade, an increasingly pervasive view argues that "the world is flat", and that location matters less and less when it comes to economic activity (Friedman, 2005). Information and communication technologies are said to be the key to understanding this trend, since they dramatically reduce the cost and increase the ease with which one moves information between geographically distant sites.

An alternative view proposes a different geography, one in which the distribution of economic activity — and in particular, knowledge-intensive and creative activity — is becoming more geographically concentrated (or "spiky") over time (Florida, 2005). The forces underlying this dynamic stem from the ability of particular places to foster the generation and circulation of knowledge among economic actors, and to provide a quality of life that is attractive to creative, knowledge-producing workers.

While there is undoubtedly a kernel of truth to each view, a more nuanced understanding of these issues emerges when one examines the key role of research universities, and explores the nature of their relationship to urban regions. Whether one considers research, teaching or "third mission" activities such as innovation and entrepreneurship, the local and global relationships that drive the success of the research university become readily apparent. At the same time, these institutions serve as key economic drivers of their host urban regions, drawing on their globally networked geographies to fuel this effect.

In this paper, I shall explore this relationship between universities and their host city-regions, arguing that it is fundamentally symbiotic. Moreover, I shall make the case that, contrary to the "world is flat" view, the importance of location has actually increased over time (rather than the opposite), and that this effect is evident with respect to all three elements of universities' mission: research, education and entrepreneurship. Notwithstanding the growing importance of location, rapidly rising new entrants have shaken up pre-existing geographies of knowledge production, thanks to major investments by the governments of emerging economies to build up research universities on a highly selective and concentrated basis. Such trends add new clusters of knowledge production to global networks, but the production of knowledge remains a fundamentally urban activity.

CITIES — PRIVILEGED SITES FOR INNOVATION

Let me elaborate, beginning with the role of cities in the contemporary global economy.

The international literature on the geography of innovation and prosperity shows that urban regions are privileged sites for innovation, entrepreneurship and the flourishing of ideas and opportunities. (See, for instance, Glaeser et al. [1992]; Storper & Venables [2004]; and Gertler [2003].) The forces underlying this connection are many and varied, originating from both the supply-side environment cities offer and the demand they generate.

Cities offer a geographically concentrated, deep pool of inputs that support entrepreneurship and the development of new products — including a wide array of specialized services and, of course, human capital. Indeed, there is growing evidence that the most talented, creative and entrepreneurial members of the labour force prefer to live in urban settings offering a high quality of place: cities that are culturally vibrant, physically appealing, safe, with good schools, and open to newcomers and new ideas.

Urban regions are home to large concentrations of sophisticated and demanding customers and deep, diverse and highly competitive markets that spur innovation. By providing interesting and important problems to solve, cities naturally stimulate new ideas or products to address them. Furthermore, because it is now widely recognized that, in many sectors, innovation is an interactive and iterative process, not a linear one, cities foster innovation particularly well. They bring technology users and producers together in a close, productive dialogue.

Similarly, cities foster the circulation of knowledge among firms — including those in the same or related industries, as well as those in seemingly unrelated industries. The capacity to facilitate such "knowledge spill-overs" and localized learning provides tremendously fertile conditions for innovation, even in a time when information technologies make it easy for information to be shared instantly over long distances.

These and other features of cities confer significant advantages for innovation, entrepreneurship, economic opportunity and growth, and social well-being.

Accordingly, public policy in many countries has moved increasingly to exploit the intimate connection between cities and a nation's capacity for innovation, resilience, and long-term prosperity. In the last 10-15 years, we have seen a growing recognition that cities are in fact increasingly critical national resources. They are now appreciated as drivers of innovation, and prosperity — not just locally, but at the national level.

The Right Honourable Greg Clark M.P. (then Minister for Cities and Constitution, HM Government, U.K.) and Greg Clark (Global Fellow, Brookings Institution/JPMorgan Chase Global Cities Initiative), make the point in *Nations and the Wealth of Cities* that "cities now aggregate the productive assets that shape competitiveness…" (Clark & Clark, 2014, p. 20). But at the same time, they continue, "the processes of metropolitan growth have, in many cases, taken place without clear economic understanding or strategic institutional guidance" (Clark & Clark, 2014, p. 20). In response, leaders from Brazil to the United Kingdom to Germany to Hong Kong are moving to provide that missing economic understanding and strategic guidance.

The same international literature to which I referred earlier makes equally clear that the goal of urban economic development strategy should be to enhance and support those local firms and sectors that demonstrate unique capabilities and competencies, based on their innovative activities. In a world of highly globalized production systems and supply chains, the only reliable source of sustained prosperity is to focus on those activities whose competitive advantage is difficult to replicate by other firms or in other regions.

The starting point in the endeavour is to acknowledge that those activities with the greatest innovative capacity are not evenly spread across the national landscape, but are instead highly concentrated in a relatively small number of city-regions. Public sector investments designed to stimulate innovation ought to be similarly concentrated, rather than allocated in a diffuse and overly dispersed way. And, as I shall argue below, such investments should target both physical and knowledge infrastructure — that is, research universities.

CITIES — PRIVILEGED SITES FOR RESEARCH UNIVERSITIES

This brings me to the second element in the interrelationship highlighted in the title: research universities.

One way governments have helped develop a region's competitive advantage is by investing in institutions of higher education and advanced research. In this connection, it is worth highlighting that the same features that make cities privileged sites for innovation, entrepreneurship and the flourishing of ideas and opportunities also make cities ideal sites for the flourishing of universities and other research institutions.

For example, universities thrive in part by solving problems brought to them by demanding local customers — who become partners in an interactive innovation process. The creativity and ingenuity of their faculty and students are enhanced by their exposure to interactive learning opportunities and rampant knowledge spill-overs locally.

The ability of universities to attract their most important inputs — faculty and students — depends directly on the quality of life in the city around them. Those same creative, energetic and entrepreneurial people, who can choose where they want to live, often decide to live where there are good schools and hospitals, vibrant neighbourhoods, stable property values and so on. So quality of place becomes a crucially important determinant of the long-term success of research universities.

In fact, it is evident that cities and universities thrive in the same environments and fuel the same outcomes. Indeed, the partnership between cities and universities has a *propulsive effect* — whereby each enhances the strengths of the other. This means that if cities are going to achieve their full potential, they will need to leverage the advantages of nearby universities or research institutions, and *vice versa*.

This relationship is *symbiotic*. A strong university helps build a strong city, and a strong city helps build a strong university. Leveraging this relationship creates mutual advantage, leading to prosperity for both the university and the city-region that hosts it. To put it even more directly: cities foster the development of world-class research institutions and universities, while at the same time universities and research institutions foster world-class cities.

The following observation supports this hypothesis. Of the top 100 universities ranked by *Times Higher Education* in 2014, 89 are situated in the environs of an urban region with a population greater than a million people — and all but one of the top 30 (*Times Higher Education* 2014).

The correlation is equally pronounced when you consider *Times Higher Education*'s ranking of the world's top young universities, the "Top 100 Under 50". Of the top 100 universities under 50 years old, 83 are situated in the environs of an urban region with a population of a million or more — and *every one* of the top 50.

While the mutually beneficial connection between research universities and their host city-region is strongly evident, this intensely local relationship is complemented by critically important global connections. Leading

Figure 1: Leading Urban Regions by research publication productivity 2011-2013.

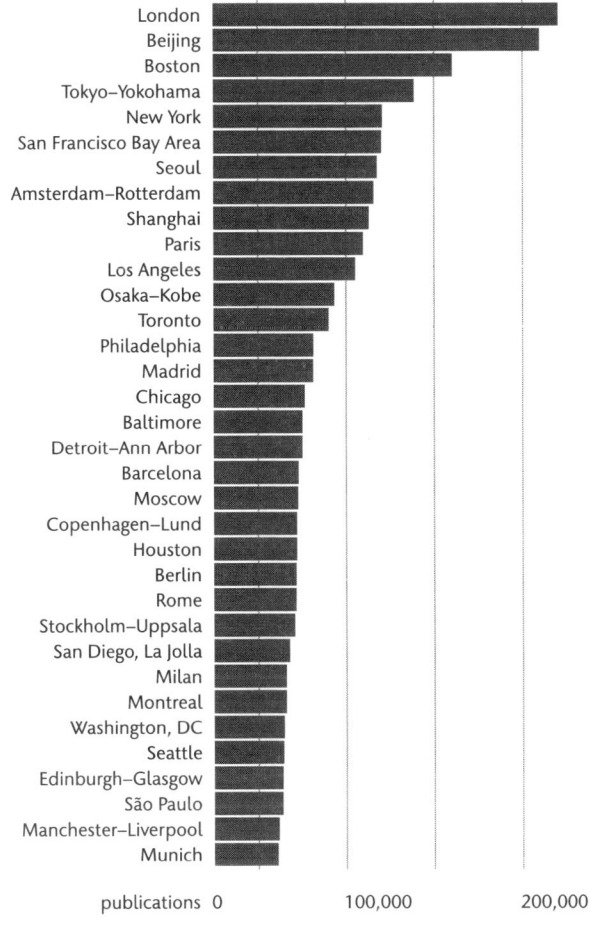

Source: Web of Science ® This data is reproduced under a license from Thomson Reuters (2014); and the University of Toronto, Office of the President.

urban regions with leading institutions of education and research are interconnected.

Figure 1 shows the world's leading centres of research productivity based on the number of publications produced between 2011 and 2013. Clearly, the world's leading research-producing regions are also the world's most dynamic metropolitan economies, demonstrating the extent to which research enterprise depends on the qualities of the urban regions in which they are situated — and vice versa.

However, it is important to note that these regions do not thrive in isolation. Collaboration (and co-publication) between scholars in different locations is becoming more pronounced over time, and increasingly this collaboration is *international*. So this phenomenon is also global in nature. Moreover these international partners are *not* randomly distributed around the globe, but are most frequently found at other elite institutions, located in other major urban regions around the world. In the words of a recent editorial in *Nature*, "Excellence seeks excellence, so elite national universities are also leading international collaborators" (Adams, 2013, p. 558).

Consider that the London urban region produced more than 195,000 research publications between 2011 and 2013, the largest number of any urban region in the world. Other urban regions among the world's top 15 research producing centres include Boston (135,000+ publications), Tokyo (113,000+ publications) and Toronto (65,000+ publications). These publications were produced in collaboration with tens of thousands of institutions in thousands of metropolitan regions. Remarkably, just these four regions — London, Boston, Tokyo, and Toronto — collaborated variously on more than 15,000 publications in that same three-year period. The institutions of education and research in these regions are the all-important gateways connecting their host city-regions to global knowledge networks.

Forward-looking governments around the world are increasingly recognizing the value of participation in these global knowledge networks. Consequently, as noted above, many national and sub-national governments have clustered their investments, building upon the strength of select regions' universities (and the regions themselves). Notably, they are concentrating capital funding for infrastructure, differentially investing in fundamental research at leading institutions, and attracting and retaining talented students and faculty, not just locally but internationally (see, for instance, Yang & Welch, 2012).

Moreover, the investments are clearly working (see Figure 2). Between 1996 and 2013, while the research output of the London region grew by 60%, the rate of growth from emerging research powerhouses was simply astonishing. Research output in Shanghai grew by 970%, in Seoul by 450%, in São Paulo and Singapore by 340%, and in Hong Kong and Mumbai by 200%. Collaborations among these urban regions and other knowledge-producing hubs around the world have also been skyrocketing, to the advantage of all cities that take part in this activity.

Why does this matter? Quite obviously, in London, Boston, Tokyo, and Toronto — *as in every other region* — our present and future prosperity depends on our ability to access and use knowledge; not just knowledge produced locally, but also knowledge produced in other leading centres of research and innovation around the world.

Hence, leading metropolitan regions are vital knowledge hubs. They are gateways, exchanging and developing innovations and ideas with partners around the world and, in the process, advancing our collective prosperity. A

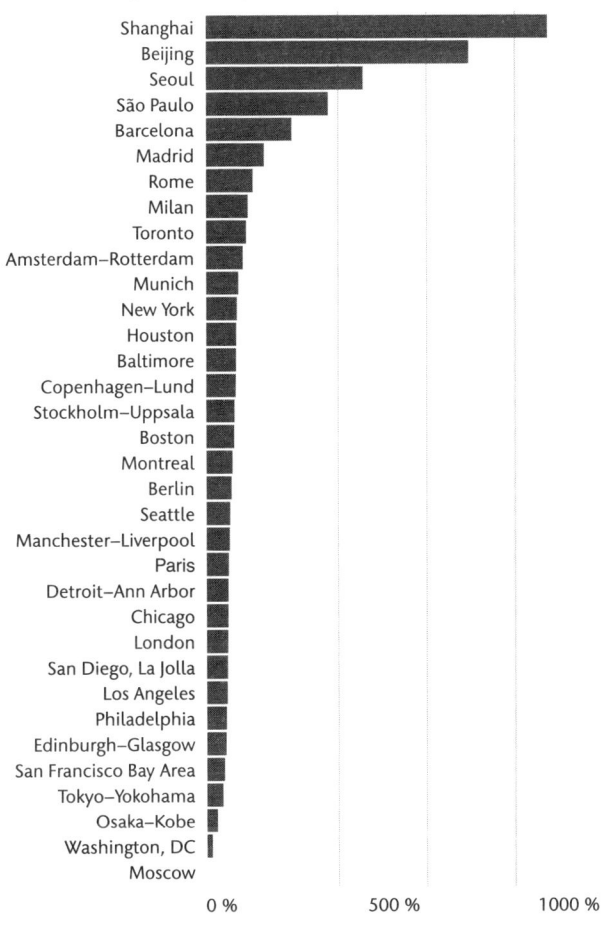

Figure 2: Leading Urban Regions by research publication productivity % change, 1996 to 2013.

Source: Web of Science ® This data is reproduced under a license from Thomson Reuters (2014); and the University of Toronto, Office of the President.

paper in the *Handbook of Creative Cities* captured this idea succinctly: "[W]ell connected research cities are likely to be important cities in the global economy; nodality in research often corresponds to nodality in other parts of the local economy" (Matthiessen, Schwarz & Find, 2011, p. 227).

In other words, well-connected, globally networked centres of knowledge production are increasingly coming to the fore as the world's leading economic centres. Venture capital and other forms of mobile investment now seek out these special places and the opportunities that are signalled by their world-leading research, talent and partnerships.

EDUCATION

Do the same analysis and conclusions derived from universities' research mission also apply to their education mission? Many would argue that the importance of location has declined over time when it comes to the teaching mission of our institutions. After all, information technology provides virtually instant communication, allowing seamless remote collaboration, and education offers a striking example. Enrolment in Massive Open Online Courses (MOOCs) has exploded. *Coursera* counts over 12 million users; *edX* over 3 million users; and over 4 million students are enrolled at Indira Gandhi National Open University in India. The numbers are continuing to grow.

In this regard, there has been considerable discussion of a revolution in post-secondary education driven by advances in digital technology. The focus of much of the discussion, particularly in the media, has been that innovation in digital pedagogy is liberating universities and students from the expensive constraints of real estate. This will drive participation and improve access — and certainly the numbers quoted above would seem to support this thesis.

It should be acknowledged that the possibilities afforded by advances in communications technology are momentous. Increasing access to education, the most powerful and progressive force in human history, is a wonderful development. Moreover, it is clear that we have only begun to appreciate the scope and scale of the possibilities that digital technology will enable.

In a 2013 survey of MOOC faculty from the *Chronicle of Higher Education*, there was overwhelming support (86%+) for the idea that MOOCs would eventually reduce the cost of education — and nearly three quarters of those surveyed reported that one of their primary motivations in signing up to teach a MOOC was to increase access to higher education (Kolowich, 2013).

Hence, these observations about the digital disruption in post-secondary education would appear to challenge the future of the symbiotic relationship between universities and cities. With access to education increasingly available online, the co-location of top universities and major urban regions revealed in the global rankings would seem to be endangered and likely to weaken over time.

In fact, I think that *just the opposite* will happen.

There is no question that post-secondary education is being disrupted. But not necessarily in the way that the media have articulated and popular imagination might believe. In this connection, it is interesting to note a tension in the modern post-secondary landscape. The rise of online learning is having a surprising effect: it is compelling us to ensure that the value of "being there" in person, in the classroom, in the library, in the lab, or on the playing field, is sufficiently great to compete successfully against purely digital modes of teaching.

Indeed, we are already seeing that new tools and technologies are helping us rethink the way we teach in the classroom. Paradoxically, digital challenges to traditional education are helping us reimagine traditional, campus-based education. This was apparent to those most closely involved right from the beginning. According to that same 2013 *Chronicle* survey, about three quarters of surveyed instructors who have taught online courses report that they have been inspired through this experience to change the way they teach in the traditional classroom.

More recently, efforts to study the pedagogical impact of technology-enhanced learning have produced some intriguing results suggesting how in-person forms of teaching and learning may be transformed and strengthened in the process. For example, researchers in the Department of Computer Science at the University of Toronto have observed important differences in learning methods and outcomes between students taking a traditional introductory computer science course and students taking an inverted introductory computer science course covering exactly the same material. In an inverted (or "flipped") classroom, students are first introduced to new material online through video clips or screencasts. Students then achieve a deeper understanding of the material through in-class problem solving, discussions and active learning, often in pairs or small groups and with the face-to-face help of professors and teaching assistants. Homework consolidates what a student has learned and helps prepare for subsequent classes and in-class or online quizzes and examinations (adapted from Bruff, 2012, and Horton *et al.*, 2015).

According to the Toronto research, overall rates at which students in traditional and inverted classes drop, fail or pass their respective courses do not differ significantly. However, students who failed the midterm and continued in the course did *substantially* better in the inverted class than those in a similar position in the traditional class. And similarly, students in the inverted class did significantly better on the final exam than their counterparts in the traditional class (see Campbell *et al.*, 2014; Horton *et al.*, 2014; and Horton & Craig, 2015).

This is a new field of pedagogical research and more study needs to be done. Nevertheless, early results such as those from the University of Toronto cautiously suggest that students in inverted classrooms benefit from the active-learning environment and face-to-face interaction with peers and instructors in the time traditionally reserved for lectures. In particular, it appears that students in the inverted classrooms are making better decisions regarding course persistence, getting individually tailored extra help, and addressing student-specific challenges. One plausible inference is that these benefits stem from increased opportunity for instructor-student and peer-to-peer face-to-face interaction.

Going beyond the confines of the classroom or the lab, universities can help foster the development of our students by harnessing the opportunities of the urban regions in which they are situated.

Experience-based learning and service learning, for example, are critical elements of post-secondary education that are inextricably linked to location. Co-op programs, internships, inter-institution collaboration, industry partnerships and urban research are activities that are fundamentally dependent on location. Universities situated in major urban regions are able to take advantage of such opportunities more readily because they are literally on their doorstep. Thus, urban regions themselves become important elements in post-secondary education.

In these ways, the value of *being there* is heightened, the educational experiences and outcomes for our students are improved, and the prospects for innovative solutions to global challenges are increased. A research-intensive university's setting is not electronically replicable.

SOCIAL IMPACT AND ENTREPRENEURSHIP

Increasing attention has been paid in recent years to universities' so-called "third mission": fostering broader social and economic impact by cultivating knowledge mobilization, innovation and entrepreneurship. Here too, I would argue, research universities situated in major urban regions have an important competitive advantage.

Let me offer the following example. According to the 1911 Census of Canada, 35% of Toronto's workforce (in a sign of the times, aged 10 years and older) was employed in the manufacturing sector, and the clothing and textile industries constituted the majority of the sector. Indeed, according to the Census, clothing and textile workers outnumbered bankers 50 to 1 and for every accountant in Toronto in 1911, there were five musical instrument makers (*Fifth Census of Canada, 1911*, 1915).

Today, the Toronto Census Metropolitan Area is the third largest technology hub in North America, comprising some 43% of Canada's technology sector by investment (City of Toronto, 2015). The region is the third largest financial services centre in North America (City of Toronto, 2015), and one of the top three largest life sciences clusters on the continent (Canadian Trade Commissioner Service, 2014).

Like Boston, New York, London, Hong Kong and dozens of other metropolitan regions, the Toronto region has reinvented itself continually over the course of its history. Where does such resilience come from? There are many forces at work, of course. However, among the most important is the partnership between the region and its institutions of higher education.

To be sure, the primary form of knowledge mobilization or technology transfer from universities to their host urban regions occurs through the production and graduation of well-educated human capital. This has been very much the model in Toronto. The graduates of its universities have been the backbone of an educated, diversified and highly creative workforce for years. It is this mutually enriching partnership, more than anything else, that has sustained Toronto's enduring prosperity, as it has in Boston, New York, London, Hong Kong and other major urban regions.

But this is only part of the story. Leading metropolitan regions are increasingly powering a surge in entrepreneurship, the very essence of urban resilience and reinvention. Between 2007 and 2013, the Association of University Technology Managers (AUTM) has reported an increase of nearly 50% in the number of start-ups reported to them (Association of University Technology Managers, 2015). University faculty and students play a vital role in innovation and entrepreneurial clusters, actively creating companies, jobs and entirely new industries.

Moreover, as Figure 3 demonstrates, these clusters thrive in urban regions. Conspicuously, 82% of the start-ups reported to AUTM during this same time period were spun out of universities within the environs of urban regions with populations greater than half a million people. This is no accident, of course. Start-ups depend for their success upon the multi-sectoral, convergent strengths found only in urban regions. New ventures of all sorts require access to capital, marketing, design, advertising, IT services, product development and testing, IP lawyers, management, packaging, logistics and highly qualified personnel. These elements provide an essential catalyst for entrepreneurship and a powerful spark for innovation.

In a virtuous circle, new businesses in turn spawn investment, employment, and partnership opportunities, along with local spill-over and knock-on effects. They open research and educational opportunities and build a region's capacity to absorb and harness the knowledge, discoveries and — most importantly — highly qualified personnel being generated by the higher education and advanced research sectors. And they create international affiliations with institutions in other jurisdictions, leveraging global knowledge networks for local advantage. These complex interrelationships form the engine of the world's most innovative regions, ecosystems where scholars, scientists, students, entrepreneurs, venture capitalists and industry leaders translate knowledge into prosperity.

CONCLUSION

To recapitulate, the relationship between universities and their host city-regions is fundamentally symbiotic and confirms the importance of location for research, education, innovation and entrepreneurship. This observation has important ramifications for public policy.

Success in a knowledge-based economy requires thoughtful, strategic support for a nation's urban regions *and* for its leading institutions of advanced

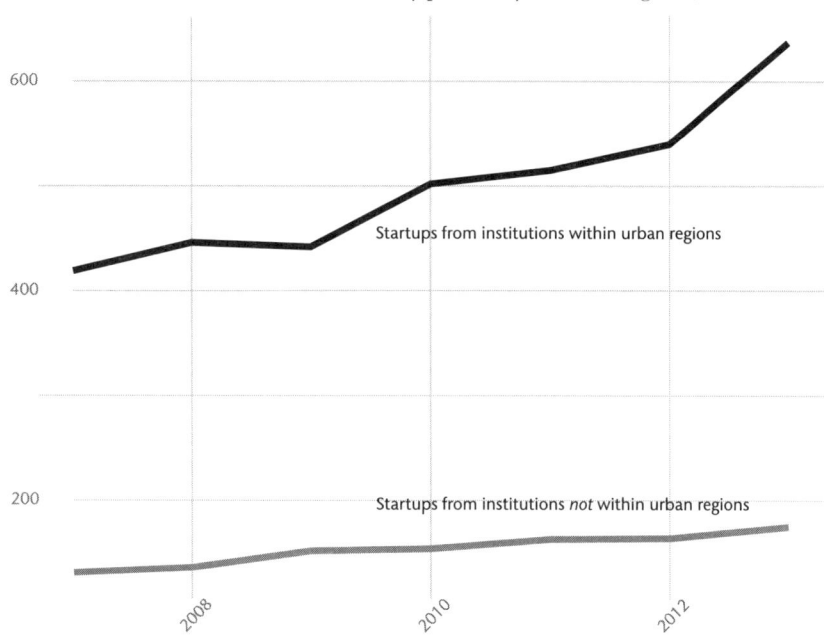

Figure 3: The Geography of Entrepreneurship (Stratups reported to AUTUM, 2007 to 2013 by proximity to urban regions).

research and education. Moreover, these leading institutions are most likely to be located in such urban regions. Public policy aimed at enhancing local and national prosperity, as well as higher education policy aimed at enhancing the global standing of a nation's universities, should acknowledge and leverage the relationship between these critical national assets. This idea stands in stark contrast to the status quo in many national and sub-national jurisdictions, where the political logic of distributing investments geographically and treating all universities as equal often exerts a powerful force over economic development and higher education policy.

This analysis also holds important implications for university leaders, at a time when the financial sustainability and reputation of many institutions are at risk (Baldwin, 2013). It is becoming clear that, for research universities in major urban regions, the ability to leverage the benefits of their favourable location — to advance their research, teaching, entrepreneurship and outreach missions — constitutes an increasingly important source of competitive advantage. Moreover, as they do so, these institutions also enable their host city-regions to address their biggest social, economic and environmental challenges, and achieve their full potential. As this mutually beneficial dynamic takes hold, the urban foundations of research universities' success become ever more strongly accentuated.

REFERENCES

Adams, J. (2013). "Collaborations: the fourth age of research", *Nature*, vol. 497, no. 7451, pp. 557-60.

Association of University Technology Managers (2015). *Statistics Access for Tech Transfer* (STATT), < http://www.autm.net/source/STATT/>. [April 2015].

Baldwin, W. (2013). "Moody's has bad news for colleges", *Forbes*, 13 March, <http://www.forbes.com/sites/baldwin/2013/03/13/moodys-has-bad-news-for-colleges/>. [April 2015].

Bruff D. (2012). "The Flipped Classroom FAQ," *Center for the Integration of Research, Teaching and Learning*, <http://www.cirtl.net/node/7788>. [April 2015].

Campbell, J., Horton, D., Craig, M., & Gries, P. (2014). "Evaluating an inverted CS1," *Proceedings of the 45th ACM technical symposium on Computer science education* (SIGCSE '14), ACM, New York, NY, pp. 307-312.

Canadian Trade Commissioner Service (2014). <http://www.international.gc.ca/investors-investisseurs/cities-villes/toronto.aspx?lang=eng>. [April 2015].

City of Toronto (2015). <http://www.toronto.ca>. [April 2015].

Clark, G. & Clark, G. (2014). "Nations and the Wealth of Cities: A New Phase in Public Policy", *Centre for London*.

Fifth Census of Canada 1911 (1915), vol. VI, "Occupations of the People," Ottawa.

Florida, R. (2005). "The world is spiky", *The Atlantic Monthly*, pp. 48-51.

Friedman, T.L. (2005). *The World is Flat: A Brief History of the Twenty-First Century*, Farrar, Straus and Giroux, New York.

Gertler, M.S. (2003). "Tacit knowledge and the economic geography of context, or the undefinable tacitness of being (there)", *Journal of Economic Geography*, vol. 3, no. 1, pp. 75-99.

Glaeser, E., Kallal, H., Scheinkman, J., & Shleifer, A. (1992). "Growth in cities", *Journal Of Political Economy*, vol. 100, no. 6, pp. 1126-1152.

Horton, D., Craig, M., Campbell, J., Gries, P. & Zingaro, D. (2014). "Comparing outcomes in inverted and traditional CS1," *Proceedings of the 2014 conference on Innovation & technology in computer science education* (ITiCSE '14), ACM, New York, NY, pp. 261-266.

Horton, D. & Craig, M. (2015), "Drop, Fail, Pass, Continue: Persistence in CS1 and Beyond in Traditional and Inverted Delivery," *Proceedings of the 46th ACM Technical Symposium on Computer Science Education* (SIGCSE '15), ACM, New York, NY, pp. 235-240.

Horton, D., Craig, M., Campbell, J., Gries, P. & Zingaro, D. (2015). "Persistence and outcomes in inverted and traditional CS1," *Research In Action poster*, University of Toronto.

Kolowich, S. (2013). "The Professors Behind the MOOC Hype," *The Chronicle of Higher Education*, <http://www.chronicle.com/article/The-Professors-Behind-the-MOOC/137905/>. [April 2015].

Matthiessen, C.W., Schwarz, A.W. & Find, S. (2011). "Research Nodes and Networks", in *Handbook of Creative Cities*, Andersson, D. E., Andersson, E. & Mellander, C. eds, Edward Arnold Publishers Ltd, Cheltenham, U.K.

Storper, M. & Venables, A.J. (2004), "Buzz: face-to-face contact and the urban economy", *Journal of Economic Geography*, vol. 4, pp. 351-370.

Times Higher Education (2014). *World University Rankings, 2014,* <https://www.timeshighereducation.co.uk/world-university-rankings/2014-15/world-ranking>. [April 2015].

Times Higher Education (2014). *100 Under 50 Rankings 2015,* <https://www.timeshighereducation.co.uk/world-university-rankings/2015/one-hundred-under-fifty>. [April 2015].

Yang, R. & Welch, A. (2012). "A world-class university in China? The case of Tsinghua," *Higher Education*, vol. 63, no. 5, pp. 645-666.

CHAPTER 17

University Leadership and Governance

Chorh Chuan Tan

In a world faced with profound challenges and opportunities, and driven by rapid disruptive change, universities can play important transformative roles. This paper argues that to be able to do so successfully a key requirement is for <u>universities to have a high degree of autonomy, tied to adequate and diversified funding, competition for resources and clear lines of accountability to stakeholders</u>.

A WORLD OF BIG CHALLENGES, OPPORTUNITIES AND CHANGE

The major global challenges the world faces are familiar to most, ranging from climate change and environmental sustainability, to population pressures and demographic shifts, to income inequality and profound socio-political changes. (U.S. National Academy of Sciences, 2015)

The university landscape too has been impacted and transformed by powerful global drivers, particularly globalization, intense competition across all sectors, the quickening pace of technological innovation and fundamental changes in demographics and societies.

These drivers have contributed to the re-shaping of the higher education sector in a number of key dimensions: (1) massification (i.e., the broadening of access to tertiary education to increasing numbers of students per birth cohort); (2) the proliferation of new, higher educational models, including private-sector providers, a much wider range of trans-national educational partnerships and new modes of learning, including on-line or blended learning; (3) greater scrutiny and benchmarking of output and impact against a global field; and (4) dramatic increases in international student mobility.

Universities are also increasingly called upon to fulfil expanded roles by building R&D strengths and translating these efficiently to drive economic growth and competitiveness, promote entrepreneurship and address major societal issues and challenges.

UNIVERSITIES: BALANCING TENSIONS, MAKING CHOICES, BECOMING MORE NIMBLE

The implications for universities are great and growing. As universities seek to redesign their education, position their research, enhance their impact and strengthen their differentiation, they would need to become better and better at making good choices, balancing tensions and responding nimbly to a fluid external and internal environment. The following paragraphs outline some of the changing contexts within which universities operate.

Massification is one of the most powerful trends that is fundamentally changing the higher education landscape. Across the developed and developing world, nations are greatly expanding access and encouraging larger numbers of students to take up tertiary qualifications. Universal access, as defined by a Gross Enrolment Rate (GER) of 50% or higher (Varghese & Martin, 2013), already applies across much of the OECD, and in parts of Asia, such as Korea and Japan.

In the year 2000, 2.38% of the world's population aged 15 to 79, or an estimated 99.5 million, pursued higher education studies. This percentage reached 3.38% in 2009, and is projected to reach 8.68% or 520 million students worldwide by 2035. A large proportion of this growth will come from Asia. In 2002, higher education enrolment in East Asia and the Pacific surpassed North America and Western Europe. By 2035, East Asia and Pacific will comprise 40% of total enrolment, with South and West Asia making up another 24% (Calderon, 2012). To illustrate, by 2020, the number of tertiary educated adults in China is projected to be equal to the total working population of the U.S. — 195 million people (OECD, 2012).

In many developed countries, the expansion of higher education, as well as slower economic growth and greater expenditures in the health and social sectors, has resulted in an increasingly resource-constrained environment for universities (European University Association, 2011). In the U.S., high tuition fees and burgeoning student debt have become major political and social issues (Bowen, 2012).

In less developed nations, the traditional structure of state-supported universities is often unable to upscale and upgrade quickly enough to support the large and anticipated influx of students. Consequently, the private tertiary education sector has grown quickly and, in some countries, has become the predominant means of access to higher education. For example, Indonesia has 83 public, but over 3,000 private higher-education institutions, accounting for more than 80% of the total market. In India, more than 50% of higher education is delivered through the private sector (Asian Development Bank, 2011).

Technology has also had a strong impact on higher education. In particular, technology offers the prospect, still largely unrealized, of enabling further massification of education with high quality and without incurring the very substantial financial outlay associated with increasing and maintaining costly higher education institutions (Christensen *et al.*, 2013).

There continues to be a positive correlation between a better-educated workforce with higher employment rates and higher wages. For example, the OECD reports, "relative earnings of tertiary-educated adults are over 1.5 times that of adults with upper secondary education, while individuals without an upper secondary education earn 25% less, on average, than their peers who have attained that level of education." (OECD, 2013). The report adds that, in particular, well-qualified young workers will be able to enter a "high-skills, high-wage" occupation stream, which will not only raise their living standards, but over time, strengthen their competitive position. Demand is expected to remain particularly high for graduates of STEM disciplines — Science, Technology, Engineering and Mathematics (Chang, 2014).

On the other hand, however, rising graduate unemployment and under-employment are a major and growing problem in both developed as well as rapidly emerging economies such as China (Qi, 2012). Substantial mismatches between the skills possessed by graduates and the needs and demands of employers have also been reported, suggesting that many universities have not kept pace with the deep changes in the nature of work. (McKinsey Global Institute, 2012)

For universities, all these shifts pose very substantial challenges while opening up interesting opportunities. These include new institutional positioning, differentiation and strategies to attract the best students who today have a much wider range of choices; to maintain high educational quality and standards for a much larger student body; and to reduce skills mismatches and prepare graduates who are well equipped for the jobs market which itself is changing very rapidly and profoundly.

In an intensely competitive and resource-constrained environment, universities also have to place a stronger focus on growing (or maintaining) and diversifying their resource base.

At the same time, universities need to balance more and more complex tensions and choices across a wider range of areas: education and research; basic research and the demands for more immediate applied research; a broad university agenda versus a more focused approach; and the relative prioritization of short-term versus long-term issues and challenges.

INSTITUTIONAL AUTONOMY MATTERS

Several studies support the view that greater institutional autonomy is associated, under certain conditions, with stronger university performance based on indicators such as global rankings and output.

In the European Union, greater institutional autonomy is considered a key strategy for its higher education institutions to restructure and position themselves to compete and thrive in a changing environment. In its Scorecard II report (Eastermann, Nokkala & Steinel, 2011), the European University Association observed that autonomy is not a goal in itself, it is a vital precondition for the success of Europe's universities.

The Scorecard Report identifies autonomy along four key dimensions:

- academic autonomy (deciding on degree supply, curriculum and methods of teaching, deciding on areas, scope, aims and methods of research);
- financial autonomy (acquiring and allocating funding, deciding on tuition fees, accumulating surplus);
- organizational autonomy (setting university structures and statutes, making contracts, electing decision-making bodies and persons);
- staffing autonomy (responsibility for recruitment, salaries and promotions). (Eastermann, Nokkala & Steinel, 2011, p. 9)

The Scorecard states that autonomy is not an objective measure, but a reflection of perceptions and indications along these four key parameters.

Interestingly, the United Kingdom ranks within the top grouping on all four clusters, which correlates with the overall sense that universities in the U.K. generally enjoy higher levels of autonomy than those on the continent.

While stressing that Europe's higher education sector needs to move away from over-regulation and micro-management of universities, the EUA has emphasized that autonomy must be balanced with accountability, and that increased autonomy does not equate to an absence of regulation.

In the Salamanca Declaration of 2001, and again in the Graz Declaration of 2003, the EUA declared that: "Universities accept accountability and will assume the responsibility of implementing reform in close cooperation with students and stakeholders, improving institutional quality and strategic management capacity." (Eastermann, Nokkala & Steinel, 2011)

In a separate study, Aghion *et al.* (2009) generated several measures of autonomy, governance and competition for research funding, and reported that university autonomy and competition were positively correlated with university research output, both among European countries and among U.S. public universities. They also found that when state universities received a positive funding shock, they produced more patents if they are more autonomous and face more competition from private research universities. The data support their hypothesis that universities that are more autonomous and need to compete more for resources are also more productive. In their words, "these hypotheses — autonomy and competition — are intertwined both in practice and logically. There is little point and possibly some danger in giving universities great autonomy if they are not in an environment disciplined by competition for research funding, faculty and students. There is little point in promoting competition among universities if they do not have sufficient autonomy to respond with more productive, inventive or efficient programs".

For Asia, the higher education landscape is very diverse, and differs markedly across different countries. More developed and mature economies, such as Japan and South Korea, have very well regarded educational systems and highly-ranked universities at a global level. Rapidly industrializing economies, such as Indonesia and Malaysia, are seeking to rapidly improve the scale and quality of their tertiary sector. Emerging economies such as Vietnam and Mongolia grapple with broadening access while raising quality, within constrained financial and manpower resources. Overall, autonomy for higher education institutions is part of a broader and more comprehensive higher education reform agenda being undertaken across Asia, with differing speeds and approaches.

In a World Bank paper comparing East Asian universities which have ranked well in the Shanghai Jiao Tong University's Academic Ranking of World Universities (ARWU), four countries were highlighted as having strong performance, after factoring their total population and annual citations per population: Singapore, South Korea, Japan and China (in order of ranking) (Fiszbein & Ringold, 2012). The paper further noted that to achieve optimal results, institutional governance should not be considered in isolation from system-wide governance. National objectives, policies and regulatory robustness are also key components to drive and support continued development. University autonomy in and of itself is "not sufficient for good governance".

THE APPROACH IN SINGAPORE

Over the past two decades, the Singapore government has progressively given the publicly funded universities more autonomy while maintaining a strong level of funding support.

In 2006, the government corporatized the National University of Singapore and the Nanyang Technological University as not-for-profit companies limited by guarantee. The key goal was to allow greater autonomy for the universities so that they could be more nimble and competitive to achieve excellence in education and research (Ministry of Education, Singapore, 2005).

Corporatization encompassed wide-ranging and fundamental changes involving organizational autonomy, financial arrangements and the evolution of the Ministry of Education's role in supervising and monitoring the higher education sector.

Of particular importance was the establishment of the University's Board of Trustees as the principal governing body. The relationship between the university and Ministry of Education was formalized through the Policy Agreement defined by the Ministry to which the universities must abide, and a Performance Agreement initiated by the university and agreed to by the Ministry, which sets out the goals, strategies and key thrusts and programs of the university over a five-year period, together with the indicators by which progress and performance would be tracked.

Corporatization was closely tied to an enhanced accountability and Quality Assurance Framework which included annual reviews by the Ministry and an in-depth evaluation of the university every five years.

I believe that this far-sighted and bold move by the Singapore government has been a major enabling factor in the continuing strong progress of Singapore's autonomous, publicly funded universities at both the local and global levels.

The next section outlines some of the most important implications and consequences of this corporatization initiative as exemplified by the experience of the National University of Singapore.

CORPORATIZATION: — THE EXPERIENCE OF THE NATIONAL UNIVERSITY OF SINGAPORE

Corporatization has impacted virtually all aspects of NUS but for the purposes of this discussion, I will highlight three areas which I feel have been of greatest significance.

Firstly, corporatization provided a powerful impetus for NUS to think fundamentally, boldly and long-term about its strategic positioning and goals. Corporatization also gave NUS the means by which these goals could be quickly and effectively translated into thrusts, programs and actions, as well as the nimbleness to adapt to changing circumstances.

Following corporatization, NUS established a new strategic planning cycle and integrated it closely with its resource allocation framework (covering funding, human resources and space). A much more robust and comprehensive monitoring system was also developed to track progress and underpin accountability. Corporatization also encouraged and enabled the much longer-term planning necessary for transformative change, while allowing nimbleness to adapt and respond quickly in the shorter-term.

In mapping our goals and strategies, a major consideration was the incorporation of national interests, objectives and concerns into NUS plans and programs. We considered this to be an essential role of a national university and part of the university's accountability to its stakeholders.

This does not imply a narrow mapping of NUS programs to articulated national goals. For example, NUS felt that it would far better serve the local community by being a global university centred in Asia, rather than an inwardly facing institution. Also, we believe it is important for the university to have within its portfolio of initiatives a good number which may be unconnected to shorter-term local interests. This is because the university needs to think independently about the future and how it can create value in the longer term.

Secondly, corporatization resulted in the substantial enhancement of professional and administrative capabilities and the creation of new competencies, necessary for competitiveness in the global higher education sector.

Nearly all functions in NUS were enhanced or revamped in the run-up to, and as a result of, corporatization. For example, the traditional Bursar's function was fundamentally upgraded into new resource planning and financial services capabilities, that today encompass all funds budgeting, long-term financial planning, a long-range capital plan that extends 15 to 20 years, efficient treasury functions, and so on. The campus infrastructure group was very substantially strengthened to enable high quality physical planning and construction, facilities renewal, integration of environmental sustainability measures over a multi-year time frame. New capabilities that had to be built included a development office to raise substantial philanthropic support and an investment office capable of providing good returns on NUS endowment investments.

Very importantly, corporatization further extended NUS human resource flexibility and responsiveness to effectively nurture, retain and attract talented faculty, staff and students in a vastly more competitive landscape.

Finally, corporatization is engendering a much stronger sense of collective ownership and participation amongst faculty, staff and students. It is important to note that when we speak of autonomy, there is a question of where the "centre of gravity" of autonomy should best lie. One key consideration in this regard is the balance between centralization and decentralization within the university. In the case of NUS, our goal is to create a system and structure which enable individual faculty and staff initiative, and which encourage Schools to be dynamic, while preserving the ability to work together well towards collectively defined goals. This is not a simple task and requires continual attention. Overall, however, while this is difficult to measure, my own sense is that corporatization has contributed in a major and exciting way, to the growing dynamism and "can-do spirit" within the NUS community.

REFERENCES

Aghion, P., Dewatripont, M., Hoxby, C., Mas-Colell, A. & Sapir, A. (2009). "The Governance And Performance Of Universities: Evidence From Europe And the US". *Economic Policy* 25 (61): 7-59 http://www.nber.org/papers/w14851 (Accessed: 14 Jul 2014).

Asian Development Bank (2011). *Higher Education Across Asia: An Overview of Issues and Strategies* | Asian Development Bank. [ONLINE] Available at: http://www.adb.org/publications/higher-education-across-asia-overview-issues-and-strategies. [Accessed 14 July 2015].

Bowen, William G. (2012). "The 'Cost Disease' In Higher Education: Is Technology The Answer?" *The Tanner Lectures*, Stanford University. http://ithaka.org/sites/default/files/files/ITHAKA-TheCostDiseaseinHigherEducation.pdf (Accessed: 14 Jul 2014).

Calderon, Angel (2012). *High Education in 2035 — The Ongoing Massification*, Available at: http://www.academia.edu/2612867/High_Education_in_2035_The_Ongoing_Massification (Accessed: 14 Jul 2014).

Chang, Li (2014). "International Student Mobility Trends 2014: The Upward Momentum Of STEM Fields". *World Education News And Reviews.* http://wenr.wes.org/2014/03/international-student-mobility-trends-2014-the-upward-momentum-of-stem-fields/.

Christensen, G., Steinmetz, A., Alcorn, B., Bennett, A., Woods, D. & Emanuel, E. J. (2013). *The MOOC Phenomenon: Who Takes Massive Open Online Courses And Why?*, Available at: http://papers.ssrn.com/sol3/papers.cfm?abstract_id=2350964 (Accessed: 14 Jul 2014).

Eastermann, T., Nokkala, T. & Steinel, M. (2011). *University Autonomy In Europe II — The Scorecard*. European University Association, Brussels. http://www.eua.be/university-autonomy-in-europe).

European University Association (2011). *Impact Of The Economic Crisis On European Universities*, Available at: http://www.eua.be/News/11-01-07/Impact_of_the_economic_crisis_on_European_higher_education_EUA_publishes_latest_update_ahead_of_major_new_report.aspx (Accessed: 14 Jul 2014).

Fiszbein, Ariel & Ringol, Dena (2012). *Benchmarking The Governance Of Tertiary Education Systems*. World Bank Group, Washington, D.C. http://documents.worldbank.org/curated/en/2012/01/24022077/benchmarking-governance-tertiary-education-systems (Accessed: 14 Jul 2014).

McKinsey Global Institute (2012). *The World At Work: Jobs, Pay, And Skills For 3.5 Billion People.* Available at: http://www.mckinsey.com/insights/employment_and_growth/the_world_at_work. (Accessed: 14 Jul 2014).

Ministry of Education (2005). *Autonomous Universities — Towards Peaks Of Excellence*, Ministry of Education, Singapore. http://www.moe.gov.sg/media/press/2005/UAGF%20Preliminary%20Report.pdf

OECD (2012). "How Is the Global Talent Pool Changing?" *Education Indicators in Focus*, (5), [Online]. Available at: http://www.oecd-ilibrary.org/education/how-is-the-global-talent-pool-changing_5k97krns40d4-en (Accessed: 14 July 2015).

OECD (2013). *Education at a glance 2013: OECD indicators*. OECD, Paris. http://www.oecd.org/edu/eag2013%20%28eng%29--FINAL%2020%20June%202013.pdf (Accessed: 14 Jul 2014).

Qi, Wang (2012). "570,000 Graduates Unemployed, And Why So?". Sina.Com. http://english.sina.com/china/2012/0611/475714.html

U.S. National Academy of Sciences (2015). *Global Challenges*, Available at: http://sites.nationalacademies.org/international/international_052200 (Accessed: 14 Jul 2014).

Varghese, N.V. & Martin, Michaela (2013). *Governance Reforms And University Autonomy In Asia*. Available at: http://publications.iiep.unesco.org/Governance-reforms-and-university-autonomy-Asia?filter_name=varghese (Accessed: 14 Jul 2014).

CHAPTER 18

The Role of Universities and Social Needs in Times of Great Change

Atsushi Seike

INTRODUCTION

It goes without saying that universities are social entities, and the very meaning of their existence is directly related to whether they can serve and benefit society. Although this may vary widely among universities, and an institution may place more importance on one philosophy over another, almost all universities are founded on the principle of making positive contributions to society. In order to realize their founding principles in the contemporary world, universities are committed to education, research and other activities including medicine, and in this respect there should be no conflict of interest between universities and society.

Often friction occurs between universities and society when there is a gap between the expectations of the two parties regarding the way universities should contribute to society. Firstly, while universities are focusing on how best to contribute to society in the long term, quite often society demands contributions with short-term results. Secondly, and this is related to the first point, universities value autonomy and independence, while society tends to think that universities should be managed and administered as a corporation or government office. It seems that this expectation gap has been widening recently.

As a part of society, universities cannot ignore its needs and demands. However, in order to take on a leadership role in society, it is also important for a university to assert and uphold its philosophy. To do so, financial autonomy is indispensable to a university. In this paper I will examine these challenges universities are facing today, using Keio University to explain some of my points.

THE FOUNDING PRINCIPLES OF KEIO UNIVERSITY

Firstly, we must consider what constitutes an ideal relationship between universities and society. This depends on how universities can apply their founding principles to the contemporary necessities of society and define the purpose of universities in today's context. As an example, for Keio University this means how best to apply the principles of our founder, Yukichi Fukuzawa, to serve the needs of society.

Keio University was founded 157 years ago in 1858 by Fukuzawa in the city of Edo, now called Tokyo. This was when Japan had just started to open its ports to the world after almost two centuries of national isolation, and it was only nine years prior to the Meiji Restoration of 1867 that brought about the fall of the feudal Tokugawa Shogunate, which had governed Japan for more than two and a half centuries.

It was a time of dramatic upheaval that greatly transformed Japanese society in many ways. Fukuzawa said of his generation who had lived through the feudal Edo period and witnessed the restoration that transitioned Japan into a modern state: "We have lived two lives, as it were" (Fukuzawa, 2008). In such a time of great change, one could no longer consider things as if they were simply extensions of past events. It was now important to understand new situations for oneself and use that understanding to form solutions.

A country will tread the path of modernization if it is able to strengthen its overall national power and improve living standards, and this is only made possible through progress in natural sciences and technology. Additionally, in order to realize a truly modern society, it is absolutely essential to understand and develop the humanities and social sciences, which aid modern political and economic systems.

In this respect, Fukuzawa realized the value of learning above all else and its particular importance in times of great change. And he particularly emphasized the importance of *jitsugaku* which was usually translated as practical science. However, for Fukuzawa it meant "science" or a scientific way of thinking as he made apparent in the *Keio Gijuku Kiji* (*Twenty-Five Years of Keio Gijuku*), a pamphlet published by Keio in 1883, in which Fukuzawa gave the *kana* reading "science" alongside the Chinese characters *jitsugaku.*

He established Keio University to foster young people who can think for themselves; and through the pursuit of learning, particularly of scientific studies, to gain new wisdom for the benefit of society and contribute to the progress of Japan. Today, Keio University's mission is to respond to the current needs and demands of society based on our founding principles.

REALIZING OUR FOUNDING PRINCIPLES IN COPING WITH THE PROBLEMS WE FACE TODAY

As a matter of fact, we are currently also experiencing great changes and internationalization, or one might say, an age of globalization where national borders no longer exist in various aspects of society such as economic activities. Societies are now experiencing great structural changes such as global warming, aging society and declining birthrates, natural disasters and frequent regional conflicts, which all question the very sustainability of our societies. Recently, in the market economy, the walls that divide nations are gradually coming down, and business corporations as well as individuals are becoming more exposed to global competition. Particularly in developed countries, we must provide more value-added products and services in order to maintain high standards of living, and, by doing so, the level and amount of competition with countries with lower wages will become tougher.

Japan is referred to as the forerunner of addressing many of these emerging issues, and is often one of the first countries in the world to experience them. The problem of an ageing population and declining birthrate is already most severe in Japan, and we have increasing risks both natural and manmade, such as risks related to volcanic hazards and to our regional security in the East Asia region.

There is also increasing necessity to provide more value-added products and services in order to maintain high standards of living in Japan due to keen competition with emerging economies in Asia. I believe this is also an opportunity for Japan because if we are first to find solutions to these issues, this may have valuable implications for other countries. Applying Fukuzawa's philosophy of contributing to society through learning, particularly through science, in the context of today means researchers and students at Keio University must work hard to find solutions to these issues that confront society. And we must nurture those who are able to cope with these emergent issues in an assertive manner. In this way we will be able to contribute to Japan and to the world.

In order to cope with these issues, Keio University created three educational and research initiatives in 2014. The first is the Longevity Initiative in which we conduct research and education to create a sustainable ageing society; the Security Initiative aims to make a safer and peaceful society; and the Creativity Initiative to promote a more creative society that can generate high added value. For each initiative, our goal is to conduct deeply-probing research, apply it to solve problems through mutual collaboration among the different disciplines, and use this process to educate students who can think for themselves. I would like to discuss this in more concrete terms using the Longevity Initiative as an example.

As is commonly known, Japan has the fastest-aging society in the world. The proportion of older people aged 65 years old and over is now more than a quarter of the total population. This proportion is continuing to increase, and in 20 years' time in 2035, more than one third of the Japanese population will be older people. To cope with such a tremendously aging population, which is unprecedented on a global scale, it is important for us to promote a Life-Long Active Society, in which the will and abilities of older people can be fully utilized. The increase in the number of active workers beyond the current retirement age would reduce the average per-capita burden and become a driving force of economic growth in the supply side as well as the demand side of the macro economy (Seike et al., 2012).

Of course, good health is a key variable in achieving a Life-Long Active Society. This is not simply about improving life expectancy, it is also important to know the potential of a society in which people lead longer and healthier lives. In this respect, Keio University's medical doctors and physiologists led by Professor Nobuyuki Hirose are conducting comprehensive research related to health and longevity including large-scale studies on centenarians ranging from their genetics to habits and lifestyles (Arai et al., 2016) Additionally, for research on regenerative medicine, a field in which Keio excels, we are accumulating knowledge and insight on how to maintain and restore the physical and intellectual capabilities of older people.

On the other hand, for many years Keio's labour economists have produced reputable research on the labour supply behaviour of older people, which has shown key variables that dictate older people's motivation to continue working. It has been understood through econometric analysis that, in addition to health, the employment system such as mandatory retirement practices, social security systems such as public pension, and educational attainment are found to greatly influence older people's motivation to continue working. Through this understanding, we can propose effective reforms of employment practices, public pension and education systems to establish a Life-Long Active Society (Seike, 2008).

By combining analytical results in labour economics with those in the medical and physiological fields, we are also able to understand to what degree investments in the promotion of health and longevity for older people affect their willingness and abilities to continue working. This interdisciplinary approach to research should allow us to deduce the implications and effectiveness of linking healthcare policies to employment policies.

This process applies also to the Security and Creativity Initiatives. That is, advancing research related to each initiative, collaborating with different disciplines at Keio University to develop effective policy solutions, and sharing more of the benefits of Keio's research with the world. By encouraging our students to play a more active part in this research, we should be able to see significant improvement in the quality of our education.

UNIVERSITIES SHOULD SEEK LONG-TERM RESULTS IN EDUCATION

Wide expectation gaps often emerge between universities and society because universities are striving for the best outcomes for the long-term future of society, while society often demands short-term results. It seems that in recent years, society's expectations for universities, especially from the business community, are becoming increasingly short-sighted. Regarding education, companies are often seeking more graduates with vocational abilities who can respond immediately and effectively to the needs at the workplace. In terms of research, they want more research projects that lead to short-term business profit, and this is where most of the funding is concentrated.

However, within society, universities are given the task of carrying out research and education with long-term prospects. In this respect, Fukuzawa wrote: "The 'guardian goose' cranes its neck to watch for danger, while the rest of the flock focuses intently on pecking their food. The scholar is also the 'guardian goose' of the nation. While people are preoccupied with the trends of the times, scholars should reflect on the past, carefully observe the developments of the present, and discuss the goods and bads of days to come" (Fukuzawa, 1874). One might also say that it is the duty of those who are accomplished in learning to make thorough and long-term assessments and deliberate on what is important for the future.

This has extremely important implications for the role of university education. Of course, universities today, particularly professional graduate schools, are expected to provide education that emphasizes practical application such as medicine and law. However, even for these professions, let alone for many other types of jobs, "work ability" or occupational competency is something that is mainly acquired on the job. At the same time, work ability is largely dependent on the kind of skills required for the technological structure as well as the state of the market for the products produced and services provided. The technological structure and state of the market may change frequently in one's long working life, so the work ability that is suited to the technology and market structure at the time of graduation from school may become obsolete sooner or later. Hence, the ability to adapt and respond to these changes becomes more important, particularly in times of great change such as the present.

In the history of Keio University, when the Fujiwara Institute of Technology, which is the predecessor of Keio's Faculty of Science and Technology, was established at the beginning of the Second World War, the first dean of the engineering school, Dr Toyotaro Tanimura, said: "A useful person now will also become useless right away," and rejected society's demands for engineers who could immediately apply their skills beyond the classroom. The then-president of Keio University, Shinzo Koizumi (1964), deeply appreciated what Dr Tanimura said, and wrote: "This should be indeed our educational principle."

This ability to think for oneself to respond to changing situations on the job will become increasingly important in contemporary society where technology and the market are changing at a faster pace. Of course, to think for oneself is not to think aimlessly but to think systematically. This is the process of learning by which students identify an issue, construct a hypothesis that can explain the issue, and test the hypothesis to form solutions. This is none other than the scientific way of thinking, therefore learning that is both broad in scope and deep will become ever more important.

In order to provide a variety of opportunities for students to engage in a wide spectrum of learning experiences, we have constantly promoted liberal arts education at Keio. We also strongly encourage even our undergraduate students to conduct academic research to experience the process of the scientific way of thinking.

UNIVERSITIES SHOULD SEEK LONG-TERM RESULTS IN RESEARCH

Long-term vision is also important for the role of universities in research. The role of universities is not to focus on research with short-term goals, that is, the kind that brings immediate benefits soon after its application. Even if the research has no market value now, researchers must undertake research that benefits humanity in the long term. In this respect, the paper published by the Global University Leaders Forum of the World Economic Forum at Davos in January 2012 that called for the support of basic research, clearly pointed out the importance of the role of universities in providing basic research, saying that "Today's applied research comes from yesterday's fundamental discoveries." It quoted the famous words of Sir George Porter, a former President of the U.K.'s Royal Society, who said: "There are two types of research; applied and not-yet-applied." Surely one important role of universities is to conduct not-yet-applied research.

Universities must take on an interpretational role, namely to connect long-term basic research to applied research or to businesses that can make ventures from applied research based on basic research. Here we should do two things.

Firstly, we should encourage our faculties and students to concentrate on what they are interested in, which often leads to pioneering and even game-changing basic research without them having to worry about money. A necessary condition of translating our basic research into something used outside the university is of course that we continuously produce interesting results in our basic research or curiosity-based research. In this we always ask governments and business communities for their generous support for basic research.

Secondly, we must attract attention from outside the university, including the business community, government and even the public as a whole. In this we have to use all kinds of networks we have developed including our alumni association. For example, if one company is interested in the application of basic research, they may donate research funds. If it really believes in the possibility of a venture based on that research, it may invest in the venture.

For example, Keio University has a research institute called the Institute for Advanced Biosciences in Tsuruoka City, Yamagata prefecture, which is located in northeastern Japan. It receives a total of 700 million yen each year in financial support from Yamagata prefecture and Tsuruoka city.

The research undertaken by the institute, which was made possible due to this governmental support, led to the creation of two new venture companies: Human Metabolome Technologies, a company which conducts metabolome analysis, and Spiber, which has developed synthetic spider silk fibre.

Human Metabolome Technologies has successfully gone public and is the only local company in Tsuruoka City to be listed on the stock exchange. In the case of Spiber, we asked an automobile parts company for its support, and the company is not only investing in the venture financially, but is also providing know-how regarding manufacturing and marketing. We have been supporting young scholars who make pioneering discoveries, in order to help them receive the financial support from local governments and companies that makes setting up venture businesses possible.

We were able to do that because we had developed credibility as a research university. So our ability to translate our basic research into projects outside the university is crucially dependent on to what extent we have truly developed our basic research and organizational sustainability.

UNIVERSITIES SHOULD MAINTAIN A NON-HIERARCHICAL ORGANIZATIONAL STRUCTURE

What makes universities different from other social organizations such as companies and governments, is the manner in which they are governed. The organizational structure of companies and governments is hierarchical with a clear chain of command, and in recent years there has been a rise in the notion of corporate-style governance of universities among politicians and business leaders in Japan.

Of course, universities, too, are organizations, so good strong governance is necessary. However, the freedom and independence of the individuals who comprise the university organization must also be respected as much as possible. This is an indispensable condition for educating university students as well as conducting advanced research.

This idea is particularly important for Keio University, which has its roots in Fukuzawa's founding principle of educating individuals to think for themselves through learning and bringing new wisdom to society by advancing scholarship. Since the establishment of the university, the non-hierarchical nature of education has been exemplified in our long-standing tradition of *hangaku hankyo* — meaning students not only learn, but also take on the role of teaching. The *Keio Gijyuku Shachu no Yakusoku* (Agreements among the members of the corporation) (Fukuzawa, 1979) established in 1871, defines this principle of *hangaku hankyo* as the following: "A man may be receiving instruction in one subject and at the same time may be teaching another subject. This man is a student and at the same time belongs to the teaching members."

In order to fulfil this spirit, Fukuzawa believed that those who learn at Keio University must all be equal. This equality between students was a matter of course, but that it must also exist between teachers as well as between teachers and students, was an extremely rare concept in a time when the rigid hierarchical structure of the feudal system made clear distinctions between teacher and students. Fukuzawa's rationale behind this concept was his firm belief that there was no end to learning, that teachers and students must learn and teach together, and mutually improve each other.

Fukuzawa also believed that only in a free and autonomous environment can learning be truly developed. In 1893, Fukuzawa wrote in an article in the *Jiji Shimpo* newspaper: "By nature, the way in which scholars love studying is akin to the way in which the drinker loves his drink — is this something one can really control? As this is something one cannot prohibit on one's own, one might suppose that letting them 'roam to graze' would suffice in some way for scholarship. However, in reality it is precisely the rules, restrictions and the like that clutter up the secular world that act as obstacles to true learning." He argued that taking an administrative approach to learning would do more harm than good in the advancement of learning, and this indeed can be seen as a caution to us university presidents who have a tendency to want to administer education.

A university functions to its fullest potential when its students and faculty members have the freedom to learn and conduct research, and the duty of the head of the university is to establish such conditions and maintain them. Their leadership is important in that he or she must steer the university to make social contributions to the fullest extent based on the founding principle of the institution, and in order to do so they must also implement optimal resource allocation. Heads of universities will only be recognized and regarded highly for their leadership role when they are able to realize an environment in which students and faculty members are given full freedom to learn and conduct research.

A SOLID FINANCIAL BASE IS ESSENTIAL

In order to maintain and develop an autonomous and active research and educational environment, we need a strong financial basis. In times of economic difficulties, when government funds have become increasingly policy-induced, and private research funds demand increasingly short-term profits, it has become more important for universities to have their own resources to conduct autonomous research and education. At present, we have four main sources of revenue, namely tuition fees, revenue from our university hospital, government funds, and revenue from asset management and donations. However, it is not an easy task to increase these revenues.

The annual tuition fee for an undergraduate student at Keio University is around $10,000, whereas for Harvard students it is around $40,000, for example. In contrast, the number of undergraduate students at Keio is around 29,000 and around 7,000 at Harvard, so if you multiply the tuition fee with the number of students, the amount for Keio and Harvard would be about the same. If Keio were to achieve the same student-faculty ratio in the undergraduate level as that of Harvard, we would need to increase our tuition fee fourfold. However, in comparison to tuition fees of other universities in Japan, our fees are already among the highest in the country, and it is not easy to increase this amount considering the backlash we may receive from the public.

Our yearly revenue from our university hospital is now 52.5 billion yen or $438 million, which is almost one third of our total income. However, under Japan's public health insurance system, hospital revenues must be proportionate to the amount of expenditure, and by definition the hospital cannot generate a large surplus earning. The surplus earning of the hospital is hardly sufficient for rebuilding or improving our hospital facilities.

In Japan there are government subsidies also for private universities, and Keio University is currently receiving 12 billion yen or $100 million annually. These include funds that cover general expenditures as well as competitive funds such as the Top Global University Project, and they support the management and operations of private universities. However, these funds only amount to less than 10% of the average operating cost of private universities, which is far from sufficient. In addition, with the financial crisis, both public and private universities have been suffering from lower government funding in recent years.

We cannot expect a significant increase in tuition fees, income from our university hospital, or government funds, so we must look to donations and revenue from asset management. If we consider that the educational service we offer to our current students must reflect how much they pay in tuition fees, we cannot use this money to invest in our facilities for future students, nor transfer it to scholarships for other students. Our general policy is that funds for future investments and scholarships must come from donations and the earnings from asset management, and it is fortunate that Keio University has always had a loyal and strong alumni community that we often call to for financial assistance.

Currently Keio University has more than 100 billion yen or $883 million in financial assets, which is the largest for a private university in Japan, and the revenue from this is 5.2 billion yen or $43 million. However, this is very small in comparison to American universities.

Of course there is always a risk of loss with asset management, and we actually suffered 53 billion yen in unrealized losses (when the difference between the book value and the current fair market value is at a minus) after the collapse of Lehman Brothers. In accordance with the accepted accounting principles, we had to declare an impairment loss of 17 billion yen (replacement of current fair market value with book value). Following this lesson, in the last six years since I became President, we have been working on gradually replacing risky assets with safer assets to create a healthier portfolio for the university. The only way to increase gains through a healthier portfolio is to increase our total financial asset, and in order to do this, we have been calling for more donations.

Universities exist in order to make various contributions to society based on their founding principles. However, each university must find the best way in which they can bring benefits to society. It must carry out education and research by taking into consideration what is best for its students and for society from a long-term, longitudinal perspective, and it must also maintain an autonomous and independent organizational structure. In order to realize this in a sustainable way, universities must possess the capability of securing a soundly sustainable financial basis.

REFERENCES

Arai, Yasumichi; Takayama, Michiyo; Inagaki, Hiroki; Gondo, Yoshiyuki; Yukie, Masui; & Hirose, Nobuyoshi (2016). "Centenarian Studies: An Interdisciplinary Research on Healthy Longevity." In: *Aging Mechanisms: Longevity, Metabolism, and Brain Aging*. ed. Nozomu Mori & Inhee Mook-Jung. Springer Japan, Tokyo. Forthcoming.

Fukuzawa, Yukichi (1874). *Minkan Zasshi*. Keio Gijuku Shuppan-sha, Tokyo.

Fukuzawa, Yukichi (1883). *Keio Gijuku Kiji*. Pamphlet, Keio Gijuku, Tokyo.
Fukuzawa, Yukichi (1893). *Jiji Shimpo*. Jiji Shimpo-sha, Tokyo.
Fukuzawa, Yukichi (1979). "Agreements Among the Members of the Corporation." In: *A History of Keio Gijuku Through the Writings of Fukuzawa Part 1*. The Hokuseido Press, Tokyo. (Original work published 1871).
Fukuzawa, Yukichi (2008). *An Outline of Theory of Civilization*. trans. David A. Dilworth & G. Cameron Hurst III. Keio University Press, Tokyo. (Original work published 1875).
Koizumi, Shinzo (1964). "Kitaerareta" Chikarazuyosa, Fujiwara Ginjiro-shi wo Oshimu. *Yomiuri Shimbun*. 18 March.
Seike, Atsushi (2008). "Pensions and Labour Market Reforms for the Ageing Society." In: *Human Resource Management in Ageing Societies*, ed. Harald Conrad, Viktoria Heindorf, and Franz Waldenberger. Palgrave Macmillan.
Seike, Atsushi, Biggs, Simon, & Sargent, Leisa (2012). "Organizational Adaptation and Human Resource Needs for an Ageing Population." In: *Global Population Ageing: Peril of Promise*, ed. Global Agenda Council on Ageing Society. World Economic Forum, Geneva.

PART V

Human Constraints

CHAPTER 19

From MOOCs to MOORs: a Movement towards Humboldt 2.0

Yves Flückiger and Pablo Achard

INTRODUCTION

Massive Open Online Courses (MOOCs) have attracted a lot of attention in the academic world in general and presidents' offices more particularly. But some worry that this model of teaching is a step back to a vertical and unidirectional model of knowledge transmission and that it breaks down the Humboldtian contract of mutual enrichment between teaching and research.

In this article, we argue that, on the contrary, MOOCs offer an interesting opportunity to reconcile teaching and research.

THE RAPIDLY CHANGING ACADEMIC LANDSCAPE

2012 was famously baptized "Year of the MOOCs" by the *New York Times* (Pappano, 2012). Nevertheless, and despite some storytelling, MOOCs were not born out of nothing. Actually, they are just the tip of an iceberg of transformations that universities have been experiencing in recent decades.

We distinguish four external drivers to these transformations:

- **Demography**: Worldwide, the number of young people is larger than it has ever been in history, mathematically increasing the need for education and more specifically for higher education. At the same

time, people live longer in good health and, at least in economically wealthy societies, old people are socially active and still seeking personal development, such as life-long learning.
- **Politics**: New Public Management policies have developed in many countries. In this context, universities are regaining a degree of autonomy that some had lost to governments and public authorities in the previous centuries. This new autonomy generally goes hand-in-hand with an increased demand for impact, performance measurement and accountability (Tolofari, 2005).
- **Economy**: First, the globalization of the economy has had impact on universities with an increase of mobility, of international collaborations, of competition. The academic playground has grown considerably. Second, many countries have seen an increase in their wealth and the development of a new middle class, eager to get more education. Particularly revealing is the case of China. Third, and maybe more importantly, the economy is more and more dependent on knowledge: "Knowledge is fast becoming the most important form of global capital" (Burton-Jones, 2001). Universities are impacted through their two core missions: teaching, as the economy needs more and more educated people; and research, as innovation is a key driver of growth.
- **Technology**: Computers have changed our ways of working, communicating, or doing research, to name but a few. More importantly, the advent of the Internet and tools like Wikipedia make entire libraries available at a mouse click and, more profoundly, modifies the role of the "experts". Professors are no longer the only source of information and today's "sage on the stage" needs to be more of a curator. Lastly, humanity produces more data in two days than it did from the birth of *homo sapiens* to the year 2003 (Lane, 2014).

This context has had a huge impact on the academic world. To highlight some of the most significant ones:
- **Massification**: The World number of students went from 0.5 to 100 million between 1900 and 2000 (Schofer & Meyer, 2005). It is expected to exceed 500 million by 2035 (Calderon, 2012). This means that a 30,000-student university has to be built every single day for 35 years to respond to this new demand. It also means that the geography and sociology of higher education are rapidly changing, moving from North-West to East and South, and from elite to mass to universal education (Trow, 2010). Of course, the expectations of this new student body are quite different from the ones of the few elite students of a century ago.

- **Online learning**: The increase of online learning happened before the birth of the MOOCs. Between 2000 and 2010, the percentage of U.S. students who took at least one online class jumped from 10% to 31% (Allen & Seaman, 2011). In this area, private for-profit universities have been particularly present. Hybrid- or blended-learning is more and more mainstream.
- **Continuing education**: In parallel with online learning, life-long learning has massively increased in the last 20 years. To take the example of the University of Geneva, the number of students enrolled in life-long learning programs or courses witnessed a 50-fold increase in two decades, before stabilizing.
- **Internationalization and competition for talent**: The advent of global university rankings in early 2000s shed light on competition among universities that is no longer national but of an international nature. Attracting the best students, researchers and professors is a key strategic issue (Wildavsky, 2012). International collaborations have continuously expanded and universities are looking beyond borders including, for example, through off-shore campuses.
- **Massification of research**: The number of scientists worldwide follows a continuous increase. Because science grows through debates among peers, this massification has, *de facto*, increased the specialization of scientists.
- **Economization of science**: Research funding has also evolved, implying more stakeholders, demanding greater accountability and, sometimes, greater and faster impact on society (Swiss Science and Technology Council, 2013; Stephan, 2012).

MOOCs are born from this context. They are not a tsunami or an avalanche. They are not a disruptive innovation brought by young challengers to oust fossilized old-timers. They are one among the many innovations that universities have adopted to face the multiplicity of challenges we just described. Having said that, MOOCs contribute to changing the academic landscape.

WHAT MOOCS ARE ACCELERATING

The University of Geneva was among the first European universities to enter into partnership with Coursera. As such, we have witnessed a number of evolutions that MOOCs are accelerating:

- **Knowledge dissemination**: Knowledge dissemination is one of the core missions of universities. MOOCs allow reaching a very wide audience, geographically, culturally and socially diverse. Nowadays, most of the MOOC participants are not actual students but life-long

learners. As such, it is a mistake to think of MOOCs as a replacement of traditional on-campus education.
- **Diversity**: Reaching large audiences, MOOCs allow the creation of two-way mentoring between people of different backgrounds who are following given courses. Hence, they can be an incubator and an accelerator for economic and social innovation. Well used, they can become an agent of empowerment and equity (Goldin & Katz, 2010).
- **Visibility**: MOOCs are a new tool in university branding. They are an open door in the classroom that permits the demonstration of competencies, excellence, high-profile topics to many stakeholders: prospective students, collaborating researchers, donors, public funders, alumni, collaborating industries, etc. They participate in the global competition we described.
- **Student selection**: If successful, a MOOC can be used not only to attract students but also the select the best ones.
- **Rebalancing teaching and research**: Research has long been the main, if not only, criteria for recruiting and promoting faculties. Providing a large visibility for teaching, MOOCs are rebalancing this status. Campuses are talking about teaching and learning as they had not for decades. This new focus on teaching is welcomed at a moment where public debate has accused universities of fooling their "customers", making them pay for star-scientists while being taught by adjunct faculty. Of course, MOOCs will create a new type of stars: teaching-stars, but universities are used to handling research-stars and should cope easily with this new challenge.
- **Teaching innovations**: MOOCs are also catalysing new ways to teach, and particularly collaborations between instructors. Just as research is nowadays a team adventure, teaching in a MOOC involves many people with different competencies. And, just like research, teaching in a MOOC can involve multiple institutions: universities, museums, media companies, experts... Following a mastery-learning philosophy, MOOCs bring also some new tools such as in-video quizzes or multiple peer-assessments. We expect to see a blossoming of interactive tools in the coming years.
- **Big data**: One domain where MOOCs can bring an important element to teaching innovations is pedagogical research. By collecting vast amounts of data on how student interact with pedagogical material, MOOCs allow improvements in efficiency. Currently, hundreds of A/B testing are being performed on the various platforms. By analysing conjunctly multiple variables, this efficiency increase will go hand-in-hand with a personalization of learning environments and learning material.

- **International collaborations**: The multiplicity of partners can extend beyond the creation of a single MOOC and partner universities can create common programs. These can be fully online or blended. For reasons of economic efficiency, the MOOCs constitute a tremendous incentive for institutional collaborations, in particular at the international level, mainly between the best universities in the world which will offer joint degrees.
- **Interdisciplinarity**: MOOCs are an efficient tool for interdisciplinary programs where students from diverse backgrounds need to get a mutual understanding of each other's domain.
- **Unbundling**: The ultimate personalization experience is a complete unbundling of higher education. Currently, campuses offer a package of services: teaching, mentoring, lab work, field work, remediation, access to libraries, sports, counseling, placement, internships, recreational and cultural activities, etc. All these activities can be offered by different institutions in different places, transforming each and every individual experience into a unique pathway. MOOCs participate in this trend by allowing classes to be taken remotely and by dividing knowledge into short learning modules. That said, a complete unbundling will be a nightmare for most students, lost in in too many offerings. Therefore universities will have to re-bundle parts of the student experience.

MOOCS AND RESEARCH

Beyond data on student behaviour collected for pedagogical research, some MOOCs have been used to collect research data in other domains. As an example, one of the instructors of Geneva's MOOC on International Organization Management asked volunteer students to send her short descriptions of Public Private partnerships, the central topic of her research. A hundred students sent her interesting case studies that she could use.

MOOC participants are also feeding research by providing feedback on new concepts, enriched by a broad cultural diversity and, very often, a good knowledge of practical situations where these concepts applies. This is epitomized by Duneier's testimonial on his sociology MOOC: "Within three weeks, I had more feedback on my sociological ideas than I'd had in my whole teaching career," he said. "I found that there's no topic so sensitive that it can't be discussed, civilly, in an international community." The online discussion forum spawned many global exchanges. Soon after Professor Duneier talked about social norms, using as his example the lack of public restrooms for street vendors — including an embedded video of New York vendors — students in

Hong Kong, India, Russia and elsewhere commented on the situation in their own cities. (Levin, 2012)

All these examples demonstrate that the arrival of MOOCs allowed the emergence of a new shape of research which would simply not be possible without this evolution creating what we may call Massive Open Online Research (MOOR).

But is there a way to better intertwine research and teaching in MOOCs? Answering this question requires first describing another movement, parallel to MOOCs, called Science 2.0.

SCIENCE 2.0

We have already evoked some of the transformations faced by science in the last decade. "Science 2.0" is one of them. According to the European Commission (European Commission, 2014), "'Science 2.0' describes the on-going evolution in the modus operandi of doing research and organizing science. These changes in the dynamics of science and research are enabled by digital technologies and driven by the globalization of the scientific community, as well as the increasing societal demand to address the Grand Challenges of our times. They have an impact on the entire research cycle, from the inception of research to its publication, as well as on the way in which this cycle is organized." Let us highlight some key domains impacted by this evolution.

First, new modes of knowledge communication arise. Preprints have long been the privilege of physicists, but are expanding to other disciplines. Scientific blogs emerged in the 2000s and continue to fuel the scientific debate. Social networks, either dedicated to scientists (ResearchGate, Mendeley...) or not (Facebook, Twitter, LinkedIn...) are being used by a vast majority of researchers (Van Noorden, 2014). So, if still dominant, the paper article in a scientific journal or conference proceeding is no longer the only way to communicate to peers or to a broader audience.

Second, a movement towards openness touches many aspects of science projects: open data, open notebooks, open codes, open access to publications... The aim of their promoters is to suppress the pay walls that prevent professionals, public bodies or laypersons from having access to the results of scientific research, vastly publicly-funded; as well as facilitating research in other laboratories or verification of published results. Although well in phase with the scientific ethos, this movement is slowed down by several issues, such as promotion practices, lack of incentives, privacy protection, and burden of data management.

Citizen science is a third expanding area. Popularizing science has always been an interesting but difficult issue. Making a non-professional audience fully engaged in the science process is even harder. Some domains like astronomy, botany or entomology, have a long tradition of amateurs collecting new data or species, but they remained an exception in the scientific field, largely restricted to professional researchers. Two projects have demonstrated that digital technologies can help close the gap between the 'main street' and the lab.

The first one is FoldIt. Researchers were facing the difficult task of folding proteins, i.e. finding their 3D structure based on their chemical composition and physical laws. The problem is too heavy to be solved by brute-force computers and too complex to rely on traditional optimization algorithms. With the assumption that human spatial reasoning was key to solve this type of problems, they invented a game called FoldIt where gamers competed to get the best possible 3D-shape for their molecules. The game was a big success and "players working collaboratively develop[ed] a rich assortment of new strategies and algorithms" (Cooper et al., 2010).

Another example of citizen science is the Galaxy Zoo project that latter evolved into the Zooniverse platform (https://www.zooniverse.org). In Galaxy Zoo, volunteer participants where asked to classify different galaxies depending on their morphology. Today, more than a million people are active in dozens of crowdsourced scientific projects, ranging from astronomy to humanities. This activity demonstrates the willingness of many citizens to be part of research projects that they find useful or intellectually interesting. By intertwining learning and research, citizen science links MOOCs with MOORs, both of them improving each other's impact on society.

COMBINING MOOCS AND CITIZEN SCIENCE

Together with a local start-up (MMOS), the University of Geneva is currently starting a project that will integrate a citizen science platform and MOOCs. The expected outcome is to improve both research and teaching.

On the research side, while tasks have successfully been completed by citizen scientists in a variety of disciplines, the commonly used platforms suffer from one major drawback: they tend to be limited to simple curation and annotation tasks that can be performed without having to teach or learn specific skills. But MOOCs provide a teaching and learning environment where the specific skills needed to gather data, to address complex data curation and annotation tasks, or to optimize model parameters, can be learned. As a result, the scope of tasks that can be crowd-sourced into MOOCs will be significantly larger than the one addressed in the commonly used citizen science platforms. As an example, one can imagine that participants in the Geneva's MOOC "Adaptation to climate change" could select beaches that seem to present risk of erosion (step 1), then enter the characteristics of the selected beach in a computational platform that quantifies these risks (step 2), analyse if the computed output corresponds to an identify level of risk (step 3) and, lastly, propose an action plan to reduce risk (step 4). A later stage will team up participants to address even more complex problems.

On the teaching side, the project developed by the University of Geneva considers MOOC participants as research and innovation partners focusing on a shared given research challenge. This stands in stark contrast to most common MOOCs that only provide students with coursework assignments whose solutions do not contribute to scientific research or innovation and whose role is limited to assessing knowledge or skills. By engaging MOOC students with data processing tasks directly relevant to novel research projects or to global grand issues, this project will not only contribute to strengthen their data-driven skills, but also reinforce their intrinsic motivations to learn and discover. By strengthening these motivations, we hope to attract additional students as well as increase the number of active ones.

TOWARDS 'HUMBODLT 2.0'

Emerging from a post-war *tabula rasa*, the Humboldt's model of university was conceptualized in the early 19th century in Germany. It is articulated around three major principles (Renaut, 2006). First, the university is autonomous and free from external pressures, namely, the Church, the State and society. Second, it intertwines two domains that were previously separated: teaching and research. Third, it encompasses all knowledge but without the dominance of one discipline over another nor the dominance of teaching over research or vice-versa.

This model was particularly successful: Germany was a scientific powerhouse by the end of the century. It was a major inspiration of the new American universities and it remained an ideal throughout the 20th century. We could argue that the model was never fully implemented. In the same manner, the research norms, formalized by Robert K. Merton, are contradicted by the history of science (Anderson, 2010). Nevertheless, it is an ideal-type that greatly influenced the "idea of the university".

This model has been challenged many times in the recent decades. But we follow Robert Anderson in that "it is better to see the 'idea of the university' not as a fixed set of characteristics, but as a set of tensions, permanently present, but resolved differently according to time and place. Tensions between teaching and research, and between autonomy and accountability, most obviously. But also between universities' membership of an international scholarly community, and their role in shaping national cultures and forming national identity; between the transmission of established knowledge, and the search for original truth; between the inevitable connection of universities with the state and the centres of economic and social power, and the need to maintain critical distance; between reproducing the existing occupational structure, and renewing it from below by promoting social mobility; between serving the economy, and providing a space free from immediate utilitarian pressures; between teaching as the encouragement of open and critical attitudes, and society's expectation that universities will impart qualifications and skills. To come down too heavily on one side of these balances will usually mean that the aims of the university are being simplified and distorted."

Today, MOOCs and MOORs, through the mediation of Science 2.0, offer an opportunity to reinvent Humboldt's model once more, to resolve these tensions differently.

In MOOCs, collaborations in teaching as well as horizontal discussions among participants lead to "**teaching feeding teaching**". In MOOCs, feedbacks from many cultures and practical experiences lead to "**teaching feeding research**". With the opportunity to combine MOOCs and MOORs and in particular citizen science, we will experience "**hands-on research feeding teaching**" as well as a new degree of research improvement by trained "human computation". These cross-fertilizations, combined with the new equilibrium between teaching and research, make us believe that the Humboldtian university will embrace the digital revolution with success. Humboldt 2.0 is just around the corner.

REFERENCES

Allen, I. E. & Seaman, J. (2011). "Going the Distance: Online Education in the United States, 2011." Babson Survey Research Group and Quahog Research Group. http://www.onlinelearningsurvey.com/reports/goingthedistance.pdf.

Anderson, Robert (2010). "The 'Idea of a University' Today." *History & Policy*, March. http://www.historyandpolicy.org/policy-papers/papers/the-idea-of-a-university-today.

Burton-Jones, Alan (2001). Knowledge Capitalism: Business, Work, and Learning in the New Economy. Oxford University Press.

Calderon, Angel (2012). "Massification Continues to Transform Higher Education." *University World News*, no. 237 (September). http://www.universityworldnews.com/article.php?story=20120831155341147.

Cooper, S., Khatib, F., Treuille, A., Barbero, J., Lee, J., Beenen, M., Leaver-Fay, A., Baker, D., Popovic, Z. & Foldit players (2010). "Predicting Protein Structures with a Multiplayer Online Game." *Nature* 466: 756.

European Commission (2014). "Background Document. Public Consultation 'Science 2.0': Science in Transition." http://ec.europa.eu/research/consultations/science-2.0/background.pdf.

Goldin, Claudia & Katz, Lawrence (2010). *The Race between Education and Technology*. Harvard University Press.

Lane, Jason ed. (2014). *Building a Smarter University — Big Data, Innovation, and Analytics*. SUNY Series, Critical Issues in Higher Education. State Universy of New York Press, Albany.

Levin, Tamar (2012). "College of Future Could Be Come One, Come All." *New York Times*, 19 November. http://www.nytimes.com/2012/11/20/education/colleges-turn-to-crowd-sourcing-courses.html?_r=1.

Pappano, Laura (2012). "The Year of the MOOC." *New York Times*, 2 November, Education/Education Life section. http://www.nytimes.com/2012/11/04/education/edlife/massive-open-online-courses-are-multiplying-at-a-rapid-pace.html.

Renaut, Alain (2006). "Le Modèle Humboldtien." Centre International de Philosophie Pratique et Appliquée. http://cippa.paris-sorbonne.fr/?page_id=1071.

Schofer, Evan & Meyer, John W. (2005). "The Worldwide Expansion of Higher Education in the Twentieth Century." *American Sociological Review* 70 (6): 898-920.

Stephan, Paula E. (2012). *How Economics Shapes Science*. Harvard University Press. Cambridge, Mass.

Swiss Science and Technology Council (2013). "'Economization' of Science." 4/2013. http://www.swir.ch/images/stories/pdf/de/economization_of_science_4_2013.pdf.

Tolofari, Sowaribi (2005). "New Public Management and Education." *Policy Futures in Education* 3 (1): 75-89.

Trow, Martin (2010). *Twentieth-Century Higher Education: Elite to Mass to Universal*. Johns Hopkins University Press, Baltimore.

Van Noorden, Richard (2014). "Online Collaboration: Scientists and the Social Network." *Nature*, 13 August. http://www.nature.com/news/online-collaboration-scientists-and-the-social-network-1.15711.

Wildavsky, Ben (2012). The Great Brain Race How Global Universities Are Reshaping the World. Princeton University Press, Princeton.

CHAPTER 20

Impact of Technology on Learning and Scholarship and the New Learning Paradigm[1]

Arnoud De Meyer

INTRODUCTION

Recently I took on the challenge of teaching a course to Undergraduate students at Singapore Management University. It had been more than 20 years since I had taught any Undergraduates, having spent most of my career at Graduate Business Schools. I did it partially because many of my younger colleagues had told me that teaching had changed tremendously. Deep down I may have felt that I was perhaps a little out of touch with what happened inside and, as I would soon discover, outside our classrooms.

I was indeed intrigued by the experience. When I entered the classroom for my first class, I was confronted with a forest of laptops, and most students had as well a smartphone if not a tablet computer on the side. The class I taught was very interactive, and I was often surprised how students would pull up additional material through the internet to complement, if not correct, what I had shared. They had done their homework and watched YouTube videos about some of the cast in the cases I taught. And often they had updated the stories discussed in the case. I also noticed that many of them had more than one website open, and were combining the discussion, my slides and other

---

1. This paper has benefited significantly from the comments of Sriven Naidu and Tan Gan Hup. I wish to thank them. But the responsibility for the positions taken in this paper is mine.

materials with an occasional glance at Facebook, Weibo or another social network site. The students admitted that there was a parallel class discussion session going on over these networks about what was happening in class. I realized quickly that even in a very interactive class I never had their full attention. But I also quickly learned that I could keep the conversations going before and after class over the same websites or our Learning Management System (LMS) and thus enrich the learning experience.

At about the same time the University went through a major review and revision of the Library, reducing drastically the number of printed books and journals, thereby also reducing the number of racks and making space for a 24/7 study and group discussion facility. We had set it up as an experiment with different types of furniture and functions, so as to see what students do with such facilities. It struck me that while students were often quietly studying in front of their laptop and with headphones deeply plugged into their ears, they also wanted to sit together, apparently studying together, or as one said, "hang out" with each other.

Technology in education is not alien to me. I have actively already participated in three waves of using technology to change the nature of higher education: the development of videos for individual learning in the early 1990s, the first interactive online programmes in the late 1990s, and blended tailor-made programmes for executives in the early 2000s. Frankly these previous waves had all somewhat mixed results. But I have to admit that what I lived through in the recent years is of a very different nature. I see the emergence of a radically different learning paradigm.

The impact of technology on learners entering university shouldn't be underestimated. Sophisticated Info-comm technology penetrates daily life at an accelerating rate. Students entering University today saw the first smartphone when they were 6 and may have been using an iPhone when they were 12. Our next wave of students will include many who used the iPhone from when they were 8. Those who are currently in primary school — well, iPhones, Facebook or Weibo, Twitter existed even before they were born.

Increasingly, each cohort of "digital natives" entering a university for a Bachelor's degree will expect that their learning experience will build upon the competencies and IT literacy they have grown up with. Such competencies will include the ability to acquire knowledge from the internet, to collaborate online synchronously and remotely, etc.

Many Universities scramble to adapt curricula to be more in step with rapidly changing expectations of employers. We may need to begin questioning more seriously how much more responsively Universities should monitor and adapt to the changing profile of the students they enrol.

Like many other Universities, we also see the growth of research about and anchored in Big Data. It seems to change the nature of the research paradigm.

Predictive Analytics and Social Technology have become the topic of the day in research methods. As many have argued, this may well change the way we perform empirical research, emphasizing much more a renewed inductive approach over the more accepted hypothesis-driven Popperian approach or model building.

These and other events have made me reflect on how technological evolution will have a lasting impact on learning and scholarship.

A FEW HELPFUL CONCEPTS

I found it helpful in my understanding of the role of technology to rely on four concepts.

The first one is Sociomateriality as proposed by Orlikowsky and Scott (2008). They make the distinction between three different research views of social and technical worlds. The first view is that humans and technology are assumed to be discrete, independent entities with inherent characteristics. The second assumes that humans and technology are interdependent systems that shape each other through on-going interaction. The third, the Sociomaterial View, is that humans and technology only exist through their temporally entanglement.

Simply put, the first view sees students and technology as independent. For example, a student does not change or act differently because of different types of classrooms. The second view implies that we recognize that technology interacts with students, and enables them to perform different activities. In this view, for example, online books or journals enable our students to consult literature independent from the place where they are, or it allows us to offer online classes which can be attended by students all over the world. But the basic experience of analysing the literature or attending a class leading to a degree does not change fundamentally.

The third view implies that through the entanglement of technology and humans, we actually become different beings. Many scholars who study the relationship between Men and Technology had observed this before. Suchman (2007) describes how engineers and designers working with Product Life Cycle Management Systems (including CAD-CAM) behave totally different than in earlier design environments, when they become immersed in a multiplicity of documents, conversations (on an international scale), virtual excursions to a project site, etc. MacKenzie and Millo (2003) noted in their analysis of the Black-Scholtes pricing model in options markets, that it was originally a mere theoretical formula, but that it enacted over time a world of computer algorithms, professional skills and financial institutions in which the human actors became very different financial professionals. In the same way, we can argue that our students are actually different: they learn differently and act differently because of their entanglement with new forms of information and communication technologies. The student who is always connected, who has access to an overload of information, who wants to express freely his or her opinion on blogs, who combines living in virtual and face-to-face networks is a different person than the one who went to lectures to take notes, who studied from printed textbooks and wrote letters. If we accept this hypothesis we need to look for *a different learning paradigm that optimizes the learning of this new student.*

The second theoretical concept that can help us is how management scholars have developed a new approach to service innovation. Barras (1986) suggested in his influential paper that, contrary to product innovation, service innovation follows a reverse product cycle. Service organizations adopt in first instance a technological platform to increase the efficiency of the service production and delivery, followed by the improvement of quality and effectiveness. Only in a third phase does the technology assist in generating wholly transformed or truly innovative services. This model was originally developed for financial and professional services, but we have shown that it can easily be applied to ICT based innovations (De Meyer *et al.*, 2001). Internet provided a technological platform on a network, where first we could share information and mails in a more efficient way, then we improved access to data and applications, and finally we created totally new services (as is illustrated by Amazon in the retail sector or Facebook in networking).

This reverse product cycle may well apply directly to what happens in the learning environment at our universities. The ICT platforms were first used to enhance efficiency e.g. by making class materials available online and by offering simple MOOCs. Later on we improved the quality of the learning environment by providing rich media information, taping lectures so that students could review the materials more easily, etc. Now we are in the phase where *truly disruptive and innovative approaches to create a new learning environment have become possible.*

A third concept that may help us is that of the Service-Dominant logic (Vargo & Lusch, 2008). This approach describes a service not as some form of an intangible product, but as "a process of using one's resources (e.g. knowledge) for someone's (self or other) benefit as compared to the more traditional conceptualization of services [...] as a unit of output (i.e. an intangible product)" (Barrett *et al.*, 2015). Learning at our institutions appears clearly to be such a process. Learning as an output of what we provide at Universities is not a discrete intangible product, but a continuing process. We need to provide an answer to how we redesign this process in the current context, where *Information technology will no doubt play a central role in the formation and functioning of our learning ecosystems* and thus in learning innovation.

The fourth concept is of a different nature. It is about the role that Big Data may play in influencing our research and research methods (Gandomi

& Haider, 2015). Big Data, characterized by the three Vs of Volume, Variety and Velocity, is expected to have a still uncertain impact on what and how we research through prospective analytics. Prospective analytics can be applied to many fields from predicting the failure of jet engines based on the stream of data from several thousand sensors, to predicting customers' next moves based on what they buy, when they buy, and even what they may say on social media. It is to a large extent based on pattern recognition and discovery of more or less complex relationships. This is very different from our traditional research methods. As Martin Rees, the former President of the Royal Society in the U.K., has said: "Big Data will allow us to mine and mash our way to unexpected discoveries and insights. It may allow us to ask new questions, one that we couldn't have asked when science depended on the work of a few people in a single lab working in a limited area of knowledge with just a few gigabytes of processing power" (Pisani, 2010). *The days of hypothesis-driven scientific endeavour may be behind us. Now it is all about pattern and relation recognition.*

WHERE WILL THIS LEAD US?

In the following sections I want to speculate on what these four concepts entail for teaching (or learning), research and the business model for the Universities.

Impact on education

Let me be clear: I will not dwell any more on the effects of technology on the efficiency or the quality enhancement of our delivery systems. Many of us have implemented online LMS, online course materials, and we may have experimented with MOOCs or other forms of distant learning. Keeping in mind that we are searching for an innovative and disruptive learning paradigm, I would like to propose five additional changes:

We are moving *from a teaching paradigm towards a student-centered learning paradigm*. I was raised in an era where Universities had a few quasi-monopolies: University faculty were the source of knowledge, University Libraries had a quasi-monopoly on information. Universities were bound by their physical location and it was our task as educators to provide knowledge (and in some cases even bits of wisdom) to the students. The only monopoly we may still have today is the right to grant degrees. But all else is widespread and competitive: geographical location and distances have become almost irrelevant, knowledge is accessible (and often relatively free) across geographical and organizational boundaries, and in many cases the educator does not know much more than what the students have easy access to. Our role as educators evolves towards that of a guide and a facilitator: a guide to help students make the difference between the good, the bad and the ugly information; a facilitator to help make sense out of the overload of information available at our fingertips. As a consequence the initiative for designing a curriculum may well shift a bit from the academic supplier to the student-user. Some have speculated that we may evolve towards a world where the student attends courses in different institutions, sometimes online, and assembles in that way the degree (U.S. Department of Education, 2006). When I see how clever some of our students are in combining our classes with some of the local and international exchange programs and independent study units, I am convinced that this is less farfetched that we might think.

The new learning paradigm will be no doubt be more *experience based*. Project based learning as a subcategory of experience based learning is not new. It was a hallmark of a lot of engineering education. The simple idea to start from a real as opposed to a stylized problem, and have the students learn from the experience they build up in solving these problems will get more and more application in other disciplines.

Related to this is the concept of the *flipped classroom* (*The Economist*, 2011) where we let the student learn the conceptual frameworks outside the classroom, thus freeing up time in the classroom to apply the concepts by solving problems, debating applications, etc. This may not sound revolutionary to those of us who have been teaching by the case study method for example. The change is no doubt in the richness of what can be done outside the classroom through rich media and social networking. As I mentioned in my introduction, it struck me as a veteran case teacher how much more I could engage with students about the class materials before and after class.

"Going to the classroom" will be less and less identified with spending time in a well-defined and constrained physical location. *The classroom has become virtual and may exist everywhere and at all times of the day*. Students collaborate and dialogue over networks during class hours and outside these specific times. They work with colleagues next to them in the Library (though still over internet), or with friends and colleagues elsewhere in the world. Geographical and organizational boundaries have less and less meaning and importance, and interaction will move much more from one-to-one (as in tutoring) or one to many (as in a lecture) to a many-to-many interaction (as in social networking).

Educators will have to spend much more effort and creativity on Learning Analytics (Greller & Drachsler, 2012). I don't want to go in a debate on the precise definition of Learning Analytics but generally it is about the use of learner data and analytics to predict and to advise on students' learning. While we may always have had some data and support systems to advise the students, it is imperative that in an environment where the responsibility for the design of the learning trajectory shifts from the educator to the student, we provide much more information to guide the student.

Impact on Research

The impact of technology on research may come somewhat slower than on education. Students' turnover is higher than that of scientists and researchers: we have a vast installed base of disciplinary research anchored in classical hypotheses based paradigm, which may slow down the shifts. But I predict four changes:

a) One of these is the *radical internationalization* of research. Future research will be networked. This is a continuation of what already exists, but the tools for communication and for research support will enhance considerably the productivity of internationally networked research. Research, design and engineering support systems, e.g. specialized social networks, Product Lifecycle Management Systems for design, cheap video communication systems or retrieval and document management systems have made huge improvements and have enabled a new generation of international research networks.

b) As mentioned before, Big Data and Predictive Analytics will make non-hypothesis based research more acceptable. Both the way we ask questions and how we solve them will be adjusted. There are huge opportunities in this, because we can study phenomena that used to be out of our reach. But there are also some risks. Pattern recognition does rarely address causality and may thus be effective in prediction, without really being able to explain why. "Fishing", a more colloquial word for data mining, is not yet accepted or acceptable by scientists. But it may only be a real problem when the datasets are too small or the sampling has been too weak to support any insights. I can foresee a future "galactic" battle between the galaxies of Big Data and Data Science and the traditional scientific approach. And the battlefield will be partially in our Universities.

c) A third trend is the emergence of what some call Social Technology, or the application of Data Science and Big Data to social problems. In social sciences we were often limited by small sample sizes and costly and difficult access to subjects for experiments. How many psychological and sociological experiments have been carried out with undergraduate students at top U.S. universities? Or how many healthcare studies were limited to small samples of a few hundred subjects. Apps on mobile devices have made it possible to transform healthcare studies to the study of tens of thousands of subjects easily (Apple, 2015). I have no doubt about the rigour with which these older studies were carried out, but one cannot but think that the samples were socially and culturally biased and generalization was therefore difficult. The rapid diffusion of sensors to capture data on all aspects of life and society, and the creation of vast, varied and fast evolving databases of user behaviour in social networks, online retailing, etc. open up tremendous perspectives for rigorous, relevant and truly revealing social sciences research. This development is not without risks. There are concerns about security, privacy and ownership of personal data. Frankly speaking I don't think that University administrators will be able to stop researchers from jumping enthusiastically on these new opportunities. But University administrators will need to overcome the issues of cybersecurity, government legislation e.g. the one on offshore information usage or data protection, and create a common international consensus on working guidelines for Big Data researchers.

d) Technology may also create more potential for interdisciplinary research on pressing societal issues. Let me take an example. Many countries are confronted with the challenges and opportunities created by an ageing population. Understanding how we can get productive and happy ageing requires research in areas as diverse as medicine, mechanical engineering, finance and economics, sociology, ethics, sensors, data processing, and many more. We also know that grasping the real opportunities of an ageing population will require the complex interaction between these different disciplines. Technology may help us to bridge these differences.

As I mentioned, I am not sure whether we as university administrators will have a big influence on these evolutions. Creative researchers and scientists will always be a step ahead of us. But we may want to think about the frameworks and the context in which these evolutions can be optimized, and performed within boundaries accepted by the professions and the society.

Impact on our 'business model'

We know that what is described above will require us to make significant investments in technology. And the costs of technology seem to be escalating. While the administrators want to keep the cost of technology down, we also know that we don't want yesterday's technology and that our students and researchers require us to constantly upgrade and improve the technology systems. We need to recognize that the technology bill will not decrease. Thus University administrators will be forced to think where else they can reduce costs to keep investing in technology.

But it is not that cost challenge that I want to focus on. There are three other issues that will require all of our attention as University administrators:

  a) *The emergence of new competition*: most of our research universities are built on the combination of the Von Humboldt model of a research institution of early 19th-century Germany combined with the teaching methods developed in Oxbridge, and refined in the top U.S. universities. It was and is a strong and performing model that was partially based on a monopoly of granting degrees (either granted by the Governments or in very few cases based on the sheer exclusivity and quality of the tuition). We know from other industries that disruptive innovations based on technology pose a risk for the incumbents, in particular when and if a university degree becomes less valued, or can be offered through means other than a government decree. Private universities pop up all over the world, and fill voids left by the traditional universities. Alternative pathways to success in the professional world are pondered upon by governments, in particular on the basis of the OECD report on Continuing Education (OECD, 2014). And actors such as Coursera offer modules by very distinguished faculty from very recognizable institutions, therefore making it difficult for others to charge premium prices for sharing knowledge. I have little doubt that the top among the traditional universities will survive, but I do fear that many of the other players in the academic sector will be forced to act more and more as a commercial operator and will have to adjust some of the values of the University as a social good.
  b) *Pricing*: Big Data and Data Analytics will allow us to radically redesign and customize courses for delivery either face to face or electronically. This may also implies significant economies in paper wastage, reduced teaching redundancy, lower administrative costs, and, as I mentioned, to some extent a shift of the design of the curriculum from the faculty to the students. Will we pass on these savings to the students? As the OECD (2014) suggests: "It is possible that there may be a growing prevalence in universities adopting hybrid pricing structures, using the fee premium from commercially viable sources as funding to provide education access for the underprivileged."
  c) *Rise in expectations*: As technology has enhanced the possibilities for learning and scholarship by research universities, we may expect our stakeholders' expectations to rise. Public funders of education may soon expect greater accountability on the return and the impact of their investments, and likely in more tangible and immediate terms. In a not very distant future, research funding agencies may expect the use of technology to track the diffusion of knowledge created through

grant-funded research. Governments may require Big Data efforts to monitor the social and economic impact of research-informed policy interventions.

An observation common to all of these trends is that there is a significant trend towards the commercialization of Higher Education and the University. We know that this is not without risk. Derrick Bok (2004) has argued that the commercialization of Universities may well jeopardize our fundamental mission by accepting more and more compromises of basic academic values. There are indeed significant risks when such commercialization would lead to more secrecy in corporate-funded research, or when customer orientation towards students and parents would lead to compromises in the rigour of the education.

SINGAPORE MANAGEMENT UNIVERSITY AS A SHORT CASE STUDY

What do we do at SMU with all these opportunities and ideas? (SMU, 2015a) We experiment in our way and we are very happy to share the results of these experiments with our peers.

While we have decided not to engage in the production of MOOCs, partially because of lack of resources, we have experimented successfully with the use of technology in learning. All of our course materials and course management can be online, though it is still a choice for our faculty how much of these opportunities they want to us. We are in the process of having all faculty go through a training to be acquainted with the process of online teaching. Furthermore we have experimented in both undergraduate and graduate programmes with a variety of technologies.

Let me give you a few examples. We organize a series of blended courses, i.e. where part of the teaching and learning happens online, but alternating with face-to-face sessions. Some of those experiments are purely internal. In other cases e.g. the blended IE-SMU MBA program, we are also happy to learn from our peers. We also have global courses where students from SMU and USC recently participated in classes from opposite ends of the world with the help of technology before they met on each other's campuses.

The experiment in our Library with different learning environments has been complemented with the development of a new three-storey facility called SMU Labs. There we have a variety of flexible project rooms, discussion areas, huddle rooms, a one-button presentation room, an active learning classroom and a white room for creative thinking. It is also a space where we are developing SMU-X standing for eXperimentation, eXploring, the X-factor or even the unknown (SMU, 2015b). SMU-X is a combination of experiential courses which are supplemented by a collaborative, co-working environment. And it is an informal/casual 24h space for student centre learning and to blur the lines of classroom and out-of-class space (to support your impact to education para), tapping into the richness of out of class experience and learning through social networking.

In Analytics and Big Data SMU's School of Information Systems has a wide range of research programmes (SMU, 2015c), some of them in collaboration with Carnegie Mellon University. The portfolio of these research programs originated in more technical research, but gradually the users of these technical capabilities in Management and Marketing, Sociology or Psychology are getting involved. Examples of such research are the high frequency internet surveys (aided by student surveyors with tablets) carried out by the Centre for Research on the Economics of Ageing (CREA) (SMU, 2015d)

CONCLUSION

I have argued that the current opportunities offered by technology may lead to a fundamental change in our learning and research paradigms. There have been waves of technology impacting higher education before. But in line with the concept of socio-materialism and the disruptive innovations that have become possible on a stabilizing ICT platform, we may have to redefine the complex system that a present day University represents.

Such a redefinition comes with risks and problems. I referred to issues of rigour in education and research, privacy protection, accountability or the threat of the pure commercialization of the University sector.

This begs the question of what we might aspire to achieve with these new emerging research and learning paradigms. Should they embrace a diversity of elites — and define those who fully embrace diversity as a new elite? In the past, research universities educated the elite of society and prepared its leaders, scientists and future statesmen to fulfil larger responsibilities. Things are different today. Participation in higher education has been "democratized" as access has increased across the world. Most governments invest significantly in research to remain competitive as knowledge-based economies. As a result, research universities today educate a significant proportion of society. Diversity on campus has thus increased on many dimensions — ethnicity, nationality, gender, socio-economic status, previous scholastic performance — and unexplored scholastic potential. Social interactions will become an increasingly important design component of programmes if on-campus education is to remain distinctive and valuable.

Perhaps a key opportunity for the new research and learning paradigms is embracing and harnessing such diversity, and allowing students to learn how they can contribute not just as individuals, but also as bridges. Bridges between cultures, disciplines, between theory and application, between stakeholders with different interests — yet keenly aware that they share the same future. University education should remain an important way to transform society. It is at risk of yielding to pressures to merely transform young adults to play a role in the workforce.

REFERENCES

Apple (2015). https://www.apple.com/pr/library/2015/04/14Apple-Announces-ResearchKit-Available-Today-to-Medical-Researchers.html, (retrieved on April 27, 2015).

Barras, R. (1986). "Towards a Theory of Innovation in Services", *Research Policy* (15), pp. 161-173.

Barrett M., Davidson, E., Prabhu, J. & Vargo, S.L. (2015). "Service Innovation in the Digital Age: Key Contributions and Future Directions", *MIS Quarterly*, vol. 39 no. 1 pp. 135-154.

Bok, D. (2004), Universities in the market place: The Commercialization of Higher Education, Princeton University Press.

De Meyer, A., Dutta, S. & Srivastawa, S. (2001). *The Bright Stuff*, Prentice Hall, London.

Gandomi, A. & Haider, M. (2015). "Beyond the Hype: Big Data Concepts, Methods and Analytics", *International Journal of Information Management*, vol. 35, pp. 137-144.

Greller, W. & Drachsler, H. (2012). "Translating Learning into Numbers: A Generic Framework for Learning Analytics". *Educational Technology & Society*, 15 (3), pp. 42-57.

MacKenzie, D. & Millo, Y. (2003). "Constructing a market, performing theory: The historical sociology of a financial derivatives exchange". *American Journal of Sociology 109*, pp. 107-145.

OECD (2014). *Skills Beyond School: Synthesis Report*, OECD Reviews of Vocational Education and Training, OECD Publishing. http://dx.doi.org/10.1787/9789264214682-en/ (retrieved on 25 April 2015)

Orlikowsky, W. J. & Scott, S.V (2008). "Sociomateriality: Challenging the Separation of Technology, Work and Organization", *The Academy of Management Annals*, vol. 2, no. 1, pp. 433-474.

Pisani E. (2010). "Has the Internet Changed Science?", *Prospect*, 17 November.

Suchman, L.A. (2007). Human-machine reconfigurations: Plans and situated actions. Cambridge University Press.

SMU (2015a). http://www.smu.edu.sg (Retrieved on 19 April 2015)

SMU (2015b). http://www.smu.edu.sg/news/2014/12/21/space-students-students (retrieved on 19 April 2015)

SMU (2015c). http://www.smu.edu.sg/area-of-excellence/analytics-business-consumer-social-insights (retrieved on 19 April 2015).

SMU (2015d). http://centres.smu.edu.sg/crea/ (retrieved on 25 April 2015).

The Economist (2011). "Flipping the Classroom", 17 September.

U.S. Department of Education (2006). A Test of Leadership: Charting the Future of U.S. Higher Education. Washington, D.C..

Vargo, S L. & Lusch, R. F. (2008). "Service-Dominant Logic: Continuing the Evolution," *Journal of the Academy of Marketing Science* (36: 1), pp. 1-10.

CHAPTER 21

Adapting the University to the Constraints, Responsibilities and Opportunities of a New Age

James J. Duderstadt

INTRODUCTION

During the years following the Great Depression and World War II, the United States launched a massive effort to provide educational opportunities to all Americans. Returning veterans funded through the GI Bill (Serviceman's Readjustment Act of 1944) tripled college enrolments. The post-WWII research strategy developed by Vannevar Bush transformed our campuses into research universities responsible for most of the nation's basic research (Bush, 1945). The Truman Commission proposed that all Americans should have the opportunity of a college education (Thelin, 2004), and California responded with its Master Plan, which not only provided all Californians with the opportunity of at least a community college education, but simultaneously created the University of California system, perhaps today the leading research university system in the world (Douglass, 2000).

America benefited greatly from these visionary investments in the future aimed at providing both the educational opportunity and new knowledge necessary for economic prosperity, social well-being and national security. Our nation saw spectacular achievements, such as sending men to the Moon, decoding the human genome and, of course, creating the Internet and the digital age. Over the past half century, our nation and, indeed, the world, have benefited greatly from the extraordinary commitments of our parents, the "Greatest Generation", to educational opportunity and the support of university research.

Yet, today, much of this earlier commitment to investment in education and research seems to have waned. Not only the quality of our primary and secondary education, but also the skills of our workforce, lag many other nations. Over the past decade, government support of our public universities has dropped by roughly 35%, putting leading research universities such as U. California, U. Wisconsin and U. Michigan at risk (Holliday, 2012). After a brief surge during the late 1990s with the doubling of the budget of the National Institutes of Health, both federal and corporate support of basic and applied research has fallen significantly, while fields such as the social sciences have been savaged by conservative political forces. And, perhaps most telling of all, the inequities characterizing educational opportunity in America have become extraordinary. (Haycock, 2010) The unfortunate reality facing young students today can be summarized by observing: "If you are poor and smart, you have only a one-in-ten chance of obtaining a college degree. In contrast, if you are dumb and rich, your odds rise to nine-in-ten!" (Vest, 2005)

More fundamentally, an extraordinary shift has occurred in the public perception of the purpose of American higher education over the past half century. In early decades following World War II, higher education was viewed primarily as a *public good* because of the critical role it played by an educated population and the knowledge generated on our campuses in determining the welfare of our nation merited strong support from public tax revenues. Today, our nation seems to no longer understand that the support of educational opportunity and campus-based research represents *investments* in the future, not burdensome *expenditures* from public resources. Instead, most Americans view a college education primarily as a *private benefit*, which enables students to compete for high-paying jobs, as evidenced in part by the rapidly increasing income differential between those with and without a college degree. Hence, it is not surprising that public policy has shifted to view a college education as something that students should pay for themselves through fees, enabled, in part, through loans and debt.

So, too, as the compelling challenges of the post-World War II economic recovery, the Cold War and the space race subsided, federal support of the research and development needed for prosperity and security has weakened in the United States. Rather than the "peace dividend" anticipated during the 1990s, the nation's R&D investment relative to the nation's GDP has dropped. Faced with the financial pressures of quarterly earnings that demand corporate priorities shift away from long-term research to product development, great research organizations such as Bell Laboratories have disappeared. Even more seriously, federal policies no longer place a priority on university research and graduate education, as basic research funding has dropped by roughly 20% over the past decade. Most recently, a conservative Congress has adopted rigid constraints, such as a sequestration on all federal expenditures, putting at serious risk not only basic research but also the capacity and quality of the nation's research universities (Lane, 2014).

Both the irony and tragedy of this situation flows from the realization that today our world has entered a period of rapid and profound economic, social and political transformation driven by knowledge and innovation. It has become increasingly apparent that the strength, prosperity and welfare of region or nation in a global knowledge economy will demand a highly educated citizenry enabled by development of a strong system of education at all levels. It will also require institutions with the ability to discover new knowledge, to develop innovative applications of these discoveries, and transfer them into the marketplace through entrepreneurial activities. Hence, current American higher education policy represents a dramatic disinvestment in its future.

Throughout most of our history, education in America has been particularly responsive to the changing needs of society during early periods of major transformation, e.g., the transition from a frontier to an agrarian society, then to an industrial society, through the Cold War tensions, and to today's global, knowledge-driven economy. As our society changed, so too did the necessary skills and knowledge of our citizens: from growing to making, from making to serving, from serving to creating, and today from creating to innovating. With each social transformation, an increasingly sophisticated world required a higher level of cognitive ability, from manual skills to knowledge management, analysis to synthesis, reductionism to the integration of knowledge, invention to research, and, today, innovation and entrepreneurship. Our nation's challenge today is to understand that once again it is time to challenge current public policy and make new commitments to education to enable our nation to achieve prosperity, health and security.

More generally, it is clear that, as the pace of change continues to accelerate, our schools, colleges and universities will need to become more adaptive if they are to survive. It is not enough to simply build upon the status quo. Instead, it is important that we consider more expansive visions that allow for truly over-the-horizon challenges and opportunities, game changers that dramatically change the environment in which our institutions must function.

To illustrate, let me suggest two intellectual trends that are likely to become increasingly important to our society over the next several decades and should intensify the public good character of higher education.

AN OLD THEME FOR A NEW GENERATION: *RENAISSANCE*

Our world is changing rapidly, driven by the role played by educated people, new knowledge, creativity, innovation and entrepreneurial zeal. The professions that have dominated the late 20th century — and to some degree, the contemporary university — have been those which manipulate and rearrange knowledge and wealth rather than create it, professions such as law, business, accounting and politics. Yet, it is becoming increasingly clear that the driving intellectual activity of the 21st century will be the act of creation itself, as suggested by Jacques Attali in his provocative forecasts for the 21st century at the turn of the Millennium: "The winners of this new era will be creators, and it is to them that power and wealth will flow. The need to shape, to invent and to create will blur the border between production and consumption. Creation will not be a form of consumption any more, but will become work itself, work that will be rewarded handsomely. The creator who turns dreams into reality will be considered as workers who deserve prestige and society's gratitude and remuneration." (Attali, 1991)

The tools of creation are expanding rapidly in both scope and power. Today, we can create objects literally atom by atom. We are developing the capacity to create new life-forms through the tools of molecular biology and genetic engineering. We are now creating new intellectual life-forms through artificial intelligence and virtual reality. Already we are seeing the spontaneous emergence of new forms of creative activities, e.g., the "maker" fairs providing opportunities to showcase forms of artistic, recreational and commercial activity; the use of "additive manufacturing" or 3-D printing to build new products and processes atomic layer by atomic layer; and the growing use of the "app" culture to empower an immense marketplace of small software development companies. In fact, some suggest that our civilization may experience a renaissance-like awakening of creative activities in the 21st century similar to that occurring in 16th century Europe.

A determining characteristic of the university of the 21st century may be a shift in intellectual focus, from the preservation or transmission of knowledge, to the process of creativity itself. If so, then vision for the university of the early 21st century should stress characteristics such as creativity, innovation, ingenuity and invention, and entrepreneurial zeal. But here lies a great challenge. While universities are experienced in teaching the skills of analysis, we have far less understanding of the intellectual activities associated with creativity. In fact, the current disciplinary culture of our campuses sometimes discriminates against those who are truly creative and do not fit well into our stereotypes of students and faculty.

The university may need to reorganize itself quite differently, stressing forms of pedagogy and extracurricular experiences to nurture and teach the art and skill of creativity and innovation. This would probably imply a shift away from highly specialized disciplines and degree programs to programs placing more emphasis on integrating knowledge. There is clearly a need to better integrate the educational missions of the university with the research and service activities of the faculty by ripping instruction out of the classroom — or at least the lecture hall — and placing it instead in the discovery and tinkering environment of studios or workshops or even "hacker havens".

Actually, as John Seely Brown suggests, today's students are already using technology to function much like artists — disciplined, focused, pushing boundaries, challenging assumptions and creating meaning (Brown, 2009). They are willing to engage with multiple viewpoints before synthesizing their own. They are engaged, first and foremost, in fostering what might be called the creative class, desiring not only to create for themselves, but also seeking others to build on their creations. The platforms they use are mostly digital, e.g., social networking, cloud-based data repositories, open source and open content technologies, and remixing the work of others through rich media capable of expressing complex ideas.

As Brown warns, in a rapidly changing world, innovation no longer depends only upon the explicit dimension characterizing conventional content-focused pedagogy focused on "learning to know". Rather, one needs to enable an integration of tacit knowledge with explicit knowledge to facilitate "learning to do", "learning to create" and "learning to be" tools already embraced by the young, if not yet by the academy. Particularly key in this effort is the earlier goal of diversity. As Tom Friedman noted in a *New York Times* column: "The sheer creative energy that comes when you mix all our diverse people and cultures together. We live in an age when the most valuable asset any economy can have is the ability to be creative — to spark and imagine new ideas, be they Broadway tunes, great books, iPads, or new cancer drugs. And where does creativity come from?" As *Newsweek* described it, "To be creative requires divergent thinking (generating many unique ideas) and then convergent thinking (combining those ideas into the best result)." And where does divergent thinking come from? It comes from being exposed to divergent ideas and cultures and people and intellectual disciplines (Friedman, 2010).

AN OLD THEME FOR A NEW ERA: *ENLIGHTENMENT*

Today, a rapidly changing world demands a new level of knowledge, skills and abilities on the part of our citizens. Just as in earlier critical moments in history when our prosperity and security were achieved through broadening and enhancing educational opportunity, it is time once again to seek a bold expansion of educational opportunity. But this time we should set as the goal providing all citizens with universal access to lifelong learning opportunities, thereby enabling participation in a world both illuminated and driven by knowledge and learning.

The challenge facing us today is to recognize and accept our responsibilities to provide all of our citizens with the educational, learning and training opportunities they need and deserve, throughout their lives, thereby enabling both individuals and nations to prosper in an ever more competitive global economy. While the ability to take advantage of educational opportunity will always depend on the need, aptitude, aspirations and motivation of the student, it should not depend on one's socioeconomic status. Access to lifelong learning opportunities should be *a right for all rather than a privilege for the few* if a society is to achieve prosperity, security and social well-being in the global, knowledge- and value-based economy of the 21st century (Miller, 2006).

So, how might we achieve such a goal in the face of the array of financial, social and political constraints faced by contemporary universities? Any vision proposing a future of the university must consider the extraordinary changes and uncertainties of a future driven by exponentially evolving information and communications technology. The extraordinary connectivity provided by the Internet already links together the majority of the world's population. To this, one can add the emerging capacity to capture and distribute the accumulated knowledge of our civilization in digital form and provide opportunities for learning through new paradigms such as MOOCs and cognitive tutors. This suggests the possible emergence of a new global society no longer constrained by space, time, monopoly or archaic laws, and instead even more dependent upon the generation of new knowledge and the education of world citizens.

Today, the rapid evolution of information and communications technologies and the new paradigms they support, such as crowdsourcing, digital archives and data mining, suggest a new learning ecosystem symbolized by the diagram of three elements: Wikipedia, Google and Watson. Imagine a triangle, with Wikipedia on the top vertex, Google on the lower right, and Watson on the lower left. So, what is this puzzle?

Interestingly enough, each of these elements addresses a key core competency of the university:

- *Wikipedia* represents the capability to create enormous learning communities with a collective ability to digest and analyse information, self-correcting and evolving very rapidly through crowdsourcing as an emergent phenomenon.
- *Google* represents a future in which all knowledge is available in the cloud, digitized, accessible, searchable — everything ever printed, measured, sensed or created — big data to the extreme.
- *Watson* (the IBM computer that used artificial intelligence to beat the champions of the game-show *Jeopardy*, and more recently used to

perform medical diagnosis) represents the capacity to use data mining and artificial intelligence to analyse information, trillions of transactions per second, identifying correlations, curating information, authenticating knowledge, certifying learning and providing ubiquitous access.

So, what does this diagram represent? A new epistemology for the 21st century? Or perhaps it is a new form of a university capable of being extrapolated to serve the learning needs of all of humanity. Or perhaps it provides a contemporary path to a second great historical theme: the Enlightenment of the 18th and 19th centuries that swept aside the divine authority of kings and clerics by educating and empowering the public, stimulating revolution and creating the liberal democracies that now characterize most developed nations. Clearly our world needs once again the "illumination" provided by distributing "the light of learning and knowledge" to counter the ignorance (e.g., today's "denier" culture) and address the challenges of our times, informed by the rigour of scholarly inquiry rather than data-mined correlations.

More generally, the goals of the Enlightenment of 18th-century Europe were to provide for a rational distribution of freedom, universal access to knowledge and the formation of learning communities. Rational and critical thought was regarded as central to freedom and democracy. Knowledge and learning were regarded as public goods, to be made available through communities such as salons, seminars and academies. These dreams of the universal and the collective, *Liberté, Egalité and Fraternité* for the French Revolution — or perhaps better articulated by Jefferson's opening words from our own Declaration of Independence: "We hold these truths to be self-evident, that all men are created equal, that they are endowed by their Creator with certain unalienable Rights, that among these are Life, Liberty and the pursuit of Happiness" — remain as important today as they were three centuries ago.

Today, the educational institution most capable of launching a new "age of Enlightenment" is the "university", with its dual missions of creating "unions" of scholars and learners and providing "universal" access to knowledge. In a sense, the word "university" itself conveys the elements of this vision: both the sense of a "union" or community of learners (i.e., *universitas magistrorum et scholarium*) and the "universality" or totality of knowledge and learning as the key to social well-being in an age of knowledge. Furthermore, since these have been regarded as *public* goods, one might even suggest that the *public* universities have a particular responsibility in providing these.

But, while the Enlightenment of the 18th century was concerned with "celebrating the luminosity of knowledge shining through the written word", today, knowledge comes in many forms — words, images, immersive environments, "sim-stim". And learning communities are no longer constrained by space and time but rather propagated instantaneously by rapidly evolving technologies (e.g., cyberinfrastructure) and practices (e.g., open source, open knowledge). The ancient vision of the Library of Alexandria — to collect all of the books of the world in one place — is rapidly becoming true — except the "place" has now become a cloud in cyberspace (e.g., the HathiTrust and Google Books). Learning communities are evolving into knowledge-generating communities — wikis, crowdsourcing, hive cultures that span the globe.

William Germano suggests yet another argument for such a theme as the possible next stage in speculating about the evolution of the "book", from the invention of writing to the codex to the printed volume to the digital revolution. As he explains:

> "Right now we are walking through two great dreams that are shaping the future of scholarship, even the very idea of scholarship and the role "the book" should play within it. Great Dream No. 1 is universal access to knowledge. This dream means many things to many people, but for knowledge workers it means that scholarly books and journals can, and therefore should, be made available to all users. New technologies make that possible for the first time in human history, and, as the argument goes, the existence of such possibilities obligates us to use them. Great Dream No. 2 is the ideal of knowledge building as a self-correcting, collective exercise. Twenty years ago, nobody had Wikipedia, but when it arrived, it took over the hearts and laptops for undergraduates and then of everyone else in the education business. Professional academic life would be poorer, or at least much slower, without it. The central premise of Wikipedia isn't speed but infinite self-correction, perpetually fine-tuning what we know. In our second dream, we expand our aggregated knowledge quantitatively and qualitatively." (Germano, 2010)

THE UNIVERSITY AS AN EMERGENT CIVILIZATION

So, what might we anticipate over the longer term as possible future forms of the university? The monastic character of the ivory tower is certainly lost forever. Although there are many important features of the campus environment that suggest that most universities will continue to exist as a place, at least for the near term, as digital technology makes it increasingly possible to emulate human interaction in all the senses with arbitrarily high fidelity, perhaps we should not bind teaching and scholarship too tightly to buildings and grounds. Certainly, both learning and scholarship will continue to depend heavily upon the existence of communities, since they are, after all, highly social enterprises. Yet, as these communities are increasingly global in extent, detached from the constraints of space and time, we should not assume that the scholarly communities of our times would necessarily dictate the future of our universities. For the longer term, who can predict the impact of exponentiating technologies on social institutions such as universities, corporations, or governments, as they continue to multiply in power a thousand-, a million- and a billion-fold?

But there is a possibility even beyond these. Imagine what might be possible if all of these elements are merged, i.e., Internet-based access to all recorded (and then digitized) human knowledge augmented by powerful search engines and AI-based software agents; open source software, open learning resources, and open learning institutions (open universities); new collaboratively developed tools (Wikipedia II, Web 2.0, the "Internet of Things"); and ubiquitous information and communications technology (e.g., inexpensive network appliances such as iPhones, iPads or smart watches). In the near future, it could be possible that anyone with even a modest Internet or cellular phone connection will have access to the recorded knowledge of our civilization along with ubiquitous learning opportunities and access to network-based communities throughout the world.

Imagine still further the linking together of billions of people with limitless access to knowledge and learning tools enabled by a rapidly evolving scaffolding of cyberinfrastructure, which increases in power one-hundred to one thousand-fold every decade. This hive-like culture will not only challenge existing social institutions — corporations, universities, nation states, that have depended upon the constraints of space, time, laws, and monopoly. But it will enable the spontaneous emergence of new social structures as yet unimagined — just think of the early denizens of the Internet such as Google, Facebook, Wikipedia …and, unfortunately, Al Qaeda. In fact, we may be on the threshold of the emergence of a new form of civilization, as billions of world citizens interact together, unconstrained by today's monopolies on knowledge or learning opportunities.

Perhaps this, then, is the most exciting vision (albeit threatening to some) for the future of knowledge and learning organizations such as the university, no longer constrained by space, time, monopoly or archaic laws, but rather responsive to the needs of a global, knowledge society and unleashed by technology to empower and serve all of humankind. And all of this is likely to happen during the lives of today's students. These possibilities must inform and shape the manner in which we view, support and lead higher education. Now is not the time to back into the future.

REFERENCES

Attali, Jacques (1991). *Millennium: Winners and Losers in the Coming World Order*. Random House, New York, NY.

Bush, Vannevar (1945). Science, the Endless Frontier, A Report to the President. United States Government Printing Office, Washington, DC.

Brown, John Seely (2009). "Minds on Fire", Educause, January/February.
Douglass, John (2000). *The California Idea and American Higher Education*. Stanford University Press, Palo Alto, CA.
Friedman, Thomas (2010). "Broadway and the Mosque", New York Times, 3 August.
Germano, William (2010). "What Are Books Good For?" The Key Reporter. Phi Beta Kappa Society, New York, NY. Winter.
HathiTrust Website: http://www.hathitrust.org/community
Haycock, Kati (2010). Opportunity Adrift. The Education Trust, Washington, DC.
Holliday, Chad (2012) (chair). Research Universities and the Future of America: Ten Breakthrough Actions Vital to Our Nation's Prosperity and Security. National Academies Committee on Research Universities. National Academy Press, Washington, D.C.
Lane, Neal *et. al.* (2014). Restoring the Foundation: The Vital Role of Research in Preserving the American Dream. American Academy of Arts and Sciences, Cambridge, MA.
Miller, Charles (2006) (chair). A Test of Leadership: Charting the Future of U.S. Higher Education. National Commission on the Future of Higher Education in America ("The Spellings Commission"). Department of Education, Washington, DC.
Rhodes, Frank (2009). Universities and the Innovative Spirit. Glion Declaration II. Glion Colloquium, Geneva.
Thelin, John R. (2004). *A History of American Higher Education*. Johns Hopkins University Press, Baltimore, MD.
Vest, Charles M. (2005). Clark Kerr Lectures, The University of California. University of California Press, Berkeley, CA.

CHAPTER

Reinventing Greatness: Responding to urgent global-level Responsibilities and critical university-level Priorities

Ihron Rensburg

INTRODUCTION

In this chapter I reflect on the contemporary significance of knowledge institutions, and particularly research universities, for both emerging and established economies and for the world as a whole, but with particular reference to South Africa and Africa.

As knowledge institutions have become ever more central to human social and economic development, and as globalization has made countries more aware of their relative positions within an interconnected world, so too have comparisons between and rankings of institutions and countries become more influential. Universities in particular are under enormous pressure, from political leaders, state bureaucrats and often their own administrators, to perform in ways which elevate their standings in terms of global rankings — heavily weighted towards research outputs and citations and the training of postgraduate research students — or to fall behind in the global development race.

The logic behind this compulsion to perform or perish is not new; it has been with us for centuries and has been spurred by successive industrial and technological revolutions. But this dominant global development logic has intensified in recent years. As universities around the world seek to catch up with or surpass their more highly ranked peers, they reinforce this logic and the assumption that greatness in terms of knowledge and research is already known and needs only to be emulated. This assumption, however, is misplaced, and the logic which underpins it is unrealistic. In our globalizing world, greatness is evolving and must evolve, in response to the multiplication and proliferation of pressing challenges with which the whole of humanity and its planet are faced. Universities, including universities which specialize in research, can no longer be ranked primarily by their research, but also by how they and their research and other activities respond to these grand challenges, in terms of cooperation, integration, inclusion, caring and civic-mindedness. Our current global development logic needs to be rethought, and replaced by a new logic: partner or perish. It is time to reinvent greatness.

THE IMPORTANCE OF KNOWLEDGE INSTITUTIONS

Given their functions of knowledge production and innovation, the training of highly skilled citizens, and the promotion of social mobility, knowledge institutions are key to delivering the knowledge requirements for development. First, this is because of the strong association between higher education participation rates and levels of socio-economic development. Second, higher levels of knowledge and innovation are essential inputs into the design and production of new technologies, and for the development of society. For instance, the number of Ph.D.s per million of a country's population is closely correlated to foreign direct investment flows that are increasingly indispensable for development. Third, the ability of a country to absorb, use and modify new or existing technologies — premised on the knowledge production capacities and skills of their institutions and citizens — accelerates development and promotes higher standards of living. Fourth, knowledge institutions can enable developing countries in particular to transition more rapidly through stages of economic development.

Last but not least, an essential role of knowledge institutions is to identify and offer solutions to the grand challenges of human development. These challenges, simultaneously national, regional, continental and global, range from sustainable development to democratization, from growing populations to scarce water and energy resources, from global IT convergence to the widening gap between rich and poor, from epidemics to financial instability, from war and civil war to transnational organized crime, from the status of women to the future of the youth, from cities for the future to climate change, and from voluntary and forced human migrations to global governance and ethics.

Indeed, all nations now face a singular emergency: regardless of their current stage of socio-economic development, if they wish to advance from a resource-based through an efficiency-based to an innovation-based economy and beyond, a globally competitive domestic system of knowledge institutions — comprising universities, science and research councils and industry research centres — is an essential ingredient. Most nations also aspire to improve and advance their knowledge institutions with respect to global rankings, and this places extraordinary strain not only on research universities but also on all the other institutions of higher education which focus on the equally if not more essential tasks of teaching and learning. Indeed, the logic of global rankings is increasingly differentiating not just universities but also nations and regions.

THE PROBLEM WITH OUR PRESENT DEVELOPMENT PARADIGM

The trouble with our present development paradigm is that it is short-term and short-sighted, and threatens to leave the poor and the less developed further and further behind. The concentration of research resources in a minority of institutions, even in the same country, coupled with vast global disparities in wealth, ensures that the majority of universities will never significantly alter their positions in the greater scheme of things.

Another problem is that it pays no heed to the consequences of unnecessary competition, and the narrow and unreflective pursuit of rankings for the sake of rankings. Improving the global competitiveness of one nation's knowledge institutions may help it increase its odds of producing more effective responses to its particular challenges, but if isolated competitiveness is the sole focus, unleavened by the cooperative production and sharing of knowledge, no coherent and effective global response to the grand challenges which affect all countries is likely.

Moreover, while the dominant development logic may have at times driven unparalleled economic growth, it has not done so for all; and all too often growth has occurred at great human cost, coupled with environmental destruction on such a scale that potentially irreversible alterations have been made to our planet's climate. Corrupt and fraudulent manipulations of financial markets recently, in 2008, also brought economic growth to a shuddering halt, after some two decades of growth, and recovery is haltingly slow.

Our current development logic also encourages both university administrators and national leaders to make investment decisions that prioritize research over teaching and learning, since research output and impact are weighted more highly by global ranking systems. This occurs despite the fact that less developed nations require equally significant investments in undergraduate education if they are to improve their societies' portfolios of highly skilled university graduates, or that more developed nations need to enhance the participation and success of poor and marginalized communities within their university systems, and especially their research universities, if they and their societies are to become more equitable. A more balanced and astute approach to investment in both undergraduate education and research development is now urgent.

A fundamental rethink of the dominant development logic should first consider the possibility of multiple, indeed, even dramatically different, national development paths; it may even ponder lower rather than higher future income development paths. More to the point, since universities and nation-states exist and evolve within an interconnected global system, purely institution-based or nationally focused development approaches are outdated and even counter-productive. The grand challenges of the present cannot be solved by any single scholar, leader, university or country working on their own.

Our increasingly integrated and interdependent world requires global-scale combined and cooperative innovations and solutions. To address our grand challenges we must place the highest premium on the pooling and networking of resources at a global level. It is both unrealistic and undesirable to expect the universities and nation-states of the South to emulate the resource-intensive developmental trajectories of their Northern and Eastern peers. What the knowledge institutions of the North and the East as much as the South require — taking into account the varied sizes, ages, profiles and developmental outlooks of their countries' populations — are a multiplication of global development partnerships, resource-intensive where necessary, but extensive, inclusive and all-embracing wherever possible.

RESPONDING MORE COHESIVELY AND COHERENTLY TO HUMANITY'S GRAND CHALLENGES

It is against this background that university leaders must regularly review their actual versus their announced missions and charters. Research universities, in particular, must now, more than ever before, reflect on both their own significance and the significance of their contributions to the world's systems of knowledge institutions, because it is in large measure dependent on these institutions to find sustainable solutions to the grand challenges of human development.

For research universities to effuse true greatness, they must elevate, and be seen and known to elevate, all of humanity, including the poor and the marginalized inside and outside their nation-states, regions and continents. Their true greatness, given the present state of our world, will reside in their ability to purposefully, coherently and comprehensively take the lead on four fronts.

First, it is necessary to establish more (and foster existing) international inter-university epicentres of critical thought and conversation, so as to provide spaces for reflection, future thinking and the development of scholarly and research-informed solutions to our grand challenges.

Institutes of advanced studies and of global studies are ideally placed to step up their respective contributions when involved in active global partnerships. So too are networks and collectives, as is evident from the European Organization for Nuclear Research (CERN) and the Square Kilometre Array (SKA) initiatives, and research intensive university networks such as Universitas 21, where institutions can pool and thus multiply their efforts within diverse and cross-continental networks. These forms of global research collaboration are certainly increasing, but hardly at the scale of global investment in research and development, which has doubled within the last 15 years to US$1.4 trillion but remains fragmented nationally, regionally and globally (Suresh, 2012: 337).

Second, and arising from such inter-university epicentres and other global research collaboration programmes, urgent action within global networks and forums is needed. To this end, Davos-like gatherings of political, business and academic leaders, equally informed by research and scholarship, must debate proposed solutions and seek agreement on the way forward, and on the roles of each of the partners involved in implementing these agreements.

Theme-focused gatherings — such as how cities of the future can overcome the challenges that cities today are facing; or how to respond more effectively the next time an Ebola outbreak occurs — will enable participants to simultaneously examine the implications of an issue for their own constituencies, understand how their constituencies are linked to others, realize how local events can trigger global emergencies, and become aware of what cooperative networks and communications plans already exist to inform policy-makers and prioritize responses. By bringing knowledge and scholarship into global public awareness, reflection and dialogue, we can make a far more significant contribution to the future prospects of our vulnerable planet.

Third, it is necessary to give concerted attention to developing and cooperatively teaching curricula which nurture more civic-minded and cosmopolitan citizens than have been produced, until now, by a narrow development logic that, in extolling resource-intensive development, has deepened poverty, widened inequality and fostered social and political conflict.

Given the avarice, fraud and collusion that led to the 2008 collapse of the world's financial markets, the values and ethics that inform our knowledge institutions' curricula clearly need revitalizing. Strikingly, our research universities are often the first to claim captains of industry as their alumni, and many university ranking systems value this aspect quite highly; we must do more to ensure that the values and ethics our universities encourage, and the conduct we incentivize, are consistent with the best traditions of civic-mindedness, cultural engagement, inclusion, caring and the nurturing of a cosmopolitan identity. Indeed, it seems to me that research universities cannot be evaluated by their research contributions alone, but must also be judged by the impact that they have beyond research, in promoting values that advance our shared humanity and that seek to uplift the most vulnerable in our societies. In addition, developing ethics-based curricula which reflect Eastern and Southern traditions and value systems as much as Northern ones can simultaneously foster greater international research cooperation.

The fourth front against which our knowledge institutions in general and research universities in particular must lead us is to enrol and embrace far higher proportions, and secure the success, of youths and minorities from poor and marginalized urban and rural communities. More often than not, the poor and the marginalized are locked out of our universities, especially the research universities, which they either cannot afford or are assumed to be academically unprepared for, or both. Sometimes, the poor are locked into a new generation of poor-quality, high-fee private higher education institutions, where their trusting belief in the value of higher education motivates them to spend resources they cannot afford. Women, who face numerous obstacles in becoming, let alone being, researchers (obstacles all too often "justified" in the name of biology, or tradition, or religion, when it is usually just chauvinism), invariably receive fewer citations than their male counterparts, even when established as researchers and the first authors of their publications (Larivière et al., 2013: 211). Entrenched gender disparities in scientific research are thus another effect of our citation-weighted global rankings.

All knowledge institutions, however, whether public or private, must be responsive to their communities. In a global context in which tuition fees are rising and state subsidies declining, and a general shift in student financial aid away from grants and bursaries and towards income-contingent loans, universities must learn to do more with less, and innovate. For example, the use of free or low-cost distance and e-learning mechanisms, MOOCs (Massive Open Online Courses) and open access materials, can reduce costs per student and expand participation. Not all research requires expensive technologies, and general methodologies of research can often be taught without any equipment. Moreover, one of the cheapest and most effective forms of including the poor and the marginalized is simply to welcome them and make them at home, by creating an enriching student-friendly learning and living experience, fostering excellent learning and teaching practices, supporting students throughout the student lifecycle, and forging a responsible and respectful academic culture and ethos.

LOCATING AFRICA, AND SOUTH AFRICA, IN THE GLOBAL RESEARCH STAKES

Africa is rising. After Asia, Africa is the world's most populous continent. By 2050 it is forecast to be home to one quarter of the world's population (or some 2.3 billion people, half of whom will be urbanized), and including 40% of the world's children (United Nations, 2014). Africa's vast mineral wealth is well known, but recently burgeoning infrastructure development, expanding agriprocessing and strong consumer demand have made the continent a favoured investment destination. Real GDP growth rates in Africa have exceeded 5% per annum over the past decade (African Economic Outlook, 2015). Mobile/cellular telephone subscriptions reached 880 million in 2014, more than either the United States or the European Union. While only one quarter of Africa's population currently has access to the Internet, usage has exploded by 6,000% in the last 15 years (MMG, 2014).

All these represent tremendous development opportunities, but they also have major implications for the continent's under-resourced knowledge institutions. Much higher and more sustained investment in higher education will be required if Africa's universities are to accommodate growing demand for higher education and lift the participation rate from its current level of 8% to the approximately 32% which was the global average in 2012 (Marginson, 2014). Africa's research productivity is also low, accounting for less than 2% of global research output: in 2008, Africa's total number of research publications (about 27,000 papers) was equivalent to that of the Netherlands (Thomson Reuters, 2010). While African researchers are more likely to co-author publications with U.S. or European peers than they are with other African researchers (Thomson Reuters 2010), much more regional and international research collaboration will be needed for Africa's essential contributions to the identification and resolving of the grand challenges of development to be disseminated to the world.

South Africa's higher education system shares many of the features of its African counterparts, although it stands out in a number of respects. There are just under 1 million students enrolled in its public universities, but 85% of these are in undergraduate programmes, and only 7% are undertaking Masters and Doctoral studies. Science, engineering and technology programmes accounted for just under one-third of all graduates in 2012 (DHET, 2013).

However, South Africa is certainly the most prolific African researcher across the majority of the main knowledge fields (Thomson Reuters, 2010). In the last decade, its research output has doubled, and its international research collaboration has tripled. The country is among the world's top five in plant and animal science research, and very productive in the geosciences, social sciences and chemistry; it also exceeds world averages in environmental and ecological sciences, space sciences, immunology and clinical medicine. From 2001 to 2012, South African authored papers indexed in Science Direct were downloaded more than 20 million times, with the U.S. accounting for 16.9% of these downloads, China for 9.7% and the U.K. for 8.6% (Elsevier, 2013). However, just as Africa's research output is the same as that of the Netherlands, South Africa's — which accounts for 40% of Africa's output — is matched by Harvard University alone.

South African universities also continue to be shaped by their colonial and apartheid pasts. Notwithstanding enormous progress, such as the doubling of university enrolments over the past decade, and the diversification of the student body (over 80% of all students are black, and almost three-fifths are women), the South African university profile still does not fully reflect national demographics. The low overall enrolment rate of 19% is further skewed in that the participation rate among the black population is only 14%, compared to 59% among whites. Universities' staff components are still mainly white and male (and aging): only 46% of instructional and research staff are African, and 45% are women. If the currently glacial pace of transformation is maintained, it is estimated that it will take at least another decade before student graduation figures match national demographics — and another 40 years before academic staff components do so (PMG, 2013).

This configuration is inimical to meeting South Africa's labour market (or even academic labour market) demands, let alone to maintaining its standing in the global research productivity stakes. Accordingly, the country's National Development Plan aims by 2030 to: increase the university participation rate to 30%, or 1.6 million enrolments; produce 5,000 doctorates per annum; increase the percentage of black academics to at least 50%; and the percentage of all academics with doctoral qualifications to 75% (from around 40% currently) (NPC, 2012).

Forward thinking, such as that contained in national development plans, is essential if countries are to advance themselves socially and economically, and high-quality research is a boon to clarifying and charting ways forward. But today's interdependent world means that development, and research, cannot and indeed should not take place in isolation. Reciprocal global research partnerships, aimed at mutually beneficial, sustainable solutions to our grand challenges, must be prioritized, not least because the pace of technological progress is often matched by the intensification of human need.

South Africa, with its large youth and working-age population and relatively few of the very old and the very young, has recently entered a demographic window of opportunity to increase its economic output and to invest in the technology, education and skills to create the wealth needed to cope with its challenges. It must seize this opportunity. Africa as a whole will enter the same demographic window within a decade, and it too must seize this opportunity. But it cannot do it in isolation. Already the consequences of large sectors of our planet being rich in resources but poor in development are becoming apparent in the huge exoduses of populations, from Morocco to Myanmar, towards lands and lives they perceive as holding out greater opportunities. The South cannot fully develop its people, let alone its knowledge, without collaboration. But the same applies to the North and East, whose economies are increasingly dependent on the importation of labour at all skill levels. The opportunities and challenges facing South Africa, Africa and the South in general are not just their own opportunities and challenges; they are opportunities and challenges for the world, and for humanity at large.

REDEPLOYING RESEARCH RESOURCES

How then might just one knowledge institution — my own institution, the University of Johannesburg (UJ) — redeploy its resources so as to engage on the four fronts where, I suggested earlier, research universities should take the lead in responding to our responsibilities and priorities? Since the second of these fronts — the nurturing of scholarship-informed debates among leaders — is precisely the defining feature of the Glion Colloquium, I shall focus mainly on the first, third and fourth.

First, it goes without saying that a research university must do research. Reflecting the pressure being exerted by national policy-makers in this era of global rankings, UJ has made considerable investments in research, and as a result has tripled its research publications within the last five years. These investments, however, have been strategically focused on areas where the institution is either already strong, or can become globally excellent, or both. UJ is also focusing on smart international research collaborations and partnerships, including joint postgraduate programme offerings and the appointment of globally renowned professors and visiting professors. A prime example is the new Johannesburg Institute for Advanced Studies, a joint venture with Nanyang Technological University in Singapore, an inter-university epicentre primed to examine the grand challenges of the present and future from a Pan-Africa-Asia perspective. While acutely aware of its many domestic challenges, UJ has also set itself the task of achieving a consistent ranking within the world's top 400 universities by 2020.

Moreover, in recognition of the considerable value of research cooperation and exchange, UJ is thoroughly involving itself in prominent research university networks such as Universitas 21 and the Council of Graduate Schools, building networks for its researchers across influential global research projects. This effort is being undertaken in the knowledge that the grand challenges we face cannot be solved by a single university or nation; that said, the better any university can equip its staff and students, the better for knowledge production in general. Hence, in addition to jointly offered postgraduate programs, the university has significantly expanded the number of its postdoctoral fellowships, and initiated a multifaceted program — replete with new assistant lecturer posts, senior tutorships and supervisor-linked fellowships — which will see the proportion of academic staff with doctoral qualifications increase to 65% by 2020.

An important sub-focus of these endeavours is an attempt to improve the quantity, quality and directionality of the global flows involving our senior students and our leading scholars. These networks could, in part, reduce the brain drain from the South by providing researchers with multiple and repeated opportunities to undertake collaborative research, share knowledge and resources, and build mutual capacities with counterparts in the North and East, without permanently relocating. With such increased interconnectivity between scholars and universities, it will be essential to develop and extend globally endorsed standards and protocols for the merit-review of research proposals and the peer-rating of scholars, such as those proposed by the Global Research Council (Suresh, 2012: 338). Over and above these efforts, by 2020 UJ aims to grow its international student body from 2,500 to 5,000, and its international academic staff complement from 12% to 20%.

Second, UJ is systematically building intellectually rigorous and ethically-based curricula which respond innovatively to the dominant development paradigm and the grand challenges of the 21st century. It is doing so by incentivizing and promoting undergraduate teaching and learning as an essentially scholarly activity, and by deepening its compulsory *Global Citizenship* programmes and its *Learning To Be* teaching philosophy, coupled with the innovative presentation of programmes built upon the phased-in use of tablets, e-books and other handheld devices. Senior undergraduate programs emphasize entrepreneurialism and preparation for the world of work, and all programs involve regular teaching evaluations by students.

Third, in order to meet its responsibility to, and ensure the success of, the poor and the marginalized of its national context, UJ is investing in academic development programs in order to improve the quality and the responsiveness of all its programs. With national unemployment exceedingly high (as much as 60% among young people, including an estimated 4 million young South Africans not in college, university, training or employment), universities cannot sit by and bemoan the continuing poor quality of public schooling outcomes. UJ is devoting a considerable amount of its free marginal assets to academically supporting and enabling poorly prepared and often first generation students to make a successful transition to the demands of university education. As much as 5% of university resources previously committed to research has been diverted to building a successful First Year Experience

Programme, buttressed by an extensive 2,600-strong tutor system and premised on early notification of underperformance.

Taking one's responsibility to the poor and the marginalized seriously can go hand in hand with being responsive to the need for highly skilled graduates. UJ's meaningful contribution to diversifying South Africa's professions and vocations is evident, for example, in the fact that 27% of all black chartered accountants are now trained at the university, with similar numbers for engineers, technicians and technologists. Research and hands-on learning experiences are also at the fore in another intervention aimed at counteracting incoming students' weak public schooling backgrounds and simultaneously, over the long term, improving the quality of future applicants: UJ's newly upgraded Soweto campus, focused on teacher education, includes a primary school doubling as a dedicated teaching school — the first of its kind in South Africa — where trainee teachers can practise their craft in an authentic setting and researchers can directly study children's learning and development (DHET, 2014).

CONCLUSION

The knowledge institution which can match its global-level responsibilities with its university-level priorities will elevate itself way beyond its standing in terms of global rankings.

The research university which includes the world in its research, which promotes and shares the flow of knowledge and scholars, which embraces the poor and does research for humanity, will be a truly great research university.

It is this kind of institution which will lead the global research community in its efforts to cooperate ever more closely in order to meet its responsibilities to itself, the planet and humanity.

It has been a truism throughout history that with greatness comes responsibility. In the middle of the 17th century, the great educational reformer John Comenius [Jan Komensky] proposed a new kind of knowledge institution, a universal "College of Light", the members of which would pay attention to themselves first and foremost, to be themselves what they should make others: enlightened (Comenius, in Piaget, 1967: 210).

The task of our research universities today is to pay attention to themselves, precisely in order to enlighten others and the world. If we must conceive of global development, and global research rankings, in terms of a race, it should not be as a race between institutions or countries considered in isolation, but as a race by humanity as a whole against the great challenges it has set for itself. Our knowledge institutions, and particularly our research universities, must be, and must be seen to be, inclusive and civic-minded, and cooperative and integrative in their efforts. There is no alternative.

REFERENCES

African Economic Outlook (2015). http://www.africaneconomicoutlook.org/statistics/.

DHET (2013) Statistics on Post-school Education and Training in South Africa 2012. Department of Higher Education and Training, Pretoria.

DHET (2014). Woza Sizokwakha! Building Higher Education: Infrastructure Renewal, Revitalisation and Development. Department of Higher Education and Training, Pretoria.

Elsevier (2013). ScienceDirect Usage Team. http://usagereports.elsevier.com/asp/main.aspx.

Marginson, S. (2014). The Social Implications of High Participation Higher Education Systems. http://www.timeshighereducation.co.uk/news/global-participation-rates-to-continue-rising-says-report/2017656.article.

MMG (2014). Internet World Stats. Miniwatts Marketing Group. http://www.internetworldstats.com/stats.htm.

NPC (2012). National Development Plan 2030: Our Future — Make It Work. National Planning Commission, Pretoria.

Piaget, J. (1967). *John Amos Comenius on Education*. Teachers College Press, New York.

PMG (2013). Equity Index in South African Universities: Briefing. Parliamentary Monitoring Group. https://pmg.org.za/committee-meeting/16621/.

Suresh, S. (2012). Research funding: Global challenges need global solutions, *Nature*, 490: 337-338.

Thomson Reuters (2010). *Global Research Report Africa*. Thomson Reuters, Leeds.

United Nations (2014). World Urbanization Prospects. http://www.un.org/en/development/desa/news/population/world-urbanization-prospects-2014.html.

Larivière, V., Ni, C., Gingras, Y., Cronin, B. & Sugimoto, C. (2013). "Bibliometrics: Global gender disparities in science", *Nature*, 504: 211-213.

CHAPTER

Intellectual Change: Creating the University of the 21st Century

Linda P.B. Katehi

Change has typically come so slowly to higher education that some educators have been known to tell a joke about a man, similar to Rip Van Winkle in the classic Washington Irving short story by the same name, who woke up after being asleep for hundreds of years to find that the only thing he recognizes from life before his extended nap is the college classroom. That's because it has barely changed from the original model of an esteemed professor, standing in front of a blackboard, Chalk, dispensing wisdom to a roomful of somewhat disinterested students.

As Jeffrey J. Selingo (2013), an editor at the *Chronicle of Higher Education*, points out in his book, *College Unbound: The Future of Higher Education and What It Means for Students*, "Change comes very slowly to higher education. Many institutions in the United States were established more than two centuries ago, with a handful dating back to the days before the American Revolution. Tradition is important at these colleges." But, as Selingo goes on to say, change is paramount today and it's coming more quickly than some institutions of higher learning are able or willing to process. "A confluence of events — flagging state support for public colleges, huge federal budget deficits, and falling household income — now makes it necessary to consider new approaches," Selingo writes.

THE UNIVERSITY AND ITS ONE THOUSAND-YEAR-OLD HISTORY

The modern American university traces its roots back to Plato's Academy and the early Greeks, with the philosophers intellectually entertaining the elite and the aristocracy, supported by rich patrons who wanted to train the future aristocrats of the day. Simultaneously, there were the sophists, whose schools taught rhetoric and other useful skills that were believed essential in attaining success. But, according to Clark Kerr, the late president of the University of California who is credited with conceiving the state's much-admired but now dated California Master Plan for Higher Education of 1960 when Kerr was president of the University of California system, the university as we know it today began to take shape in Bologna, Italy, in the late-11th century. That's when the University of Bologna, which is believed to be the world's oldest continuously operated university, was established. Bologna, Kerr points out in his landmark 1963 book, *The Uses of the University,* "developed many of the features that prevail today — a name and a central location, masters with a degree of autonomy, students, a system of lectures, a procedure for examinations and degrees, and even an administrative structure with its 'faculties'."

The University arose around mutual aid societies of foreign students called nations for protection against city laws that imposed collective punishment on foreigners for the crimes and debts of their countrymen. These students then hired scholars from the city to teach them. In time, the various "nations" decided to form a larger association, or *universitas,* thus the university we see today. The university grew to have a strong position of collective bargaining with the city, since by then it derived significant revenue through visiting foreign students, who simply departed if they were not treated well. Foreign students in Bologna received greater rights and collective punishment was ended. There was also collective bargaining with the scholars who served as professors at the University. By the initiation of threat of a student strike, the students could enforce their demands as to the content of courses and the pay professors would receive. Professors themselves, however, were not powerless. They formed a College of Teachers, securing the rights to set examination fees and degree requirements. Eventually, the city ended this arrangement, paying professors from tax revenues and making Bologna a chartered public university.

Historically, the University of Bologna, which was founded in 1088, is considered "the mother of European universities". However, this claim was made as symbolic of Italian national unity, leading some to question the legitimacy of Bologna's claim to the first university proper. If the term "university" requires that a single corporate body be made up of students and professors of different disciplines, rather than that a corporate body simply exists, then the University of Paris, founded in 1208, can truly be considered the first university.

In turn, the traditional medieval universities, which evolved from Catholic Church schools, then established specialized academic structures for properly educating greater numbers of students as professionals. These universities trained students to become clerics, lawyers, civil servants and physicians. Yet rediscovery of Classical-era knowledge transformed the university from the practical arts to developing "knowledge for the sake of knowledge", which, by the 16th Century, was considered integral to the practical requirements of the civil community. Hence, academic research was affected in furtherance of scientific investigation because science had become essential to university curricula via "openness to novelty" in the search for the means to control nature to the benefit of civil society.

As Kerr points out, however, by the end of the 18th Century, European universities had become oligarchies, "rigid in their subject matter, centres of reaction in their societies ... they stood like castles without windows, profoundly introverted". He goes on to say: "It was in Germany that the rebirth of the university took place ... [The Humboldian University]. The emphasis was on philosophy and sciences, on research, on graduate instruction and the freedom of professors and students. The department was created and the institute. The professor was established as a great figure within and without the university." This is essentially the model that has prevailed in the United States since Johns Hopkins University began to pattern itself after the German universities in the 1870s.

THE RESEARCH UNIVERSITY TODAY

Since the U.S. federal government began dramatically expanding its funding of university research during World War II, public research universities in the United States have been transformed into dynamic, indispensable sources of innovation and discovery. They contribute mightily to the nation's well-being, the U.S. economy and to the world at large. The best ones now do an extraordinary job of expanding our frontiers of knowledge and serving as a roadmap toward life-changing breakthroughs that benefit people around the world and make progress in meeting the most complex and difficult challenges of our time.

That public research universities have grown into this role is undeniable. But so too is the fact that in their evolution, they have become institutions that revolve around faculty and their scholarship. Now, with public expectations, needs and resources changed — and as our students and communities have changed as well — there stands a growing need to reinvent what it means to be a public research university in the 21st Century.

For anyone affiliated with a public research university, it is clear that change does not come quickly, easily or efficiently. This is true despite the almost constant scrutiny and self-examination to which such institutions are subjected. Our role and mission have been under discussion to one degree or another for a long time, both inside and outside our hallways and classrooms. Soon after Clark Kerr's *The Uses of the University* was published in 1963 as a series of lectures he delivered at Harvard, his ideas landed him on the cover of *Time* magazine. Similar to today, much of the public and news media were fixated on the challenges facing higher education and the role and value it has in society. Befitting Kerr's role as a true visionary, many of his observations are remarkably relevant today, almost 60 years later.

"How to escape the cruel paradox that a superior faculty results in an inferior concern for undergraduate teaching is one of our more pressing problems," Kerr noted. As research prowess grew, the quality of graduate education did as well, Kerr noted, because the teaching of graduate students is so closely tied to research, that when research is improved, graduate education is almost always bound to follow. "At the undergraduate level, however, the subtle discounting of the teaching process has been aided and abetted" by the heavy emphasis on faculty research.

We can debate whether Kerr overstated the case, but there can be little question of the need to change the paradigm for public research universities.

At the University of California, Davis, our academic and administrative structures and our intellectual priorities have very clearly been based on the concept of creating higher education as a community of scholars, where the entire organization revolves around our faculty. The university is built on the teaching paradigms they develop, on their scholarship needs and the results of their ideas about scholarship and research. That has served us well. It has been an organizational paradigm that has allowed the university to grow and flourish. It has also enabled us to make countless contributions to the greater society, as we are charged under the land grant mission bestowed upon us by virtue of the Morrill Act of 1862, a law that was signed while the nation was mired in Civil War. The Morrill Act, according to Jonathan Cole (2009), author of *The Great American University: Its Rise to Preeminence, Its Indispensable National Role (and) Why It Must Be Protected*, "created the seeds of a system of public higher education and proposed financial incentives for expansion and research".

But it has been more than 150 years since President Abraham Lincoln signed Morrill into law, as Justin Smith Morrill, the bill's author put it, to "offer an opportunity in every state for a liberal and larger education to larger numbers, not merely to those destined to sedentary professions, but to those needing higher instruction for the world's business, for the industrial pursuits and professions of life". Now, in the digital age and with an inter-connected global economy Morrill's forebears could never have imagined, we are in need of a new paradigm to meet the changing nature of our world.

Chapter 23: Intellectual Change: Creating the University of the 21st Century

At UC Davis, a top public research university with 34,000 undergraduate and graduate students and an annual budget of about $4 billion within a short drive of the California capital, we spent much of the 2014-15 academic year envisioning a new university model where the emphasis is more on our students and on learning — learning for and on behalf of students and faculty together.

For one thing, students we see today are different from students in Kerr's time, with many more choices about how and where to obtain an education after high school and prepare for the future. They can learn in many places and in many ways, both inside and outside the university. When they come to universities like ours, we are one choice for them among a diverse marketplace of possibilities competing for their attention. They understandably want places and institutions that will address their individual needs and interests.

They are also more vocal about their interests and determined to play a key role in developing curriculum and degree programs. They want more say in choices the university makes about life and activities on campus. Staff expectations have evolved similarly. The University is not as segregated and organized in silos as it had been in the past. The lines between staff and faculty have become increasingly blurred. We have highly educated staff, many of whom are participating in teaching as well as complex and vital research and community outreach. As a result, the role and orientation of faculty are, by necessity, evolving as well.

Faculty is still at the core of all that we do, but that core must now be opened up and expanded. At UC Davis, we have roughly 4,000 faculty. Less than 2,000 are members of the Academic Senate (tenure track), which shares in the university's governance. The rest of the faculty want more of a voice in decisions we make. As students have a greater expectation about participating in anything the university is doing, so do our staff and our entire faculty.

On public research university campuses in the U.S., cultural and organizational shifts, of course, come in the wake of two decades of steadily declining state support for public higher education that was reduced even more dramatically during the Great Recession related to the U.S. and global financial crises that began in late 2007. To cite just one example of the shift in public spending, in 1990-91, state of California general funds provided 78% of the funding for the University of California. In 2011-12, that had dropped to 37%. Higher education in the state now gets more funding from students and their families through tuition and fees than it does from state support, even as record numbers of students are applying to attend UC campuses because they want the education the university has to offer.

To take advantage of the opportunity inherent in these cultural shifts and deal with the public's changing priorities, we have embarked on an ambitious and comprehensive planning and community engagement process at UC

Davis. It will continue to take much of new academic year to work through as we redefine the university we want to become now and far into the future.

LOOKING TOWARD THE FUTURE: THE CHALLENGES AND OPPORTUNITIES OF THE UNIVERSITY IN THE 21ST CENTURY

Looking to the future, the University of the 21st Century should be a place where learning, teaching, creativity and translation of new knowledge are integrated into everything that takes place on its campus. A place where aspiring to achieve excellence becomes an integral part of the everyday culture and lifestyle. A lifestyle that fosters a community of learners which prepares a diverse student body to become outstanding world citizens and leaders at the same time we are creating a productive environment for our faculty to pursue their own passions and interest for scholarship and research.

Our universities should challenge their faculty, staff and students, as well as their affiliated communities, to think creatively and help transform their institutions from a 20th century university community of scholars to the 21st century university community of learners. These are communities where all members use learning to achieve excellence in themselves and for their communities and the world; where the answer to every question creates a path toward a new inquiry; where statements and demands give way to dialogue, debate and the development of a sharply honed aptitude for critical thinking. The University of the 21st Century should be a place which prepares students to be lifelong learners, nimble enough to negotiate and succeed in a future none of us can fully imagine at the moment.

Through our actions, we can demonstrate that excellence, humility and diversity can become our touchstones if we seize this opportunity to dream unconditionally, even in the midst of adversity, and if we have the discipline and academic and administrative rigour to make our dreams a reality. We can demonstrate that disciplinary boundaries can be permeable, that institutional and intellectual silos can be removed if they do nothing more than reinforce our biases and fears. We can be that rare institution that transforms itself from the 20th century university community of scholars to the 21st century university community of learners.

To be the University of the 21st Century, we will also need to become the University for the World, where our community will be extended to embrace all of its members, not just in our regions and our countries but around the globe. We will need to become global in our reach and perspective and use this attribute to change our attitudes and understanding. We can be a university where our entire campus, with all of its regional, national and international sites, becomes our classroom and laboratory. A university where our classrooms transform into wonderlands of exploration, where the truth is not an absolute or an individual pursuit, and where a journey to discovery is what we share in common.

Despite the current financial recovery and the prospects for a favourable economic environment, opportunities for upward economic mobility for young people during the past few years have been disappointing. In addition, the cost of education and health care is increasing in ways that are challenging our ability to combine quality with access. In our effort to define ourselves as the University of the 21st Century, we also need to reaffirm our commitment to our mission to provide excellence, affordability, and access to higher education and medical care, while we vow to remain global in our perspective and reach in everything we do.

At UC Davis, we are striving to achieve all this at a time when our higher education landscape is more fluid and competitive than ever. What we have learned is that, regardless of the university's location, goals, strengths and objectives, the viewpoints and individual interests of the extended university community are diverse, complex and at times conflicting. Our students and their families, being major stakeholders, have interests and perspectives that need to be heard and incorporated into our academic planning. Technological advances in educational delivery have spurred changes in the learning process and have affected the way our students interact. The "flipped classroom" is encouraging students to be more active learners. Some technologies are promoting customized learning, while others have facilitated greater access to higher education for individuals around the world.

Despite these changes, many young people say that they continue to yearn for a residential educational campus experience complete with face-to-face access to outstanding faculty members. They want the connectivity of being a member of an educational cohort of students with complementary aspirations. They want the richness of campus co-curricular organizations and, perhaps most importantly, they want the unique experience of being part of a world-class research university where we not only teach and learn, but also create knowledge through the discovery and innovation inherent in our research mission.

On our campuses our faculty and staff are recruited from around the world. They elect to join our campuses because doing so provides opportunities to expand their professional development, scholarly and clinical pursuits. They join us because they are committed to teaching and mentoring outstanding students and because they want to be members of a vibrant intellectual, research and clinical community that reflects a rich tapestry of diverse perspectives illustrative of our nature as a comprehensive land-grant university. All members of our community expect to fulfil their work life in an environment that values diversity as an enabler of excellence, provides opportunities for continuous learning and personal growth, and encourages and rewards creativity and risk-taking.

On a daily basis, students, faculty and staff on our campus work hard to advance our research, learning and public service missions. Recognizing our strengths and being cognizant of our weaknesses, we believe that this is an appropriate time to undertake a serious and aspirational community dialogue about the direction we must take to ensure the excellence of our campuses for the next 50 years. It will be important to create a vision that recognizes these realities and embraces the many innovations the future will bring in the way of tools, educational models, services and products, as well as the skills that will be needed to support the economies these innovations will drive.

At the same time, it is paramount that the University of the 21st Century fully recognizes its reach and impact, and the responsibility that comes with it. This responsibility requires the university to be socially engaged rather than insular, and externally oriented and aspiring to become a major driver in improving the quality of life of the communities it serves. For this to become the platform on which the University of the 21st Century will be built, we will have to identify its legacy strengths and build on them; recognize the importance of being bold, creative and optimistic; and embrace risk-taking as a way of freeing ourselves from past barriers.

UC DAVIS AS THE UNIVERSITY OF THE 21ST CENTURY

As part of the envisioning process we have initiated at UC Davis, we have asked the campus community and experts outside the campus to engage in discussions about the future of the university and to challenge themselves with many big questions. They include:

- a) How do we invest in the initiatives that will help us build the UC Davis of the future? How do we make the initiatives we want to invest in successful, visible and impactful to the communities we serve and to the rest of the world? What global societal challenges are UC Davis uniquely positioned to address? How can we leverage inter-disciplinary and intra-disciplinary collaborations to be a more visible and impactful leader in addressing the society's greatest challenges?
- b) What new intellectual directions, in both our educational programs and research directions, do we need to consider that will have the potential to establish UC Davis as the UC of the 21st Century? How can we ensure student success by making learning and critical thinking the core of our educational experience? How can we ensure that the educational experience of our students mirrors their diverse perspectives and needs, and supports their aspirations both personal and

professional? How can we prepare students for the world and a future we may not currently know or understand?

c) How do we create the right environment for our faculty and staff to succeed in their scholarship and achieve their intellectual or professional pursuits? How do we inspire excellence and continuous learning in everything we do? How do we recognize faculty, students and staff for their contributions to their intellectual and professional communities and for the innovation and creativity they bring to their workplaces, their classrooms and their laboratories?

As the university in a region that includes the capital of one of the world's largest and most dynamic economies, we know it is vital to our future to become more visible and impactful in Sacramento. We understand that by creating a presence that will bring together activities that need proximity to state government and access to an urban population, UC Davis can become a more vital educational leader in higher education in the nation's most populous state. So we are asking ourselves: How can we bring together our policy activities and student internship programs that benefit from being adjacent to the Capitol? How can we establish ourselves as the leader in education and clinical outreach at the nexus of Food and Health? How can we achieve these educational and research objectives and at the same time lead the region to become the fourth economic powerhouse in the state along with San Diego, Los Angeles and the Bay Area? How do we create a vibrant UC Davis City Center in Sacramento to provide our arts, humanities and sciences with an urban laboratory for their educational programs, scholarship and outreach to an urban population?

One cannot plan and envision for the future without having a firm grasp of the university's financial picture, and we are actively engaged in addressing how we can create a more sustainable financial environment. What should our priorities be in generating revenue as we try to address our immediate and long-term needs in academic programs and facilities to accommodate growth on our campus as part of our plan to add 5,000 additional students by 2020 from the numbers we had at the state of the decade? How can the university's resource model enable and fuel our academic mission? What novel perspectives can we take on the complex portfolio of revenue sources such as State of California support, tuition, philanthropy and extramural research funding? How can we best organize ourselves to be responsible stewards of the resources that we currently have through administrative efficiencies?

Hand in hand with these considerations is the need to create and nurture an environment that supports human equity. What further policies, procedures and practices can we consider to ensure that our diverse faculty, staff and students experience an organizational environment characterized by equity, inclusion, academic freedom, freedom of expression, social justice and a shared responsibility for supporting and enabling the success of others?

As we seek to become a more global university, we understand this is both necessary and not without controversy in our state, where politicians and the public demand we serve California students first and foremost. So the questions become: How do we balance our commitment to our state with our responsibility to the world? How do we help our students become global citizens? How do we have an impact on the world through our values, principles and actions? How do we have an international impact through our programs, scholarship, innovation and clinical outreach?

MOVING FORWARD: A CALL FOR ACTION

Those who say that a revolution is needed in higher education are correct. But I believe it is not going to be the kind of transformation that some are advocating or predicting where thousands or even millions of students are scattered around the world, staring into a laptop or smart phone and watching an online lecture in physical and social isolation from one another. To be sure, online and other technologies have a growing role to play now and in our future, but the coin of the realm for the future of public research universities is not going to be the "University of Everywhere", as one noted higher education analyst has predicted. The challenge is how do we evolve into a new kind of community of learners where we make all of our choices based on the needs and aspirations of everyone who is part of this community? How do we transform the university from a self-centred intellectual community into one that asks itself what are the needs of our students, of our faculty and staff working collectively? It will require us to change our priorities and the structures and processes we have built to pursue those priorities so we are a university where the emphasis is always on learning. This is no small task. We will learn much along the way that is likely to change our thinking. As with any big attempt to bring about change in an extremely complex entity, we are likely to take some false steps and make mistakes. But this is a journey we must take to keep our public research universities at the frontiers of change, innovation and higher education locally as well as globally. Our students today and in the future demand no less of us, as do our regions and countries.

REFERENCES

Carey, Kevin (2015). The End of College: Creating the Future of Learning and the University of Everywhere. Riverhead Books.

Cole, Jonathan R. (2009). The Great American University: Its Rise To Preeminence, Its Indispensable Role and Why It Must Be Protected. Public Affairs.

Katehi, Linda (2015). "An Invitation to Envision the University of the 21st Century". chancellor.ucdavis.edu/envisioning.pdf

Kerr, Clark (1963). *The Uses of the University*. Harvard University Press.

Selingo, Jeffrey J. (2013). *College Unbound: The Future of Higher Education and What It Means for Students*. New Harvest.

PART VI

Concluding Discussions

CHAPTER 24

Glion Colloquium X Summary Chapter

James J. Duderstadt and Luc E. Weber

In June 2015, the leaders of many of the world's most distinguished research universities gathered in Glion-above-Montreux to participate in the Glion X Colloquium to consider the array of responsibilities, priorities and constraints that both guide and shape their institutions. The Colloquium was organized into five topical sessions:

- The Role and Responsibility of Research Universities
- Intellectual Constraints
- Financial Constraints
- Structural Constraints
- Human Constraints

In addition, one of the participants, Peter Scott, former Vice-Chancellor of Kingston University and Glion participant, began the Colloquium with a retrospective review of the two decades of its activities. A sixth and final session was added both to allow participants to consider the most important issues and conclusions reached during the sessions and associated discussion and to provide guidance for future Glion Colloquia.

To provide a framework for the discussion in each session, participants prepared papers that were distributed in advance of the meeting. Although the format of each session allowed the presentation of brief summaries of these papers, most of the session generally consisted of open discussion of the issues raised both by the topic and the papers.

This summary chapter has been written to pull together several of the key points made by the participants and arising during the discussion phase of the sessions. These summaries have been provided in an order that conforms to the sessions of the Colloquium.

OPENING SESSION

The meeting began with a comprehensive analysis of the history of the Glion Colloquium by Peter Scott, one of its early participants and the former Vice-Chancellor of Kingston University. He observed that Glion was quite unique among university organizations since it had been sustained over such a long period of time characterized by significant change in the higher education landscape as considered by the presentation and discussions of an unusually large number of leaders of the world's major research universities. Launched in 1998 by Luc Weber, Rector of the University of Geneva, and Werner Z. Hirsch, Professor at UCLA, and with core funding initially from the Hewlett Foundation and later Hewlett-Packard Corporation, the Glion Colloquium has evolved from its initial character of a cross-Atlantic conversation between leaders of higher education in the United States and Europe into a truly global dialogue among the leaders of the world's major research universities. With the exception of the 2000 meeting held in La Jolla, California, all of its meetings have been held in Glion-above-Montreux in Switzerland, covering topics such as the challenges facing higher education at the beginning of a new millennium, university governance, the increasing engagement of the university with society, the evolving nature of the research university, relationships with business, the globalization of higher education, the importance of university research for stimulating innovation, global sustainability, and the need for universities to prepare for and adapt to change.

During this period, the key issues facing the world's research universities have changed dramatically, driven by demographic change (e.g., aging populations in the West and the growth of Asian populations and influence in the East), the shifting balance between public and private support of universities (particularly in the United States and United Kingdom), the impact of rapidly evolving technologies, such as the Internet and data analytics, on teaching and research, and the changing relationship between universities and governments demanding both education and research more directly related to economic growth and workforce needs. Scott summarizes his analysis of the impact of the Glion Colloquium as follows:

"The abiding significance of the Glion process (so far) has been the commentary it has provided on the shift from the overwhelming postwar emphasis on building mass higher education systems, certainly in response to new workforce demands from increasingly post-industrial economies, but predominantly to build more open, inclusive, opportunity-focused and perhaps more equal societies, to a 21st-century emphasis on the 'knowledge economy' characterized by global competitiveness and accompanied perhaps by an increasing degree of social pessimism as environmental risks and geopolitical threats have accumulated and older forms of solidarity have been shredded. The research university has been in a commanding position

to provide such commentary — prospectively as one of the most powerful agents of global competitiveness through its production of highly skilled graduates and outputs of research; but also retrospectively as a key institution in building national identities and shaping cultures (and also as an incubator, and preserver, of the values associated with modernity as they have emerged in the north Atlantic world over the past two centuries — and which are assumed, perhaps arrogantly, still to be transcendent)."

SESSION 1: THE ROLE AND RESPONSIBILITY OF RESEARCH UNIVERSITIES

Chair: James Duderstadt
Howard Newby: *Global Diversity in Higher Education Systems*
Bernd Huber: *The Future of Universities: Academic Freedom, Autonomy and Competition Revisited*
Rebecca Blank: *The Role of the University in Economic Development*
Alain Beretz: *The Social and Political Responsibilities of Research-Intensive Universities*
Lino Guzzella: *Reflecting on the University's Role in Society: Critical Thinking*

This session focused on what universities consider as their most important priorities and responsibilities, and how these align with both the perspectives and needs of contemporary societies at the local, regional or global level. Today, the world's research universities are pulled in different directions by demands for massification (enrolment growth), increased quality (as measured by league tables) and reducing the burdens on public financing, although with decidedly different priorities given to such demands in different regions. Aging populations in mature economies such as the United States, Japan and England are seeking to reduce public support, while rapidly growing populations and economies in Asian and African nations seek to build world-class research universities while meeting the enormous demand for higher education. The old cliché that "Europe is the past, America is the present, and Asia is the future", while perhaps true today, will likely be challenged increasingly by global forces such as demographics and emerging technologies.

In both the United States and increasingly in Europe, higher education is increasingly viewed as a "commodity", of value both to the student and to the economy, and the return on public investment is measured accordingly. Countering this utilitarian approach to the research university's role and mission may be one of its greatest challenges. There are increasing criticisms both by governments and media of the research topics, the quality of research, the sources of research funding, and international collaboration in research.

Indeed, fundamental issues such as academic freedom and the autonomy of universities in decisions on teaching and scholarship are being challenged (particularly in the United States).

Yet, it has been estimated that in the United States, growth in GDP is due 20% to the size of the labour force (now stagnant), 12% to increasing workforce skills and 68% to growth in productivity, efficiency and innovation. Hence, universities relate to 80% of growth through education and research, not to other missions such as tech transfer and workplace training. The former must remain the priority of the research university, because all of its roles (not to mention its legitimacy and authority) in society will derive from the way it sustains the quality of these fundamental missions. We must continue to make the case for these unique roles of research universities to both governments and the public at large.

Furthermore, from an economic perspective, the university system provides an ingenuous solution to an inherently public goods problem. Invention, scientific ideas, and the results of basic research offer little direct economic benefit to the inventor or to private investors, despite their long-term potential. However, by providing public support for research through a highly competitive system of grants and rewards, the university system provides a particularly efficient solution of creating inventions and progress in research to society. Moreover, academic freedom and the autonomy of universities are key pillars of the competitive mechanism to enhance the productivity of the research process in society.

Yet, it is also the case that the expansion of research activity, albeit in the public interest, requires increasing efforts of universities, research funders and research policy to maintain and improve research quality. This, in turn, critically depends on the credibility of and the public's trust in the quality of the research process. Yet, one must be cautious in making the case for the importance of the university to utilitarian objectives such as industrial innovation, workplace quality or economic growth, since the most fundamental missions of the university remain education and scholarly research. To be sure, research universities have established many mechanisms for more direct engagement with society, including joint university-industry-government applied research centres and workforce training.

But it must always be stressed by university leaders that, while important, these are not the most fundamental missions of the university. Over the long term, the research university's fundamental missions of education and scholarship will have far greater impact and should not be sacrificed to respond to near term demands nor to technology-based fads. Students still learn from human beings, not machines. Research still requires an unusual ability to think, to ask probing questions and to discover the unknown, albeit sometimes stimulated by practical problems. And the quality of a university is determined by its people, not its organization or its technology or its branding.

SESSION 2: INTELLECTUAL CONSTRAINTS

Chair: Ronald Daniels
Stefan Catsicas: Creating Shared Value through Open Innovation
Nicolas Dirks: The Evolution of Globalized Higher Education
Carlos H. de Brito Cruz: University Research Comes in Many Shapes
Patrick Prendergast: Global Research Questions and Institutional Research Strategy

This session concerned new approaches to extending the educational and research efforts of research universities to better serve the needs of society through several specific examples. The efforts of the Nestlé Company to restructure itself as the leading nutrition, health and wellness company required not only broadening its mission to include research on water resources and rural development, but also to develop a new paradigm of "open innovation" in which industry and academia join together to better understand and translate science into commercial opportunities. Although such relationships have appeared in the research cluster ecosystems in developed nations, Nestlé is interested in extending the paradigm to developing economies in South America, Africa and South-East Asia where much of their commercial activity will be focused.

A quite different approach was proposed by the University of California Berkeley, based on growing globalization of higher education. After reviewing the traditional approaches of study abroad programs, student-faculty exchanges, the development of branch campuses overseas and the creation of global networks of "consular offices" to provide a limited physical presence in various global centers, UCB has taken bold steps to create a new campus, the Berkeley Global Campus, in Richmond Bay, separate from, but close and deeply connected to, their home campus. This will involve the presence of both international and local partners — universities as well as private corporations and government agencies — joining in the design of an integrated global network of activities, programs and enterprises. In a sense, this effort inverts the usual model whereby U.S. universities establish themselves in sites around the world. At the core of this global campus will be a new College of Advanced Study that will take on issues related to global governance, global ethics, global citizenship and global relationships more broadly.

Yet another approach was described for Sao Paolo, Brazil, in building clusters for translational research that draw from the transformative research conducted by research universities. While society expects intellectual impact from university research, it places increasing priority on economic and societal impact such that the value of scientific research should include intellectual or cultural knowledge. However, for this to be successful, it requires that the core basic research programs of the university be strongly supported, since they are key to the success of applied activities.

Trinity University of Dublin is embarking on yet another approach based on defining "Global Research Questions (GRQs)" that address fundamental challenges to a region's resources or security that cannot be solved by a single discipline or within a single country. Examples of GRQs include water shortage, energy provision, climate change, poverty, migration, inequality, aging populations and conflict resolution. To identify such GRQs as key priorities, a strategic process has been developed that extends beyond traditional scientific research to identify the interdisciplinary, international research collaborations necessary to address such challenges and then put into place the necessary supranational programming and funding.

SESSION 3: FINANCIAL CONSTRAINTS

Chair: Chorh Chuan Tan
Patrick Aebischer: The Business Model of the 21st Century European University
Leszek Borysiewicz: The Importance of Philanthropy
Ronald Daniels: The Convergence of Public and Private Universities
Luc Weber: The University of the 21st Century

This session began with a discussion of the emerging financial challenges in nations with aging populations and stable enrolments where the public support of higher education was increasingly challenged. The experience of the public research universities in the United States was of particular interest where student fees had increased dramatically to compensate for the loss of 30% of their state support over the past decade. Despite strong support for student financial aid by the federal government, student debt and public concerns had risen dramatically. The sense was that many of the nation's leading public research universities were at considerable risk, in sharp contrast to private universities, which continued to benefit from high tuition revenue, private philanthropy and endowments.

Although both adequate public support and low tuition policies remained in place in most European nations, there were early warning signs from the rising tuition and debt characterizing English universities that suggested that the American experience of the shift of public perception of higher education — from that of a tax-supported public good to a student-support private benefit — might occur elsewhere. Hence, there was strong interest in exploring alternative financial models, similar to the mixed public-private model of the United States. Of particular interest was the growing importance of philanthropy and endowment in achieving financial sustainability of major research universities. Yet, for most nations, while research-intensive universities would draw from an increasingly balanced mix of public and private income sources, e.g., gifts, endowments, charitable income, business partnerships and expansion of international students, there continued to be confidence that, in the end, the leading research universities would owe their success and financial stability to public support.

However, Cambridge and Oxford do provide strong evidence that the American approach to philanthropy deserves more attention in Europe. These institutions view philanthropy not only as a buffer to public finances increasingly burdened with debt, low growth and aging populations, but also as key both to institutional autonomy and the vital seed investment in intellectual breakthroughs. Fortunately, the U.K. is beginning to implement tax incentives for both private giving to charitable causes and endowment earnings, but universities still need to develop both the culture and capacity for sustained fund-raising, similar to the learning curve experienced by public universities in the United States. Cambridge, with both large fund-raising experience and a sizeable endowment of £1.3 billion, is providing an important model of how rapid fund-raising can become an extremely important part of a university's financial portfolio. Enabling philanthropy is not just a supplement to public support, but it has rapidly become an obligation for universities if they are to fulfil their mission.

The United States is fortunate in possessing a unique combination of world-class public and private research universities. While there has long been an ebb and flow in the benefits and challenges each face, today, with the erosion in state support (suspected to be of a permanent nature) and the increasing efforts of private universities to address public needs, there are signs of a convergence of both financial character (with private support now exceeding state support for many public universities) and public engagement (as private universities accept more responsibility for activities such as health care, technology transfer and economic development). Taken together, the privatization of publics and the publicization of privates suggest that American public and private universities are tending to converge on a single model of higher education that blends elements of both: the public-regarding private ("PRP") research university.

Of course, even if this is a possible endpoint, it does not necessarily follow that the transition to this model will be equally easy for public and private research universities. Origins matter, and it is here that the legacy of state ownership and control of publics impairs organizational evolution in a way that is less true of the privates. The challenge for policy-makers is how to adopt principled and politically feasible arrangements that still confer autonomy and resources on America's great public research universities, so that they can compete on a level playing field with increasingly publicized privates. One possible route is to adopt a mechanism proposed by the University of Oregon to convert the stream of state appropriations into servicing the loan for a debt-financed endowment that would provide state universities with financial autonomy. Of course, there would still be the issues of state regulation and politically determined governing boards to address, but the model of a public research university without public ownership but with a private endowment that throws off funds comparable to the public investment is an interesting model to explore.

More generally, the real question is whether today's research universities will be able to adopt to the new world that is opening up, and whether they will be able to do this quickly enough to preserve the quasi-monopoly they currently enjoy in terms of higher education and basic research. The challenges are those of globalization, competition, the increasing pace of scientific and technical progress, and the emergence of the knowledge economy. The capacity to respond depends strongly upon regional characteristics, such as the eroding priority for higher education funding given by aging populations and level student populations in North America and Europe, or the rapidly growing populations and need for economic development in Asian and African nations. In both cases, adapting to the imperatives of a new era will require rapid attention and adaptation. Put another way, universities face a double challenge: First, innovate, modernize and restructure to keep their quasi-monopoly for discovering new knowledge and transmitting it. Second, be capable of doing this with stagnant or decreasing public budgets. This situation will be very challenging for both the governance and the leadership of institutions.

SESSION 4: STRUCTURAL CONSTRAINTS

Chair: Linda Katehi
Tony Chan: Impact of China's Economic Rise on Global Higher Education
Meric Gertler: Cities, Universities, and the Economic Geography of Innovation
Chorh Chuan Tan: University Leadership and Governance
Atsushi Seike: The Role of Universities and Social Needs in Times of Great Change

The discussion began with a review of the remarkable progress of higher education in China as its government realized that developing a modern and effective higher education system is essential to drive the nation's economic goals: the development of human capital, investment in research, cultivating an entrepreneurial culture, and building a new economy based on innovation rather than low-cost labour.

As one of the world's largest higher education systems, China has close to 2,500 accredited universities and colleges, with a current student enrolment of 35 million producing 7.5 million graduates a year. It faces the challenge of providing adequate faculty for this large system, and beyond building more research universities capable of faculty development, it is making efforts to attract back to China the large diaspora of talented students who have gone overseas for study and graduate education, many of whom are now established faculty members at Western universities. It also must address the challenge of a rising middle-class in which many families can send their children overseas for university studies, often paying full tuition. Although China has adopted many of the characteristics of the Western model of research universities, it is likely to merge these with both a unique culture (e.g., its Confucian philosophy) and national character to achieve a new model. There was a strong sense that the rapid growth and change in the Chinese higher education system are not only good for Chinese citizens, but also present tremendous opportunities for universities worldwide.

Looking more broadly at university development around the world, the case was made for the impact of urban resources on universities located in major cities. Beyond cultural and economic strengths, urban regions are privileged sites for innovation, entrepreneurship and the flourishing of ideas and opportunities. The relationship between universities and their host city-regions is fundamentally symbiotic and confirms the importance of location for research, education, innovation and entrepreneurship. Success in a knowledge-based economy requires thoughtful, strategic support for a nation's urban regions and for its leading institutions of advanced research and education.

But if universities are to play important transformative roles in addressing the challenges and goals facing society, a key requirement is for them to have a high degree of autonomy, tied to adequate and diversified funding, competition for resources, and clear lines of accountability to stakeholders. The university landscape has been impacted and transformed by the powerful forces reshaping the societies that they serve: globalization, intense competition across all sectors, the quickening pace of technological innovation and fundamental changes in demographics and societies. These forces are reshaping the higher education sector in several key dimensions: 1) massification; 2) the proliferation of new higher education models included private sector providers, a much wider range of trans-national educational partnerships, and new modes of learning including online or blended learning; 3) greater scrutiny and benchmarking of output and impact against a global field; and 4) dramatic increases in international student mobility.

Studies support the view that greater autonomy is necessary to address these challenges, including academic autonomy (over teaching and research), financial autonomy, organization autonomy and staffing autonomy. The National University of Singapore (NUS) provides an interesting model of how this has been achieved. The Singapore government corporatized NUS (and Nanyang Technology University) as not-for-profit companies limited by guarantee to provide them with greater autonomy. This requires wide-ranging changes in organizational autonomy, financial arrangements and the supervision role of the Ministry of Education. It also enabled NUS to think fundamentally, boldly and long-term about its strategic positioning and goals and how these could be achieved. It enhanced the professional and administrative capabilities of NUS. And it engendered a much stronger sense of collective ownership and participation among faculty, staff and students.

An interesting contrast was provided by a discussion of Keio University, the oldest private university in Japan, that was engaged in a strategic process to conduct research through a Longevity Initiative concerning aging populations, a Security Initiative for a safer and peaceful society, and a Creativity Initiative to promote more innovative research that can generate high economic value. The private universities in Japan face a competitive challenge from the national universities, which receive much greater public support from the government. But private universities such as Keio benefit from greater autonomy and the ability to set their own course.

SESSION 5: HUMAN CONSTRAINTS

Chair: Patrick Aebischer
Yves Flückiger: From MOOCs to MOORs: A Movement Towards Humboldt 2.0
Arnoud De Meyer: Impact of Technology on Learning and Scholarship
James Duderstadt: Adapting the University to a New Age
Ihron Rensburgh: Reinventing Greatness: Responding to Global Responsibilities
Linda Katehi: The University of the 21st Century

This session began with a broad discussion of the role of technology in reshaping the nature of teaching and research. A particular example was the major commitment of the University of Geneva to the use of MOOCs in expanding the educational programs of the institution. Although this online technology was used externally primarily for lifelong learning, it has already shaped much of the new thinking about how learning occurs, how knowledge is disseminated to wider audiences, and how students interact with one another both to learn and to reshape their learning environment. The MOOC process also provided the opportunity to use analytics to study learning data, thereby providing an important tool to improve pedagogy.

A second example of the impact of technology on the activities of research universities was provided by the growth of research about and anchored in "big data" that seems to change the very nature of the research paradigm. Predictive analytics are influencing the way we perform empirical research. It is also reshaping the way we view student learning and designing the learning paradigm. Finally, big data and predictive analytics have become an important tool in radically internationalizing research.

The discussion then shifted to a final discussion of both the challenges and new responsibilities faced by research opportunities. It was noted that in the

United States, the perspective of the missions of education and research had shifted from those of public goods benefiting all of society to private benefits for students and industrial patrons of universities that should be expected to pay directly for the services of teaching and research, rather than being heavily subsidized by public tax dollars. Hence, it was becoming increasingly apparent as the pace of change continues to accelerate, our schools, colleges and universities will need to become more adaptive if they are to survive. It is not enough to simply build upon the status quo. Instead, it is important that we consider more expansive visions that allow for truly over-the-horizon challenges and opportunities, game changers that dramatically change the environment in which our institutions must function.

Among these were the importance of considering a possible shift in the intellectual focus, from the preservation or transmission of knowledge, to the process of creativity itself, as the powerful tools of creation in areas such as creating objects atom-by-atom, genetic engineering to new life forms, and artificial intelligence. But perhaps more profoundly, it was time once again to seek a bold expansion of educational opportunity, setting as the goal to provide all citizens with universal access to lifelong learning opportunities, thereby enabling participation in a world both illuminated and driven by knowledge and learning. This will require new paradigms for learning and scholarship, but the rapid evolution of information and communications technologies, evolving at rates of 1,000-fold or more every decade, make even these goals more achievable.

Such ambitious goals will be necessary in any event to meet the massive needs for higher education, particularly in underserved regions such as Africa, experiencing rapid population growth. After Asia, Africa is the world's most populous continent. By 2050, it is forecast to be home to one quarter of the world's population (or some 2.3 billion people, half of whom will be urbanized), and including 40% of the world's children. Much higher and more sustained investment in higher education will be required if Africa's universities are to accommodate growing demand for higher education and lift the participation rate from its current level of 8% to the approximately 32% which was the global average in 2012.

In fact, given their functions of knowledge production and innovation, the training of highly skilled citizens, and the promotion of social mobility, knowledge institutions are key to delivering the knowledge requirements for development. Knowledge institutions in general and research universities in particular must lead the effort to enrol and embrace far higher proportions, and secure the success of youths and minorities from poor and marginalized urban and rural communities. More often than not, the poor and the marginalized are locked out of our universities, especially the research universities, which they either cannot afford or are assumed to be academically unprepared for, or both.

The knowledge institution which can match its global-level responsibilities with its university-level priorities will elevate itself way beyond its standing in terms of global rankings. The research university that includes the world in its research, which promotes and shares the flow of knowledge and scholars, which embraces the poor and does research for humanity, will be a truly great research university.

The final discussions turned to achieving the appropriate balance between education and research, between the desires of the faculty and the needs of the students. To be sure, over the past half-century, universities have become dynamic, indispensable sources of innovation and discovery. They contribute mightily to our economies, our welfare and the world at large. But in their evolution, they have become institutions that revolve around faculty and their research. Our academic and administrative structures and our intellectual priorities have very clearly been based on the concept of creating higher education as a community of scholars, where the entire organization rotates around our faculty. As Clark Kerr, the leader of the University of California in the 1960s, put it: "How to escape the cruel paradox that a superior faculty results in an inferior concern for undergraduate teaching is one of our more pressing problems." As research prowess grew, the quality of graduate education did as well, Kerr noted, "because the teaching of graduate students is so closely tied to research, that when research is improved, graduate education is almost always bound to follow. At the undergraduate level, however, the subtle discounting of the teaching process has been aided and abetted by the heavy emphasis on faculty research."

Yet, today's students are much different than during the formative years of the research university. They can learn in many places and in many ways, both inside and outside the university. When they come to universities like ours, we are one choice among a diverse marketplace of possibilities for them. They understandably want places and institutions that will address their individual needs and interests. Staff expectations have similarly evolved. The university is not as segregated and organized in silos as it has been in the past. We are challenged to foster a community of learners which prepares our diverse student body to become outstanding world citizens and leaders at the same time we are creating a productive environment for our faculty to pursue their own passions and interest for scholarship and research. We must transform our campuses from a 20th-century university community of scholars to the 21st-century university community of learners — a university where all of us use learning to achieve excellence in ourselves and for our communities and the world.

Those who say that a revolution is needed in higher education are correct. But it is not going to be the kind of transformation that some are advocating or predicting where thousands or millions of students are scattered around the world, staring into a laptop or smart phone and watching an online lecture in physical and social isolation from one another. The challenge is how do we evolve into a new kind of community of learners where we make all of our choices based on the needs and aspirations of everyone who is part of this community? How do we transform the university from a self-centred intellectual community into one that asks itself what are the needs of our students, of our faculty and staff working collectively? It will require us to change our priorities and the structures and processes we have built to pursue those priorities so we are a university where the emphasis is always on learning.

SESSION 6: A GENERAL DISCUSSION

The Glion Colloquium concluded with a final session of open discussions among the university leaders, both to identify the key themes and possible conclusions that had arisen during the meeting, as well as to provide guidance on future efforts. Among the most important topics considered were:

- University autonomy and accountability
- Financial sustainability (with a particular focus on the importance of private fund-raising and endowments)
- Intergenerational equity of educational opportunities (particularly in nations with aging populations)
- Providing affordable and sustainable higher education to regions characterized by major population growth (particularly in Africa and Asia)
- Mission differentiation (e.g., comprehensive universities vs. technical institutions vs. workforce training)
- Impact of rapidly evolving disruptive technologies
- Achieving a balance between competition and cooperation in addressing global issues
- How to project the importance of research universities and influence their support

An array of possible topics for future Glion Colloquia were also suggested:

- How research is changing, and its implications for the faculty.
- What is the role of elite institutions for access and equity?
- What are the political strategies to advance university interests and address social challenges?
- How do we accommodate faculty and students who run against the grain (i.e., "essential singularities")?
- A more focused discussion on achieving appropriate governance and leadership of 21st-century universities.

The concluding remarks from the group expressed strong support for the existing Glion paradigm:

- The priority given to inviting participants currently serving in university leadership roles.
- The request for advance drafts and final papers from each participant both to inform the discussions and to provide material for a widely distributed book concerning the meeting.
- The importance of a balance between brief presentations, extensive discussion during planned sessions and ample opportunity for informal discussions during dining and other planned events for the participants and their partners.
- Continuing to host the meetings in the Hotel Victoria in Glion-above-Montreux.

There was strong agreement among the participants about the value of the Glion experience for their institutions and higher education more generally. They expressed their strong encouragement and support for the continuation of the Glion Colloquium as an extremely important resource for world's research universities and the global society that it serves.

Cet ouvrage a été achevé d'imprimer en décembre 2015
dans les ateliers de Normandie Roto Impression s.a.s.
61250 Lonrai (orne)
N° d'impression : 1505927
Dépôt légal : décembre 2015

Imprimé en France